Really Not Required
Memoirs 1939 to 1946

This 'crest' was developed and drawn by Ula Dashwood Howard, the artist sister of my best friend, for a 'Christmas Card'.

The bird is the crest of HMS *Osprey* with the motto 'He shall not pass' (ASW School). At the base is the Alsatian dog 'Flash' who served aboard from 1940–1945.

You will note the 'halo' over his head. Also the ship's motto: 'Nae bather at all!'

There is the 'wavy' braid of the RNVR and the 'rocky' or lattice RNR braid.

Really Not Required
Memoirs 1939 to 1946

Colin Warwick

The Pentland Press Limited
Edinburgh • Cambridge • Durham • USA

First published in 1997 by
The Pentland Press Ltd.
1 Hutton Close
South Church
Bishop Auckland
Durham

British Library Cataloguing in Publication Data.
A catalogue record for this book is available
from the British Library.

ISBN 1 85821 477 7

Typeset by CBS, Felixstowe, Suffolk
Printed and bound by Antony Rowe Ltd., Chippenham

DEDICATION

For all those Mothers' darlings – the ship's
companies of HMT *St Loman* 1939–1943,
and HMS *Rushen Castle* 1943–1945

The First Lieutenant of 'The Fighting Saint' wrote these verses for inclusion with the Christmas Cards mailed from the ship when on the East Coast of the USA.

CINDERELLA SHIPS
Lt 'Ossie' T. Dodwell RNVR

In Britain's vain attempt to check the Führer's mighty host
Destroyers did heroic work on Norway's icy coast
They served both at the landing and at the evacuation,
But, dammit, so did trawlers, the destroyers' poor relation.

And on the shores of Dunkirk, midst the rain of shot and shell
The Navy did a sturdy job, both valiantly and well.
By stirring deeds destroyers earned the plaudits of the Nation
But, dammit, so did trawlers, the destroyers' poor relation.

Then from the bloody coast of Crete to Iceland's Arctic Waste
Destroyers grimly battled on wherever challenge faced,
Chancing any kind of odds, facing annihilation.
But, dammit, so did trawlers, the destroyers' poor relation.

And so the war moved westwards; took our cousins unaware,
They found they had not got enough destroyers 'over there'
At first to guard their convoys the destroyers weren't in station
But, dammit, there WERE trawlers, the destroyers' poor relation.

Contents

Illustrations

CHAPTER I

It is Sunday 3 September 1989 as I sit down in my Washington office to write to my son Richard in England. The sun is shining in a clear blue sky flecked with small white fleeces of cloud, just as fifty years ago in Brook, Surrey, England where a group of the locals had gathered outside the garage opposite the small country pub at around 11 a.m. waiting to hear the radio report just coming through. Germany had marched into Poland confident that Britain and France would again take no action. This time it was different, Great Britain had given its word to Poland. Now England, Scotland, Wales and Northern Ireland declared war on the German invader. We knocked on the door of the pub until the publican put his head out of an upper window.

'War has been declared so open up and let us have a drink on it!'

The publican shook his head. 'War or no war, twelve noon is the lawful opening time on Sunday,' and with that he closed the window.

'He might have made an exception,' someone remarked. 'Matter of principle you might say, just like us declaring war on Germany this morning!'

At noon the publican opened his doors and we all trooped in, ordered our respective pints and halves then looked at each other rather thoughtfully.

In the distance an air raid warning signal quavered but was followed later by the steady all clear note. A false alarm, but making the statement that the country was ready and alert, as it was to remain for six long years.

That afternoon after watching the white vapour trails of Spitfire fighter aircraft high in the cloudless blue sky I went inside and wrote to my Lords Commissioners of the Admiralty giving details of my three years' apprenticeship in the Royal Mail Steam Packet Company and my commission as a midshipman Royal Naval Reserve on leaving the Nautical College Pangbourne.

A few days later I received a response saying that my services were not required at this time and my name would be put on the Merchant Navy reserve list.

By now the marketing clients I had been handling at the 7 Park Lane, London offices of the Wallace Attwood Company, a small firm of management

1

consultants, were getting involved in war production work. My senior partner, Wallace Attwood, was joined by his son Bedford who, after creating and heading the British Market Research Bureau of the J. Walter Thompson Company at a then fabulous salary, had been given 'indefinite leave of absence for the duration' by the American agency. He brought with him several former associates interested in getting into essential war production work.

My activities were now channelled into making rather cold calls on companies engaged in war production work and I succeeded in obtaining several worthwhile projects for the boys in the back room.

Visiting my mother in Surbiton I found my sister-in-law's brother, Ian Mackenzie, who had been studying at Edinburgh University, in the uniform of a Royal Naval Volunteer Reserve sub lieutenant on leave from the training school at Brighton. At home that evening I wrote to the Lords Commissioners of the Admiralty stating that as my brother-in-law, who did not know one end of a ship from another, was now a RNVR officer my services must be very badly needed!

I received a reply by return mail requesting me to have an interview with an Admiral Potter at an address near Victoria Station, London. It was an old office building and, entering the small ante-room, I found a dozen men of about my age all with blue Burberry raincoats beside them, the hallmark of the merchant navy officer.

My turn came soon. Admiral Potter, a tall, spare man greeted me with: 'Sorry about your brother-in-law, Warwick. How did he get in?'

I told him that Ian Mackenzie was offered a commission at his university.

'Ah, yes! All the universities were offered commissions for their student bodies and now our destroyer captains are asking us what is this horse meat we are sending them as watchkeeping officers! At the same time we found that there were a great number of former merchant navy men with Mates' and Masters' tickets who, as you did, left the sea to work ashore and like you wrote us rather rude letters regarding our neglect of their services! What we need are men who can take ships to sea now for minesweepers and anti-submarine trawlers. Anti-submarine ships would be my recommendation to you!'

Six to eight weeks at HMS *Osprey*, the A/S Warfare School at Weymouth, and then to command of a deep-sea A/S trawler was the schedule. I received my commission or appointment a few days later to report to HMS *Osprey* as a Royal Naval Reserve sub lieutenant, thus retaining my former professional merchant navy officer status with the distinctive lattice pattern braid. At that time it was commented that the straight band of the Royal Navy indicated 'officers and gentlemen', while the wavy band of the Royal Naval Volunteer

2

Reserve meant 'gentlemen trying to be officers'. The lattice stripes of the Royal Naval Reserve meant just 'sailors'! Incidentally, I later found that the executive curl duplicated the Cross of David, as a Jewish host informed me in New York!

A Friday afternoon in late November found me on Paddington station to take the train to Weymouth and a meeting with a RNR lieutenant with whom I travelled. I learned that he was a pilot from South Shields and we arranged to share a hotel room as we had been advised that no quarters were available at the A/S School. A helpful railway porter who took our bags at Weymouth suggested a room at a nearby station pub, a short walk away.

The next morning I reported to the wardroom of HMS *Osprey*.

'Have a gin, Warwick,' the RN commander welcomed me. I remarked to him I had been told that the A/S course was about six weeks or so.

'Six weeks! We got the last group through in two weeks and as we are now working weekends you'll be through in nine days.'

That Sunday morning the initial classroom sessions began with the introduction to the ASDIC, or anti-submarine detection device. In brief, the most secret part of this A/S gear was the oscillator, painstakingly built by hand from small sections of quartz, in plus and minus formation and fixed to a steel plate or diaphragm. Upon an electrical current of about 1,000 volts being passed through the diaphragm, the latter oscillated and when submerged sent a reverberation through the water as a very narrow beam of one to two degrees in width for a distance in good conditions of 2,500 to 3,000 yards. Striking the hull of a submerged vessel produced an echo similar in sound to that obtained from striking a metal can. The diaphragm, acting as a hydrophone, would record the echo as another electrical impulse that was shown by the dark mark made by the moving stylus on the sensitized paper roll similar perhaps in appearance to that in a lie recorder. It seemed that two or three years before the Admiralty had been able to get the Treasury Department to fund the construction of new deep-sea trawlers, with their prospective owners providing for a reinforced keel plate which could be easily cut to provide an opening for the asdic to be lowered and protected by a dome fastened to the outside of the trawler's hull. Reinforcement was specified in addition on the trawler's bow to enable the fitting of a platform and mounting of a 4-inch First World War naval gun. No reasons were given for these construction specifications, and trawler owners complying with them received a grant in aid of their new ship construction.

The asdic operator sat in a 'high chair', tuned in to his oscillator-hydrophone with earphones and operated by hand a small wheel which turned the oscillator to make a 'sweep', with the narrow asdic beam sending out reverberations and listening for any echo or contact that could be a possible U-boat. The direction and compass bearing of the asdic beam was shown by a lighted line on the compass rose. Thus the bearing and range of a potential U-boat contact was indicated and the ship's course altered to that of the compass bearing. It was planned to be simple for simple sailors. You ran in at your trawler's maximum speed of 10-12 knots on the asdic compass bearing until the reverberations and subsequent echo became shorter as the range decreased. On joining the two, you should find the ship was over the target and dropped a pattern of five depth charges.

The five-charge pattern was made by dropping or rolling three depth charge drums off the stern of the ship from a dispenser rail in which they were stored and held ready for use. The other two charges were fired from a mortar-type thrower. These throwers were fitted on either side of the ship about amidships. The depth charge drum was held on the end of a steel 'stalk', and the reverse end was inserted in the barrel of the thrower. These 'T'-shaped depth charge holders for the throwers were stowed on the deck alongside the engine room casing with the reserve supply of depth charges. The light steel 'T'-shaped holders were manhandled into the throwers when reloading and the depth charges hoisted onto them and secured with a lashing. A simple block and tackle located over each thrower was installed.

The depth charge consisted of a simple steel drum containing about 250-300 lb of explosive with a steel tube in the centre. Here a water-pressure-operated detonator was inserted. On the detonator was a 'key' for making the required settings, starting with 50 feet and going down to a maximum of 500 feet in 50-feet steps. Following three days of classroom instruction our class was divided into two groups and assigned to the practical application on board two A/S trawlers to pick up, track and make dummy attacks on two 'tame' submarines submerged in Weymouth Bay.

Saturday morning was the end of our training session and for briefing as to our future appointments. My friend had his brief interview ahead of me.

'What is the situation?' I asked him.

Lieutenant White told me, 'They want to know if you are able and prepared to take command of one of these trawlers. The extra pay is two shillings a day hard-lying money for small ships, and three shillings a day command money.' The answer was a quick 'Yes!' by both of us!

Commander Frank Mason RN, a former submariner, was the personnel officer in the A/S Warfare division of the Admiralty and was writing up the appointments for my class at HMS *Osprey*. 'You were due for a command, Warwick,' he told me, 'but I have an urgent request from Lieutenant Commander Martyn Butt Sherwood RN, now senior officer of the Fifteenth A/S Striking

Force and an old shipmate, who tells me that it is essential for him to have his present RNVR lieutenant replaced by an RNR officer as a temporary appointment in his A/S trawler *Cape Passaro*. You are the only available RNR officer thus you will be reporting on board *Cape Passaro* in Aberdeen forthwith.'

During the depression years of the early 1930s, regular RN officers had been given 'early retirement' by the Geddes axe, as the latter was termed, Geddes apparently being the minister who 'swung the axe' terminating Lieutenant Commanders, Commanders and Captains. These retired officers were now being recalled or 'dug out', the latter being the colloquial description. There were several in our group. We reservists asked them just what was meant by 'reporting forthwith'. The reply was to the effect: 'Of course, you have to go home to get the rest of your sea-going gear together. This may take two or three days, after which you travel to the base ship to take up your appointment.'

Two days later I was reporting to the Naval Officer in Charge at Aberdeen and found that HMT *Cape Passaro* was still in Hull being fitted out and due in Aberdeen in about a week's time. It seemed that officers awaiting the arrival of their ships became temporary staff for the base signals office presided over by WRNS Officer Kennedy, whose office was on the top floor of an old office building. This proved to be a very educational assignment by getting familiar with the correct addressing of naval signals, the use of coding and decoding, and action to be initiated on reports from ships at sea; for example, when local minesweepers were attacked by German aircraft then the RAF fighter base at Dyce near Aberdeen was to be informed with the minesweeper's position. During that week a minesweeper based on Aberdeen was bombed and sunk with all hands. Miss Kennedy lost a close friend among the officers and took it very hard, while the rest of us waiting to join our ships and working in the signals office had the impact of sudden death and loss of friends brought home very sharply with the realization that this war was to be no gay adventure, and that the trawler armament of two or three 1914-18 Lewis guns was poor deterrent for German aircraft; .303 armour-piercing bullets were not available either.

At last HMT *Cape Passaro* docked in Aberdeen and I reported aboard to Lieutenant Commander Sherwood RN, a somewhat legendary character who with three other submariners had sailed an Admiralty ketch, built in Hong Kong, to Plymouth in 366 days to complete the voyage, making it through the Panama Canal, and had written a book, *The Cruise of the Taimo Shan*. Over a pink gin Sherwood commented that his RNPS (Royal Naval Patrol Service) crew of Hull, Grimsby, and Fleetwood deep-sea trawlermen, seemed a little 'mutinous' regarding his yachtsman RNVR No. 1's handling saying, 'He

5

screams at them and they fart back at him!'

I began to understand Commander Mason's 'urgent request' from his old friend and former shipmate, and found the former first lieutenant packing his gear in the little wardroom and two-bunk cabin partitioned from the seamen's mess deck in the former trawler fish hold which had stretched from midships to the forecastle in peacetime. He introduced me to Sub Lieutenant Robert Marshall RNVR, a former England rugby forward, who was awaiting an appointment to motor torpedo boats and getting rather morose at the waiting time aboard an A/S trawler. My next contact was the RNPS Second Hand or Coxswain. My lone RNR lattice stripe told him that I was a professional, former merchant navy officer, but not that it had been nine years or more since I had been at sea.

Rogers, the coxswain told me that my predecessor had refused to handle a problem regarding body lice or 'crabs' with which most of the seamen had become infected by their female contacts in Hull. 'Have all the seamen shave off their body hair and dispose of it, and I will see the base doctor about getting some blue ointment to rub on their personal parts,' I told Rogers.

The surgeon commander at the base had no supplies, but gave me a prescription for 'mercury ointment' which I took to the nearest chemist shop in Aberdeen. Handing it to the young lady pharmacist I commented, 'This isn't all for me. I need enough to take care of about thirty uncomfortable sailors!'

Smiling, she replied, 'Of course, Lieutenant, I understand!'

The next situation that I inherited was the concept by the RNPS ratings that as was the custom, when commercial fishing trawlers made port, everyone could make it ashore to the nearest pub. This is quite contrary to the *King's Rules & Regulations & Admiralty Instructions* known as 'KR & AI'. This 'bible' covered every facet of life and duties in RN ships. To quote from the other bible: 'The rules of the Medes and Persians which altereth not!' The British Board of Trade has some comparable regulations for the guidance of merchant navy captains, but nothing like the detail contained in KR & AI. For example, the latter has a regulation covering the permission to grow beards, and/or to remove them.

In some years gone by it had been the custom, particularly in the days of square-rigged sailing ships, for the master of the vessel to address his crew and give them the facts of life under his command. It was a good custom which I decided to emulate in explaining how this first lieutenant would work with the crew and what he expected of them in return. Later on at a social gathering Martyn Sherwood remarked to the captains of some other ships, 'My chaps were a little mutinous at first. I don't know what Warwick did, but he stuck out his jaw and went down to the mess deck, and things were different afterwards!'

The A/S Striking Forces, as they were termed, consisted of groups of four A/S trawlers with a retired or 'dug-out' former RN captain, commander or lieutenant commander as the senior officer commanding each group. Originally it was planned for these striking forces to patrol the NW approaches to the British Isles and be based on the bleak and inhospitable Scapa Flow naval base from which they would operate.

Martyn Sherwood, together with the other group commanders, disliked the prospect of 'hard lying' in small ships at sea combined with returning to the bleak anchorages in Scapa Flow, where store ships, colliers and oilers were anchored semi-permanently for servicing the fleet with great disfavour. Working through their old friends and former shipmates at the Admiralty, they had matters revised so that the groups would be based on Aberdeen for repairs and boiler cleaning as a home port, while being operated from the operations base at Scapa Flow. This was a great advantage for the ships companies as the A/S Striking Forces would return from the A/S patrols off the north and north-western area of Scotland, and the Orkneys and Shetlands about every five to six weeks for boiler cleaning when due, and for minor repairs and storing.

The ocean convoy system was far in the future, and at this time merchant ships were still sailing independently. The 15th A/S Striking Force, consisted of four A/S trawlers – *Cape Passaro*, now nicknamed 'Cap Pessary' by the seamen, commanded by Lieutenant Commander Martyn Butt Sherwood RN, the senior officer; *St Goran* commanded by Lt Cdr William McGuigan RNR; *St Kenan* with Lt Jimmy James RNR; and *St Loman* with Lt Cambridge RNVR, who was also on the waiting list for a MTB.

Adjoining our working area was the 16th A/S Striking Force with Cdr Sir Geoffery Congreve Bt. RN in *Aston Villa* as senior officer, with the A/S trawlers *Arab*, *Angle*, and *Gaul* completing the group. Sunderland flying boats of Coastal Command made daylight sweeps and reported any U-boat sightings. The January/February gales were still blowing themselves out with dreary periods of grey tumbling seas and driving rain, but occasionally interspersed with brief sunny days giving way to calmer seas of shining blue and white-flecked waves.

On one such rare day we passed in our A/S sweeps close to the great thumb-like rock island of North Rona, which juts out of the North Atlantic well away from the NW coast of Scotland. Scanning the rock with our glasses, we could see groups of seals clambering up a sloping shelf of rock to side down into the sea again like children enjoying a swimming-pool slide.

The 16th group came into sight as our asdic operator reported a potential submarine contact. The merry, sliding seals were forgotten as Martyn Sherwood,

7

watching the asdic recorder and compass bearing of the target, conned *Cape Passaro* over it to drop a five-charge pattern of depth charges, and followed up by another run for a second depth-charge attack. Congreve in the *Aston Villa* now came in with a third five-charge pattern. Both ships then remained with engines stopped as diesel oil began forming in a circular patch of unbreaking wavelets. Three seamen previously actively reloading their depth-charge throwers were leaning over the side viewing the growing oil patch through which *Cape Passaro* was now moving slowly to traverse the U-boat target. 'Poor bastards! Such a pretty day too . . .' I heard one of them remark.

Samples of the oil and water were collected and forwarded with the U-boat sinking report. A coded signal report was sent to C-in-C Western Approaches, repeated Scapa Flow, and NOIC Aberdeen.

Towards the end of February 1940 all A/S Striking Forces were recalled from patrols to Scapa Flow. Here some 30 A/S trawlers in their respective groups made fast to buoys in the Scapa anchorage while making visits to the various storeships, and colliers. This small fleet had been given the code name of 'The Nikolayev Party', and scanning our atlas we found a small port in the Black Sea near to Odessa. This created speculation that we might be destined for the Black Sea and a trip through the Mediterranean, but the issue of warm clothing seemed to discount this possibility. Coaling and storing were completed within a week and sealed orders were delivered to the various group commanders.

German air reconnaissance had not been idle and having reported the unusual collection of small ships, the Luftwaffe delivered an air raid resulting in a fine fireworks display of tracer and AA bursts from the destroyers and cruisers anchored in Scapa. German radio claimed bombing a 'large battleship' which proved to be the First World War *Iron Duke* sitting comfortably on the mud after a previous torpedo hit by the U-boat commanded by Captain Prien, making an entrance unguarded by nets. Later it was found that he had been piloted in by a former German watchmaker established as a respected citizen in the town of Kirkwall since around 1918. The tides rose and fell in the 'tween decks of the *Iron Duke* while the upper deck was being utilized as base staff offices and facilities. It was reported that the recent bomb hole in the upper deck had opened up an internal fishpond below.

Shortly after the air raid orders came to return all the warm clothing issue to the storeship and the sealed orders back to Operations. Now it was back to our A/S patrols as before. We were to learn later on that the destinations for the various A/S Striking Forces were to have been the Norwegian ports of Trondheim, Bergen, Andalsnes, Namsos, and Narvik, from which the A/S trawler groups would have been making their asdic sweeps of the U-boat routes to their hunting grounds in the North Atlantic through the Norwegian Sea, North Sea and Arctic waters.

The Norwegian Government, after some indecision, had refused to sanction this proposal to provide even limited storing and refuelling services that could offend the Germans, who responded to this consideration at the end of March 1940 by docking German merchant ships in the major Norwegian ports, with troops under their cargo hatches from which they streamed ashore taking over the port facilities.

This time there was no secret about where we were destined to sail. Four A/S Striking Forces based on Aberdeen were recalled from their patrol areas. Each trawler was to be fitted with a gun platform aft to take a 30mm Oerlikon AA gun of which we heard only 30 were available in England. Extra rounds were supplied for our 4-inch naval gun together with 3,000 rounds of Oerlikon shells, and .303 armour-piercing ammunition for the two First World War Lewis guns below the bridge amidships.

Plenty of 'Dutch courage' was ordered and delivered by Saccone & Speed, the major wine and spirits suppliers to naval wardrooms, and many parties were in progress every evening aboard the ships, the most notable host being Martyn Sherwood aboard the *Cape Passaro*. Here Commander Frank Mason, from the personnel department of the Admiralty, now appeared to make revisions in officers' appointments. Sub Lt Robert Marshall obtained his promised MTB command, but Lt Cambridge was told that his relief for command of *St Loman* was not likely to be available in time. Faint heart never won fair lady – nor a command, I thought. 'I want the *St Loman*!' I broke in with at once.

'Then that's it!' Mason responded at once. 'Warwick takes over the *St Loman*, while Cambridge goes to MTBs.'

'But Warwick's my number one,' Sherwood cried out.

'You don't want to lose him, Martyn? That's a good enough recommendation from his commanding officer! I told you that he was due for a command when you asked me to get you an RNR officer as first lieutenant to get your lot sorted out. I'll get an RN lieutenant for you instead!' Mason promised. We all had another pink gin on that solution for the 15th A/S Striking Force.

Lieutenant Cambridge had just returned from leave in London where he had visited the Admiralty regarding his MTB command, and I got the impression that he could hardly wait until the morning to get packed, off the *St Loman* and away from the prospects of this Norwegian adventure, to an MTB based in a British channel port.

Martyn Sherwood had me doing double duty in command of *St Loman* and as his first lieutenant until such time as Billy Pedlow, his promised RN lieutenant, reported aboard. He arrived a couple of days before sailing date and proved to be a former Fleet Air Arm pilot and very reticent about how or why he had been assigned from air to sea.

Prior to my appointment and Mason's visit, Queen Elizabeth, now the Queen Mother, was due to pay a visit to Aberdeen and hearing of it Martyn Sherwood, ever the entrepreneur submariner, had arranged with the Naval Officer-in-Charge, Aberdeen to have his ship inspected by Queen Elizabeth. This was a fine opportunity to get *Cape Passaro* spic and span above decks, with the crew cleaning up their mess decks, although any inspection of the latter was planned to be avoided at all costs!

The seamen's and stokers' mess deck and sleeping quarters had been crudely and quickly converted from the former trawler fish hold underneath the foredeck section. Lavatories and wash basins or 'heads' were on the deck under the forecastle head. Entry was by a covered companionway, as was the case with the officers' cabin and wardroom, made from the after end extension of the seamen's mess deck, separated by wooden panelling. The best that could be said for the arrangements was 'adequate but lacking in creature comforts'. A small cabin area contained two officers' bunks, leading off from the 'wardroom' which contained an 'L' sofa fitting with two chairs and a small table. Heating of both mess decks and wardroom was by two potbellied iron stoves with chimney pipes through the deck above. Their smoke competed with that from the black, soft coal funnel smoke from the engine room aft.

By comparison, the original trawler skipper's cabin was fit to entertain a queen. The cabin itself was about 16 feet square and located underneath and reached from the wheelhouse above. Two large brass-framed ports looked out on the foredeck with other ports either side. At the side of the companionway a small bathroom could be seen fitted with a short but deep bathtub, a washbasin, and hot and cold fresh water as well as salt water. Across the fore end was a large mahogany sideboard with cupboards underneath. On the starboard side ran a sofa with large chart drawers below. Two small swivel chairs were set at a 6 ft square mahogany table fixed to the deck in front of another sofa running across the aft end of the cabin. On the port side was the skipper's bunk above a three-drawer chest unit. When lying down in his bunk the skipper could watch the helmsman's course by a large magnetic compass hung above the head of the bunk from the deckhead. Of course the cabin was carpeted. There were curtains for the ports and the bunk. Trawler company owners pampered their skippers for their knowledge of the fishing banks in the deepsea fishing grounds around Bear Island and the White Sea adjacent to the Arctic Circle.

Over our drinks in the evening before the Queen's visit, Martyn Sherwood had waggishly commented that he understood the handbag carried by the Queen was most likely to contain gold sovereigns, and in consequence he would try and get hold of it and be rewarded on its return.

Next day Queen Elizabeth was driven down the Aberdeen dockside accompanied by the NOIC or Naval Officer-in-Charge to the cries of 'Hooray for our Scotch Lizzie' by the fishergirls lining the dock and taking off from their fish filleting for the occasion. The troops and petty officers, together with Sub Lt's Robert Marshall and Colin Warwick, were lined up on the foredeck for inspection while Sherwood and the NOIC entertained the Queen in the Captain's quarters.

Commander Sherwood now appeared escorting the Queen and as she hesitated at the top of the ladder leading to the wheelhouse, offered to hold her handbag which he tucked under his arm to come down the ladder with the Queen. Marshall and I looked at him meaningfully, and he was hard put not to break out laughing!

From now onwards, every day could be our sailing day for Norway, and every 'night before' was an occasion for shipboard drinking parties entertained by the group commanders. Martyn Sherwood was especially gregarious and entertaining, and the direct opposite of the 16th commander, who set himself somewhat apart on being introduced by responding: 'Commander Sir Geoffery Congreve, RN, Baronet, have your signalman make a note of it!' Rumour had it that Commander Congreve was inhibited with planning to live up to the reputation of his father, a highly decorated naval officer in the First World War. Subsequently, he seemed to be always 'seeking the bubble reputation even in the cannon's mouth' as Shakespeare put it – an activity seldom if ever appreciated or understood by his ship's company.

CHAPTER II

On the Wednesday evening of 24 April 1940, the eight trawlers of the 15th and 16th A/S Striking Forces sailed from Aberdeen for Norway and Namsos. We heard something about cooperation with the Army and that submarines were as plentiful as flowers in spring. Thus we visualized ourselves catching a U-boat or two before breakfast, the fish for that meal being provided by the blasting of the sub. Then as the misty dawn cleared away, the 4-inch gun would go into action against shore batteries; this might continue until late afternoon when once more we would hunt for our evening catch.

So with Tuesday evening concluding with such happy expectations, and fuelled with many pink gins, whisky and beer chasers, we made ready to sail with the evening tide from Aberdeen, sailing north with our asdics sweeping as we went, until the dim outline of the Horse of Copinsay of the Orkney Islands loomed up out of the misty horizon and we headed east for a landfall on Vaeroy, the southern tip of the low-lying Lofoten Islands, and the Vestfjord leading up to Narvik. On Saturday evening the snow-capped mountains of Norway glinted in the rays of the setting sun. Down below, they put on another shovelful or two of soft coal, and out poured the black trawler smoke from eight eager ships, till we smothered the nearby troop and supply convoy which, despite our full speed 12 knots, came up and quickly passed by leaving us well astern.

The ships of the 16th got together for what looked like a group commander's conference as we made our landfall on Vaeroy and altered course to the south-west to find the cleft in the mountains that led to Namsen Fjord. It was in the arctic circle twilight that we nosed our way into Namsen Fjord. A faint pinprick of a shaded morse lamp stabbed the twilight: 'Come alongside transport for ammunition and stores for Namsos,' it told us. One by one our ships edged alongside the base bulk of the transport and out of it came men and stores.

Soon we were away and as dawn came, it revealed to us low snow-patched hills on the southern shore with high and sheer rugged cliffs veined with cascading waterfalls fed by the melting snow on the northern side. Beyond were hills and mountains covered with firs and evergreens.

We steamed for 20 miles through the mirror-like waters of the fjord until the white wooden houses and wooden pier at the head of Namsen Fjord lay before us, while guarding the bay like a gigantic greyhound, lay the AA cruiser HMS *Carlisle*. The scene appeared most peaceful and attractive until we came closer, and then we saw that the church had no roof or windows, the bank was in ruins and the main street was a mass of smouldering rubble. 'Dirty dogs!' exclaimed someone, and it did seem rather unreasonable, but we had business in hand and soon all four ships of the 15th group were alongside each other and against the pier. After unloading the ammunition and stores some of the crew went ashore to examine the damage, but also to inspect the small pier warehouse with possible acquisitions in mind such as the shipping cartons that were visible inside the broken walls. These proved to contain excellent rolls of soft, white toilet paper and most appropriate to our Norwegian adventure as it turned out!

There were a few French and British troops about and one very dejected Norwegian policeman, but no one seemed to be very concerned about it all until a signal came through telling us that an air raid was imminent and to disperse around the fjord as soon as possible. The signal came from HMS *Bittern*, an AA sloop apparently assigned to provide AA cover to Namsos, whereas HMS *Carlisle* came and went with the Admiral of the Fleet, the Earl of Cork & Orrery, nicknamed 'Bottle Tops', and 'Ginger Boyle' by the sailors in his commands.

Half an hour later the eight ships of the 15th and 16th groups were scattered around the fjord near Namsos, when the irregular beat of German aircraft engines could be heard to the southward. The aircraft appeared to be a mixture of twin-engined Heinkel bombers and Junkers 87 dive-bombers. The latter really knew their business, diving to within 500-700 feet of their targets as they released their 500 lb bomb, and only being vulnerable when pulling up from their almost vertical dives. As six aircraft passed high over us and on to Namsos, AA guns boomed from *Bittern* and *Carlisle* and the sky beneath them was pockmarked with shell bursts, then came the scream of the dive-bomber engines and the whistle of falling bombs followed by the dull thud of their explosions. Smoke arose over Namsos as the planes faded away into the cloudless horizon.

'Well, that's that,' we thought. 'Of course they're not interested in us, just the town.'

During the morning three more Heinkel's came, and, to our great satisfaction one appeared to have been hit by HMS *Carlisle*'s AA fire and disappeared over the hills. 'This is none of our business,' we said. 'Let's go and look for some submarines in the approaches to Namsen Fjord.' So off we went with the *St Goran,* leaving the *St Kenan* and *Cape Passaro* to finish their interrupted unloading.

That evening we returned to the fjord entrance after sweeping the approaches, and once again 'Jerry' came over, this time down to within 3-4,000 ft to look at us. As we let go with our new Oerlikon gun, one of them swerved violently. 'Ha! he doesn't like it,' we said and as the planes flew on towards Namsos, we suddenly noticed that the water was full of sizzling splashes from incendiary bombs. We were being noticed after all! By now the planes were over Namsos and down they went in screaming vertical dives. They did their business well as two hours later we reached Namsos and saw the results – the wooden pier was on fire, the warehouse and coke dump were blazing fiercely, while the ammunition dump crackled and spat small-arms fire. In the glow of this huge bonfire we edged alongside the end of the pier, gently pushing *St Goran* to the side of it, then swinging alongside her ourselves. It was a delicate procedure as the only mooring for four ships, bow on to the pier head, was the one remaining lamp standard in the main street.

Watched by what appeared to be a British Army staff officer in his khaki greatcoat, motor coaches came and went in an endless stream, and stocky Frenchmen of the Chasseurs Alpins, bearing enormous packs but missing their ski equipment, began coming over our bows; painfully slow they were in climbing down our 4-inch gun platform ladders, despite the encouraging shouts of 'Allez oop!', 'Hokey Pokey!' and helpful guiding arms of our crew, most of whom were heaving on board boxes of ammunition, bombs and machine-guns in a far too familiar manner.

The Frenchmen flowed over our foredeck to fill the *St Goran* to standing room only whereupon she cast off to look for the transport waiting at the entrance to Namsen Fjord, and the trawler *Arab,* commanded by Lt Stannard RNR, nosed in between our port side and the pier to start loading passengers.

My two officers, Sub Lt H.O.T. Bradford RNVR and Sub Lt Frederick Osborn RANVR were already directing hoses onto the burning pier, and we suggested to Stannard that he and his first Lieutenant Max Lees RANVR might do the same on the ammunition dump area which was now close to them, as otherwise we might have little or no pier to come alongside during the next evening session being scheduled for us. This worked out very well and substantially reduced the crackling and spitting of the dump, while dousing the flames on the supports of the wooden pier. The army officer was most impressed with this exercise. Later we identified him by the black patch he wore on one eye as being Major General Sir Adrian Carton de Wiart VC, commanding Mauriceforce.

Dawn was threatening as we cast off with over 550 men on board, and found their transport the *Amenois* hove to at the mouth of the fjord where we began the hauling and prodding of our cargo up a small rope ladder, and another wooden ladder across the bows. Many slipped, but none fell and as daylight came the last and fattest man of all wobbled safely across the ladder.

The *St Kenan* and *St Goran* had joined us at the mouth of the fjord and now, directed by HMS *Carlisle*, we swept the approaches clean with our asdics for the coming convoy leaving Namsen Fjord. Once again the sky was blue and cloudless, and the sun shone like brass, as we followed the fast-moving convoy out to the westward. Six planes came up the land from the south of us and dived onto the convoy. AA guns boomed from the cruiser and escorting destroyers, bombs burst around them but without a hit. As the convoy dipped over the horizon we turned back to rendezvous with HMS *Bittern* and continued our A/S patrol until evening came once more. Then we set watch across the fjord entrance and 'pinged' with our asdic until morning.

There was little, if any, real darkness and at 4 a.m. we were away in broad daylight. As the sun came through to burn off the mist over the cliffs, we made our asdic sweeps of the approaches to the seaward once more with *St Goran* leaving the *Gaul* on patrol near the fjord entrance.

It became another flawless day, without a cloud or breath of wind. Returning at 0815 we found that the *Gaul* had been bombed, hit, and beached. Four aircraft appeared over the hills to the southward. The *St Goran* was steaming at full speed up the fjord for Namsos. On the bridge I was identifying the planes which appeared to be dive-bombers. Danny Morrison, the gunner slung in the harness of the Oerlikon gun aft, was training on the leading bomber starting to slide down towards us. Morrison knew his job; mine was to con the ship and try to take evasive action. I had my binoculars trained on that 500 lb bomb beneath the now diving bomber waiting to see when the pilot detached it. Slowly the bomb parted from the belly of the aircraft and now was the time to order 'hard to starboard', as the bomb, free of the plane, was set on an irrevocable course. Single-screw ships swing more readily to starboard than to port, and as the ship's bows swung the thought went through my mind: 'Perhaps the pilot would have missed and my evasive move may have put the falling bomb on target?' There was a loud whistle as a column of black smoke and water went up 50 yards away and the ship's helm was put to amidships. Our Oerlikon gunner and his mate were putting another pan of 30mm shells on the gun, while my signalman was extricating himself from the coffin-shaped steel box which had been fitted on the bridge for the captain to stand inside and con the ship through 1½-inch slits. A happy thought by a shore-based designer perhaps, but completely useless from my viewpoint. My two officers, Osborn and Bradford, had assigned themselves to the port and starboard .303 Lewis guns of 1914-18 vintage, mounted on 5ft high steel cylinders of about 12 inches diameter. As they put it: 'You can hardly ask the men to stand there with that amount of protection. Besides it gives us something to do during air attacks!'

The frustrated bomber was disappearing over the hills as I set course to put the ship under the overhang of the 1,500 ft cliff under Mount Hamneshuken on the northern shore. Reaching the cliff we slewed the ship under the slight overhang and lay a few yards off the shore, which was steep too, with over 100 fathoms below. Depths in the middle of the fjord were recorded as 900 fathoms and over, some 5,400 feet.

This location we considered would make the ship a more undesirable target to the dive-bomber pilots who would have to come in from one set direction and be unable to perform their almost vertical 700 ft dive with a 1,500 ft cliff wall in front of them on pulling up. Thus we were not bothered except from some incendiary bombs from some Heinkels, at which we banged away now and again when we estimated they were within Oerlikon range.

The *St Goran*, steaming away in mid-fjord with a beautiful wake on the calm waters, must have been an irresistible dive-bomber target. One plane swooped down to within 4-5,000 ft, then as the pilot dived, looking through the glasses, we saw the bomb swing loose and ten seconds later exploded in the water close to the starboard side of the *St Goran*'s bridge and wheelhouse, as I said a prayer for Billy McGuigan who would be there. It looked like a near miss. The plane climbed steeply and out of the funnel smoke; the *St Goran* steamed on and was lost to sight round the point.

About half an hour later *Cape Passaro* came steaming round the point and up the fjord. When she was abeam of us an enemy bomber coming from the south across the fjord, at a height of over 7,000 ft, let go a salvo of six bombs of the depth charge type. These fell in perfect line in her wake, moving up by spaces of 20 yards at a time, with the sixth falling 50-75 yards from her stern, which lifted with the explosion.

We signalled: 'Any damage?' to Martyn Sherwood and after several minutes received his reply – Martyn liked to handle the Aldis lamp – 'Sorry for the delay, but I had to go below to change my trousers. No damage done otherwise!'

Three hours later we heard the boom of AA guns and amid our welcoming cheers HMS *Carlisle* entered the fjord from seaward and two remaining aircraft, which were circling overhead, climbed steeply and disappeared.

16

In the evening we received a report from HMS *Carlisle* that an entry might be forced on the fjord by an enemy destroyer and three submarines. This news had an exhilarating effect on the whole ship's company, all of whom were now itching for an opportunity to get within striking distance of the enemy after acting as a 'sitting' target all day. A/S watch was set for submarines coming down the fjord; the 4-inch gun was loaded with HE and trained on the entrance to the fjord, a range of 1,300 yards, alarm rockets and skeleton guns' crews were kept at their stations on two-hour watches throughout the night. Unfortunately we were disappointed.

Once again next morning we went out with HMS *Carlisle* to make a complete sweep of the outer approaches. To a bystander, probably, it would have seemed amusing to see one small A/S trawler manoeuvering ahead of a large cruiser whose signal halyards were fluttering with signals throughout. Although this necessitated all three officers being on the bridge to deal with the signals and navigation of the ship, it seemed to serve as quite a tonic to feel that once again we were really doing our specialist job of work in true navy fashion.

At 8.30 a.m. HMS *Carlisle* made a possible asdic contact and let go a pattern of depth charges; seldom had we heard sweeter music. Then we received orders to act independently and return to Namsos for transporting troops at night. We spent the day making A/S sweeps around the coast, cloaked in friendly fog banks; above, from time to time, we could hear the irregular beat of the Heinkel bomber engines. An active search was being made for us as the troop evacuation from Namsos built up.

By evening those friendly fog banks had become so thick that had it not been for our echo-sounding equipment and asdic we would not have found the fjord entrance easily. As it was we were able to steam in at 10 knots to find that owing to the fog the embarkation orders were delayed for a further 24 hours. Thus we made our way alongside the protective cliff side making fast to a lone fir tree and a rock pinnacle.

As we entered Namsen fjord, we noticed that the *Arab* was lying alongside the *Gaul* and understood that she had been damaged by incendiary bombs. This left the three remaining ships of the 15th group, *St Loman*, *St Kenan*, and *Cape Passaro* to complete the evacuation of troops from Namsos.

Lt Cdr Sir Geoffery Congreve's 16th group was no longer operational. Congreve's ship *Aston Villa* had been damaged by a near miss during the first day at Namsos. On reporting to the admiral that his ship was disabled, he was instructed to open the sea cocks and sink her in Namsen Fjord. Our telegraphist reported that Congreve had replied to the effect: 'While my ship stays afloat, I will fight her!'

17

The terse response from old 'Bottle Tops' was: 'You will do as you are told!'

Angle and *Gaul* had suffered near misses early on, were no longer operational and suffered the same fate as *Aston Villa*. The invaluable Oerlikon guns were removed and a depth charge set to 150 ft placed next to the asdic gear to prevent possible salvage by the enemy, an unlikely event in 4,000 ft depth of the fjord where the ships were sunk.

That morning our A/S gear, which had been running constantly, night and day, for over a week, burnt out and there being no further point in our trying to carry out a patrol without an operational asdic sweep, it was decided to camouflage the ship with evergreens and small fir trees growing on the mountain side. For three hours, from 7.30 a.m. we uprooted shrubs and covered our decks and rigging, and at 10 o'clock sent all hands ashore, with the exception of the Oerlikon gun's crew, officers and the telegraphist, to take cover under the overhanging rocks on the cliff side. Possibly not very effective, but it kept the hands busy.

All that day the sun shone and there was not a cloud in the sky. Enemy aircraft seemed to be overhead all the time. Obviously they could see us as there were one or two attempts at trying to dislodge the cliff on top of us by dropping heavy bombs on land. However, they seemed to reserve most of their fire for the *Arab* and the *Gaul* lying not far distant from us, thus our camouflage must have been fairly effective after all.

The German aircraft were operating from the captured Norwegian airfield at Trondheim, south of Namsos, and during the two days that the St Loman was alongside the cliff side we became aware of the fact that we could expect a morning raid at 8 a.m., and another at midday around noon; thus to avoid disruption of our usual breakfast at 8 a.m., and lunch at noon, we advanced our mealtimes by an hour to enable everyone to eat after the scheduled air attacks. The daily rum issue for the crew was around 11.30 a.m. and standing by the voice pipes on the bridge the aroma floated up from below. I joined my two officers in the little wardroom below the foredeck for a gin or whisky around the same time.

On one such occasion all three of us were about to raise our full glasses when an air raid alarm was sounded. Bradford and Osborn went up on deck immediately to their Lewis gun stations. I emptied my glass and went up on the bridge. After the raid was over all three of us went down to the wardroom, my two officers picking up their untouched glasses remarked: 'You finished yours!'

'It might have been the last one . . .' I replied.

On the next such occasion all three of us, in the tradition of Sir Francis

Drake, perhaps, deliberately finished our pink gins before going to our respective battle stations. Occasionally we had an opportunity of getting our own back when an enemy aircraft would come a little too low over the cliffs, and in one such case we had the satisfaction of seeing the red tracer bullets from our Oerlikon gun flying past the nose and into the tail of one bomber which headed south for Trondheim immediately.

By this time the crew were over their initial nervousness, and, in fact, many of them slept through most of the raids during the day we were alongside the cliffs. The general reaction amongst the ship's company to the constant bombing attacks was mainly exasperation at not being able to do anything really effective to hit back, and the enforced inactivity on the last day, which was essential if the ship was to be kept operational for transporting troops at night, was perhaps the hardest of all to bear.

On 30 April the Germans were aware of the evacuation taking place from Namsos and the Luftwaffe stepped up their attacks; when the anti-aircraft sloop *Bittern*'s guns were practically shot out, a direct hit was scored on her and she sunk in the fjord.

On the evening of 1 May and early morning of 2 May, we were alongside the remains of the pier at Namsos for the last time with *Cape Passaro* and *St Kenan*. The *Gaul* had been lost and the *Arab* receiving damage was to return with the convoy. In less than four hours we later learned, our three ships loaded 500-600 men for each of two trips to the transports, and the cruiser HMS *York* evacuated about 4,200 troops, including a British detachment of two Bofors anti-aircraft guns originally destined to go north on a destroyer to Mosjoen. These two Bofors guns remained on the foredeck until we returned to the UK. The Chasseurs Alpins had several bicycles on which our sailors cast envious eyes hoping that they might be left on board, but the Frenchmen refused to be parted from them as they struggled up the transport's ladders, and instead left their French Foreign Legion machine-guns and tripods behind, together with their carbines and ammunition. Both of the latter were in poor condition, as we found later, as the machine-guns had a tendency to jam frequently, and the magazines of the carbines were almost all defective, so that to operate them the cartridge had to be loaded single shot at a time. The 1914 British service rifles we carried on the bridge were most superior weapons by comparison and condition!

As dawn came on the last day at Namsos, we buried our dead, Lieutenant Commander W. McGuigan RNR, commander of the A/S trawler *St Goran*, and four of his crew, all of whom were killed instantly by a bomb splinter from the diver-bomber attack we had witnessed. Lieutenant Commander Martyn

Sherwood softly read the age-old burial service of the sea. Their canvas-shrouded forms, with steel fire bars at their feet, dived to rest many fathoms deep in Namsen Fjord. 'Billy Mac', as we had called him, was a great favourite with all hands; we mourned him like family.

With *Cape Passaro* and *St Kenan* we now followed the convoy, escorted by the cruiser HMS *York* and two destroyers, out to the open sea, then turned north up the Norwegian coast to a rendezvous anchorage in Skjelfjord where we were to replenish our coal bunkers from a collier. Here we found the cruiser HMS *Penelope*, looking rather like a porcupine from the many wooden plugs filling the shell holes in her sides gained at the second battle of Narvik, at anchor with two Polish destroyers, and the British Tribal class destroyer HMS *Eskimo*, whose bow had been blown off by a German destroyer's torpedo and now had the bulkhead sealed off with a cement block. Thus, during air raids, her AA guns were not fired for fear of breaking the seal. It was a quiet night and all hands had a precious, sound sleep.

The next day was a Sunday and a bright sunny afternoon. After seeing that the first lieutenant of the Polish destroyer *Grom* had his men painting ship overside, we heard the drone of visiting Heinkels. The Polish sailors jumped up from their painting stages to man and open fire with their ship's anti-aircraft guns in response to the high-level bombing coming close to them. The aircraft disappeared, and to the great astonishment of our crew, the Poles went back overside to continue their painting job. Formidable indeed!

With the evacuation of the Allied forces at Namsos the Luftwaffe were now free to step up their operations in the Narvik area, and with land targets becoming scarce, were concentrating on the British ships in the fjords, where it was difficult for us to take avoiding action. The cruiser HMS *Aurora* was caught in a narrow inlet with no room to turn. A bomb from one of the attacking Heinkels landed on a gun turret, causing casualties, so that the *Aurora* went out to the open sea to patch up the damage and bury her dead. The Polish destroyer, *Grom*, caught in a similar situation, was sunk on 4 May after leaving the Skjelfjord anchorage.

Having evacuated the troops we now received orders to contact two transports due to arrive near Lodingen near the head of Vestfjord, and after taking the troops on board, take them to Harstad. The small-scale chart indicated a narrow, winding channel, lacking any lighted buoys or shore beacons, to be navigated in the dim half-light twilight of the northern night.

On the way to take on water at a Norwegian village with one unpaved street and only two wooden piers for our three ships to berth, a submerged object was contacted on the asdic, and, it having the earmarks of a possible U-boat, *St*

Leading Seaman S.D. Fred Houghton DSM RNR. Page 3 refers: 'This Listener' in his high chair on the bridge of HMS St Loman. *His tea mug handy on the A/S Recorder top.*

HMS Eskimo *after the 2nd Battle of Narvik. Anchored in Skjelfjord. Waiting return to UK steaming stern first.*

21

Loman and our two consorts made three depth-charge attacks to split it apart in some 20 minutes. By 9 p.m. that evening our watering was completed and we sighted the two transports. One of the four German aircraft which had been buzzing around made a half-hearted attack and, after dropping three bombs all wide of their marks, made off in the gathering dimness of the night approaching. Our three trawlers followed the transports to a temporary anchorage in a small fjord and went alongside to take on the troops and their baggage. My first Lieutenant, H.O.T. Bradford, counted close to 600 officers and men aboard, and being the first ship loaded we had the doubtful honour of being the pilot ship leading the way to Harstad. The officers went down to our wardroom where they made casualties of our remaining whisky supply, while the Brigade Major stayed up on the bridge with me. I had a prior conference with our chief engineman, Jimmy Dell, and warned him that there might be occasions when I would ask for 'full astern' on the engine-room telegraph, as we would be proceeding cautiously, running the echo sounder continuously to check the depth of shoaling, with the asdic rating training the oscillator to 'ping' for any possible obstructions ahead in the narrow ship channel.

There was literally 'standing room only' on the decks of *St Loman*, and the very thought of the ship going aground with this amount of human cargo was terrifying. As we steamed steadily towards Harstad, the major commented: 'You seem to know your way around here very well!' Little did he know that it was a first-time trip, and I replied that we had the charts and sounding equipment to help us in these waters.

Dawn was starting to break when we arrived at Harstad, and the main quay was packed with men, equipment and stores. Some Norwegian nurses in white uniforms had the men on the dock lined up for a mug of hot tea and buns, just like a Sunday school treat. Our contingent of troops disembarked and joined the tea and bun line-up, and we were about to have their baggage put ashore when the major returned to speak with me.

'A mug of tea and buns was organized for us here, but our billets are on the other side of the bay. Would you mind taking the men across when they have finished their tea? It will save us a march of about three miles at least. And could you take about a hundred extra who were here when we arrived?'

The officers and men were Territorials fresh out from England, and had not experienced any of the ministrations delivered by the Luftwaffe in Norway from dawn to dusk. Harstad was still smoking in a few places from the previous day's raids. I thought of the coming visit by a reconnaissance plane, the mass of men and equipment exposed on the quay, the target that would be reported, and how I had been hoping to be away down the channel from this inevitable non-stop daylight bombing invitation to the Heinkels. 'Very well, sir. Get them back aboard as soon as they have swallowed their tea, have them bring the buns back with them to eat on board and we'll do our best to make space for that extra hundred down below and up on the engine-room casing and gun platforms.'

I felt that although we had had enough trooping for the day, it was essential to break up that crowd on the quay before the Heinkels arrived to do it with bombing. So back they all came with the hundred extra, and we ferried them across the bay looking like a crowd of pilgrims bound for Mecca. The German reconnaissance plane could be heard high in the clouded sky, and two hours later German aircraft were passing over us on their way to bomb Harstad as we were making the bend in a very narrow channel, with no room to take the slightest avoiding action. One of the Heinkels could not resist screaming down to drop a bomb some fifty yards away before taking off again for the town. We were going full astern to avoid running ashore and as the bomb landed we grounded on a shallow rock shelf making a nice stationary target. Luckily it was low water at this time, no other aircraft came to attack us and three hours later the tide put us afloat again whereupon we continued on our way south to Lodingen.

At Namsos we would not have been so fortunate, but the bombing in this new operational section of the Norwegian coast seemed more casual by comparison, as if the German airmen had orders to spread their bomb loads evenly as there were more ships and shore targets in this area adjacent to Narvik. Three or four near misses throughout the day were not regarded as serious individual attention, although unpleasant to experience.

I had been on the bridge of *St Loman* for many watchful and stressful hours, and on putting the ship alongside the wharf at Lodingen I went down to the trawler skipper's cabin, hoisted myself up into the big bunk and slept for six or seven hours. Waking at eight o'clock by the cabin clock, I had to think for several minutes about whether it was morning or evening, there being little difference between the light at dawn or dusk.

The operations HQ of the Norwegian Navy was in the only hotel and with the only telephone link to the outside world. With my two officers, Bradford and Osborne, I went ashore to report to the Norwegian NOIC, and having 'made our number', so to speak, visited the hotel bar to quench a desire and thirst for beer that was very longstanding. Just as we were putting a wonderful Norwegian lager to our lips, a young Norwegian naval officer hurried in with a signalled report of a U-boat being suspected in the vicinity. We had observed that the hotel's beer supply was rapidly approaching vanishing point, thus we could not help feeling that the NOIC might have concocted the submarine report to get us away from the bar before we made further inroads into the last of the precious stock of beer. Perhaps our suspicions were unjustly founded, for there was a submarine periscope sighting report in the fjord, and the dozen officers of the three ships in our group dutifully downed their beer before taking our ships out to sweep the fjord. We swept and we swept with our asdics or sonar gear, but all to no avail. With our half-quenched thirsts we remained suspicious of the validity of our assignment.

Eventually we received instructions to return to Skjelfjord for coal and await further orders. On the way we were hailed by a Tribal class destroyer asking on her loud hailer: 'Have you any mail for us?'

'No,' was our response.

To which came the query: 'Haven't you come from Scapa?' and, receiving another negative asked, 'Where are you from?'

'Namsos,' was our reply.

The reply came over the destroyer's open microphone: 'Christ!'

Later on we sent a small delegation with the wireless operator and his coder to get up to date on their signals and navigation notices to the battle cruiser *Resolution*. On returning, our W/Tel D. Crowsley reported with some pride in his voice: 'You know, sir, they've got notices up in that ship about panic in air raids!' No doubt about it, the ship's company were considering themselves as real veterans under fire!

About the same time, we became senior officer of the 15th A/S Striking Force by the process of elimination. Lt Jimmy James RNR, commanding the *St Kenan*, had collapsed completely during an air raid and had been taken to hospital, while as Lt Cdr Martyn Butt Sherwood RN commented to me: 'It was the third bomb that hit *Cape Passaro*. Will you make the report to the Admiralty for our group, if you get back?'

Narvik had been captured on 28 May 1940 and on 7 June had been evacuated as the last British naval units had reached the high seas. While lying in Skjelfjord, which my Australian officer had dubbed Hell Fjord due to the regular high-level bombing, we received orders to return to the UK with the cruiser *Penelope*, the damaged destroyer, *Eskimo*, and the Polish destroyer together with a small assortment of supply and troopships forming a small convoy, which was to sail at night so as to get well into the open sea before the daily aircraft visit. Fortunately, visibility was poor, and low cloud cover, together with fine, misty rain, shrouded our exit from Skjelfjord, but cleared a little during the next three days when we could expect the daily call from the German Heinkels. Luckily their bomb aiming was a lot worse than previously, but on the last of these attacks several of the aircraft pressed home their attacks at low level and I found were machine-gunning the ships' bridges, when making their run-in to attack, as I had been watching for the bombs to start to fall from an attacking aircraft prior to making any helm order.

Glancing around as the aircraft passed over, I found no sign of anyone with me. Then the signalman, Sid Wain, clambered out of the protective steel 'coffin' with the bridge lookout and my first Lieutenant, H.O.T. Bradford, appeared from the wheelhouse ladder commenting: 'By God, Sir! You've got guts standing up here when they're machine-gunning us!'

'Machine gunning?' I queried.

'Look at those bullet holes in the bridge woodwork!' he replied. He was right, no doubt about it.

'Look at my legs,' I said.

'Are you hit?' he asked.

'No,' I replied, 'but I want you to tell me if you see any movement and if they are straight up and down.'

'Your legs look as though you are standing still,' Bradford said, 'but why?'

'I'll tell you,' I said. 'My knees feel as if they are knocking together and my legs are about to turn to jelly and drop me down on the deck!' He laughed, but I really meant it. No one believed me!

On this final attack the destroyer *Eskimo*, which was travelling stern first with her engines going astern to avoid stress and strain against the remaining bulkhead of her lost bow, had not opened fire during the previous raids, but let go with everything she had at the diving aircraft. Fortunately, her bow bulkhead held fast as she continued steaming stern first.

The weather was now closing in with protective rain and mist as we approached the Shetland Islands. But now there was a new note in the sky – British fighter aircraft, the first we had seen or heard in over a month. They were a great and cheering sight. Our little convoy made for the Pentland Firth and the entrance to Scapa Flow, when we were detached with orders to proceed to Aberdeen, arriving there about two days later. Only when we went ashore, feeling firm cobblestones of the fish dock under our feet, did we realize the tension under which we had been working for the past month or more. A terrific feeling of elation came over me and my two officers as, shining, shaved, and in our No. 1 uniforms, we strode up the dock towards the Naval Base in the offices of the Imperial Hotel down at the harbourside.

The *St Loman* was due for boiler cleaning and five days leave to each of the two watches, so my next visit was to the paymaster's office with my ship's crew list. I handed my list to the paymaster lieutenant requesting that pay for the *St Loman* be made up to date.

'*St Loman* is sunk!' he replied, pointing to a blackboard on the wall behind him, with the names of the 15th A/S Striking Force having strike-out lines through *St Loman*, *St Kenan*, and *Cape Passaro*, while *St Goran*, also at the bottom of Namsen Fjord, remained afloat according to his records.

I told him that I was quite sure that the *St Loman* was afloat and now alongside the dock in Aberdeen, that he should strike out *St Goran* and reactivate the *St Loman*, while getting confirmation from Operations, if he wanted to be reassured.

We had received mail for *St Loman* when we first arrived at Skjelfjord, which was regarded as a rendezvous location for Narvik ship operations. I had received two letters, one of which was from my wife Betty, who was imagining herself in love with a nearby gentleman farmer named Dalgeish and asking me 'to be a dear, sweet, kind boy and give her grounds for a divorce'. The other letter was from the Canada Life Insurance Company to say that as the quarterly payment on my 'all risks' life insurance policy had not been made it was being cancelled. In reply to my wife I had regretted that there were no opportunities for getting a co-respondent, much as I would have welcomed the opportunity in my present situation, but on the other hand she might become a pretty little widow at any time which would entail a minuscule pension, in all probability.

I sent the Canada Life letter to Barclays Bank who were paying my premiums by banker's order, informed Canada Life, and commented that their company might want to sell me life insurance after this war. In my mail at Aberdeen was an apology from Canada Life, and a note from Betty commenting that 'you will always get back all right!' It did look that way, of course.

At the same time as Narvik was captured on 7 June and was being evacuated by the last British naval units, the German Army made its breakthrough to the British Channel ports where about 300,000 Allied troops, most effectively protected in the air by the RAF, were evacuated from Dunkirk between 26 May – 4 June, 1940. I went down to Surbiton in Surrey to spend my leave with my mother and father, and visit my son and his mother, who had moved from the small farm cottage at Brook to stay with her mother and father near Hampton Court.

After a day at home I went up to London to report to the A/S Warfare Division at the Admiralty, and as I had promised Lt Cdr Martyn Sherwood, as the commanding officer of the surviving ship of the 15th A/S Striking Force and its senior officer by default, I asked for Cdr Frank Mason and was given a guide to take me through the warren of Admiralty corridors to his office. My debriefing, to use the US Navy term, was most informal, the Navy captains and commanders called me by my surname, and I said 'Sir' to them in our conversations regarding the Norwegian operations. In one operations room there was a large map of northern Norway showing the location of an announced Allied minefield. 'That's not where the Admiral's signal gave it to us,' I observed, 'but this way.'

'Oh, that's where he's got it,' replied the operations officer, adding, 'it doesn't really matter because there is nothing there. It is a proposed minefield which has to be declared.' He proceeded to alter his chart according to my information.

Mason then took me to a Commander Fawcett who was responsible for the monthly Anti-Submarine report, produced by the Anti-Submarine Warfare Division at the Admiralty. Fawcett was most interested in the anti-submarine patrols that I had carried out with the *St Loman*, and our asdic sweeps made of the approaches to and from the entrance to Namsen Fjord. 'All the other chaps have told us about the intensive and continuous bombing by German aircraft, but you have been carrying out anti-submarine work in spite of it. Now, would it amuse you to write up the experiences of A/S trawlers in Norwegian waters for the May 1940 issue of the staff report?'

I thought for a few minutes and then put the question: 'What you would like me to present, sir, might be termed "the truth appetisingly told"?'

'Exactly!' Fawcett replied.

I went to work and mailed the copy to Commander Fawcett RN, Anti-Submarine Warfare Division, Room 9, South Block, Sub-Ground, Admiralty. Fawcett later wrote to me in a letter dated 22 July 1940.

Dear Warwick,

I am afraid you must think me an awful stinker for not having written to thank you for your account of the Norwegian Operations. I have been flat out with one thing and another.

I am glad to say that I obtained permission to include your account in the May edition, untouched. I am very grateful to you, as it is far away the brightest and best thing I have been able to publish, and I feel you have done your fellow Norwegians a service in producing a permanent record of the hectic time you all had.

I am now doing another job as well as the book, and so should never have had time to piece together anything that would have done your experience justice.

Again many thanks, and good luck. Don't fail to look me up next time you are this way.

I did look him up several months later when Fawcett told me that in response to his request to have me assigned to him for a project on which he was engaged, the terse reply was: 'On no account is this officer to be taken from sea!'

Before I left the Admiralty, a young RN commander in Frank Mason's office asked me for the names of some officers and men of above ordinary skill, courage and devotion to duty. I commented on Lt Stannard RNR and his first Lieutenant, Max Lees RANVR, of the *Arab* damping down the burning ammunition dump with the ship's hoses when evacuating the Chasseurs Alpins at the burning pier at Namsos.

As to the *St Loman*, my first lieutenant, Sub Lt H.O.T. Bradford RNVR, and Sub Lt Frederick Meares Osborne RANVR, my asdic officer, had unhesitatingly manned the anti-aircraft Lewis guns, which lacked any effective protection against enemy fire. The Oerlikon gun, with little better protection, was manned by Sea Gunner Andrew Morrison RNR, Seamen W. Wilson, and Alexander Graham RNR, while Eng W. McCallum RNR continued to pass the ammunition to them. Leading Seaman Robert G. Mackenzie RNR carried out the duties of coxswain, keeping the crew ready for action and manning the ship's wheel for fast and effective course alterations during air attacks. Throughout all activities and actions W/Tel D. Crowsley RNVR maintained W/T communications.

These were the men, setting an example 'as to how every man should do his duty', I told the young RN commander. The gossip mill had it that he had divorced his wife, married Lady Alexandra Haig, and was regarded as an officer on his way up in the Royal Navy, with a reputation as an outstanding destroyer commander.

When in the operations office, I was taken to join a little group of staff officers to listen to a commander they all envied because he had been sent to Holland with a staff of demolition experts and explosives in order to blow up various dock gates, dikes and other useful installations that would be taken over following the German advance, but that the Dutch just would not destroy of their own volition.

On returning home from my visit to the Admiralty I found my younger brother Ian, now a captain in a Territorial regiment of the Royal Engineers and a budding architect, visiting my parents. He had been evacuated through the French port of Le Havre, where he had expected me to be to bring him back across the channel!

* * *

It was quiet in England after Dunkirk, as if the country had received a winding blow and was now sitting back to regain its breath. My father's import business had closed down and the three houses which had been converted into flats just about paid the mortgages with the tenants' rents. 'Why don't you three boys take over the properties and pay your mother a monthly allowance?' he suggested one evening.

'That's not a very practical arrangement,' I said, 'I am at sea in the Navy, Ian is in the Army, and our brother Alan is in India running the gun carriage factory in Jubblepore. You know what your living costs amount to roughly, so what I think would be the simplest solution is to divide that by three and each of us boys will pay a third share each into mother's bank account every month. I will write to Ian and Alan and advise them of the arrangement we propose and you don't have to make any changes in handling the property, rents, tenants, etc.' As the middle brother it always seemed to me that I was expected to take over the responsibilities of the eldest son, possibly because I had gone to sea after leaving college and thus the first to be out in the world!

My two brothers agreed with my suggestion. Alan and I duly made bankers orders, but my young brother Ian compromised by giving my mother the signature on his bank account, which of course my mother would never use if it could be avoided, and of which, I remarked to him in later years, he was fully aware!

My father seemed rather relieved with my solution. He was now approaching his nineties and not too well a man besides, nevertheless he always endeavoured to be bright-eyed and cheerful. As my mother had once remarked to me: 'When your father acts more cheerful than usual, I'm always suspicious that things are bad in the business!' Mother was right of course, but my father had taught this son a valuable lesson about how one should behave when the going gets tough and even dangerous.

The days of my leave passed quietly. I visited my son staying with his grandparents at their great Hampton Court house surrounded by a massive brick wall with iron-barred entrance gate. Leaving in the early evening, I often went to the New Inn pub a little way up the street for a quiet beer before taking the bus back to Surbiton. One night I went into the small Confectioner/ Newsagent/Tobacconist across the street from Grove House, run by a rather nice young woman, to buy cigarettes. As the bus went past she said, 'That's your last bus!' Then, smiling, for we had met in the shop before, she added, 'Why don't you stay over and take one in the morning?' We both needed each other, and so I did.

CHAPTER III

My five days leave passed all too quickly and I returned to Aberdeen where the *St Loman* had been in dry dock for the refitting of the asdic dome covering the asdic oscillator which had been leaking slightly, and for a periodic boiler-cleaning operation. Sub Lt H.O.T. Bradford had received his desired MTB assignment and was leaving to take up his command working out of a channel port. In his place came Sub Lt Gilbert Neville Jones RNVR, a rugby football enthusiast good enough to be approached for a base assignment so that he could play scrum-half for the Royal Navy, an opportunity he passed up to be on active sea duty. Then on a temporary assignment came Sub Lt Gott RANVR, a very young Australian whose father had won a Victoria Cross in the first World War.

Aberdeen was getting its share of attention from German bombers, as was evidenced by what happened to two blocks of county council flats or apartments. They had been designed so that two bathrooms were on each of the six stair-landings, one assigned to an apartment on either side. Near bomb misses on either side had caused the outside walls of the upper sections to fall away to expose the baths and WCs on the three upper floors, with the stairs and stair wells left intact, providing a somewhat indecent exposure.

I received orders to escort a small coastal convoy from Aberdeen to Duncansby Head, leaving the convoy when it entered the Pentland Firth to proceed to Baltasound on the island of Unst, the farthest north of the Shetland Islands, marked by the Muckle Flugga lighthouse. Sub Lt Gott was on the bridge with me when we cleared Aberdeen harbour and moved ahead of the little column of merchant ships. 'When do we practice action stations?' he asked me.

Gott looked a little askance when I remarked, 'That's not too necessary in our experience.'

About that time a couple of German bombers appeared out of the low clouds. I pressed the button for action stations, which was really not too necessary as 'Flash', the gunners' Alsatian dog, was already barking and nipping the heels of the gun crews as they poured up from the mess deck. A couple of bombs fell near the leading ships of the convoy, and one of the aircraft came close enough for us to exchange a short burst of machine-gun fire. The aircraft disappeared in the clouds with the sound of their engines fading as 'Flash' ceased barking to go below as the gun crews stood down. The stokers continued to dump the ashes from the engine room over the side and Leading Seaman Robert Mackenzie organized his hose crew to clean the decks of harbour dirt.

About an hour later, there was a repeat performance by a single bomber, after which Gott commented, 'Now I understand what you meant about the necessity for practice!'

A couple of days later found the *St Loman* entering the long stretch of Baltasound and making fast to the end of the little wooden pier to which the island ferry from Kirkwall came every two weeks with mail, passengers, and supplies for the little villages of Yell, Mid Yell and Burravoe, and a dance was held in the small community hall at Baltasound.

The Naval Officer-in-Charge, or NOIC, was a Royal Navy Fleet Air Arm commander whose flight consisted of an antique 'Walrus' flying boat flown by a RN lieutenant and his Leading Seaman telegraphist and gunner. *St Loman* was the guardship on which the commander and the pilot gathered with us in the little wardroom for the traditional midday pink gin of gin and angostura bitters. It was June/July with long, pleasant summer days when the nights were as daylight at dawn. It was considered that after reoccupying northern Norway the Germans might initiate a landing on the Orkney and Shetland Islands, thus the daily 'Walrus' flight was the advance patrol nearest to the coast of Norway.

'Freddy' Osborne had been a lawyer in Sydney, New South Wales, who felt that if he did not get 14 hours sleep out of 24 he did not feel really at his best, but had cheerfully lost a lot of his sleep during April and May 1940. On going ashore, his first priority was always the dining room of the best hotel available. His friends in Sydney had provided a multiplicity of introductions to friends and acquaintances of theirs forming a wonderful address book, and even on the island of Unst he had an introduction to the local minister. After entertaining Freddy to dinner, the minister had suggested that the crew of his ship might attend the church one Sunday. When Osborne relayed this invitation, I countered by suggesting that the minister hold a service on board as I doubted that there would be many volunteers wishing to walk five miles or more there and back on a Sunday! Nevertheless he might discuss it first with Leading Seaman Mackenzie, who was acting as Coxswain. 'Mac' made it known that all were welcome at the church on a Sunday, but the 10-mile walk proved too much distraction for all hands.

As Captain of the guardship, I received a Sunday evening dinner invitation from the Laird of Baltasound and presented myself at his low, ranch-style house with a bottle of my duty-free Scotch whisky. After dinner of boiled mutton followed by a roly-poly suet pudding, the laird's wife excused herself while her husband and I sat on the sofa by the French windows looking out on the sound and pleasured ourselves with the good Scotch.

In days gone by, Baltasound had been a busy place when the shoals of herring moved in an almost solid tide up the east coast of England, commencing near Yarmouth where they were met by the fishing boats catching and transporting the silvery fish to the waiting Scotch fisher girls to be filleted for drying and kippering. As the herring shoals moved up the coast, so did the fishing boats at sea and the fisher girls at their tables on the fish docks. It seems that Baltasound enjoyed the maximum concentration of the north-sweeping herring shoals, and a low-lying complex of now-deserted brick-packing and curing sheds presented a hive of activity during the season. Then, for some unknown reason or whim of nature, the herring shoals came no more. The laird and I talked over and discussed such matters as we looked out over the sound, until the northern lights and twilight faded into the early-dawning light outlining more sharply the almost horizontal foliage and limbs, streamlined from west to east by the winds of winter, of the small fir trees which clung tenaciously to the heather-covered earth and rocks.

The days passed quickly and were a welcome relaxation with walks along the crests of the steep, rocky cliffs of the island. Initially, some of the hands carried their Chasseurs Alpin carbines to shoot at the black arse-up ducks and cormorants down below. This activity had to be discouraged as the NOIC received some complaints of ricochets off the rocks startling the populace, who never seemed to be in existence, but were there just the same.

A small grassy field served as a practice soccer pitch, culminating with an exhausting challenge match between the mess deck versus the wardroom and POs.

The wardroom and PO's mess won, principally due to the sustained and spirited leadership of Sub Lt Jones, the former potential scrum-half for the Welsh rugby team. As I soaked my aching limbs in a hot seawater bath I made a resolution not to do this sort of thing again!

After some two weeks of our guardship duty, the Commander (A) came aboard for his noonday gin with a signal from Scapa Operations to the effect that he and his staff were to pack up and return to Scapa, while *St Loman* was to depart for Belfast and, being based there, would be operated by the Commander-in-Chief, Western Approaches Command. C-in-C W.A. was now responsible for the Western Ocean, Gibraltar, and also coastal convoys for merchant ships bound for ports in Scotland and the north-eastern coast of England.

The Commander (A) was rather concerned as to whether the aged Walrus flying boat could take off with the heavy load of himself, the pilot and his seaman gunner plus all their personal gear and records. However, the RN lieutenant seemed hopeful and confident, although it was a very long taxi down the smooth waters of Baltasound, the next day, until the Walrus cleared the water, wobbled a little, then ascended gradually into the sky at the extreme end of the island waterway, accompanied by a small cheer from the crew of the *St Loman*, who now began hauling in the mooring ropes for their departure to Belfast.

The following morning found the *St Loman* being swept through the swirling cauldron of the west-bound tide through the Pentland Firth which flows east and west through the ragged rockbound shores of the firth at 4-5 knots with each changing tide. All the rocks are steep-to, as navigators say, thus a small vessel losing power would just continue being swept through by the eddying tides clear of the rocky piles.

Soon the *St Loman* was rising to the heavy swell of the Atlantic Ocean and, turning south around Cape Wrath into the North Minch passage between the Outer Hebrides and north-west Scotland, we met our assigned coastal section of an inbound Western Ocean convoy. *St Loman* took up station on the starboard side of the two-column procession of miscellaneous merchant ships stretching about two miles, while another A/S trawler, also on passage to Belfast, took station on the port side. These were the thin days of the war when convoy escorts were a bit lean.

The passage through the Minches was uneventful as the convoy again met the Atlantic swells and set course for the North Channel entrance to the Irish Sea.

The merchant ship acting as commodore and leading the starboard column started turning to port to take up the easterly course and put Inistrahul island and lighthouse abeam. As the ship swung slowly, 'boom' went the gun on her stern manned by her armed guard crew, followed by the shell splash where a periscope had been sighted. The U-boat had been waiting for the turn, putting the convoy columns broadside on. The engine room telegraph was rung for full speed as *St Loman* headed for the point at which the merchant ship fired. As the alarm bells were ringing the hands were already at their action stations and up the voice pipes came the broad Scots voice announcing that the depth charges on the stern rails and the midships throwers were ready and requesting depth settings. 'Set to one hundred feet,' was the response and back came that Scots voice of Seaman S.D. Sullivan repeating the order. He had good reason to be keen on this job. The previous winter, as a fisherman working out of Granton, he spent a bitter hour and a half in the cold water of the North Sea when a U-boat shelled and machine-gunned a defenceless fishing fleet. Sullivan did not need telling to get ready. That experience of last winter had changed him from a fisherman to a fighting man with a score to settle. Seaman S.D. Houghton, perched on his stool at the asdic set on the bridge, was impassively listening to the reverberations of the sonar beam as the 'ping's were sent out as he swept the wheel, turning the oscillator in the bow section of *St Loman*'s keel. He made two-degree sweeps from ahead to abeam on either side indicated by a light beam under the compass card in the binnacle. 'Echo and hydrophone noises,' reported Houghton as he started moving his sonar beam to the right and left measuring the extent of his target. Freddy Osborne put on the asdic officer's headphones and nodded assent as I brought the ship onto the target bearing, and 'Bunts' Wain, my signalman, warned the engine room of a pending depth charge attack which would rattle up the engine room dynamos with their concussion. The moving stylus marked the echoes on the asdic recorder paper.

As the range came down, so did the time between the reverberations, and the metallic 'clonk' of the echo from the U-boat hull shortened.

'Fire one!' yelled Freddy into his voicepipes, and the first depth charge with its 250 lb of explosive set to go off at 100 feet depth rolled off the stern rails.

'Fire two!' from Freddy, releasing the second charge off the stern rails and the 'stalks' from the midship throwers on either side made their parabolas with depth charges attached.

'Fire three!' completed the five-charge pattern similar to the Five of Clubs on a playing card, with the third charge being dropped off the rails. The exploding pattern made the whole ship shudder as a dog shaking himself when he comes out of the water. I took *St Loman* about a thousand yards from the target spot, reduced speed to slow ahead and turned the ship so as to bring the U-boat bow on. Seaman S.D Sullivan, with joy in his Scots brogue, reported that both throwers were reloaded and ready for settings.

The 4-inch gun crew were looking a little despondent, feeling no doubt that they were not in on the act. So for the next attack I shouted from the bridge: 'The next lot is for Namsos!' The gun crew brightened up and smiled again.

Robert McKenzie, at his action station at the helm in the wheelhouse below the bridge, reported 20 fathoms on the echo sounder, and the next five-charge pattern was set at 125 feet. Houghton and Freddy Osborne were lining up for the run-in on the target and 'full ahead' was rung on the engine room telegraph. When the next pattern exploded, some black pieces of debris swirled to the surface and disappeared. There was a bloodthirsty cheer from Seaman S.D. Sullivan aft on the depth-charger rail release. Running out from the target area and turning to steam slowly over the spot there was a strong smell of diesel oil accompanied by huge jellyfish-shaped belches of air. Jimmy Dell, the chief engineman came up from below to ask dourly, 'Any bodies yet?' Jimmy's brother had been lost on a minesweeper the previous week.

McKenzie, the coxswain, had been relieved on the wheel to organize the anchoring of a dan buoy with a large red flag and a lantern to mark the spot as we proposed to keep contact, as instructed, until daylight next morning when a destroyer was due to come and investigate. So we remained through the night, keeping bow on to the U-boat hull, watching the light on our dan buoy bob up and down in the slight swell. Twenty fathoms below men might have been dying a slow death, choking on the gas from the mixture of seawater and battery acid as the shattered lights dimmed within the damaged hull.

At dawn the promised destroyer arrived to confirm our diagnosis and steamed off on her patrol. During the action our 'Sparks', W/T D. Crowsley, a peacetime bank clerk, had sent out a brief running commentary reading something like this: 'Periscope sighted and marked by gunfire by convoy . . . investigating probable U-boat contact. First and second attacks made. Oil patches and debris seen on surface. Position buoyed, propose holding contact and standing by for 24 hours.' Later Crowsley was able to post up in the mess deck a simple signal response from Commander-in-Chief, Western Approaches: 'Well done *St Loman*.'

When the situation permitted, A/S ships liked to remain in contact with bottomed U-boats until it was fairly evident that there was no life left on board. Quantities of oil and air coming to the surface were not sufficient hard evidence in themselves. U-boat captains had been known to discharge oil, air and clothing from a torpedo tube to play possum and delude the hunters. Thus engineman Jimmy Dell asked, 'Any bodies yet?'

We sailed into Belfast feeling justifiably self-satisfied. *St Loman* had done the job for which she was destined, but instead of two or three days in harbour to rest and celebrate the occasion, we found the base in a 'flap.' Invasion from the channel ports was imminent. We had 12 hours to coal and sail for Portsmouth. Thus we left that night to see if all we had heard about the German E-boats was really true, and as we made our way down the Irish Sea we fell in with other A/S trawlers from other bases all heading for the Channel ports, where facing us in France, it was reported that the Germans were assembling fleets of barges.

After the North Atlantic and coastal convoys, our particular anti-invasion patrol down south was not really arduous. By day, in clear weather, we remained at anchor and at dusk would go out on patrol in the centre of the channel, while our Motor Torpedo Boats, and Motor Gun Boats, patrolled between us and the French coast, hoping to contact German E-boats and also to report the first signs of any invasion armada, which we were required to tear into with our 4-inch gun, light Lewis machine-guns and our indispensable Oerlikon guns, for as long as we could survive. A signal from the base Admiral in Portsmouth exhorted us, in the words of Admiral Horatio Nelson, to the effect that: 'When in doubt no captain could do better than to lay his ship alongside that of another.'

I had mustered the hands in the mess deck after our arrival and briefing in Portsmouth to put them in the picture as to our assignment. After reading the admiral's recommendation I had commented that we would first take advantage of the range of our 4-inch gun, and that the time to put the ship alongside, or rammed into, a barge full of Huns armed with automatic weapons would be when out of 4-inch shells.

At dusk RAF bombers would be flying south, and an hour or two later German aircraft would start coming over. The night would be filled with their droning, and on either side of the Channel would appear the stabbing silver beams of the searchlights and the flicker of anti-aircraft gun bursts. Occasionally on the French side, we would see a flash and feel a dull concussion as our bombers did good work, and often a dull red glow would flicker up and grow. During daylight hours Coastal Command aircraft did our sentry job, except when the weather thickened and we had to grope our way out to patrol our beat once more.

As we lay at anchor off the South Coast during the day there were daylight raids on Portsmouth and Southampton to watch, but much to our aggravation, we had only one chance to fire effective shots. It was a fine sunny day and four of our ships were lying head to tide watching the dogfights between our fighters and the enemy bombers overhead. Suddenly a German fighter-bomber, trying to throw a Spitfire off his tail, went into a power-dive and, flattening out, roared across the sterns of four waiting ships. Four Oerlikons and twelve Lewis guns pumped lead into him. He probably never knew what hit him as he went plunging into the sea. The Spitfire pilot may have been annoyed at being cheated of his rightful prey, but he might have recalled that he had not had to take so much as we had without being able to retaliate effectively.

* * *

A few weeks slipped by and the invasion threat faded. There was a 'buzz' that a group of invasion barges, putting out from the French coast either on an exercise or probing thrust, had been bombed by the RAF with petrol, or incendiary fluid containers, setting the sea alight around the barges which were full of potential invasion troops, causing horrible casualties and panic. Concentrations of invasion troops and barges were reported being dispersed and burned bodies being washed up on the British Channel beaches. Whether true or false we never learnt, but we went back to be based at Belfast and our convoy duties varied between coastal operations, under our own orders, and Western Ocean convoys, working with destroyer and corvette escort groups based on Greenock, where we were ourselves based later on.

That invasion patrol from dusk to dawn was both a monotonous and rather edgy time. I would be on the bridge from dusk until dawn broke, when my two eyes were the only 'radar', as the issue of that invention, developed by the Navy, had been delayed due to RAF night fighters having first call on its production. The captain of another A/S trawler remarked to me: 'Warwick, you worry too much!' Possibly he was right, and one worry was that in the event of losing my ship I would have to be writing to the 'next of kin', telling Margaretina Morrison why my gunner, Andy Morrison, would not be coming home to her, for instance – after making out many crew lists for paymasters I found I could recall the wives' names of all long-term crew members. It did not occur to me that I might not survive to write those letters. Perhaps I unconsciously believed my own wife's 'You'll always get back!' response to my letter from Norway, in her 'Dear John' letter to me.

Of course there were no shore navigational lights and the only aid to getting a check on the ship's position was to use the fishing skipper's method of taking a run of echo-soundings to be matched with the ship's compass course on the Channel chart. When dawn did break, the *St Loman* was more often than not rather closer to the French coast than necessary for diverting German aircraft on their way back from a night-bombing raid to dump unused bombs prior to landing. While the danger of invasion faded, the U-boat commanders had not been slow to take advantage of the temporary absence and weakening of our convoy escorts.

A brief review of anti-submarine operations in the first six months of the war showed that the convoy system was the outstanding point in these operations, and was the best defence against direct attacks by U-boats. This success was by no means unexpected, as experience in the First World War proved the great value of the system. Out of 164 ships that were sunk by U-boats during the first six months, only 7 were in convoys which were escorted by A/S vessels. These results were achieved in spite of the fact that the A/S escort rarely consisted of more than two vessels, and frequently only one. It seemed that the U-boat had a marked antipathy for attacking convoys, preferring lone neutrals, and stragglers from convoys. Thus the convoy obviously provided the best kind of 'bait' as an attempted or successful attack revealed the presence of the U-boat within reach of one or more A/S vessels and the hunt for her would begin. The first six months of the Second World War showed that if the position of a U-boat were revealed close to A/S vessels, the chances of destroying it were high. The main problem was one of initial detection, mainly due to the short range of our asdic which entailed using a large number of vessels, unless the U-boat could be persuaded to reveal herself within reach. Other problems were the 'non-sub' echoes, i.e. objects other than submarines, and the shortcomings of the asdic when it failed to indicate the depth as well as the range. This led to the development of depth-charge patterns of greater intensity in attempting to cover all the depths at which a U-boat might be lurking.

At this time there was not enough information to provide any really positive evidence about the habits of German U-boats, although it was usually possible, when reliable reports of U-boats in the North Sea were obtained, to determine whether they were bound to or from the Atlantic. The estimated and logical routes used by U-boats to and from the Atlantic (see p. 39) were through the North Sea, then through the Fair Island Channel between the Orkney and Shetland Islands at night before turning southward and setting a course to pass north of Rona. They would then continue almost directly south, passing to the west of the Flannan Isles and St Kilda off the Outer Hebrides to operate in the North Atlantic. The outward track of the U-boats was designed to provide potential contact with inward-bound merchant shipping, most likely to be unescorted neutrals. Their average speed when passing through the North Sea to the North Atlantic was described by the survivors of 'U-63' who stated that on passage she dived all day and proceeded on the surface at night. In order to get her batteries charged up within a reasonable time of 6 hours, she had to proceed at 350 revolutions giving a speed of about 11 knots with a running charge on both diesel engines.

The scarcity of North Sea sighting reports, despite the numerous Coastal Command patrols, confirmed that U-boats dived during daylight hours. In January and February this might have been from 0700 to 1700, thus the 500-ton U-boat, with a cruising speed of 11 knots, might spend 10 hours submerged at 3 knots followed by 14 hours at 11 knots on the surface when her batteries could be recharged. Average speed could increase during bad weather unsuitable for flying, while decreasing as the days got longer. While being hunted, the U-

Plate. 3

C.B.04050/40 (1▸2)

OUTWARD & INWARD TRACKS of "U"-BOATS

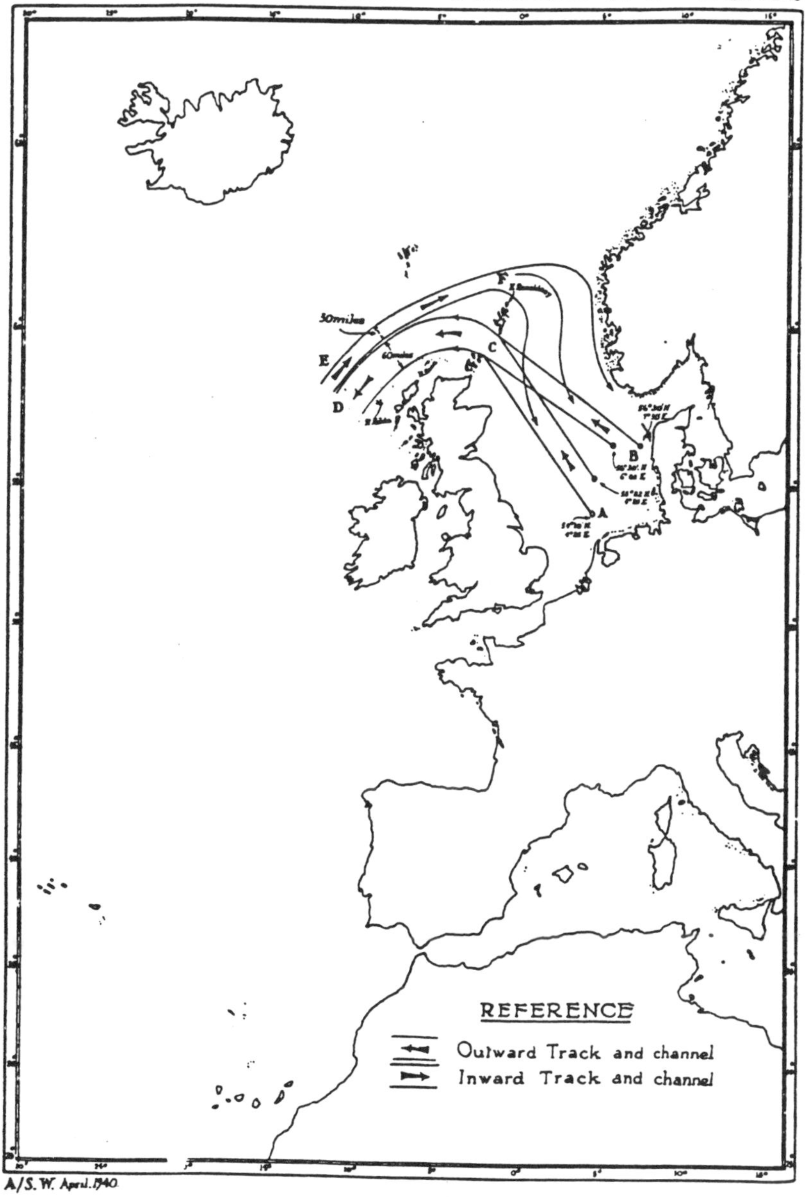

REFERENCE

◄═══ Outward Track and channel
═══► Inward Track and channel

A/S.W. April.1940.

boat generally remained stopped on the bottom at a safe depth, if possible. German submarines carried air-purifying plant and oxygen to last for 48 hours.

The electric torpedoes used were seldom fired from much outside an estimated range of 2,500 yards as their range of 3,280 yards (3,000 metres) would fall off if the battery had not been charged recently. The low speed of the electric torpedo (30 knots) made an attack from before the beam of the target preferable. Attacks on escorted convoys tended to be made during the hours of darkness, and often in fog, mist, and falling snow or heavy rainstorms when a U-boat had the best chance of escaping on the surface, running both engines at estimated full speeds of 17 to 18 knots, although cruising normally at greatly reduced speeds.

German air torpedoes left a track and being much more expensive than electric ones, tended to be used mostly for practice purposes. Nevertheless they had a range of 6,000 yards at 38 knots, and 8,000 at 32 knots. Air torpedoes were carried aft, in an upper-deck tube, as in this position it was impossible to haul back an electric torpedo to recharge the battery. While the invasion threat across the Channel faded, as we returned to our Belfast base, it became apparent that following the fall of France, and with the availability of the French ports of Dieppe, Le Havre and Cherbourg in the English Channel area, with Brest, Lorient and St Nazaire in the Bay of Biscay, the arduous and time-consuming North Sea passage for the U-boats would be much reduced, thereby affording maximum time and effort for the coming Battle of the Atlantic.

On returning to Pollock Dock in Belfast a collision mat, which I had requisitioned a couple of months previously, was delivered on board. In the morning gale and a black squall, a specialty of the Scottish coast, just as the *St Loman* had been picking her way out of an anchorage, a merchant ship about ten times her size had come bearing down. Putting the helm hard over to starboard, I had been able to make the bow of the oncoming ship graze past our stern with the loss of a few yards of paint and rust from the *St Loman*'s hull. Lt Trevor Blore RANVR, my other Australian and a former editor from Reuters Press Association, had tumbled down the iron ladder of the gun platform on the fo'c'sle head to check for any damage aft. Blore had reported just a scrape on the hull, with an off-watch engineman still fast asleep in one of the box-like bunks of the after-cabin, despite the merchant ship's having scraped the hull within a couple of feet of where he had lain.

This incident had prompted me to get a collision mat, which is a coir pad resembling a huge coconut fibre doormat about 12 ft square, secured by fan-shaped ratlines at the top and bottom, as found at the head and foot of a hammock, and made fast to two steel rings.

The new collision mat was opened for inspection, then rolled up and stowed on the foredeck under the whaleback. The next procedure was to lower the light steel chain over the ship's bow, like a skipping rope, bring it aft under the keel to a position amidships, haul the chain tight like the belly band on a horse, and secure it with lashings through the shackles on each end of the chain. The principle of the collision mat being to stem the flow of water into a ship's hull through cracked plates and have the coir fibres drawn in to fill the cracks opened in the hull. My coxswain Robert Mackenzie and the leading seaman gunner, Andrew Morrison, did a workmanlike job in rigging the chains for any future emergency.

St Loman was assigned to pick up a north-about coastal convoy lying in Loch Ewe at the head of Loch Fyne and bound for the Firth of Forth. It was an uneventful passage north through the Minch's, then rounding Cape Wrath to sail east through the boiling cauldron of the Pentland Firth past Stroma to Duncansby Head, then south for the Firth of Forth where the *St Loman* went alongside at Granton, the fishing port near Leith.

Leading Seaman Alexander Graham made a request for 'two days' passionate leave'. It seemed that his fiancée, also from Stornoway, was a nurse at the Edinburgh hospital and this was a chance for them to get married. Graham was a former merchant navy seaman and had been in the Oerlikon gun crew in Norway.

I told him: 'I understand what you mean by "passionate leave", but what I suggest is that I give you a week's compassionate leave as the Navy understands it, then you can rejoin the ship in Belfast where we shall be due after delivering the merchant ships from the Firth of Forth to the Lock Ewe ocean convoy assembly point.' The men of Stornoway, in the Isle of Lewis, sign on as able seamen to travel the ports of the world, but when getting married it is almost always to a girl from Stornoway, and one thing both always have in common is the Gaelic language, which they can both speak and write. It is a beautiful soft tongue.

At the informal convoy conference I recognized the commodore and addressed him by name: 'I know you, don't I?' he said.

'Yes, you do, Captain Berry,' I replied. 'I was the junior cadet on the Royal Mail Steam Packet's cargo ship the *Nariva* sailing out of Cardiff in September 1929 for the West Coast of the US and Vancouver. You were the Chief Officer and I was making my first trip to sea as an apprentice.'

We shook hands warmly as he responded with '. . . And now you are the senior officer of my escort!'

41

It was early December and the weather that evening was promising a wet and rough stormy night as the double column of some eight assorted merchant ships began to slowly start assembling as they came from their anchorages in the Firth of Forth. It was a ragged bunch and I had arranged with the other A/S trawler escort to lead them out, while *St Loman* rounded up all the stragglers into the rear of the column. By the time the little column had formed up, *St Loman* was about a mile astern of the last two ships. The convoy had already rounded the Isle of May and the leaders were passing abeam of the Bell Rock off the Firth of Tay. It was a night as black as the insides of a sick cow, blowing half a gale with occasional rain squalls. Lt Trevor Blore had been relieved with me on the bridge by my comparatively new first lieutenant, another RNVR officer assigned temporarily until his MTB command came up. At around 2200, I told Lt Atkinson to slowly close up to the rear ships of the convoy columns, which would take about two hours and to call me at midnight, when I proposed to take the *St Loman* to a station on the starboard beam of the convoy. I needed that two hours below and as I went down through the wheelhouse I was happy to see that my coxswain, the dour and level-headed Robert Mackenzie was on his watch there with the helmsman. 'Old Mac' as the wardroom officers called him, had better eyes and far more experience at sea than my first lieutenant on the bridge above.

Lying on my bunk fully clothed, lulled into a restful doze by the steady pulse of the engines, I was jarred fully awake by a shuddering crash, followed by a lesser one canting the cabin sharply to port. As I made it up the bridge ladder I saw the huge bulk of a merchant ship clearing the *St Loman*'s stern. We had been hit on the starboard bunkers amidships; fortunately they were full of soft coal and that cushioned the shock. If it had been 12 feet further forward, then it would have cut into the wardroom and Lt Blore, who had taken the chance to change into his pyjamas and sleep in comfort from midnight until seven o'clock. He hardly needed the lookout relaying my message asking him to get up on deck quickly.

Sid Wain, my signalman, had already contacted the merchantman with his Aldis lamp to get the information that she was a straggler from the southbound convoy and was cutting across the rear of our convoy bound for the Firth of Forth. Using the strong beam of the Aldis lamp as a searchlight I saw three sailors trying to cut loose the Carley float made fast to the rigging of the foremast. Swinging the beam to the starboard side amidships I could see where the merchantman had struck and bounced down the *St Loman*'s side. Fortunately the seaboat had not been swung out, and more fortunately still, Mackenzie, looking out of the wheelhouse and seeing the black bulk of the other ship looming down, had swung the wheel quickly to hard-a-starboard so that the *St Loman* was already rolling with the coming punch of the pending collision. Lt Atkinson was saying that he was 'sorry'.

'Don't let's worry about what has happened, Atkinson. Get on the chart table and give me the compass course to about a couple of miles off a sandy-pebble shore, and then north close to the coast towards Aberdeen.' Then grabbing back the Aldis lamp from Sid Wain I hailed to Lt Blore as I trained the lamp on the Carley float: 'Get those bloody young fools off that Carley float. Get that fucking collision mat from under the whaleback and start getting it rigged on the starboard side. Tell them we're not going to get our feet wet and lose all our gear. We can keep her afloat and if need be run her ashore. 'Flash' has more sense than all of them. He's up here sitting in the sternsheets of the boat ready to go ashore!'

Mackenzie and Morrison, the gunner, were already struggling with the collision mat helped by the three sailors off the Carley float to pull it over a massive dent in the starboard side plates, then starting to haul on the chain under the ship's keel to secure it in place, with the mat of oakum and coir backed with canvas over the cracked plates and sprung rivets.

Now the boat was swung out and readied for lowering if required; 'Flash', the gunner's Alsatian, remained crouched in the stern. Jimmy Dell, the Chief Engineman reported water rising disturbingly in his stokehold and engine room.

'You'd better go below and keep an eye on it,' I told Lt Blore. 'Tell the Chief that I'll be making for Aberdeen. If we make it, we can't go in until daylight and we've got to keep going to have that collision mat tamped in, so we might as well make for a place I know the way into. I'll stand in towards the beach and be ready to run her up if she does start to sink. Whistle up the voice pipe every half-hour or so, and let me know what's happening down below.'

I took *St Loman* westwards to within about one mile of the beach with the echo sounder running in the wheelhouse as the ship was headed north, parallel with the shoreline, with the sounder checking on the 5-fathom line shown on the chart. Lt Osborne had been checking on his asdic gear and now came up on the bridge to spell Lt Atkinson, who was rather shaken by the events.

'Keep her going as she is headed now, Mr Osborne. Check the distance from the last position to be off Girdle Ness. Steaming at about five or six knots. Let me know when I come up from visiting the engine room as to what time that might be,' I ordered.

So I went down the bridge ladders and aft to the engine room. Going down I could see the three crankheads of *St Loman*'s reciprocating engines throwing spray over the engine room every time they dipped in the slowly rising water.

Lt Blore was in the stokehold handing out cigarettes from time to time. The stokers, both from Aberdeen, had heard from the Chief where we were headed and were cheerfully shovelling coal into the furnaces as the wet fuel splattered off their shovels. 'Think we'll make it, Chief?' I asked Jimmy Dell.

'Aye, sir. She's still gaining a little, but not too much. Could we turn the condenser intake to draw from inside the ship? It might be just what we need to keep the water where it is now, about six inches below the main fires.'

'Don't worry about the rule book, Chief, put Engineman McCallum on it right away,' I answered.

Jimmy Dell's suggestion worked out and the water intake held below the main fires. Returning to the bridge, I found some of the hands had come to the fiddley grating to stare down into the engine room and ask questions. As they heard the reassuring answers, a speculative look came into their eyes, and grins began to wrinkle their faces. I knew what that meant. They were calculating how much leave the repair job might give them. It was getting near Christmas and they began to realize that this night's accident could mean Christmas at home for them.

Alfy, our boy steward from Lowestoft, was clambering up and down the greasy iron ladder to bring mugs of hot tea down to the engine room. An atmosphere of optimism and cheerfulness prevailed and grew as the light of dawn broke. The wind had dropped and the sun was struggling to rise above the horizon to reveal low, gently-breaking green- and white-flecked waves.

By the time breakfast was finished we were in sight of the Aberdeen signal station and, making our number, flashed a signal requesting permission to enter at high tide. The wireless signals we had sent during the night had warned them to expect us and have a fire brigade pump on the dockside. Replying to the suggestion that we should anchor until high tide, I explained that the *St Loman* had to be kept steaming to operate the converted condenser-intake pump fully or else the water would rise flooding the stokehold and extinguishing the boiler fires. Thus we cruised backwards and forwards off the entrance to the harbour waiting for high tide, as the men came on deck looking eagerly towards the roofs and spires of Aberdeen in the distance.

We then had a meeting on the bridge, and I asked Lt Blore to take down in his news reporter's shorthand my questions to the Officer of the Watch, and his replies. The night had been dark with low visibility, but Atkinson had been able to make out the southbound convoy passing inshore of the tail of our northbound ships, when suddenly the 5,000 ton black bulk bore down out of the darkness, as the straggler headed across the wake of the northbound convoy to get inshore to join the ships bound for the Firth of Forth. The *St Loman*'s sidelights and masthead light were flashed on in warning but the collision was seen to be inevitable.

'Mr Blore, make a note here,' I added to Atkinson's evidence. 'Seeing that the merchantman was about to strike us just forward of the crew's quarters, Lt Atkinson ordered the wheel over to hard a-starboard, so that the *St Loman* was swinging towards the merchantman as she struck us and thus 'rode the punch' of the five-thousand-tonner as her bow crashed into our side below the crew quarters then, sliding down *St Loman*'s hull, cleared us with a passing punch on the quarter. At the same time Seaman Sullivan, who had been operating the asdic wheel on the bridge, slid down the ladders to render the depth charge of the starboard thrower completely safe while the great stem of the merchant ship crashed into the starboard bulwarks buckling the deck plates beneath his feet. Then he had hurried forward to assist those hands ordered to rig the collision mat. Coxswain Robert Mackenzie in the wheelhouse had already anticipated the hard a-starboard order from the bridge so the *St Loman* was swinging when the order came.'

The subsequent court of inquiry held in Aberdeen to determine the cause of the accident took the view that in bad weather, visibility and ships steaming without any navigation lights the collision was an unfortunate wartime incident. Nevertheless the watch on deck of the *St Loman* had possibly saved the ship by good seamanship and initiative, as my report had indicated to the naval court.

At high tide we swept into the inner harbour to make fast alongside the wharf of the fish dock with the fire engine pump drawing the water out of *St Loman*'s cracked hull. *St Loman* was to be boiler-cleaned and dry-docked for hull repairs in Aberdeen, which meant Christmas leave for all hands. Personnel at the Admiralty had initiated changes in my officers. Lt Atkinson was to be relieved (to take up his promised MTB command) by Lt Oswald T. Dodwell RNVR. My Australian officer Lt Trevor Blore RANVR had obtained the Admiralty Press Division appointment for which he had been angling, while Lt Frederic Meares Osborne RANVR was to join a new corvette as first lieutenant, and a Canadian, Lt Willis RCNVR, was to replace him as A/S officer. Thus only Sub Lt Gilbert Neville Jones RNVR remained unchanged. I was beginning to suspect that Commander Frank Mason RN at the Admiralty was using *St Loman* as a 'training ship'!

'Ossie' Dodwell, as my new first lieutenant was to be called in the wardroom, turned out to be a very fortunate change for me. Ossie was a former merchant navy officer holding a 2nd Mate's certificate. He had 'swallowed the anchor' and several sea-going years to manage a free house public house owned by his wife's family and located in the Liverpool dockside. Shortly after the outbreak of war he told me that he had remarked to his wife: 'I think that it's time for me to get into the Navy'.

He received the reply: 'I wouldn't think much of you if you didn't!'

Before taking Christmas leave I took Dodwell out to dinner with an Aberdeen girl I had been dating. Carol Kidd worked in an Aberdeen insurance office and had many attractive girlfriends, all in their early twenties, who liked to meet and mingle with the young navy and airforce officers in the cocktail lounges of the best hotels with the avowed objectives of getting engaged and married. As one forthright friend of Carol's stated: 'If he's engaged he can break it. If he's married he can get a divorce!' In consequence I kept my status unknown. Carol lived with her widowed mother, a trained nurse whose husband, the former regimental sergeant major of a Highland regiment, had been killed in action during the First World War. Mrs Kidd had nursed a bitter hatred through all the ensuing years. 'Kill Germans!' she would implore me.

Christmas leave with my mother found my father in a nursing home and far from well, but as optimistic as ever. I visited my son now living with his grandparents in the big house surrounded by its walled garden in East Molesey, across the Thames from Hampton Court, and spent the night with my friend, their neighbour. I was rather glad to be back in Aberdeen standing by the *St Loman*, visiting the shipyard daily to check on progress and living in a room at

Sub. Lt. Atkinson   Ch.Eng, J.P.T. Dell DSM RNR   Lt. O.T. Dodwell
Sub. Lt. G.N. Jones   Eng. W. McCallum DSM RNR

the naval base section of the Imperial Hotel on the Aberdeen harbourside.

I relieved Ossie Dodwell to go on leave to Liverpool. It seemed that he had introduced Carol Kidd to an old shipmate, a Lt Chesterman RNR and that he appeared to have been a matchmaker. Chesterman was an Australian and it seemed that Mrs Kidd was prepared to go to Australia with her daughter and prospective son-in-law after the end of the war. Aberdeen girls moved fast!

New Year's Eve shrouded Aberdeen in the traditional 'Scotch Mist', a damp, clammy breath wetting the pavements of the unlit streets to a slippery sheen. It seemed appropriate that my first year in command of *St Loman* had begun and ended in Aberdeen. A section of the old Imperial Hotel had been commandeered by the Royal Navy overlooking the waterfront. The RN 'dugouts' and staff commanders, with their base captain, were very comfortable in their hotel rooms some of which were assigned to seagoing officers standing by their minesweepers and A/S trawlers under refit and repair. All these officers had their meals in the hotel dining room, the RN paymaster having negotiated for the officers' lodging and victualling allowances to offset the cost of their room and board in the Imperial Hotel. This was a beneficial arrangement for all concerned, and as might have been expected the Imperial Hotel bar and lounge never lacked for free-spending customers from the Navy, Army, RAF and civilians.

Aberdonians, enjoining the reputation, to use the American idiom, of 'squeezing the quarter until the eagle screams', proved to be the most hospitable people bellying up to any bar in the world. Indeed it was never easy to buy your own beer, much less to buy a reciprocating round of the 'hoffs and hoff pints' or 'big hoffs', meaning a single shot of whisky with a half-pint beer chaser, or a double whisky followed by a pint of beer. The traditional Scotch custom was to first down the whisky to create a flaming throat, to be quenched at once by the following draft of beer.

As might be expected tongues loosened fast and former strangers became instant friends. Thus, all around the bars, there were cheerful voices telling many good tales, for this was the sailormen's world in the harbour bars designed to welcome thirsty sailors and their captains returning from the sea.

Many engaged in the Scotch custom of 'First Footing'. After midnight on New Year's Eve, young men would visit family parties being held in their homes, enjoying 'tea and drams'. Lt Hamish Edgar RNVR of the Aberdeen base staff, and a native Aberdonian, owned the doubtful asset of an automobile, and now enlisted three of the seagoing officers to make up a 'first footing' party to visit friends and neighbours.

'First Footing' gives an excellent opportunity for young and unattached men to start the coming year with new friends and acquaintances. Your group must have its bottle, or preferably bottles, of Scotch whisky, and include the essential dark-haired man who must be the first to enter the home when the door opens to his knock. On entering, the dark man proceeds to kiss all the ladies, young and old, and is followed by the rest of the group doing likewise. Having established this delightful initial social contact the visitors now offer a drink from their bottle which will be reciprocated by a return response by the folks in the home visited.

For our opener we had Lt Chrichton RNVR, known in the ships' wardrooms as 'bedroom eyes'. This tall, slim, dark-featured and essential ladies' man made our initial entry and the well accepted passes, closely followed by the flaming red-headed, freckled face of Hamish Edgar, the anti-climax being the two blonde heads of myself and Lt Norman Hartnell RNR, commanding the A/S trawler *Northern Dawn*.

Hamish Edgar had many friends' houses to visit, so it was perhaps fortunate that his old auto had a flat battery, as after every first-footing visit and consumption of several drams came the sobering effort of pushing the car to get it started while keeping on our feet. When Hamish ran out of addresses we knocked on the doors of several houses emanating from which was the sound of song and music through the blackout-curtained windows.

Dawn was lighting the streets when we made it back to our beds in the Imperial Hotel through the damp, deserted streets. My hotel bed had never looked more restful and inviting. I undressed and closed my eyes for what seemed just a few restful seconds, when there came a loud hammering on my door and the orders: 'Everyone down to the shelter,' accompanied by the wavering, warning wail of the air raid sirens.

'Just like the bloody huns to make a useless air raid on this granite-built city during the Scotch hangover on the morning of New Year's Day,' I grumbled, dressing and going downstairs to the accompaniment of some dull thuds of bombs and AA gun fire, soon followed by the steady welcoming wail of the 'all clear'.

Resting for a while I got shaved, fully dressed and went down to breakfast. Then, walking down to the shipyard where *St Loman* was in drydock, I saw where one small house of granite blocks had received a near miss. The walls still stood firm while just a few slates were disarranged on the roof giving the 'very dour' appearance of resistance and determination.

During the past year, *St Loman* with its hard-bitten but happy crew had replaced my home and family, for my son Richard was now being brought up by his grandparents while his mother was being employed on a Ministry of Food project, living with a girlfriend in London during the week and spending weekends at her brother's house in Chobham, Surrey. Rice's Farm, which we had rented in Brook, Surrey, while it was more secure from the now more intensive bombing raids was an understandably dull location for an attractive and vital young woman, compared to the more exciting wartime atmosphere of London.

St Loman was soon moved out of drydock to the harbour dock-side for coaling and storing, as all hands and officers returned from their shore leave. Steam had been raised so that once again the ship became a living thing.

While changes had been made in the officers, crew members were as before. I learned from the 'galley wireless' that their wives considered *St Loman* a 'lucky ship' to stay with. So far that had been the case and as one of my more frequent dates observed to me: 'You love that ship more than you love any woman, which is right because she will never let you down!' I was not sure whether this was a complaint or a compliment.

Later, recalling her observation, I mentally reviewed some of the most prominent members of my ship's family. First and foremost G. Mackenzie DSM RNR, the very salt of the earth and sea and a father to all seamen he supervised as their bos'un. Often, after making a shy knock on my cabin door, 'Old Mac' would introduce a suggestion or recommendation with; 'I was thinking, skipper'. Or, contacting Lt Oswald Dodwell RNR in the wardroom he would say, 'Mr Dardsen, I was thinking . . .' He was never able to get the first lieutenant's name correctly, nor did we ever correct him! Mackenzie came from the small Scotch fishing village and port of Wick on the north-east coast, graduating from drift-net fisherman to deep-sea sailor on merchant ships.

The Leading Seaman Gunner, Andrew Morrison DSM RNR, was Mackenzie's right-hand man. Another deep-sea sailor and sometime bricklayer from Edinburgh, owner of 'Flash' the talented Alsatian dog who, it was rumoured, had gone to sea to avoid the dreaded accusation of chasing and killing sheep, and the punishment of death, if proved. Thus Flash was without 'home leave' for the duration, in banishment to the seaman's messdeck. Andy had clean-living and sober habits, but possessed an effective and very fast right-hook silencer for the noisier inebriates returning from shore leave.

The former Oerlikon gun crew of Leading Seaman Alexander Graham DSM RNR and Able Seaman William Wilson DSM RNR now manned a twin-barrel .50 calibre machine-gun. I recalled how Wilson had overstayed his leave and Mackenzie had brought him up on Captain's Defaulters. I asked the dark, curly-haired Grimsby trawlerman: 'You were a day late, Wilson. Everyone else made it on time. Why did it happen?'

'Well, sir, it was like this. We had four days leave, and on the first night, second night, and third night there were air raids and the wife and I were down in the cellar with the two kids.' There was a brief silence. Mackenzie and Lt Dodwell were trying to keep straight faces.

'What about the fourth night? No air raids?' I asked.

'That night the bed went through the floor!' answered Wilson. There was another silent period. Mackenzie and Dodwell were wearing broad grins.

After a judicious pause, I observed: 'So you took another and more pleasant night and were a day late because of it? Dismissed with a caution on compassionate grounds, coxswain!'

The morning watch was turned out with the cheerful shout of 'Wakey, wakey, rise and shine, you've had your time, I want mine!' That was Leading Seaman T.W. Cuthbert RNPS, a former Hull fish filleter who had finagled his RNPS entry and rank with a fake discharge written by a shipping clerk friend signing off a trawler crew in Hull.

Down below, in the engine room, ruled the chief engineman and senior petty officer, James Peter Thompson Dell, DSM RNR, a trawler engineer from Fleetwood, Lancashire, where his parents had moved from Shields, Northumberland. Fleetwood knew Jimmy for one of its brightest harbour lights. He stood a little over five feet tall and topped a lean steel and whipcord frame with a Norwegian-cast face inherited from his grandfather, which was always twisted into a cheerful look of roguery.

Jimmy's second engineman, William McCullum, DSM RNR, was his shore-going drinking companion. 'Mac' was an Aberdonian, skilled in finding and acquiring any scarce bits of gear that might be needed at some time on board. As bombs were falling fast and near, in Namsos, he came up from the engine room to volunteer carrying ammunition to the AA gun's crew, strolling calmly and leisurely along, singing very much out of tune: 'Every time it rains, it rains pennies from heaven'. Sober or 'drink taken', the oddly-matched pair would roll off and return with the same heaving gait much to the disapproval of 'Old Mac' the coxswain.

On another occasion in Belfast, when *St Loman* was standing by for guardship duty at the entrance to the lough, Mackenzie reported all hands on board with the exception of enginemen Dell and McCullum who had stepped ashore and were reported to be in 'that sink of iniquity the Gibraltar Bar'.

'Tell Andy Morrison to take a taxi and bring them back,' I ordered.

Some twenty minutes later as the shore lines were being hauled in, the taxi arrived at the dock side. From the bridge I saw Morrison get out on the far side of the taxi to come around and pay the driver. Then he opened the door facing the ship and out tumbled two sorry figures making their way up the gangplank on hands and knees to disappear from sight. 'How much was the taxi?' I asked Morrison, as he reported his charges on board.

'McCullum paid for it!' he replied.

'Why McCullum could hardly make it aboard, let alone get his hand in his pocket!' I exclaimed.

'Oh, I put my hand in, and I gave the driver a good tip as well!' replied Andy.

As I rang down 'Stand by on engines' I knew that third engineman Christopher Stuthridge, a stoker petty officer of the Royal Fleet Reserve on loan to the Patrol Service, was down there in charge. Chris, but for some freak of drafting, should have been serving on a fleet destroyer or cruiser. In peacetime he worked as a factory engineer at Aintree, Liverpool, and in wartime as a modest, conscientious petty officer of the Royal Navy.

The dead opposite of Chris Stuthridge was Stoker Stuart RNPS, reputed to be one of the best workers in the stokehold by his chief engineman, but reported to be the worst drunk ashore by my dour coxswain, Mackenzie. I had once received a letter from his wife, addressed to the Commanding Officer, *St Loman*, which began: 'Oh, Sir! It would make your eyes weep and your heart break to see his little children without good clothes to their backs or shoes on their feet . . .', then asking that her husband should be made to increase her allowance.

Stuart had requested through the coxswain to see me on 'a personal matter', and on being ushered into my cabin opened up with: 'It's like this, skipper. I drink and my wife drinks. She just spends everything she gets on drink, and the children are not being looked after properly. The ladies of the Edinburgh Children's Benevolent Society will see that the children are taken care of if you can arrange for my wife's and my childrens' allotments to be paid to the Society. They will give my wife her proper allowance.' I handed Stuart his wife's letter.

'This request from your wife was addressed to me as your commanding officer. What you suggest now does seem the best possible solution to your family drinking problem. I will make the arrangements with the paymaster at the base, and then inform your wife of the action taken at your request. Incidentally, the chief says you are the best man he has in the stokehold, but the coxswain reports you are the worst drunk returning from shore leave. Will you try to improve that situation for me as well as for your children?'

Stuart did show a little improvement in his drinking habits, but his wife told his crew mates in a pub: 'That skipper of yours is a right bastard!'

Such were some of the characters now regarding me as a 'father confessor' to sort out their problems and grant them 'compassionate leave' on occasions. Nevertheless with 'the first turn of the screw' they became a fighting ship's company.

CHAPTER IV

During December 1940 I had the opportunity to study the monthly Anti-Submarine Reports by the Naval Staff of the Anti-Submarine Warfare Division. These were prefaced with: 'SPECIAL CAUTION. It is particularly emphasized that as the enemy has very little knowledge of our Asdics, this subject should never be discussed where there is any chance of an unauthorized person being within hearing.'

There was little doubt that U-boat commanders were very much aware that we possessed some sort of precision equipment enabling A/S vessels to make contact with submerged U-boats, hence the preference by their commanders to avoid attacks on escorted convoys and instead concentrate on sinking unescorted ships and neutrals. It was interesting to learn that during our involvement in the Norwegian operations there had been a marked lull in U-boat activity throughout the whole month of March 1940, and that such activity as had occurred was concentrated around the Shetlands and Orkneys in the last ten days of March. The most striking feature was the absence of all enemy submarines in Atlantic waters after about the 12th. This disappearance of U-boats, although temporary, was total.

Early in April every available U-boat left Germany to take up patrol positions for operations against Norway which were imminent. The smaller U-boats were dispersed between Norway and the Orkneys and Shetlands, with the exception of two stationed to the eastward of North Rona. The larger U-boats occupied positions north-east of the Shetlands and off the Norwegian coast, extending as far north as the Lofoten Islands, Vest Fiord and Vaags Fiord.

The number of U-boats off Norway was at its maximum in the second week, and thereafter dwindled. The April report claimed that one U-boat was known to have been sunk in the Norwegian operations and two or three sunk or damaged. Later the Germans admitted to the loss of six U-boats.

The large number of U-boats concentrated in Norwegian waters did little damage. The diagram of U-boat warfare for April (see pp. 54-6) presents an extraordinary picture of the concentration off Norway and in the northern

North Sea. The shipping sunk by the U-boats was negligible and the number of reported attacks on U-boats was not large. They sank five unescorted neutral merchant vessels, attacked three warships without success, also three submarines, two unescorted vessels and an escorted convoy. Their failure to get results is more explicable when comparing conditions off the Norwegian coast with those on the Western Approaches trade routes where the traffic was more confined to lanes and the area of operations much smaller, with targets moving at much slower speeds. It is probable that at the beginning of the Norwegian operations the U-boats were anxious to avoid disclosing their positions and may have had orders to attack only large warships, although none of our capital ships were attacked.

From the point of view of the war on our shipping, the German occupation of Norway and Denmark was by no means entirely to their advantage. While able to base U-boats in Norway to shorten their passage to the Atlantic, their action had resulted in bringing under our control a considerable amount of modern Scandinavian shipping not previously under Allied charter.

Home Fleet destroyers operating in the area had little opportunity to hunt U-boats, being occupied with the escort of fast troop convoys and the first and second battles of Narvik. Thus A/S trawlers carried out the essential sweeps of the approaches to the fjords by day, and troop landings and evacuations by night. German Stuka dive-bombers and Heinkel bombers concentrated on their elimination, winning them recognition from Winston Churchill as 'the little ships that went through hell'.

U-boat activity had broken out afresh from around 20 May and continued throughout the month of June. Tonnage lost during the month of 260,479 reached the highest point since the war began. In the North Sea there was very little activity, the greatest being the area enclosed by the parallels of 45°N and 51°N and the meridians of 8°W and 15°W. On 11 June, a U-boat operating farther south stopped and threatened the United States liner *Washington*, then on the 21st and 25th ships were sunk as far south as the latitude of Lisbon and Cape St Vincent. On two occasions a U-boat appeared further west, as far out as 17°-18°W.

During the month the German 'Ace' Kapitanleutnant Prien cruised to the southern Western Approaches (see p. 59). Leaving Germany on the 10th and going as far south as 45°N, he followed a convoy north-eastward towards Ushant and returned northabout to claim a record tonnage of 66,587. Prien may have still been in 'U-47' or in a newer boat making its first cruise. Early on the morning of 19 June he opened his operations by attacking convoy HGF 34 north-west of Finisterre and torpedoed three ships, *Baron Loudoun*, *British*

"U"-BOAT WARFARE.

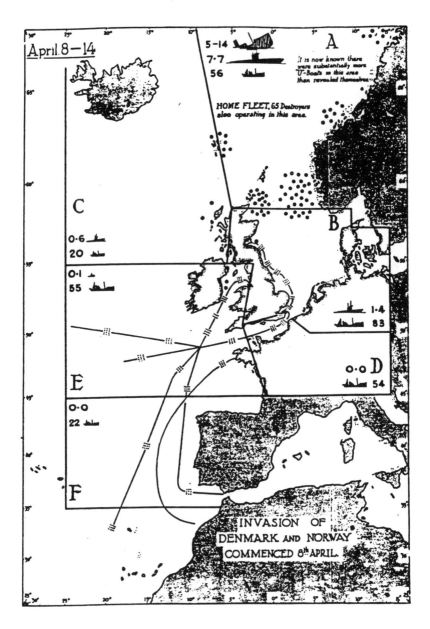

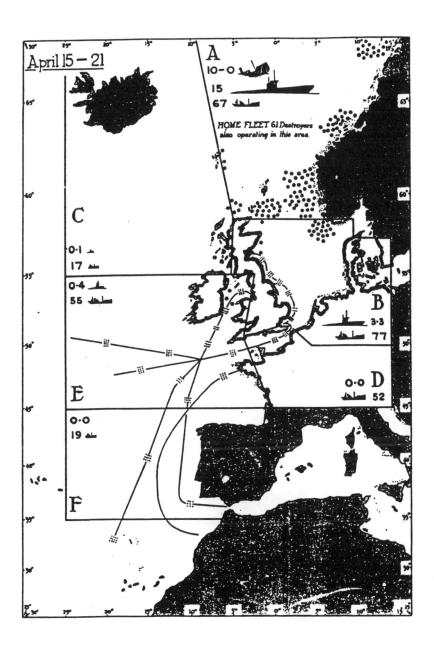

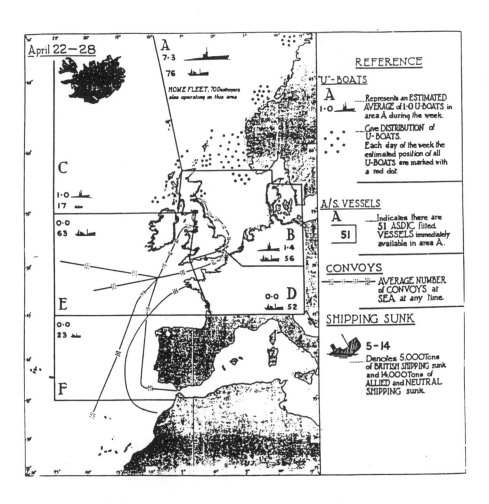

Monarch, and *Tudor*. Following the convoy northwards it is possible that an aircraft dropped two bombs near him on the evening of the 20th at 1835. Two hours later Prien torpedoed *Otterpool*, while the *Fellside* opened fire on the U-boat and made her escape, claiming to have registered two hits. Turning north-westwards Prien torpedoed the tanker *San Fernando* in HX 49, escorted by two sloops. Following up the convoy on the same evening, he torpedoed and sank the Norwegian *Randsfjord*. Then turning westwards again, he met another U-boat which had sunk the Norwegian tanker *Eli Knudsen* from the same convoy.

Prien and his men enjoyed a quiet period for five days until the afternoon of the 27th when the Dutch *Leticia* was torpedoed and sunk, then, after torpedoing the Greek *F.B. Goulandris*, Prien set course for home. The *Arandora Star* crossed his track when north-west off Ireland on the morning of 2 July, and was torpedoed without warning with heavy loss of life including many German and Italian internees carried on board.

Prien then returned through the Fair Island Channel at an average of 10 knots and was sighted by aircraft on 4 July. He arrived home on the 5th, broadcasting a short account of his cruise on the 6th. Though not mentioning the names of the ships he sank, his broadcast formed this list of his victims:

Ship		Date	Position	Tonnage
Norwegian	*Tudor*	0230/19	45° N 12° 21W	6,607
British	*British Monarch*	0100/19	45° N 12° 21W	5,661
British	*Baron Loudoun*	0037/19	45° N 12° 21W	3,164
British	*Otterpool*	2143/20	48° 47'N 7° 50'W	4,876
British	*Prunella*	0652/20	49° 44'N 8° 52'W	4,443
British	*San Fernando*	2012/21	49° 20'N 10° 23'W	13,056
Norwegian	*Randsfjord*	0100/22	50° 45'N 7° 45'W	3,999
Dutch	*Leticia*	1700/27	50° 09'N 13° 46'W	2,580
Greek	*F.B. Goulandris*	1600/29	50° N 11° 52'W	6,701
British	*Arandora Star*	0710/2	56° 21'N 10° 40'W	<u>15,501</u>
				<u>66,588</u>

Although U-boat activity was intense during the month of June, particularly in the Western Approaches, there was no corresponding intensity of A/S operations because of the lack of A/S ships due to military exigencies requiring small craft for evacuation duties which left only a bare minimum of A/S vessels for escort duties, and practically none for offensive use. Secret Standing

Orders by Admiral Dönitz undoubtedly contributed to the more intensive activity: 'Tactics Against Convoys – (a) In the first place, attack, and keep on attacking. If the boat is temporarily forced away or driven under water, follow up in the general direction of the convoy, try to get in touch again, and once more, ATTACK! (b) On sighting convoys or *other* valuable targets against which other boats can also operate without detriment to your own attack, report as soon as possible, even before making your own attack, and between your attacks send further reports to enable contact to be maintained. The sinking of the vessel is invariably to be by torpedo.' Kapitanleutnant Prien certainly carried out his standing orders to the letter.

During July there were two distinct phases of U-boat activity. Until the middle of July the Western Approaches between the latitudes of 48° North and 51° North was the most active area. After the rerouting of convoys through the North Channel the enemy lost no time in reorganizing his U-boat patrols to meet the increased traffic in the North-Western Approaches.

Prior to this time attacks made on shipping off the north of Ireland resulted from encounters with U-boats on passage to or from their patrol areas further south. Thus, on 2 July, the *Arandora Star*, carrying prisoners of war and internees to Canada, passed across the homeward track of Kapitanleutnant Prien, when north of Ireland, who sunk her with his last remaining torpedo. A very important innovation in U-boat strategy now occurred. Lorient, a port to the south-east of Brest and Brest itself began to be used as a base for U-boats spending only a very few days in port for renewing supplies and, in particular for replenishing torpedoes. In the last week of July the presence of at least two U-boats in Lorient was established by two German broadcasts narrating, in a garbled form, the exploits of Kapitanleutnant Rollman and Kapitanleutnant Kretschmer. Rollman was the first U-boat commander to enter a port of north-west France. This was an occasion celebrated by a broadcast on 22 July, the commentator standing on the quay as Rollman's U-boat came in, proclaiming the successful attack on the destroyer *Whirlwind*, sunk south-east of Ireland on 5 July.

During August U-boat activity was closely concentrated in the North-Western Approaches with constant attacks on shipping, almost exclusively in this area, using new tactics of attacking at night, and presumably firing from and certainly withdrawing on the surface. On 15 August the German Government proclaimed a complete blockade of the British Isles and called upon Neutral Governments to forbid their ships to sail through the Anglo-German war zone

CRUISE OF KAPITÄN LEUT. PRIEN.

June 10th. July 5th. 1940.

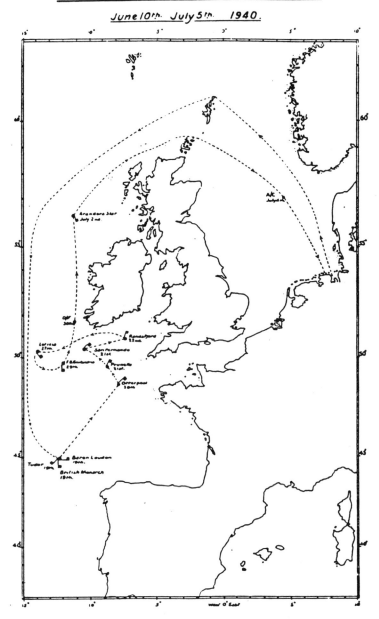

A/S.W.Div.July 1940.

under risk of being destroyed.

On the patrol by Kapitanleutnant Kretschmer it was claimed that he sank 65,137 tons of shipping between 28 July and 7 August (see p. 61). His patrol commenced on 26 July from the new U-boat base at Lorient in northern France. After only two days at sea, when 60°W of Dingle Bay, south-west Ireland, Kretschmer sank the unescorted British motor vessel *Auckland Star* of 13,212 tons. Then, proceeding northwards, he met another unescorted vessel, the British steamship *Clan Menzies* of 7,336 tons which he sank on 30 July. During the daylight hours of that day he made an 8 knot dash to a position 40° south-west of Barra Head to sink the British *Jamaica Progress*, a 5,475-ton steamship. Next he ran south to meet an outward-bound convoy, OB 191 to sink the British steamship *Jersey City* of 6,322 tons, and follow the convoy westward for some 36 hours. After the escorts had left, he torpedoed three more ships, *Alexia*, *Lucerna*, and the Norwegian *Strinda*, but fortunately, all being tankers in ballast, they returned to harbour.

On his homeward journey, Kretschmer attacked convoy HX 60 and torpedoed the British *Geraldine Mary* of 7,244 tons. He continued keeping west of 15°W as was normal for U-boats on patrol, making his way north of the Shetlands. When north-east of Muckle Flugga his U-boat was attacked by aircraft, but reached port going into Stavanger. Kretschmer subsequently boasted his successes, adding for good measure a 50 per cent addition to the tonnage of his victims.

U-boat attacks on convoys had become bolder and July marked the beginning of serious attacks on convoys while asdic-fitted escorts were present. In general these attacks were on large convoys which, owing to the shortage of escort vessels, were guarded by only two asdic-fitted ships. By now, American destroyers being made available under 'Lend-Lease' were due to start arriving in England. These 1,200-ton flush-deck destroyers were completed in 1919-20. They had shallower draft and were less in the beam than British wartime destroyers. Their turning circle was said to be about 1,000 yards, not too desirable for anti-submarine attacks.

During the early days of the anti-submarine war at sea, there were occasions when it appeared that Nazi-indoctrinated U-boat commanders on passage through the North Sea, going north of the Shetlands or through the Fair Island Channel, while making speed on the surface in the early evening or in thick weather, to run on their diesels and also to charge batteries, would encounter small fishing fleets on which they seemed to vent their spite by shelling and machine-gunning the little unarmed fishing vessels. This practice was not exclusive to the U-boats. It was also common in German aircraft returning

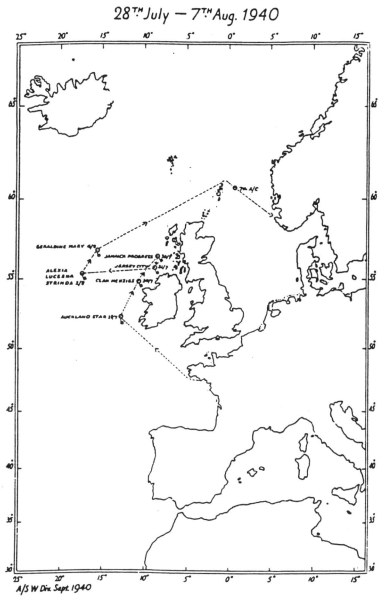

CRUISE OF KAPITAN LT KRETSCHMER
28TH July — 7TH Aug. 1940

A/S W Div. Sept. 1940

61

from raids on the north-east coast ports.

The bitterness thus created in the RNPS crews of A/S trawlers was most apparent when their ships were making depth-charge attacks on a suspected U-boat. At such times hands were likely to arm themselves with rifles hoping to see a U-boat's gun crew breaking the surface with the conning tower. On 18 June 1940, the Italian submarine *Galileo Galilei* had sunk the Norwegian tanker *James Stove* off Aden and was being hunted by the two sloops *Kandahar* and *Shoreham* which were searching a position given by a RAF fighter shadowing the submarine until the arrival of a bomber, whose bombs missed, the stopped and charging submarine diving when attacked.

Meanwhile the A/S trawler *Moonstone* was patrolling a line (060° Aden 7 to 25) as *Galileo Galilei* surfaced from 0155 to 0222, 20 June, hidden in monsoon weather from a dawn search by Blenheims of 203 Squadron covering an area 90 by 100 miles. At 1137 HMS *Moonstone* obtained a contact at the very extreme range of 5,000 yards, and 14 minutes later attacked with one depth charge set to 150 ft, the depth of the water being 37 fathoms. A full five-charge pattern could not be dropped because the ship's speed against the sea and swell was insufficient. Owing to the long range at which contact was obtained the submarine probably heard *Moonstone* and dived deep. The trawler regained contact at 300 yards and at 1220 attacked with another charge set to 150 ft, speed again not being sufficient for a full pattern. Six minutes later another charge was dropped and after this the submarine broke surface 2,000 yards astern. *Moonstone* turned as quickly as possible, while the submarine opened fire. The trawler kept bows on to the enemy and returned such a fierce fire with her two First World War .303 Lewis guns that the Italian gun crews, after some erratic shooting, were driven from their guns. When the range closed to 500 yards, all spare hands in the *Moonstone*, armed with rifles, assisted the Lewis gunners in subjecting the enemy's decks to sustained and accurate fire.

A direct hit by the *Moonstone*'s 4-inch gun on the base of the conning tower, followed by another at the top, finished the action. The whole Italian crew rushed on deck, hauled down the colours, and frantically waved white clothing. *Moonstone* ceased fire at 1255. HMS *Kandahar* arrived to put a prize crew on board, eventually getting the engines running and *Galileo Galilei* entered Aden Harbour under her own power, flying the White Ensign.

At this time the majority of U-boat commanders did not torpedo unescorted merchant ships without warning. Notable in this regard was U-26, commanded by Kapitanleutnant Scheringer, when stopping SS *Niederholm*, by two shots across her bows in position 50° 50'N 14° 10'W, about 150-200 miles south-west of Ireland. The crew took to their boats in a rough sea and saw the grey-green conning tower of the U-boat 1½ miles to starboard. Twenty minutes later the U-boat, moving abeam of *Niederholm*, fired a torpedo which struck forward of the bridge causing the steamer to break in half. Then the U-boat came within 100 yards of the lifeboats and fired a shot taken as a warning not to try returning to the wreck whose fore end sank in 2½ hours, with the after part remaining afloat for some time longer.

Another victim during this third cruise of U-26, was the SS *Langleford*, a wheat ship of 4,622 tons, torpedoed without warning at 0915 on 14 February 1940. After sinking the ship the Captain of U-26 signalled the steamer's Captain to come alongside. He refused to comply and the first officer went alongside the U-boat to be questioned. The German Captain expressed regret when told that two men had been lost by his sinking of the *Langleford*, without warning, but explained he did so because she carried a gun. He gave the British seamen a sack containing two bottles of rum, two hundred cigarettes, six boxes of matches, a large package of bandages, and a ten-pound box of ship's biscuits. He also gave a bearing to assist them in reaching the nearest land, 70-80 miles away.

On her homeward journey U-26 was attacked in the Atlantic by aircraft, and when near the Shetlands she was depth-charged by destroyers unsuccessfully. Reaching Wilhelmshaven during the third week in February, she underwent a long refit period and missed the Norwegian operations. The fourth and fifth cruises of U-26 were spent mainly in escort and transportation activities on the Norwegian coast.

The sixth and last cruise of U-26 began when she left Wilhelmshaven on 20 June, passing north of the Shetlands for the Atlantic, steering west of the Hebrides and Ireland to the Western Approaches. On Sunday 30 June, U-26 sank the unescorted Norwegian SS *Belmoira* by torpedo and gunfire, and at 1730 on the same day torpedoed the Estonian SS *Merkur* in position 48° 26'N, 10° 58'W, 200 miles south-west of the Scilly Islands. The Captain of the *Merkur* described a conversation with the enemy commander, and stated that a Mickey Mouse caricature was painted on the conning tower.

U-26 now embarked on the operation which led to her destruction. Warned by W/T from Germany that an outward-bound convoy would pass her operational area on 30 June, she therefore lay in wait. When first sighted the convoy was zigzagging very markedly. It seems that U-boat commanders took this to be a sign that the convoy was unprotected.

The convoy was part of OA 175. HMS *Gladiolus*, the Flower class corvette escort was zigzagging ahead of the line of advance when at 2100 the Commodore's ship sighted the U-boat diving about five miles distant, bearing

280°. *Gladiolus* went at full speed to the estimated position, searched to about one mile north of the convoy's path and altered course 16 points to sweep to one mile south, but with no result. This took one hour and by then the convoy had reached the position where U-26 had submerged.

At the same time, U-26, manoeuvring for position, had seen the convoy turn away from her, then shortly afterwards alter course again towards her, presenting a very favourable position. Her Captain and other officers, excited at the excellent targets, had a brief discussion about which ship should be their first victim. They agreed to torpedo a 12,000-ton British tanker followed by the British SS *Zarian*, 4,871 tons, the rear ship of the outside column of the convoy.

At 2318 the U-boat fired two torpedoes from the surface within a few seconds of each other. The first, an air torpedo, missed the tanker, and the second, an electric, hit SS *Zarian* aft causing serious damage.

After firing her torpedoes U-26 did not dive immediately but watched the SS *Zarian*. The U-boat Captain subsequently described the damaged ship as having her entire stern under water and refused to believe that she had been towed into Falmouth, giving the opinion that she would have sunk after being towed for three miles.

HMS *Gladiolus*, attracted by Very lights fired by *Zarian*, headed in her direction. As soon as the U-boat saw HMS *Gladiolus* turn towards the *Zarian*, she dived to a depth of 190-230 ft. Her starboard motor was running badly and the Captain was of the opinion that to make good his escape the port motor would have to run at three-quarter speed and the starboard at half speed. The compass was found defective preventing the maintenance of an exact course. The gyro compass was not switched on in order not to give away her position.

HMS *Gladiolus* obtained asdic contact at 1,200 yards, set depth charges to 500 ft and 350 ft alternately and ten minutes after the U-boat had fired her torpedoes made a full five-charge pattern. Regaining contact after this attack at 1,200 yards, *Gladiolus* dropped another full pattern with similar depth settings at 2340.

Asdic contact was lost for over an hour. At 0102 on 1 July contact was made again and at 0109 a third full pattern of charges was dropped. Contact was not regained until 0232, resulting in the fourth pattern being dropped at 0239. Regaining contact at only 800 yards range a fifth pattern was dropped at 0309. Finally at 0343 good contact was obtained with hydrophone effect which ceased suddenly when a sixth and last five-charge pattern attack was made.

No movement or contact was subsequently detected after a very thorough search. A strong smell of oil became evident after the final attack and at daybreak a vast patch of oil was found. Nevertheless, in spite of an accumulation of defects resulting from the attacks, the U-boat survived. Later, prisoners described the depth charges as being well placed and extremely close to them. They were amazed at the strength of construction of their U-boat. The depth settings on the charges being too deep may have attributed to the failure to completely destroy U-26, although it was clear that the persistent attacks by *Gladiolus* severely damaged her and so demoralized the crew as to make her eventual destruction inevitable.

Apparently the lights in U-26 were extinguished by the first attack, leaving only the emergency lighting. According to the crew, much water entered at some time during the action, due to damaged bow and stern caps, and the after torpedo-operating tank also filled because the tube drain had been left open. Thus the U-boat lost trim and she went down by the stern, so that the crew were moved forward to endure most of the attacks crouching together between the bow torpedo tubes. The defective main starboard motor became more ineffective while the circulating system of one main engine was put out of action, with the result that upon surfacing later the circulating pump of the other engine had to be cross-connected to work on both sides, limiting the U-boat's speed very considerably. The battery was almost completely discharged. Very little air was left in the compressed-air bottles with only one of the two compressors in action. An external oil tank, thought to have been damaged, accounted for so much oil coming to the surface. The rudder could not be moved to its full limits, and as so much water had entered the boat it became necessary to trim on the midships main ballast tanks.

An hour and fifty minutes from the last depth-charge attack, at about 0520, U-26 surfaced and, sighting a destroyer right ahead, 800 yards distant, turned slowly to port, started up a diesel and, without being seen, made off towards the dark horizon in the west. She ran her compressors to fill the almost empty bottles and was attempting to charge batteries when the junior officer on watch sighted another 'hunting craft' ahead. U-26 turned away to leave the two British ships astern, when a Sunderland flying boat was sighted on the starboard bow. The U-boat was still down by the stern, although much of the water that had penetrated during the attacks had been got rid of, and attempts had been made to get a correct trim. The Captain now ordered the entire crew into the bows of the boat. U-26 had not been sighted by the flying boat and might still have made good her escape if only her batteries had been charged.

HMS *Rochester*, on her way to close *Gladiolus*, sighted the U-boat on the surface at 0605, making so much smoke that in the early morning light she appeared to be a merchant ship hull down on the horizon. The destroyer saw the Sunderland moving in that direction. U-26 crash dived at 0613 and the flying boat, sighting the disturbed water two miles distant turned and dropped four 250-lb, A/S bombs, whereupon the U-boat surfaced almost at once, the crew assembling in the conning tower. The aircraft made a left-hand circuit and attacked again with four more bombs which burst about 40 yards from the conning tower.

Realizing that there was now no chance of escape the German Commander gave the order to abandon and scuttle the boat. The crew emerged, assembled abaft the conning tower and then jumped into the water, whilst the Engineer Officer flooded the boat. He escaped from the conning tower just as U-26 went down with one hatch open and engines running at half speed.

HMS *Rochester* closed and opened fire at a range of 1,100 yards in an effort to prevent the scuttling, however, on observing the U-boat sinking the destroyer reduced speed and picked up survivors.

The Captain of U-26 made a better impression than many officers captured at an earlier date. He behaved in a polite manner and was reasonable and intelligent in conversation, although an ardent Nazi. His personality and maintenance of discipline may account for the fact that before capture his crew not only destroyed all documents, notebooks, letters and other matter which might have been of use to their captors, but also presented a stubborn and continuous resistance to interrogation.

My study of the 1940 monthly Anti-Submarine Reports confirmed my experience that the German U-boat was a very tough 'nut' to crack and that persistent depth-charge attacks must be carried out in rapid succession while asdic contact was held. When escorting a convoy it was essential to ensure that the U-boat commander be forced to 'keep his head down' until the convoy had passed clear and the escort could return to its position in the A/S screen. This was an escort commander's usual standing order. Two or three depth-charge patterns in quick succession tended to make the U-boat dive deep from its periscope depth position and remain inactive astern of the convoy.

CHAPTER V

After the fall of France the main preoccupation of British naval forces in Home Waters had been the threat of seaborne invasion. This confined large numbers of destroyers and other A/S vessels to the east and south coasts as illustrated on 16 September 1940 chart (see diagram on p. 69). The almost exclusive concentration of U-boat activities in the North-Western Approaches reacted unfavourably on British anti-submarine activities. The transfer in July of all convoy routes through this area had made the provision of air escort for convoys difficult owing to the lack of adequate landing facilities in the area. Long-range German reconnaissance aircraft could now work from facilities in the south of France and increased the quantity and effectiveness of their reports on convoys, locations, number of ships and escorts both to the U-boats on patrol and Admiral Dönitz at his operational headquarters in Berlin.

Of the 59 ships attacked in North-Western Approaches, 40 were in convoy (see diagram on p. 70); 71 per cent of the total were night attacks. The period of greatest activity was between 16 and 22 of September when a concerted attack was made on Atlantic convoys. This was the period of, and immediately following, the full moon.

During October, Lorient was the principal U-boat operational base. The average time U-boats spent at sea was between two and three weeks. Once more activity was confined to the North-Western Approaches and the heaviest casualties occurred during four days, 17-20 October, when two inward-bound convoys were very heavily attacked. During 18-19 October alone 31 ships were hit. Once again an important feature of U-boat tactics during October was the concentration of most aggressive operations into the middle phase of the 'Hunter's moon'. Every night attack on a convoy was made during moonlight, and the period of greatest activity followed the 15th when the moon was full. At this time when the moonlight hours were the longest, conditions were most favourable to U-boats for prolonged chases and for manoeuvring before, after and between attacks. Logically enough, Admiral Dönitz sent out his boldest and most skilful U-boat commanders.

67

Prien took part and claimed to have sunk eight ships out of two convoys. He returned to Germany round Muckle Flugga and was the target for a strong attack by three Hudson aircraft off Egersund on 25 October. Damage to his U-boat was proved by the fact that she took two full days to travel 150 miles into the Skaggerak and crept in by the back door, rather than risk further air attack by continuing on her way to Wilhelmshaven.

Kretschmer, whose total of sinkings had been calculated by German mathematicians as 217,000 tons, was at sea during this intense U-boat activity and sank eleven ships before returning to Lorient.

Frauenheim sank ten ships, and Endrass, who took part in an attack on one of the convoys which suffered severely, raised his total claim for the cruise to 44,000 tons. Moehrle, whose exploits were first broadcast on 10 October was reported to have sunk seven ships.

The U-boat tactics were to make their attacks from periscope depth and escape on the surface at high speed after making their attack and in some cases submerged by day. Tactics vary with individual U-boat commanders but in the September and October convoy attacks appeared to be often as follows:

> The U-boat gains contact with the convoy during the day, either as a result of reports from long-range German reconnaissance aircraft, reports from other U-boats or by sighting smoke, and then proceeds to shadow at extreme visibility range on the bow or beam. When darkness has fallen, the U-boat, trimmed down low on the surface, closes the convoy and endeavours to reach a position broad on its bow. A very careful watch is kept for escorts to pass astern of those stationed on the bow of the convoy and press home the attack as close as the U-boat captain dares. In some cases the boldest have achieved a firing range of about 600 yards. Reaching a firing position on the beam of the convoy, most U-boats would increase to full speed, fire a salvo of four torpedoes, turn away at full speed, and retire as rapidly as possible in the safest direction. If their retreat is unseen, U-boats will continue along the line of advance of the convoy some miles off and, if weather permits, reload their torpedo tubes on the surface. Subsequent attacks may then be made on the same convoy, in the same manner, at intervals throughout the night.

With U-boats on the surface, echo contact by asdic could not normally be expected, but with U-boats passing escorts at speed, hydrophone effect could be obtained.

When I was at the Admiralty with Captain Fawcett in the A/S Division, he

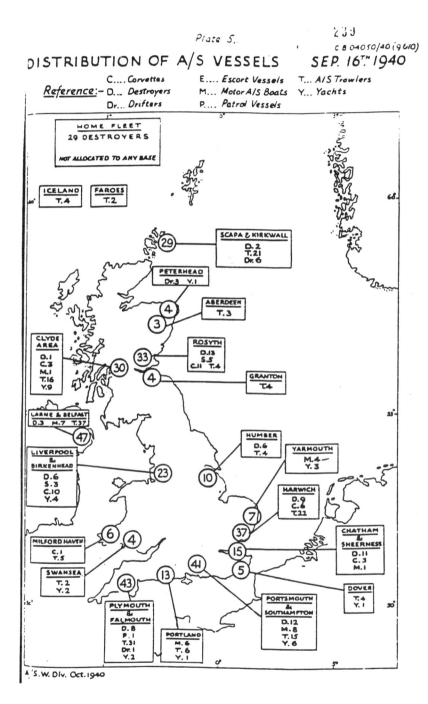

Plate 5.

2 3 9

C B 04050/40 (9610)

DISTRIBUTION OF A/S VESSELS   SEP. 16ᵀᴴ 1940

Reference:-
C.... Corvettes
D... Destroyers
Dr... Drifters

E.... Escort Vessels
M... Motor A/S Boats
P.... Patrol Vessels

T... A/S Trawlers
Y... Yachts

HOME FLEET
29 DESTROYERS
NOT ALLOCATED TO ANY BASE

ICELAND
T.4

FAROES
T.2

(29)

SCAPA & KIRKWALL
D. 2
T. 21
Dr. 6

PETERHEAD
Dr.3   Y.1

(4)

ABERDEEN
T.3

(3)

CLYDE AREA
D.1
C.3
M.1
T.16
Y.9

(33)

(30)

ROSYTH
D.13
S.5
C.11   T.4

(4)

GRANTON
T.4

LARNE & BELFAST
D.3   M.7   T.37

(47)

LIVERPOOL & BIRKENHEAD
D.6
S.3
C.10
Y.4

(23)

HUMBER
D.6
T.4

(10)

YARMOUTH
M.4 —
Y.3

HARWICH
D.9
C.6
T.22

(7)

(37)

CHATHAM & SHEERNESS
D.11
C.3
M.1

MILFORD HAVEN
C.1
T.5

(6) (4)

SWANSEA
T.2
Y.2

(43)

(15)

(13)

(41)

(5)

DOVER
T.4
Y.1

PLYMOUTH & FALMOUTH
D.8
P.1
T.31
Dr.1
Y.2

PORTLAND
M.6
T.6
Y.1

PORTSMOUTH & SOUTHAMPTON
D.12
M.8
T.15
Y.6

A 'S.W. Div. Oct. 1940

Plate 1   CB. 04050/40 (9810)

BRITISH ALLIED ᴀɴᴅ NEUTRAL SHIPS SUNK SEPT. 1940

REFERENCE   +   British ships sunk.
            o   Allied and Neutral ships sunk.

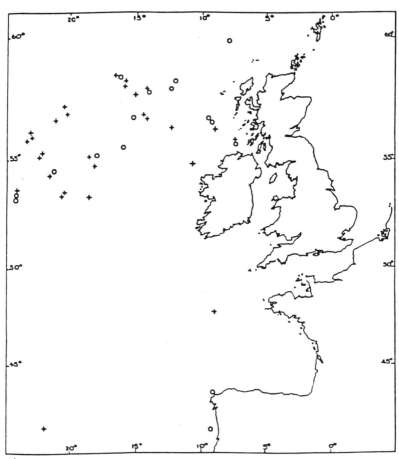

A/S.W. Div Nov 1940

70

commented that great efforts were being made to develop and equip all convoy escorts with radar apparatus that would enable them to locate a U-boat on the surface at night beyond visible range. It seemed that while the Navy had pioneered this development, equipment priority was given to the RAF for guiding night fighters to German bombers in their raids on London. On making contact with the target, the night-fighter pilot would see a round blob appear on his radar screen and home in on it until the blob grew stubby wings. This was the signal to press his firing button. Looking up he would find the tail of the bomber dead ahead, blasted with his eight wing-mounted machine-guns, or the alternative cannons. One story put out in the media for the Germans to ponder over was that the RAF night-fighter pilots had been put on a special diet of carrots which resulted in exceptional night vision!

Convoy escorts lacking the facilities of radar or ASV apparatus had to depend on good eyes, constant vigilance and ensure a most efficient lookout, particularly on bearings abaft the beam, as the most likely ways to achieve success in sighting and destroying the enemy. It now became possible to improve the tactical efficiency of the destroyers, sloops, corvettes and trawlers as escorts for convoys; these ships were being formed into groups to work under their own senior officers. As far as possible, ships of one group would always work together.

In January 1941 *St Loman* was assigned to the Clyde convoy escort base under Captain D. Greenock, joining an escort group made up with three destroyers, *Beagle*, *Hesperus*, *Boadicea*, and with the A/S trawlers *Lady Elsa*, *Lady Madeline*, and *Angle*. Two Free French-manned Flower class corvettes had been made part of the group, but seldom, if ever, seemed able to get ready for sea because of engine or A/S equipment defects delaying their sailing with the group. On the rare occasions that these corvettes did get to sea, it was not long before a return to Greenock became essential because of mechanical problems.

The senior officer of our group was the commander of the destroyer *Boadicea*, Captain Alfred Turner RN, known in the service as 'Flash Alf, and for any woman except his wife!' Turner also enjoyed the reputation of a hard-driving taskmaster as an escort commander, whipping his miscellaneous group of ships into an effective and efficiently coordinated escort group. Turner arranged for me to act as liason for the operations and requirements of the A/S trawlers, while he acted for the destroyers and corvettes himself. 'Flash Alf's' communication exercises were somewhat demanding with the trawler complement of one radio operator and one signalman to three or four times that number on the *Boadicea*, nevertheless it was our pride that we could match the destroyer bridges in quick response.

After a couple of convoy trips on Western Ocean convoys Captain Turner joined me for the traditional pink gin after an inspection visit to *St Loman* and the other A/S trawlers, and after sipping his drink remarked: 'I must apologize to you people. I just did not realize what you have to work with in your ships compared to my complement on the *Boadicea*, and only three watchkeeping officers.' I replied, 'You don't have to apologize, sir! We consider that we should be able to do anything that your ship can do, except thirty knots!'

Turner laughed and agreed.

Neither effective U-boat captains nor their British A/S hunter commanders came ready-made. Prior to attaining command of a U-boat the potential captain learned the basics of his craft as a first lieutenant on one or more operational patrols, preferably under the tutelage of a 'Star' commander. Both navies seemed to adopt a similar principle judging from my experience in the *St Loman*!

It was not until the latter part of 1940 that the first German 'Star' commander was captured with the sinking of U-32 (see p. 80) when on her eighth and last cruise with her Captain, Oberleutnant-zur-See Hans Jenisch, a 27-year-old native of East Prussia, making his sixth operational patrol as her Captain.

The early history of U-32, a 500-ton U-boat, began when her keel was laid down at Bremen on 1 April 1936, before being launched early in 1937 and completed on 15 April 1937. Her first Commanding Officer was Kapitanleutnant (Lieutenant Commander) Werner Lott, who was taken prisoner after the sinking of U-35 on 29 November 1939. This officer was replaced by Kapitanleutnant Paul Buchel, who remained in command until 31 January 1940. U-32 was known to have been in Spanish waters in 1938, from 5 February to 8 May, and again from 5 October to 24 October. During June 1939 she took part in tactical exercises in the Baltic and shortly before the outbreak of the Second World War was used as a training U-boat for six to eight weeks at Neustadt. U-32 put to sea either for training purposes or for trials from 7 August to 29 August 1939. During this time a refit was found to be necessary, as she did not leave on her first operational patrol until early in September 1939. Other U-boats of the same flotilla, namely U-28, U-29, U-33 and U-34 all left Wilhelmshaven on 19 August 1939.

U-32 left Wilhelmshaven to begin her first patrol on 4 September 1939, carrying eight mines and seven torpedoes. She proceeded north of the Shetlands, not through Fair Island Channel, to lay mines south-west of Ireland. According to Admiralty information, mines were laid in the British Channel at about this time. U-32 did not sink any ships during this cruise and returned to Wilhelmshaven on Saturday 30 September, when her Captain, Kapitanleutnant Buchel was awarded the Iron Cross, Second Class; thence the U-boat went to Kiel for torpedo tube repairs. A refit was also required, after which U-32 was expected to leave on her next cruise towards the end of October. The engines were not working properly and it was necessary to fit twelve new cylinder blocks.

On the completion of this work U-32 carried out trials in the Baltic to test her surface and submerged speeds. This work and trials occupied a considerable time, and U-32 remained in Germany until after Christmas 1939. During this period the first lieutenant commenced a special course of instruction for command at Warnemunde, but returned to his appointment as first lieutenant before the course had ended.

On Thursday, 28 December 1939, U-32 left Wilhelmshaven on her second operational patrol, carrying ten mines and a number of torpedoes fitted with magnetic pistols. She passed north of the Shetlands, but was unable to lay the mines in the intended area, owing to the presence of British A/S trawlers described as 'small guard ships', and proceeded for about five hours westerly (280°) and then laid the mines. The Norwegian SS *Enid* of 1,140 tons was sunk on 17 January, six to seven miles north of Muckle Flugga. During this cruise U-32 was frequently attacked by aircraft, but was never hit. The U-boat returned to Wilhelmshaven on Sunday, 21 January. The Admiral commanding U-boats was dissatisfied with Buchel, her commanding officer, for having laid his mines in the wrong place, and replaced him by Leutnant Jenisch who had served in the U-32 as first lieutenant. The normal stay in Germany was a little over a month.

The third operational patrol commenced on Sunday, 28 February. U-32 again carried mines which were to be laid in the same position as the minelaying operation of the previous patrol. She passed through Fair Island Channel and on 2 March 1940 sank the Swedish MV *Lagaholm* about 55 miles north of Cape Wrath. After rounding the south-west coast of Ireland, U-32 laid her mines near St George's Channel. Repeated attacks from the air always missed the U-boat.

On returning to Wilhelmshaven on Saturday, 23 March 1940 U-32 was seriously in need of a refit, otherwise she would have been made ready in the ten days remaining before the commencement of the Norwegian operations. Every available U-boat was being utilized for these operations, including the oldest 250-ton training boats.

On Saturday, 27 April 1940, U-32 left Wilhelmshaven for Trondheim with a cargo of ammunition. Her torpedo tubes were loaded but she carried no spares. U-32 did not carry her own gun, but transported an 8.8 cm gun with ammunition. The U-boat proceeded north to Christiansand Fjord and then kept close to the Norwegian coast on her way to Trondheim. It was reported that British A/S trawlers made an unsuccessful depth-charge attack on Thursday, 2 May.

On or about Sunday, 5 May the U-boat reached Trondheim to dock near to the 1,000-ton ex-Turkish submarine known as 'UA', which had also taken a cargo of ammunition from Germany. No ships were sunk on the return trip, and U-32 arrived back in Wilhelmshaven on Monday, 13 May 1940 with an engine missing badly on one cylinder, but the dockyards and repair shops were so crowded that she was ordered to proceed through the Kiel Canal, where repairs were effected within three days.

U-32 returned to her base and remained in Germany until 3 June 1940, when she began her fifth operational patrol. This time she carried five torpedoes in her tubes and six spares, but no mines. She passed north of the Shetlands into the Atlantic and proceeded down the west coast of Ireland to the Western Approaches. On this outward leg U-32 sank three ships totalling about 22,000 tons. One of these was in a convoy and two proceeding independently. Five additional ships were sunk south of Ireland near the mouth of the English Channel. These eight sinkings were achieved between about 10 June and 17 June 1940. After a patrol of exactly four weeks, U-32 returned to Wilhelmshaven on Monday, 1 July 1940 for a refit, including diesel repairs.

U-32 left Wilhelmshaven on Thursday, 15 August on her sixth patrol, again carrying eleven torpedoes. She passed north of the Shetlands to the Atlantic and operated in the Western Approaches. Only when she was well at sea did the crew learn that the patrol was to end in France. U-32 took about five days to reach her operating area, and patrolled for some considerable time without success. During this time the U-boat came across a lifeboat of the Belgian *Ville de Mons* of 7,463 tons, torpedoed by another U-boat on 2 September 1940 about 150 miles west of the Hebrides. U-32 gave water to the men in the boat and indicated the nearest land, before going on to sink three ships out of the Halifax Convoy HX66A, and two or three ships later.

On 8 September 1940 U-32 arrived at Lorient, where some minor repairs were carried out, and some below average crew members were replaced from the pool of U-boat personnel at that port. Ten members of the crew received the Iron Cross, 2nd Class; the first lieutenant, the junior officer, one petty officer, and one rating were awarded the Iron Cross, 1st Class.

A rest period of only ten days was allowed before U-32 commenced her seventh operational patrol on 18 September accompanied by a minesweeper as far as the harbour entrance, and proceeded to her operational area, which was described as being some hundreds of miles out in the Atlantic where other U-boats were operating. There she attacked the remains of a convoy previously attacked by Kapitanleutnant Schepke.

In a surface engagement with the British SS *Collegian* on 22 September, in position 55° 14', 16° 40 W, there was no moon and it was very dark at 0550. The Captain put his ship's stern towards the U-boat, stopped zig-zagging and opened fire. U-32 returned fire with two guns, the nearest shot being about 200 yards off target. The *Collegian* fired 10 rounds, with the last shell landing very close to U-32. After 20 minutes the U-boat disappeared after firing a torpedo which missed.

HMS *Lowestoft* was 15 miles away, saw the flashes from this gunfire and proceeded to the position. At 0829 a search for U-32 commenced with HMS *Heartsease*, and later with *Skate* and *Shikari* assisting.

After about an hour *Lowestoft* made contact at 1,400 yards range, but lost it when closing. The position was crossed, and after turning *Lowestoft* regained firm contact at 1,300 yards range with a target extent of 9° and slightly opening inclination. She attacked at 0920 with six depth charges set to 250 ft, 350 ft and 500 ft, the depth of water being 500 fathoms. After the attack contact could not be regained. A search was carried out in company with *Heartsease*, but nothing further could be detected. Later it was learned that no damage was inflicted on U-32 which used the evading tactics of crash diving to 60 metres, then, proceeding at depth, she had steered west.

On 26 September, in position 53° 47'N, 24° 19'W at 0140, the 6,863 tons British SS *Corrientes* was sunk by U-32. Two days later another British ship, the *Empire Ocelot* of 5,759 tons, bound from Liverpool to the United States in ballast was torpedoed when about 700 miles west of the coast of County Mayo. She was struck in the boiler room almost amidships by a torpedo travelling very fast, about 6 ft below the surface. The ship stopped and the crew took to the boats. There was a moderate swell at the time. Shortly afterwards the survivors saw U-32 go alongside the *Empire Ocelot*, but not long enough for anyone to board the steamer. The U-boat moved round onto the port quarter of the steamer and fired about eight shells at the sinking ship.

The British SS *Darcoila* of 4,804 tons which left Milford Haven on 20 September 1940, had not been heard of again until prisoners from U-32 admitted having sunk her. There were no survivors.

The Dutch SS *Hanlerwijk* of 3,278 tons was missed by a torpedo fired by U-32 at 1130 on 30 September. The U-boat then followed the steamer and sank her by gunfire at 1920 on the same day. As the *Hanlerwijk* was sinking, U-32 approached her at periscope depth, as the Germans wanted to read the name of the ship. The sun was shining into the periscope and Jenisch misjudged the distance, with the result that the U-boat came into collision with the sinking ship. Although U-32's bow was damaged the torpedo tubes were not affected, but she proceeded to her base, reaching Lorient on 3 October.

The German High Command announced in a communiqué of Friday, 4 October that Jenisch's total on this cruise was 42,644 tons. Three Iron Crosses, 2nd Class, were awarded to ratings on 3 October and it was officially announced on 10 October that Jenisch had been decorated with the Knight Insignia of the Iron Cross.

Shortly after returning to Lorient, half the crew of U-32 went on leave to Germany. Some travelled together by train, which skirted Paris and passed through Luxembourg, the journey to Wilhelmshaven taking two and a half days. Others went to Germany by air. When returning from leave the men travelled separately. A few inefficient members of the crew were replaced from the pool of U-boat personnel at Lorient. While the crew were there they sat out four air raids in cellars for shelter.

The eighth and last patrol of U-32 began on 24 October. A minesweeper accompanied her to the entrance of Lorient harbour for the last time. U-32 carried eleven torpedoes, nine of which were air and two electric. Five were in the tubes and of the six spares, four were housed in the bilges under the deck plates, and two wrapped in canvas above the deck plate of the forward compartments.

The crew took their few possessions with them and also presents bought in France for their relatives and friends in Germany, as it was hoped and expected that their boat would return home to Wilhelmshaven at the end of the cruise.

U-32 proceeded to her operating area off the North-Western Approaches. Bad weather was encountered about the second or third day out, and the patrol became dull and uncomfortable.

About 0815 on Saturday, 26 October, the SS *Empress of Britain* was bombed and set on fire by German aircraft when about 50 miles off the north-west coast of Ireland. The ship had to be abandoned, but later, after the fire had been brought under control, was taken in tow by two tugs. German naval authorities then sent out a W/T signal to U-boat commanders, advising them of the position and probable course of the ship in tow. Jenisch, near whose operating area the *Empress of Britain* was to pass, decided to attack her.

Apparently U-32 had to enter the operating area of U-31 in order to intercept the quarry. She proceeded to a position well ahead and lay waiting on the surface in the darkness with her engines running at the slowest speed. The U-boat lay almost exactly in the course of the big ship, and the risk run by Jenisch was very high. The two escorting destroyers preceding the *Empress of Britain* passed zig-zagging, one on either beam of the U-boat. The Germans thought that their boat must be seen at any moment. Then two tugs passed towing the damaged ship, and Jenisch, with characteristic intentness of purpose and cool judgement, waited until the very last moment before increasing the speed of his engines and firing three torpedoes almost simultaneously from a range of 600 metres.

U-32 was on the port side of the *Empress of Britain*. One of the torpedoes hit on the port side abreast of the foremost funnel, and another hit the engine room further aft. The third torpedo exploded prematurely.

The U-boat turned away and made off, still on the surface, at emergency full speed. The *Empress of Britain* was enveloped in a large cloud of steam, and when this thinned, some four minutes later, the torpedoed ship had already sunk. At one stage during the attack a Sunderland flying boat flew about 300 feet over the U-boat, but did not see her.

Nothing further of importance happened until shortly after midday on 30 October. Visibility was poor on this day, the sea was high and there were heavy rain squalls. In spite of this, U-32 sighted the British SS *Balzac* in position 55° 37'N, 13° 26'W, about 150 miles north-west of the coast of County Mayo. The ship was zig-zagging at the time and her kite was not seen by the Germans as her Master supposed.

The U-boat was extremely suspicious of the *Balzac*, thinking that she might be a U-boat trap or 'Q' ship. One torpedo was fired while submerged at 1240, but this missed the ship and exploded on her starboard side 50 yards abeam of her mainmast. The explosion caused a large disturbance in the water and a blue haze was observed. As *Balzac* did not know the cause of this she reported that she was being shelled.

Balzac's report was received by HM ships *Harvester* and *Highlander*. At the time HMS *Harvester* was searching for the Commodore of Convoy SC8; after meeting the Commodore at 1230, *Harvester* proceeded to look for *Balzac*, approaching the position from the southward at 25 knots.

HMS *Highlander*, which was in position 45 miles 270° from *Balzac*, swept down from the northward and met *Harvester* at 1610.

At 1740 *Balzac* was sighted on the port bow by *Harvester*, which closed and interrogated her about the U-boat attack earlier in the day. *Highlander*, then about ten miles distant, steering to intercept the convoy, was kept informed.

In the meantime the Captain of U-32, after missing the *Balzac*, became increasingly puzzled by the behaviour of the merchantman, and followed her submerged.

Between 1300 and 1400 GMT the radio officer of the *Balzac* heard a pulsing sound on his receiver and the Master, concluding that this might be due to the presence of a U-boat, altered course several times and ran into rain squalls. The gun's crew and all lookouts were standing by. U-32 continued to follow the ship and came to periscope depth, but dived at once upon sighting destroyers and submerged. She then pursued the *Balzac* at full speed submerged. The men at the listening apparatus reported to the Captain that they thought they heard suspicious sounds. The Captain gave the laconic reply: 'Rot. That is our own noise, we are travelling at full speed.'

Jenisch, intent as ever on his purpose, apparently ignored the presence of hostile warships and continued to follow *Balzac*.

At 1812, HMS *Harvester*, about 1,000 yards on *Balzac*'s port bow, obtained asdic contact on the port bow at very short range. Before the contact had been classified the periscope of a U-boat projecting about two feet out of the water was sighted bearing Red 30.

The Captain of the U-boat stated that for some time *Harvester*'s hydrophone effect had been indistinguishable from the *Balzac*'s. He raised his periscope and saw *Harvester* very close indeed and at once ordered a crash-dive. U-32 was then about 80 yards off *Harvester*'s port beam.

After signalling 'S' (submarine in sight) the Captain ordered full astern port, full ahead starboard with his rudder hard-a-port, with the intention of ramming, the range of the periscope being such that this manoeuvre appeared possible. As *Harvester* turned, it was appreciated that the U-boat was going about five knots and thus came inside the ship's turning circle. Engines were reversed to swing the stern over the U-boat.

At the moment when the U-boat crash-dived, engines were stopped in *Harvester*. Full ahead was then ordered and a pattern of six charges with deep settings was dropped. The pattern would have had an effect on the U-boat had she turned to port, but in fact she turned to starboard. The crew of the U-32 heard the explosion of the depth charges fairly close, but no serious damage was caused.

HMS *Harvester* was turned at 1,000 yards and asdic contact regained. *Highlander*, which was closing, was given the range and bearing. *Balzac*, being in the way and preventing an immediate attack, was informed that she was standing into danger and was given a course to steer.

Harvester then lost contact, possibly due to the target being end on. Meanwhile, *Highlander* obtained a good contact and passed over it at slow speed, giving range and bearings, and also dropping a calcium flare.

At 1848 *Highlander*, while turning, signalled that she would attack if *Harvester* obtained good contact. Shortly afterwards *Harvester* did obtain contact at about 1,850 yards, being at that time at right angles to *Highlander*'s track. However, before she could confirm and report the contact, a signal was received from *Highlander* to attack, whereupon *Harvester* moved in at 18 knots, but as the other vessel was seen to be doing the same thing, *Harvester* reversed engines, but held the contact until *Highlander* dropped a 14-charge pattern. The position of the charged agreed with *Harvester*'s contact, which became confused with echoes from the detonations of the charges, and was lost. *Harvester* turned parallel to *Highlander* and continued on a course of 120° to sweep the area in case the attack had been unsuccessful.

After *Highlander*'s 14-charge pattern had been fired at 1853, the range was opened to 1,600 yards by plot and the ship turned to starboard. At this moment a track was seen on her port bow. Visibility was bad as there was a dark rain squall and daylight was fading, but course was altered towards this track which gradually resolved itself into two tracks, thought to be torpedoes. At this moment large air bubbles were seen and asdic contact was gained.

At 1908, 15 minutes after the depth charges had been fired, the U-boat surfaced, moving at about 7 knots, stern well down. *Highlander* informed *Harvester* and opened fire with her 4.7s at point-blank range. It was difficult to assess the effect of this as it was almost dark, but one shot was seen to hit the conning tower. Fire was opened with machine-guns in a further attempt to prevent the Germans from scuttling their boat; several of them were seen to be abandoning her. Owing to the darkness it was impossible to tell how many had jumped overboard, and the possibility of ramming was considered in case the U-boat was shamming. However, it was soon apparent that the U-boat was finished, as her bow, high in the air, was caught in the beam of *Harvester*'s searchlight, and she was seen to sink stern first.

Harvester closed the position ready to drop a 14-charge pattern, but shouts from the water showed that the majority of the crew were out. She therefore reversed engines and stopped in the middle of the swimming men. HMS *Harvester* rescued twenty-nine survivors and HMS *Highlander* four. Nine men lost their lives including the junior officer.

After her crash-dive U-32 had done some rapid manoeuvres, including reversing engines, in her efforts to escape. The men at the listening apparatus had been puzzled by the way in which they were being hunted; at times they could only hear a faint sound which they took to be a ventilating plant or refrigerator; at other times the 'tapping' noises of the destroyers' asdic transmissions could be heard.

The 14-charge pattern had come as a highly unpleasant surprise and caused considerable damage in the boat. The lighting system failed and all electrical instruments were put out of action; valves refused to function and a junction of the compressed air leads was fractured, causing excess pressure in the U-boat. Some small leaks were started and the after ballast tanks were crushed in on both sides and put out of action. The depth gauge was smashed and the electric switch gear, which broke away, was seen hanging by its wire connections.

The crew were sent forward and orders were given to blow all tanks. An attempt was then made to surface by using the hydroplanes, but the motors would not function. U-32 finally surfaced with her stern well down. The Captain thought that he might be able to dive again and shouted orders to the Engineer Officer, but there was no more compressed air. The idea of firing torpedoes at the attacking destroyers had also to be abandoned owing to the complete lack of compressed air.

The Captain then gave the order to abandon ship. The crew escaped through the conning tower and jumped into the sea. One of the wireless operators described how he found the conning tower suddenly empty, so he clambered out, but saw the Captain about to carry up ammunition onto the outside deck; he then saw another officer jump into the sea, and the wireless rating followed suit. The Engineer Officer opened the necessary valves to make sure the U-boat would sink.

The German prisoners displayed an attitude which had not been so evident in previous cases. All were fanatical Nazis and hated the British intensely. As had been previously noticed, they had been warned against disclosing any information which might be valuable. Once again it was apparent that the policy of the German High Command was to maintain a high degree of secrecy by allowing officers and men to share only such knowledge as was essential to carry out their duties. Various men knew the details of their job only, and had no idea of the work of other members of the crew.

They were advocates of unrestricted warfare, and prepared to condone all aggressive violence, cruelty, breaches of treaties and other crimes, as being necessary to the rise of the German race in Europe. German successes during 1940 appeared to have established Hitler in their minds, not merely as a God, but as the only God. They maintained that Germany was at present only 'marking time' until after the consolidation of a series of political victories and 'corrective adjustments' in the Balkans and elsewhere. They thought, whenever it was deemed suitable, that a German attack on Great Britain would be overwhelmingly successful, and professed to be amazed at the British failure to see the inevitability of eventual utter defeat at the hands of Hitler.

In spite of their insistence on the supremacy of the German race, they were remarkably sensitive to anything which might be construed as a slight on their dignity as officers, and made constant demands for various favours. This attitude did not quite conform with their declared approbation of the treatment meted out to a British officer prisoner of war in German hands, who asked for different food and was promptly put on half rations.

The officers were impressed by the treatment they received in the British destroyers which rescued them, but they were not very well educated according to British standards and though reasonably polite to British officers, behaved somewhat arrogantly to NCOs and men, when they thought that they could do so with impunity.

The Captain of U-32, Oberleutnant-zur-See Hans Jenisch, the first German 'Star' commander to be captured, gave the impression of being a determined, possibly obstinate U-boat Captain, and was criticized by other officers of U-32 as being difficult or impossible to influence. They also deplored the fact that his concentration on a specific attack, or detail of a plan, prevented him from taking into consideration other factors. He was without doubt a brave and cool-headed officer, but personally was an uninteresting, and not very intelligent human being, although reasonably polite and well-mannered.

He had entered the Navy in 1933, and after the usual period of training had been promoted to Leutnant-zur-See (sub lieutenant), on 1 October 1936, being transferred to the U-boat branch in 1937. On 1 June 1938 he was promoted Oberleutnant-zur-See (Lieutenant), having qualified as a torpedo officer, and was appointed to the 2nd U-boat Flotilla.

He joined U-32 some months before the war as first lieutenant. The Engineer Officer was not at all arrogant, and seemed grateful for small kindnesses. Although cautious in his conversation, he was polite and gave the impression of being more interested in his profession as an engineer than the political aspects of the war. He had formerly served on the lower deck and had only recently joined U-32.

The junior officer, who was lost, seemed to have been a popular and efficient Leutnant-zur-See. After two years in the Navy he transferred to the U-boat service in 1938. He had been awarded the Iron Cross, 2nd Class, and the

1st Class of the same order on 8 September 1940. He had served in U-32 for a considerable time and was due for promotion to Lieutenant.

It was probable that a second 'star' commander was eliminated in an attack by three Hudson aircraft on 25 October. The U-boat attacked was thought to be U-47, commanded by the 33-year-old German 'star' commander Kapitanleutnant Prien.

At 1145, when the three Hudsons were on armed reconnaissance off south-west Norway, in position 58° 21' N, 04° 22' E, about 45 miles south-west of Obrestad, a U-boat was sighted on the surface from a height of about 6,000 ft. The weather was fine, with no cloud. Wind was 110° 25 knots and visibility 20 miles, tidal stream 35° 1-2 knots. The depth of water was just over 100 fathoms.

Aircraft 'E' attacked first and dropped ten 100-lb bombs, all of which fell near the U-boat, one scoring a direct hit abaft the conning tower. Aircraft 'K' followed and dropped two 250-lb bombs, which fell 20 ft on either side of the U-boat; the rest of 'K's' bomb salvo failed to release. Aircraft 'J' then dived to attack, but all bombs failed to release, however 'J' got an excellent view of 'E's' bombs falling and confirmed the direct hit. Icing at 6,000 ft probably accounted for the failure of the bomb-release gear. The U-boat was observed to list to port and appeared to be in a sinking condition. A few minutes later her stern lifted out of the water and she disappeared altogether, but from Admiralty information of the subsequent movements of the U-boat it was known that she surfaced after this attack.

The U-boat was probably quite seriously damaged as she took two days to travel 150 miles on passage through the Skagerrak to her base, avoiding the risk of further attack incurred in the shorter North Sea route.

It was believed that the U-boat opened fire on the aircraft, indicating an initial determination to face the attack on the surface. The bomb hit caused a quick change in tactics and the crash-dive.

The position and course of the U-boat fitted in reasonably well with the established fact that Prien took part in the attack on HX79. At this time there could be no certainty about Prien's presence on this occasion, nor whether, if it was his U-boat, he was wounded or killed by the bomb. It was noteworthy that no subsequent report of the deeds of this much publicised figure was broadcast to Germany as part of the internal propaganda. Prien was mentioned in external broadcasts as though still active against British shipping, but without any convincing details of his supposed activities.

CHAPTER VI

German internal broadcasts provided this list of the more successful U-boat Commanders who had been awarded the Knight Insignia of the Iron Cross. Oberleutnant-zur-See Hans Jenisch was the first 'Star' U-boat Captain to be captured.

Name	Rank	Date of Award	Remarks
Prien, Gunther	Kapitanleutnant	17.10.39	Awarded Oak Leaves 21.10.40
Schultze, Herbert	Kapitanleutnant	2.3.40	
Schubart, Otto	Kapitanleutnant	18.5.40	
Rollman, Wilhelm	Kapitanleutnant	2.8.40	
Kretschmer, Otto	Kapitanleutnant	8.8.40	
Lemp, Fritz Julius	Kapitanleutnant	21.8.40	
Liebe, Heinrich	Kapitanleutnant	22.8.40	
Hartmann, Werner	Korvettenkapitan	2.9.40	
Rosing, Hans	Korvettenkapitan	3.9.40	
Frauenheim, Fritz	Kapitanleutnant	5.9.40	
Endrass, Engelbert	Oberleutnant-zur-See	10.9.40	
Kuhnke, Heinrich	Kapitanleutnant	20.9.40	
Schepke, Joachim	Kapitanleutnant	26.9.40	
Jenisch, Hans	Oberleutnant-zur-See	10.10.40	
Bleichrodt, Heinrich	Kapitanleutnant	29.10.40	Prisoner of War
Oehrn, Viktor	Kapitanleutnant	29.10.40	
Luth, Wolfgang	Oberleutnant-zur-See	29.10.40	

In regard to the personnel and manning of U-boats during this first year of the war at sea it was understood that promotions, illness and retirement, temporary or permanent, from active participation in operational patrols robbed the U-boat branch of a number of successful commanders, including Hartmann, Liebe, Lemp, Schultze, Buchel and Rollman. Casualties and capture further reduced their numbers.

Officer prisoners of war admitted frankly that the strain of U-boat warfare affected their nerves, and it was obvious that many of the prisoners captured in the latter part of 1940 were nervously and physically exhausted. Dissatisfaction was evident at the relentless way in which crews were forced to work. It was maintained that only the minimum time was now allowed in harbour for essential repairs, and that they were then sent to sea again at the earliest possible moment.

In order to fill and strengthen the ranks of U-boat officers, the German naval authorities had transferred a number of officers from other branches of the Navy to be trained intensively for U-boats. Officers up to and including the rank of Lieutenant Commander were selected for this training. The more senior were intended to take command of U-boats after taking their preliminary U-boat courses and completing one or more patrols under instruction with an experienced U-boat captain.

On conclusion of these cruises these senior officers were given command of a new U-boat. A few weeks of trials and a working-up period for the crew followed in the Baltic prior to the U-boat proceeding on patrol. Kapitanleutnant Wentzel who was in U-32 for training, would have been given the command of U-77 had he not been captured.

The training of these officers from surface ships helped to fill the gaps in the ranks of U-boat commanders and other officers, but the lack of essential experience among these transferred officers proved to be an immense disadvantage, as one or two patrols under instruction did not compare with several years' service in U-boats.

A growing shortage of experienced petty officers was another cause of anxiety in the U-boat branch of the Navy. There was now a higher proportion of junior ratings with little or no training for U-boats, and among these men there were scarcely any who had volunteered for this branch of the service.

The monthly Anti-Submarine Report for November 1940 indicated that the 17 'star' U-boat commanders had been responsible for the major share of merchant ship tonnage sunk since the outbreak of the war.

While U-boats had been recalled from their North Atlantic patrol areas for reassignment to the Norwegian operations for transportation of guns, ammunition and supplies to German army units moving up the coast from Trondheim to

Narvik, during April and May 1940, early in June they were returning to their patrol areas in the Western Approaches. This was not the case with the large number of British A/S trawlers carrying out similar duties in cooperation with the British and French expeditionary forces facing the invading German army units. Losses from intensive German air attacks probably represented at least two thirds of these little ships.

Those A/S trawlers surviving did not return to A/S operations in the Western Approaches as did the U-boats, but were assigned to carrying out anti-invasion patrols in the channel until the anticipated threat of invasion had faded by early October with the autumn gales. Meanwhile, U-boat activity flared up again from the end of May.

In common with the German U-boat service the Royal Navy was anticipating similar trained-manpower shortages. At the end of 1939 a 'training college' had been established at Brighton in a former school, and named HMS *King Alfred*, to provide the basic officer training for the potential junior deck officers, who were dubbed '90-Day Wonders' by the regular navy destroyer captains to whose ships they were assigned as 'watchkeeping officers'. The British Army had followed a similar system, and after the first year's experience both services issued orders that all candidates for commissions must have served as rankers or ratings and be recommended by their commanding officers. Commanders of all ships were now requested to recommend ratings for training as potential reserve officers.

My coxswain, leading Seaman R.G. Mackenzie RNR had been recommended for promotion to 2nd hand in the Royal Naval Patrol Service and was due to leave for the RNPS manning base at Lowestoft as soon as his replacement reported on board.

Three other candidates I selected for officer training were the following:

W/T D. Crowsley DSM RNVR, the *St Loman*'s wireless operator. A reserve rating and peacetime bank clerk.

Ldg. Seaman Alexander Graham DSM RNR, a deep-sea merchant navy reservist from Stornoway, Isle of Lewis.

Ord. Sig. Sidney Wain RNVR, a peacetime clerk in the Birmingham Gas Works' office.

A number of British banks, insurance companies, and municipal offices had undertaken to make up their former employees' service pay to the level of their peacetime earnings. Both Crowsley and Wain were fortunate in this respect.

Crowsley and Graham had been decorated for their services during the Norwegian operations on board the *St Loman*, and all three men had exhibited that coolness, courage and devotion to duty required of a naval officer under fire, and in very trying conditions at all times.

Crowsley was the first to be sent down to my cabin. 'You have read the Admiralty Fleet Order put up for information on the mess-deck noticeboard, I expect?' I said. 'I would like to put your name forward, Crowsley . . .'

'As you know, skipper, the extra pay and prospects are not very important, but the wife has been on to me suggesting that if I get a commission, with my signals and wireless experience, I might get a shore-base job and we could live together again,' he replied.

'Crowsley, just warn your wife that with my recommendation, your DSM and W/T background, you are most liable to end up as a signals officer on a foreign service cruiser, rather than a UK base job!'

Later my prediction proved correct, Crowsley got both his commission and foreign service cruiser.

Alex and Kenina Graham cutting the cake at their Golden Wedding anniversary,
17 August 1992.

Sidney Wain was the next to come down, with a broad smile, resulting, I suspected, from being warned by his friend Crowsley.

'All my best friends are those on board this happy ship. She's based on Greenock now for regular convoy escort schedules. Boiler cleaning every two to three months means at least a week of home-leave for two watches, and the watch aboard can get shore leave in Greenock with an opportunity of night leave in Glasgow at weekends. I appreciate the opportunity, skipper, but I'd just as soon stay with the ship.' Thus Wain excused himself, and Alexander Graham was my last prospective candidate.

'Graham, you're an RNR reservist and a deep-sea sailor, merchant navy. Going to sea is your chosen profession. As of now you have the required four years' sea time that enables you to sit for the Board of Trade, second officer's certificate that will qualify you for third or second officer with a shipping company after this war. You can study for the exam and take it while you are in the Navy as an officer. I want to recommend you as the man this navy needs as an officer, as of right now. If I can put your name forward then Captain 'D' Greenock will have you interviewed by a board of destroyer commanders. They will pass you for drafting to your manning base and to HMS *King Alfred* training school.'

Graham looked thoughtful. After a short silence he nodded. 'I'll take your recommendation, skipper, the way you put it to me.'

Men from the Isle of Lewis most often go down to the sea in ships and make their living on the great waters, and when they return it is to marry a woman from Stornoway. Graham was no exception to this custom for when *St Loman* had docked in Granton, the port of Edinburgh, he and Kenina MacKay of Calbost village, then a hospital nurse, had been married (see p. 86). I knew because I had granted the 'passionate leave' he had requested. As I had forecast, Alexander Graham was highly recommended by the interviewing board of regular Royal Navy captains and commanders of destroyer escorts in Greenock.

Shortly after his arrival at the manning base I received two missives, a personal letter from Graham to say that the staff captain at the manning base had recommended that he should forego my recommendation for a commission as he did not have a personal income to supplement his pay. The other was a memorandum from Captain 'D' Greenock stating that Leading Seaman Alexander Graham DSM RNR had been recommended and was agreeable to forego his prospective commission as an officer RNVR as he did not have private means.

I proceeded to undergo a 'slow burn' and wrote two responses:

To: Captain 'D' Greenock, Repeated Commander-in-Chief, Western Approaches, Admiralty.

Reference: Recommendation of Leading Seaman Alexander Graham, DSM RNR for a commission as a RNVR officer.

Ldg. Seamen Graham was awarded the DSM for his skill, courage and devotion to duty as an anti-aircraft gunner during his service on board HMS *St Loman* during the Norwegian operations. My two RNVR officers, Sub Lt H.O.T. Bradford, and Sub Lt F.M. Osborne both received the DSC. Neither of these officers had private means and were solely dependant on their service pay and allowances. The fact that these officers had no private incomes had no bearing on their ability as fighting ship's officers in wartime. I confirm my recommendation and would be happy to have Ldg. Seaman Alexander Graham under my command as a ship's officer.

Lieut R.C. Warwick DSC* RNR
Commanding Officer HMS *St Loman*

I also wrote a personal letter to Alexander Graham advising him not to forego his commission under any circumstances as he had received my recommendation and that of a board of destroyer captains. In addition he would be equally able to live on his officer's pay and allowances as was the case with Lieutenants Bradford, Osborne, and myself.

Over a year later, at the offices of the RN Paymaster in East London, South Africa, the staff officers greeted me with:

'Commanding Officer of the *St Loman*, we've heard about you!' Then they showed me the letter to Captain 'D' Greenock which had been reproduced in Admiralty Fleet Orders in regard to the importance of qualified candidates being recommended despite their status in peacetime.

Shortly after, Graham was drafted from *St Loman*. My new coxswain, 2nd Hand Pym Grace RNPS, informed me that Ord. Seaman Michael Foster wished to see me on a 'personal matter', and in due course escorted Seaman Foster down to my cabin and, announcing him, retired. Seaman Foster was a graduate of a British public school and obviously his parents were well-to-do; nevertheless, he was always of slovenly appearance, and as he appeared to consider himself as being 'above the common seamen', had become the butt of some practical jokes by his messmates. He had fallen for the old joke of being sent to the chief engineer for 'a bucket of revolutions', and later, when a diver was overside, being sent to the engine room for a lantern as the diver could not see underwater.

I told Foster to take a chair and tell me what was on his mind.

'Do you know a Captain in the Admiralty (giving the name)? Well, he was at my parents to dinner when I was last on leave and said that by now I should have been recommended for a commission. My brother is now a major in the Army.'

'Your brother was undoubtedly well qualified and in addition, recommended by the commanding officer of his regiment. As far as you are concerned, Foster, I cannot recommend you for advancement from ordinary seaman to able seaman, much less leading seaman. Compared to these "common seamen", as you may regard your messmates, you are completely useless baggage aboard this ship and appear to be unwilling to learn anything about the duties of a seaman. You are slovenly in both habits and appearance.

'What you are trying to tell me, Foster, is that if I don't recommend you for a commission, then your parents will be pulling strings in the Admiralty to get me to make the required recommendation on your behalf, regardless of your qualifications.

'When the coxswain comes to see me with an opinion that you may now be advanced to a leading seaman, then I would be prepared to recommend you for a commission. You have the background and education, and are not entirely unintelligent, despite what I have heard. If you are not prepared to go to work, then go ahead and have your parents "pull strings" and see where it gets you.'

About a month later the secretary to Captain 'D' Greenock asked me to see him. He handed me an Admiralty memorandum to Captain 'D' which read:

Reference Ord. Sea. Michael Foster. HMS *St Loman*. Is it being considered that he should be recommended for a commission? Report is requested.

On the memorandum Captain 'D' had pencilled: 'Why?'

'What is Foster like?' asked the secretary. 'You have to reply.'

'He's completely useless right now,' I said, picking up the memorandum to reply to it, as follows:

To: Captain 'D' Greenock, Repeated Admiralty, C-in-C Western
    Approaches.
At the present time I am unable to recommend Ordinary Seaman Michael Foster for promotion to Able Seaman. I do not consider it to be in the best interests of the service to recommend him for a commission until such

time as he can be advanced to leading seaman.
Lieutenant R.C. Warwick DSC* RNR
Commanding Officer HMS *St Loman*

Captain 'D' Greenock noted: 'Approved forwarded Admiralty, repeated C-in-C Western Approaches'. The response from the Admiralty was: 'Report in six months'.

After receiving the comment from the Admiralty I sent for Michael Foster.

'Well, Foster, so you pulled the strings and you see where it got you?'

'Yes sir! I am sorry now that I did, as it turned out just as you said.'

'Very good, Foster. You know where you stand. If you want to get that recommendation, now you have to work for it.'

About a year later Foster made leading seaman when *St Loman* was on the South African station and I made the promised recommendation. Then I wrote a note to his father in England:

I understand that you have some connections in the Admiralty which might arrange for your son Michael Foster to return to the UK for training at 'King Alfred' as he has passed for leading seaman, and as promised, I have made the required recommendation.

I received a note of thanks for my suggestion, and the comment:

'I think that you have made something of him!' As I had suspected Michael had been 'mother's boy . . .'

CHAPTER VII

During 1940 *St Loman* was credited with the destruction of two U-boats, the first being on 18 July 1940 in 55° 40'N, 6° 56'W, and the second on 11 September in 56° 01'N, 11° 12'W. At the time *St Loman* was based on Belfast, Northern Ireland, where Admiral Richard King RN was the Naval Officer In Charge (NOIC). Rumour had it that when dug out of his retirement, he had been most solicitous for the welfare and safety of his wife, as Belfast, with its industrial complex and shipyards, could become a natural target for German bombers. Thus Mrs King had been lodged safely away in the countryside of western England, while her husband faced the Luftwaffe's anticipated raids on Belfast. In fact, three minor raids did take place during 1940, the first of which caused the terrified population of the Belfast slums to gather their nearest belongings and stream out to the countryside.

My army captain brother, whose engineer regiment was now encamped near Belfast, said that this evacuation resembled the clogging of the roads in France as the German Army swept round the Maginot Line. There were some loud noises and much anti-aircraft fire, but very little bomb damage resulted. After experiencing their first air raid the citizens just remained at home, or inside the pubs. I spent a most pleasant evening in the cellars of the Midland Hotel, near to Pollock Dock, being regaled with drinks on the house in the excellent company of some fellow officers and attractive army nurses who had been in the upstairs lounge bar. A 500-lb bomb did fall in front of the 'Pollock Club' but was very well encased in thick black mud under the jetty, with its fins just visible. After it was inspected as a curio the following morning, its apparent delayed-action fuse exploded, hurling a mass of mud over the cafe entrance in the afternoon.

Admiral King thrived on the dangers and apparent hardships of his post and earned the nickname 'squeegee Dick' from the socialite girls frequenting the officer's club, because of his curious habit of playing an imaginary accordion with his right hand up and down the tender backs of his dancing partners.

The Belfast officers' club had been the headquarters of the pre-war League of Health & Beauty and now suffered from the embarrassment of a profit surplus from its bar trade conducted adjacent to the dance floor, where Admiral King could be seen squiring the red-gold-haired Marchioness of Dufferin & Ava. The marquis was away in the Army, and Maureen, formerly one of the famed 'Guinness girl' beauties, ran the 'Pollock Club' cafe for the officers and men of the A/S trawler base during the day, waiting on tables and passing the time of day to all and sundry without discrimination.

A custom in the First World War had been for ships sinking U-boats to paint a gold star on their funnels. '*Pour encouragez les autres*', as I put it in my bad French. Seaman Sands, with an apparent gift for signwriting, had painted two such stars on the *St Loman*'s grey funnel.

Admiral King's staff captain had asked me for recommendations in connection with the U-boat sinkings and my present first lieutenant, Trevor Bennett RNR, received a 'Mention in Dispatches', while a DSM was awarded to each of the asdic ratings, Seamen Houghton and Sullivan. I received a Bar to the DSC awarded for the Norwegian operations.

My wife's cousin, Mary Woodsford, was a 'sob sister', or reporter on the *Daily Mirror* tabloid and I found that it was due to her that my photograph and that of Captain Lord Louis Mountbatten appeared side by side in the *Illustrated News* and *The Tatler* with the captions: 'Captain Lord Louis Mountbatten RN, Bar to the DSO. Sub Lt R.C. Warwick RNR, Bar to the DSC.'

About one third of *St Loman*'s crew had been decorated and one evening I heard through my open cabin port the quartermaster on the ship alongside sing out, '*St Loman*'s watch ashore going clank! clank! clank! with their medals . . .'

The 'Royals' visited navy and army installations and *St Loman* received visits from the Duke of York and the Duke & Duchess of Gloucester in Belfast, both parties being escorted by Admiral King.

I was actually on leave when the Duke of York made his inspection, but my new first lieutenant Oswald Dodwell remarked: 'You didn't miss anything, skipper, the Duke was as drunk as a skunk when he came aboard!'

Mary Woodsford had related a story regarding the recent marriage of the Duke & Duchess of Gloucester. It appeared that one of the *Daily Mirror*'s editors had been able to negotiate a contact on the staff of Norman Hartnell, the couturier to Royalty, to be stationed behind a screen in the fitting room when the future Duchess of Gloucester's lingerie could be seen. In due course the woman editor returned to the *Mirror* offices to be surrounded by her staff chanting, 'Tell us what it was like. Is it really glamorous?'

Throwing down her purse and notebook in disgust, the editor replied, 'It's woollen combinations! Buttoned up at the back! Buttoned up at the front! Now glamorize that if you can!'

I had received a signal from Admiral King that the ship would be inspected by the Duke & Duchess of Gloucester at 1500 hours. By noon the ship and crew were ready for the big event, and whisky, gin, soda water and angostura bitters set up on my cabin table, as would be expected by Admiral King. *St Loman* was alongside the jetty and outside her was the *Stella Polaris* commanded by Lieutenant Ward DSC RNR, a peacetime fishing skipper, and one of the hardest drinkers in the port of Hull. 'Come aboard, Colin, I've got a bottle of Drambuie to kill!'

'Wardie, we've got an inspection by the Admiral and the Duke of Gloucester this afternoon,' I said.

'Then you'll need a drink before that! Time enough to go, man . . .' When it came to entertaining Skipper Ward was not to be denied, so Lt Dodwell and I went aboard the *Stella Polaris* to join Ward and his two officers with the bottle of Drambuie. It was a very large bottle of that potent liqueur, rightly called 'The spirit of the '45 rebellion'. Lt Dodwell and I returned to our ship well fortified for the pending inspection.

Admiral King, leading the Duke in his regimental colonel's uniform and with the stylishly dressed Duchess, was piped aboard. After inspecting the officers and men lined up on the foredeck, the Admiral, with an imperceptible lick of his lips remarked: 'The Duke and Duchess would like to see your quarters.' I led the way up to the wheelhouse and to the top of the steep companionway with the Duchess, followed by the Admiral and the Duke.

The Duchess was carrying a handbag and hesitated at the top of the ladder. 'Shall I take your bag?' I asked.

'If you would, please.'

Then as she was looking down the stairs, I added, 'Shall I lead the way?'

'Please do!'

So I led the way down and stood at the foot of the stairs as the royal legs felt their way carefully down. Then Mary Woodsford's story came to mind and I raised my downcast eyes for an all encompassing glance. The Duke very obviously had made some changes in the lingerie since his fiancée's visit to Norman Hartnell's fitting room!

Some months later, nine to be exact, the *Stella Polaris* passed us on passage flashing the signal: 'Duchess of Gloucester gave birth to a son this past week. Congratulations *St Loman*!'

About this time an investiture for officers was being scheduled at Buckingham Palace, and Admiral King decided that by travelling on RAF transport I could make it with 48-hours' leave, to travel from Belfast to the London airfield (which has since become Heathrow) and return the next day when *St Loman* was due to sail for a convoy rendezvous.

Seating on the Dakota transport was basic in the extreme. There was a steel bench on either side of the cargo area with miscellaneous aircraft parts and mailbags in between. I picked a spot where I could look out of a window or small port. This was my first time up in any aircraft, and when halfway across the Irish Sea I saw a destroyer below us flashing the challenge. Then all of a sudden my rear end felt tense and vulnerable until the pilot fired his recognition flares. I had had experience in being below an aircraft, and now I knew how an airman felt when knowing that a ship below had him in its AA gunsights.

Heathrow was a mere airstrip with a couple of Quonset huts at one end where a RAF car and driver were parked. The mailbags were loaded in the back and I got in the front to make the first stop at Buckingham Palace and the midday investitures.

Quiet efficiency reigned in the ante-rooms to the great reception hall of the palace. Dark-suited servants took care of the coats and gas-mask bags, and hung them in the cloakrooms assigned to each of the services. Then they took each of us to the washrooms and brushed off our uniforms before I received my brief instructions as my assistant fitted a small silver hook in my left lapel. 'The merchant navy officers will be the first in the waiting line. As you have two decorations you will be the first navy officer to be called, announcing your rank, name, and decoration to be received. His Majesty will be standing on the dais. When your name is called you will walk in front, turn left to face His Majesty and salute. As you are receiving the DSC and Bar, His Majesty may say a few words to you.'

The merchant navy, Royal Navy, army and air force officers were now being assigned to their places. I was particularly impressed that the merchant navy officers took precedence over the senior service.

When I came face to face with King George VI, he took my decoration from the cushion held by a chamberlain standing at his right hand side and neatly placed its ring on the waiting hook in my left lapel. Now came the few words predicted: 'Where did you get the first one?

'Norwegian Operations, sir!'

'And the second?'

'Two U-boats, sir!'

'Good show!' replied the King as I stepped back, saluted and joined the small waiting crowd of friends and relatives. A chamberlain retrieved the hook from my lapel, and placed my decorations in a small leather-covered box marked 'D.S.C.' on its lid.

I found my Aunt Mabel with my son Richard. My aunt and godmother explained that my mother had been too frail to accept one of the two limited invitations sent to her and my wife. My silly mother-in-law had told her daughter that as her divorce decree nisi had not been made absolute it was just impossible for her to take my son to Buckingham Palace with all those press photographs being taken. My aunt took my about-to-be-wife's invitation in order to bring my son to the palace.

We waited to see the completion of the investiture, and I also wanted to meet Squadron Leader E.H.P. Clarke DFC RAF who had been in my term at Pangbourne College. He too had been decorated that morning. Clarke was very tense. 'They've got most of our term – Cooper, Dundas, Charlton, Mansfield . . .' he rattled off the names as if they were posted on a board in his memory. 'The RAF have me on training now, but I want to get back on operations.' We shook hands and he went off to find his wife. If Clarke had the score correctly, then there were only three or four of our term left, but he got his wish to go back on operations. Shortly afterwards he was gone too.

I took the train from Waterloo to Surbiton with my son and Aunt Mabel, where I spent the night with my mother and where my wife came to claim our son. Early next morning I was away to catch my RAF ride to Heathrow from the RAF offices in the Strand.

Back in Belfast that afternoon I reported back to HMS *Caroline* based at Pollock Dock and to pick up my sailing orders for that evening. It was back to convoy escort and business as usual!

CHAPTER VIII

The former Commander-in-Chief of Western Approaches Command had been Admiral Dunbar Nasmith VC, a gallant and intrepid submariner from the First World War, who had taken his submarine through the nets and minefield of the Dardanelles in the ancient-named Hellespont strait joining the Aegean and the Sea of Marmara, torpedoed Turkish battleships and made his way out as he had entered. His successor as C-in-C WA was Admiral Sir Maxwell Horton RN, snidely dismissed by his RN contempories as 'A common little man who has made good!' and reputed to have married a red-haired barmaid in his youth. Nevertheless Maxie Horton, as he was referred to by his staff and escort commanders, had most efficiently organized the convoy system in the Western Approaches from his headquarters in the Liver House on the Liverpool dockside.

Escort groups for Western Ocean convoys were based in Greenock, and those for the Gibraltar convoys in Liverpool. C-in-C WA's jurisdiction extended to 45° West, where Canadian navy escort groups based on Halifax, Nova Scotia, and Argentia, Newfoundland, escorted UK-bound convoys assembled in Halifax and Argentia, and were starting to be met by the UK-based escort groups with the westbound merchant ships. The Canadians parted company with their eastbound convoys which were taken over by the now eastbound British escorts, and returned to Canada with the westbound ships.

The Plimsoll mark, named after the British statesman Samuel Plimsoll who was instrumental in having legislation passed against overloading vessels, shows the lawful submergence level 'WNA' for Winter North Atlantic, providing the highest freeboard of all the marks painted on the sides of British merchant ships. Foul weather, gale-force winds, heavy seas, rain, fog and mist, and overcast skies were the order of the day and night. The best that could be said for the miserable rainstorms was that they tended to flatten the breaking seas and wind whipped off the heavy Atlantic swells.

The converted deep-sea Hull and Grimsby trawlers were designed with a high flare to their bows to meet the brutal short seas and the rough arctic waters of Bear Island and the White Sea areas. When dry-docked these trawlers showed the lines of a yacht-type keel, giving a draught of 12-14 ft aft and 8-9 ft forward in order to offset the pull of their heavy peacetime deep-sea trawl beams and nets.

St Loman and her sister ships made light of the worst North Atlantic weather and despite their low freeboard amidships, little water was taken on the foredecks. The fleet destroyers with their shallow draught and knife-like bows made heavy going in the usual rough weather, severely reducing their cruising speed to avoid taking heavy seas forward.

Parting from our westbound convoy to a Canadian group, 'Flash Alf' Turner in HMS *Boadicea* signalled his course and speed at 12 knots to make the position of the eastbound convoy that his escort group was to take to the UK, and to take up position on his beam with the destroyer HMS *Beagle* in a line abreast formation making an asdic sweep as we went. The A/S trawlers *Lady Elsa* and *Lady Madeline* formed abeam of *St Loman*. Only with the best coal and a full head of steam could the A/S trawlers maintain a speed of 12 knots, thus as the three destroyers *Boadicea*, *Beagle* and *Hesperus* began to draw ahead in the line; 'Flash Alf's' aldis lamp flashed:

'You'll have to do better than this to make the convoy!'

Then the westerly gale blew much harder than before. The three destroyers were making heavy weather as their bows cut down into the breaking waves and their speed reduced. Now the three trawlers, rising high over the heavy swells and breaking seas, began to draw ahead of the destroyers in the line-abreast formation, and it was our turn to make a signal to *Boadicea*: 'You will have to do better to make the convoy!' It was acknowledged without response.

On this particular convoy assignment four army commando volunteers had been put on board as passengers, 'For toughening', I had been told. Outside one of my open cabin ports the army sergeant was talking to one of the seamen under the overhang of the bridge asking: 'Is it always like this?'

'Like what?' replied the sailor.

'Well all this bloody rain, mist, cold, fog. The f**king ship rolling and pitching up and down, throwing bloody spray in your face. That's what!'

The seaman was silent for a while before replying, 'Well, yes! Most of the time it is like this, but sometimes the seas go down quite a bit and the sun comes through the overhanging clouds around noon.'

'Well f**k this for a life!' the sergeant ended.

Heavy weather and poor visibility were not entirely unwelcome. The fog and overcast assisted in hiding convoys from the searching eyes of the enemy's Focke-Wulf aircraft, while most U-boat commanders stayed submerged during very heavy weather and still showed a preference for seeking out and sinking unescorted merchant ships, many of which were neutrals.

Sightings by German aircraft went to Admiral Dönitz's headquarters in Berlin. The sighting position with the estimated course and speed of the convoy would then be relayed to U-boats patrolling in, or near, that area with instructions to make a sighting contact at extreme visibility, then to take a position astern of the convoy, monitor its position, course and speed for transmission to other U-boats which might be in position to join in an attack.

U-boat commanders acted on their own initiative and planned their attacks independently of other U-boats in the area of the sighted convoy, which would be named by Berlin after the U-boat commander making the initial sighting. Thus if the latter happened to be Kapitanleutnant Wilhelm Rollmann, the code name would be 'Rollmann'.

The speed of most convoys did not exceed that of the slowest ships, usually an average of 6 to 7 knots. Convoys termed fast would make 10 to 12 knots. A U-boat could make 15-16 knots with her diesels on the surface, and after shadowing a slow convoy from a position 5 to 10 miles astern, depending on the visibility, could proceed at dusk outside the convoy to take up a position well ahead. Then, trimmed down to periscope depth, she could await the arrival of the convoy columns, and hope to slip undetected through the A/S screen of the convoy escorts. When positioned outside the port or starboard side of the convoy columns, she could fire torpedoes as the merchant ship targets passed by. During the confusion created by one or more successful attacks, the U-boat commander would retire at speed on the surface using his diesels, which might also be geared up with the U-boat's electrics for a maximum burst of speed.

With three or four U-boats converging on a convoy, radio signals between them might be exchanged for one or two days, then radio silence, intimating that the attack on the convoy was imminent. The favourite time for a U-boat attack tended to be an hour or two after sunset in the evening, or an hour or two prior to dawn breaking in the early morning.

The primary function of a convoy escort group was to ensure absolute protection and safe passage for ships in the convoy; not to seek out and hunt U-boats that might be planning to make attacks. Thus the escort commander would position his escort ships so as to provide the most effective A/S screen around the convoy.

We were escorting an eastbound convoy entering the approaches to the North Channel of the Irish Sea. Captain Turner in HMS *Boadicea* had stationed his destroyer ahead of the four columns of the convoy with HMS *Beagle* and HMS *Hesperus* on the starboard and port beams of the convoy. A/S trawlers *Lady Madeline* and *St Loman* were positioned bearing about 45° off the outside convoy columns and abeam of *Boadicea* zig-zagging across the head of the convoy.

As dawn was starting to break behind a shroud of damp mist, there came the clout of a 4-inch gun from *Boadicea* as the short-wave radio on *St Loman*'s bridge barked, 'Submarine on surface starboard side.' Already at action stations, Seaman Houghton was tracking a U-boat contact bearing about 45° on *St Loman*'s port bow at about 1,500 yards range. Assuming that the U-boat had just crash-dived a five-depth charge attack was made with 100-ft settings.

The leading ship of the convoy's starboard column was closing *St Loman*'s attack position and the contact faded in the wake of the convoy. HMS *Beagle* on the starboard side of the convoy gained a contact astern of the convoy and attacked with a 14-charge pattern. After this contact could not be regained, indicating possible destruction of the U-boat.

Both *St Loman* and *Beagle* now resumed their stations on the convoy escort screen. Whatever the results of the two depth-charge attacks the U-boat commander had been forced to 'keep his head down' as the convoy cleared the potential danger area.

On reaching the North Channel entrance to the Irish Sea the convoy was dispersed for the merchant ships to make their ways independently to Loch Ewe, the Clyde, Liverpool and the Bristol Channel. *Boadicea* flashed the signal. 'Proceed independently to Greenock' as the whitewash boiled under the sterns of the three destroyers in response to 'Full ahead' being rung down to their engine rooms. Black coal smoke belched out from the funnels of the *St Loman* and *Lady Madeline* as their respective engine rooms started working up to 110-120 revolutions on their 'three-legged up-and-down jobs', as their reciprocating engines were called.

The rising wind had dispersed the mist and was whipping up unruly, tossing waves. Above in the low, grey, overcast clouds we could hear the uneven beat and chocking of an aircraft's engines as a RAF Blenheim finally broke through the overcast, diving into the sea about half a mile distant from *St Loman*. 'Flash Alf' in *Boadicea* had seen the crash, and both ships closed its position only to see the bomber disappear below the waves as the sole survivor's yellow 'Mae West' life jacket could be seen bobbing up and down.

'We are lowering our whaler,' flashed *Boadicea*. From *St Loman*'s bridge we saw the boat drop unevenly into the rough sea alongside the destroyer.

'Will you be lowering the boat, sir?' asked my coxswain, Mackenzie, regarding the *St Loman*'s one lifeboat already swung out below the bridge on the starboard side for use as an 'accident boat'. This is the custom of merchant navy ships when putting to sea. Mackenzie had the boat's crew in their life jackets and the hands ready to lower. It was 9 July 1941, but those rough green seas of the North Channel were as cold as charity.

'No, coxswain! That navy whaleboat crew have lost a couple of oars already and are in trouble! We'll put the ship alongside the man in the water making a lee for him on our starboard side. Now get the Jacob's ladder over the side amidships. Andy Morrison wants to go overside with a heaving line fast to his waist to get hold of the pilot so that the hands on deck can haul them both to the ladder. We need another volunteer at the bottom of our Jacob's ladder to fend Andy and the pilot off the ship's side, then for both to push the survivor up the ladder so our hands on deck can help all three of them on board and over the bulwarks.'

With a quick 'Aye, aye, sir!' Mackenzie was down to the foredeck to get the rescue equipment and hands organized. Sub Lt Gilbert Jones, the rugby scrum-half for Wales had come up on the bridge to join Lt Dodwell on watch.

'Mr Jones, if and when we get that pilot on board, he's likely to be frozen stiff, and Andy Morrison and Seaman Brown, who has volunteered to get down overside on that ladder, are not going to be much better. Take all three of them down to the stokehold, the warmest place on the ship, strip off their clothes and wrap them in blankets. You know the life-saving drill to get the water out of the pilot, and all three of you start to massage him. Use some rum for rubbing alcohol, putting some in each of them as well!'

I had learnt how to handle the reciprocating engines of a deep-sea Hull trawler. Ringing for 'Full ahead' and 'Full astern', and vice versa, without the 'Stop engines' in between, avoided the risk of stopping on 'top dead centre', as it was called. Then, putting the helm 'Hard to starboard', with 'Full astern', would stop the ship, swinging the bows sharply to starboard.

While the rescue members readied themselves on the starboard bulwarks amidships, *St Loman* came up head to wind about 30 ft past the man in the water, then went full astern with the helm hard over to starboard to hold the ship, making a lee, and with the engines now stopped, starting to drift towards the survivor. Morrison, with the line around his waist, dived in when close to and clasped his arms around the pilot as the hands on deck pulled both men to the Jacob's ladder, where Seaman Brown cushioned them both against hitting the ship's side with his own body. Willing hands pulled all three aboard into the care of Sub Lt Jones and his massage programme in the stokehold.

Using the same technique *St Loman* was put alongside the *Boadicea*'s whaler to tow it back to the destroyer. The whaler's crew were looking very sorry for themselves and unable to make any headway in the tumbling seas.

Leading Seaman Gunner A. Morrison RNR and Able Seaman L. Brown

RNR were awarded the Bronze Medal of the Royal Humane Society.

Sub Lt Jones's massage programme combined with the injection of navy rum had the RAF sergeant pilot of the ditched Blenheim in excellent shape by the time *St Loman* reached the head of the Firth of Clyde and received orders to anchor off Gourock pier until the usual berth at Greenock became available. The RAF's air-sea rescue launch came alongside as soon as the anchor dropped to collect their survivor.

Later in the afternoon my coxswain, Robert Mackenzie, came down to the wardroom with the suggestion that the watch due for shore leave might be taken by the ship's lifeboat to Gourock pier at 1900 to return at 2300. Ldg. Seaman Donald MacDonald would be in charge of the lifeboat and remain at the pier landing. Closing time for the pubs in Gourock was 2230, thus half an hour gave time for the 'one for the road' back to the landing at the pier.

MacDonald was one of the four seamen from Stornoway on the Isle of Lewis, who with Alexander Graham, Donald Morrison, and 'Big John' Smith crewed the lifeboat. All of them 'had the Gaelic' as their first language proving most fortunate for a recent recruit coming from the Isle of Islay, where he and his parents were the lighthouse keepers at Port Ellen at the Gigha Passage. It was some time before he learnt to speak English!

Just after 2300 the coxswain reported to the first lieutenant, Oswald Dodwell, that the watch ashore had reported back on board, but Ldg. Seaman MacDonald was missing. My official report stated that MacDonald had left his post at the landing to round up the crew members on shore leave in the pubs and get them on their way back to the pier landing by 2300. Crossing the road in the blackout, at the street corner, a city bus making the sharp turn had knocked down MacDonald who was killed almost instantly while on duty.

It was likely to be the truth of the matter that MacDonald had taken his 'duty visit' to the pubs just before closing time as an opportunity to down several 'big hoff's' in rapid succession and in fact was 'absent without leave ashore'!

Thus in the space of 24 hours the St Loman had saved a man at sea and lost a man ashore, but the last tragedy came as no surprise to the other Stornoway men. 'MacDonald was fey' they claimed factually, in that unusually excited or gay state believed to portend sudden death. As was the custom, MacDonald's sea gear and effects, which included a very new uniform, were auctioned in the messdeck by the coxswain.

Shortly after I had mailed my letter of condolence to his elderly parents and enclosing the money order, I received a letter from a firm of credit tailors regarding the overdue instalment on the new uniform ordered by MacDonald. It was duly regretted by the commanding officer that due to his death on active duty no such action requested could be taken.

CHAPTER IX

During December 1940 there had been a pronounced lull in the U-boat campaign. Enemy tactics and strategies appeared to have undergone a revision. The initially successful night attacks made by U-boats on our convoys were heaviest in October, but declined rapidly in November. Only two convoys were attacked in December, because the Germans may have realized that their methods were now understood, and U-boat captains were fearful of the intensive hunts by A/S escorts.

In addition it was possible that the intense star shell illumination created by the escorts on the beam of the attacked convoys had a greater psychological effect upon U-boat captains than might have been expected. Silhouetted in a flash of bright light when making a fast surface retreat to escape after making a torpedo attack, the natural impulse could have been to crash dive to avoid detection. Now most vulnerable to contact by the asdics of the searching escorts, the U-boat was no longer a threat as the convoy columns moved out of the danger area.

New evasive routing measures had been put into effect on 20 December 1940, as a counter to the development that U-boats in the North-Western Approaches had been attacking our convoys in longitudes 20° to 25°W, an area beyond the point which could be reached by our escorts, particularly in bad weather.

The following measures were therefore adopted and put into effect:

1. Maximum utilization of dispersion to the extent permitted by the endurance of merchant ships and the limitation of the North-Western Approaches.

2. Spreading the routes of the HX-Halifax convoys between about 63½° and 57°, and the routes of SL, SC, the Sierra Leone and Gibraltar convoys between about 57° and 54°N, 54°N being as far south as the danger from air attack could be accepted. The routes for outward-bound convoys conformed.

3. With the exception of Gibraltar sailings, to open out the cycle of all convoys with the objective of reducing strain on the escorting forces.

4. In summer, making the maximum use of northern waters, in order to obtain the high degree of protection against night attacks by U-boats afforded by the almost perpetual daylight.

5. Enable escorts on the more northerly routes to proceed further to the westward by establishing refuelling bases for escorts at Loch Ewe and at Hvalfjord in Iceland.

6. Make use of the Minches for some outward- and homeward-bound convoys.

Another very possible reason for the lull in German U-boat activity could have been the almost constant attention paid by the RAF to the U-boat base at Lorient.

Early in December, a westerly movement of U-boats became noticeable, as previously the enemy had operated mainly to the eastward of meridian 15°W. This new disposition showed that most U-boats were as far out as 20°W, the Germans to the northward and the Italians to the southward. This movement may have been inspired by a healthy respect for air attack combined with an attempt to intercept our convoys before the A/S escort arrived, as on the nights of 1 to 3 December three ships were sunk in Convoy OG 46, which was escorted by only a single A/S ship. One straggler from this convoy was sunk also.

After this date no escorted convoys were attacked, and the losses sustained during the remainder of December were thus:

Dispersed from convoy or after escorts left	14 ships
Stragglers	6 ships
Routed independently	5 ships

Italian submarines assisting the Germans in the Atlantic achieved greater success in December than in previous months. One Italian submarine torpedoed the 5,000-ton SS *Ardanbham* on 27 December in latitude 59°N, an achievement loudly proclaimed in the Italian press, as it was further north than their submarines had ventured previously.

Information supplied by the Anti-Submarine Warfare Division indicated that Italian submarine captains had no stomach for continuing evasive tactics submerged after being exposed to two or three depth-charge attacks. This may have been due to some lack of confidence in the construction of Italian submarines. German U-boats were able to take considerable punishment from depth-charge explosions and at depths of at least 4-500 feet, and at the same time throw off the listening asdic operators of the hunters by the creation of apparent 'non-sub contacts' by means of alternate bursts of ahead and astern on the propellers making a blanketing 'wash' around the then motionless U-boat. German U-boat survivors who had been subjected to the massive 14-depth-charge attacks made by our destroyers had expressed great, and often surprised, admiration for the toughness of their U-boats under pressure at extreme depths.

The standard complement of depth charges for such A/S trawlers as *St Loman* was 50 of the 250-300-lb drums, made with a hollow tube in the centre, into which a 'pistol' detonator, operated by water pressure, was inserted in each charge. A detachable brass 'key' made the required depth setting in a selection of 50-ft depths from 50 ft to 500 ft, and retained for proof of setting prior to firing from the amidship throwers, or being dropped off the rails aft, making a 'five of clubs' playing card design coverage over the target.

Destroyers attacking at speeds approaching 15 knots tended to lose contact for an appreciable time after carrying out an attack, taking some time to regain it. My experience with *St Loman* making a maximum of 10-11 knots and running out about 1,500 yards from the target, having made a five-charge attack, was that my asdic operators quickly regained firm contact as the ship was turned with the helm put hard to starboard, to come bows on ready to run in for a second depth-charge attack with both the amidship throwers already loaded, with the depth-charge pistols charged and ready for the required settings and the 4-inch gun crew looking hopefully for a surfacing target at the same time. Firm contact being regained after making a second five-charge pattern attack gave the opportunity to deliver three hammer blows in quick succession of, for example, depth settings of 150 ft, 250 ft, and 500 ft.

Hydrophone operators in U-boats quickly picked up and identified the quick beat of a destroyer's propellers, whereas those of the single-screw A/S trawlers were identical to those of a merchant ship. Turning to starboard for preference combined the right-handed thrust of the trawler's single screw to turn almost in a ship's length and in any sort of weather.

The shallow-draft destroyers carried their oscillator diaphragms higher in the water than those of the A/S trawlers, and exposed them to greater turbulence when reversing their course, and making a larger turning circle.

It was apparent to me that an A/S trawler escorting a Western Ocean convoy could not have the luxury of investigating a potential U-boat contact at leisure, but, relying on the experience of the asdic operator, could make an immediate

105

depth-charge attack with the officer of the watch directing it. Thus my standing orders were to the effect that in the event of the asdic operator classifying a contact as a possible U-boat, then he was expected to ring for 'action stations' and when I reached the bridge the *St Loman* should be lined up on an attacking course to deliver the first depth-charge attack.

It was the usual procedure for the officer of the watch to first call his commanding officer, and the latter would decide whether to order 'action stations'. I had my critics in this respect, but I had decided that I had complete confidence in my officers' judgement, and I was not about to give a U-boat captain an extra five or ten minutes to line up his torpedo attack on the convoy column. The contact might turn out to be a whale, but an excellent 'practice action stations' nevertheless – even if 'my face might be red!'

On the subject of whales the A/S Warfare Department had these observations to offer:

A/S vessels have wasted time and depth charges in attacks upon whales because asdic contact and visible indications convince Commanding Officers of the presence of a U-boat.

A study of the characteristics of whales proves that the behaviour of some species, especially the Killer whale, does, in fact, resemble the indications of a U-boat.

A whale's back has several times been mistaken for a U-boat surfacing on her side or upside down before sinking.

In addition, oil rises to the surface from the whales that have been depth charged, and a large specimen has been known to produce as much as 40 tons. This has no smell, but is said to resemble olive oil.

Normally, whales rise to the surface and spout every 8 or 9 minutes, but a frightened animal can hold its breath under the water for above 30 minutes. The spouting causes a rumbling sound, especially in good weather.

Sleeping whales remain motionless, with nose and fin above water, acting like a boat drifting and wallowing in the swell.

Fig. 1 (see p. 107) is a photograph of a whale spouting. This was at first thought to be a U-boat blowing her tanks, and the fin of a whale nearby was thought to be the U-boat's periscope.

Fig. 2 shows an oil patch on the surface after a whale had been depth charged, and another whale in the vicinity spouting.

Figs. 3 and 4 show the Killer whale. This species is found anywhere from the Arctic to the Antarctic, but particularly in low latitudes of the Southern hemisphere, usually travel in shoals of 5-50. They are not more

PHOTOGRAPHS OF WHALES

Fig. 1.

Fig. 2.

Fig. 3.

Fig. 4.

Fig. 5.

Fig. 6.

107

than 30 ft in length; the dorsal fin is 6 ft high on an adult male and about 3 ft on a female.

These whales sometimes move at speed with only the fin visible, which from some angles, looks like a periscope. The wake of the fin, especially when seen from the air, closely resembles the wake of a periscope.

Fig. 5 illustrates two different types of whales diving. The Hump whale which has a small hump instead of a fin, about 45 ft long, shrugs at the end of the dive and throws its tail out of the water.

The Blue whale, 65 ft long, with a small fin does not show its tail when diving.

Fig. 6 shows the Finn whale, which is also a fast-moving whale with a dorsal fin, and the Sperm whale, another humped-back species, that shows the whole of its tail when diving. The Sperm whale spouts forward instead of upwards.

All types of whales, when feeding, stand on their heads with tails waving slowly from side to side in the air.

The Basking shark, a 40-50 ft fish, has a dorsal fin nearly 7 ft high. This type of shark remains motionless on the surface, down by the stern and with nose awash. At a distance the fin might possibly be mistaken for a periscope; it would be motionless or moving forward slowly, not dipping as would be the Killer whale's fin.

Basking sharks are to be found in all temperate seas, particularly the North Atlantic, appearing off Wales, Ireland and the West of Scotland in the spring and moving off to the Norwegian coast in August. Except during the breeding season, when as many as 50 may congregate, they are generally seen singly or possibly in pairs.

Another large fish with a dorsal fin 2 ft 6 in. high which might be mistaken for a periscope is the Sunfish, an extremely sluggish type of fish which appears off the British Isles in the summer months.

Despite the A/S Warfare Department's comments on wasted time and depth charges, while I did not propose to waste time, but in order to be safe rather than sorry, I arranged at the *St Loman*'s refit in Aberdeen to have deck fittings for an additional 45 depth charges installed thus increasing attack capacity from 10 patterns of 5 charges to 19.

The A/S Warfare Review for March 1941 commented that:

In March the Germans made a determined effort to launch the intense U-boat campaign of the long-threatened Spring Offensive.

At least twelve U-boats were sent to sea commanded by some of the enemy's most skilful U-boat captains.

Their tactics included a repetition of the concentrated night attacks upon convoys, and six convoys were attacked during the month, with the consequent torpedoing of twenty-four ships, four of which were subsequently brought into port.

Previous ideas of general enemy policy have been confirmed. U-boats usually operate in groups of three to five, each vessel being given a small individual patrol area in the water covered by the whole group. The first U-boat to locate a convoy shadows and reports and will not normally attack until at least one other U-boat has concentrated for attack.

Shadowing U-boats make signals which can be D/F'd by others to 'home' themselves on to the convoy. Alternatively a Focke-Wulf aircraft obtaining the initial sighting will make similar signals to 'home' the nearest U-boat to shadow.

Operations against U-boats had been more successful in March 1941 than in any other month of the war.

There was clear evidence of increased efficiency of A/S escorts and the U-boats which attacked adequately escorted convoys were dealt with effectively.

Fifty attacks on U-boats or supposed U-boats were made during March, thirty-nine by surface vessels and eleven by aircraft.

The most interesting occurrence of the month followed the attack on Convoy HX 112. Two and possibly three U-boats were sunk that night, one as the result of an ASV contact.

After being depth-charged by the escorting destroyers U-100 surfaced and might have escaped in the darkness had she not been detected by HMS *Vanoc*'s ASV. The destroyer rammed this U-boat and while she was picking up survivors another escort obtained asdic contact in the vicinity. Although it was considered unlikely that another U-boat would remain as close, the A/S Control Officer and operator were so convinced that their classification was correct that HMS *Walker* fired six depth charges. This attack was extremely accurate and brought U-99 to the surface almost at once.

These successes resulted in the death and capture of two of Germany's star Commanders.

The effect of the loss of two of the enemy's most skilful U-boat captains was soon apparent: the U-boats were once more forced westward. Thus the chief problem of the Navy has been that of extending A/S escort as far west as possible.

In regard to my proposed tactics of making immediate depth-charge attacks on suspicious asdic contacts when escorting convoys, it seemed that some officers, being economy-minded, had a wrong impression of the cost of depth charges, as the A/S Warfare Review commented: 'Apparently some officers have a wrong impression of the cost of depth charges; a depth charge, complete with explosive and pistol, costs £37. The supply position was very satisfactory and reserves at home and abroad exceeded 24,000. The average monthly expenditure was 1,200 charges.'

The above-mentioned depth charge cost, complete with explosive and pistol given in the March issue of the A/S Report was stated in error being revised in the April A/S Report as £22 10s. 0d for a Mark VII depth charge complete. If fired from a thrower, the cost, including carrier and cartridge was £27 10s. 0d.

CHAPTER X

During the winter of 1940-41 weather in the North Atlantic was exceptionally foul, and our slow convoys became even slower than usual, as for instance one escorted by us in Captain Turner's group averaging 24 sea miles on two days of gale-force winds and heavy tumbling seas.

However there was a good side to this combination of gale-force winds, overcast, and unruly seas, which the occasional rain squall served to pat down somewhat. The resulting poor visibility made the planned 'wolf pack' or group U-boat strategy of Admiral Dönitz impossible.

U-boats assigned to patrol the anticipated convoy routes were constantly frustrated by this adverse weather during their daylight searches for convoys, which when sighted had to be shadowed from astern. U-boat command would now name the target convoy after the sighting U-boat's captain.

Thus as the sighting U-boat tailed along at extreme visibility distance from the rear ships of the convoy, the convoy escorts could often hear the position, course, and speed estimates being transmitted by the U-boat to the German command in Berlin. Other U-boats in the vicinity would now receive this information and instructions from U-boat command to join the shadowing U-boat astern of the convoy. When German radio signals stopped, this meant 'Tonight is the attack night' to the listening escort commander.

U-boats would gather astern of the convoy, proceed on the surface at full speed and travel up either side of the convoy unseen to positions well ahead of it, then turn to await their prospective victims' approach at nightfall. Trimmed down to periscope depth, maintaining steerage weigh they would manoeuvre to fire their torpedoes as the merchant ships passed by, then try to slip away undetected in the wake astern of the convoy during the ensuing confusion, most often escaping at their full surface speed of 16-17 knots.

Flower class corvettes with a capability of 15-16 knots, and coal-burning A/ S trawlers making 10-12 knots under the best conditions were unable to overtake these attackers, which, reaching a safe distance, could reload their torpedo tubes on the surface and possibly make another attack on the convoy before dawn.

One most important factor at this time was the British Admiralty's ULTRA intelligence information making U-boat positions known and enabling convoys at risk to suddenly change course, thereby avoiding the U-boat lines. Thus although the average number of U-boats operating in the Atlantic during 1941 increased from 12 in February to as many as 36 in August, the number of ships they succeeded in sinking fell drastically.

Captain Alfred Turner, the senior officer of our escort group and in command of the destroyer HMS *Boadicea*, required that each commanding officer of the ships in his group should know what was required of them during anti-U-boat operations and without the necessity of signalled orders.

My standing orders in *St Loman* carried down this concept to the officer of the watch. Every officer was capable of initiating and carrying out a depth-charge attack on a probable U-boat contact. Thus I expected the officer of the watch to call me by ringing for action stations, and when I arrived on the bridge, he was expected to be on an attacking course with the *St Loman* ready to deliver the first five-charge pattern on the suspect contact.

In actual fact I was seldom off the bridge from before dusk to first light in the morning, taking my brief sleeping hours on a 'donkey's breakfast' straw mattress. This served in preserving my night vision and avoided the temporary blinding effect of a flashlight or cabin light being switched on by a bridge lookout sent down to call me. Other commanding officers did not always agree with me and preferred the order for action stations to be their own decision, having evaluated the situation on the bridge. 'Warwick, you worry too much!' one commented to me. Perhaps he was right, but it did not change my mind!

In order to expedite an initial five-depth-charge attack, the explosive 'pistols' were inserted in all depth charges, both those carried on the rails aft and the thrower reload charges lashed down amidships and on the deck. Pistols for the initial five-charge pattern were primed and inserted ready to fire. Then the depth settings were made for each individual charge with a detachable 'key'. A depth had to be set before the key could be detached and returned to the shore base as evidence.

Lieutenant Walter Sadgrove RANVR was one of a small volunteer group of Australian A/S-trained officers arriving from Sydney early in 1940 to serve in A/S ships of the RN, and recently had been given command of the A/S trawler *Stella Capella*. His wife Wilcie had joined him in Belfast from Australia, and they were a welcome and attractive couple in our wardroom. Late in the evening Wilcie would look at her husband, saying, 'Oh, Walter!' At which we would all burst out laughing and tell him to take her home. They had an agreement that if Wilcie got pregnant then she had to return to Australia. Of course the inevitable happened!

St Loman was being boiler-cleaned in Belfast, when my coxswain, Ldg. Sea. Robert Mackenzie, provided a temporary relief on board the *Stella Capella* for a coastal convoy of short duration. It seemed that when on passage back to Belfast, a potential U-boat contact was obtained, but lost again during the long delay in priming depth charges, as Sadgrove had observed to me in our wardroom over the inevitable 'pink gins'.

Later, I asked Mackenzie what had caused the delay and in his soft, deprecating voice he said: 'It was due to those wooden plugs used to close the centre tubes of the charges being swollen by the sea spray and water, and making it very hard to remove, so that the firing pistols could be inserted and primed.'

I gave Mackenzie a puzzled look of surprise. 'Mac, are you telling me that a five-charge pattern had not been armed and ready?'

'That's the way we have it on *St Loman*, but Mr Sadgrove will not have the pistols inserted in any of the depth charges until action stations. He considers it a necessary precaution against premature explosion on board.' Mackenzie shook his head, doubtful it seemed.

A few months later *Stella Capella* was reported torpedoed and lost with all hands off Iceland. It seemed that a U-boat commander took advantage of the delay on hearing an asdic contact being made.

A monthly A/S Warfare Journal report around that time indicated that a RN destroyer commander blessed with his regular navy crew could be found as unprepared as a reservist in command:

A Destroyer Misses a Magnificent Opportunity

Whilst four destroyers were carrying out an A/S sweep at daybreak, one of them sighted two white Very lights or rockets ahead, followed some time later by a single light. It was assumed that these were fired by U-boats making a rendezvous, and course was set to investigate.

In a little over an hour a U-boat was sighted fine on the port bow at about 800 yards range, and simultaneously asdic contact was obtained. The enemy was proceeding at 8 knots steering the same course as the division.

The destroyer at once turned to port at full speed to ram, ordering fire to be opened with SAP, depth charges were set to 50 ft.

The U-boat increased speed and turned to starboard. The destroyer conformed until, at about 100 yards range, the U-boat was at right angles crossing from port to starboard.

When the gun-layers could see the target, fire was opened with maximum depression, but the effect could not be seen owing to the blinding gun flash.

The U-boat just cleared the destroyer, either by speed or a crash dive, and the conning tower was seen to pass down the starboard side about 30 yards clear of the bridge.

The destroyer's Commanding Officer gave the order to fire depth charges when he considered the enemy was in the right position, but as the ready lamps were not burning the gunner only pulled the lever controlling the trap, no charges were released, and it was then discovered that the safety bar was in place. Later, contact was momentarily regained but lost in heavy quenching.

From the behaviour of the U-boat and her apparent reluctance to dive, it is considered probable that she had been damaged previously and this wonderful opportunity of destroying her was lost, due to the unpreparedness of the ship's depth charge armament.

Poor Walter Sadgrove lost his ship with all hands!

By the end of 1941 Captain Alfred Turner in HMS *Boadicea* enjoyed an unblemished record for his escort group by delivering all the convoys escorted without the loss of any merchant ships. The motto of the A/S Warfare Division was that of an osprey with a fish in her talons and the words '*Ne exeat*' or 'He shall not go forth!'

Every escort made immediate depth-charge attacks on every suspicious or probable U-boat contact to ensure that U-boat commanders kept their heads and periscopes down while the convoys passed, turning their attack plans into those of self-preservation. Our two group destroyers *Hesperus* and *Beagle* swept well ahead and astern prior to dusk and first light at dawn, then covered ahead and astern of the convoy as the group swept the bow, beam and flanks.

In December 1941 Captain Turner received recognition of the results obtained by his hard-driving efficiency by way of a command of an assault ship which had been converted from a requisitioned ocean ferry, together with its merchant navy crew and officers, under what was termed a 'T124X agreement' for a period of six months. This agreement enabled the former officers and men to be retained to operate the former ferry ship for an agreed period while receiving their merchant navy pay and status.

'Flash Alf' termed it a promotion, with a problem for him.

'How do you merchant navy officers keep discipline aboard your ships?' he asked when coming aboard *St Loman* to announce his 'promotion'. 'Logging a man and fining him five shillings, to be disputed by the Seamen's Union when he signs off, doesn't seem much of a deterrent!'

'The mate, as I think you call him, told me, "You are going to find things a little different to where you have been, Captain Turner. There's only one thing they understand aboard this ship. This!"' Holding up his clenched fist, 'Flash Alf' continued: 'Last Sunday I made my first captain's inspection. Down in the engine room I asked one of the hands working there: what do you do?

'"I'm a fucking greaser!" he replied. "Then a word of advice, when you reply to your commanding officer you say Sir!" The greaser spat out in reply: "None of that bleeding nonsense about me!" I thought of what the mate or first officer had told me. Then I knocked him down on the engine room bed plates, and carried on with my inspection.

'My captain's cabin is below the bridge with ports that open above the head of the gangway. Sitting there I heard a new crew member coming up the gangway ask the quartermaster "What's the old man like?"

"He's all right! Knock you down as soon as look at you!"'

On 9 December 1941 *St Loman*, detached from an inward-bound convoy, was sailing up the Clyde to Greenock in the bright winter sun, past the height of Aisla Craig, when the BBC Home & Forces programme announced briefly the Japanese attack on Pearl Harbour.

'What do you think that means, sir?' asked my signalman Sidney Wain.

'Just that every one of the major powers are now in our war. That's all!'

It did mean a little more than that as it was going to extend our Battle of the Atlantic even further westwards, because for Admiral Dönitz, his U-boat war was always a war against Allied merchant shipping, to win the race between him sinking our ships and our building of new ones. That this success could lead to the weakening and final collapse of the British economy and its defences was Dönitz's firm belief. Thus it did not matter to him where a merchant ship was sunk, but what did was where the greatest successes could be achieved through the shortest operations and the least loss of U-boats. This he termed 'the economical employment of U-boats'.

It applied now to the sea lanes along the eastern seaboard of America which, considering the long approach of over 3,000 nautical miles, promised to be a rewarding area of operations for as long as shipping remained uncontrolled and unprotected, and as long as the US Navy had little experience of A/S warfare.

* * *

On 11 January 1942 five of the larger type IXB and IXC German U-boats, possessing a great sea endurance range of 13,000 nautical miles at 10 knots, and each with a large stock of 22 torpedoes, reached the American east coast. Within two weeks they had sunk 15 ships totalling 97,242 tons. Now the US Navy became our friend in need. February-March 1942 saw 26 British A/S trawlers taken from their Western Ocean escort groups and assigned to work under the orders of the US Navy.

Following the dispersal of an inward-bound convoy and over two weeks at sea, *St Loman* came alongside on a Saturday afternoon in Greenock to find about 70 tons of steam coal waiting in trucks on the dock to top up the ship's bunkers. Water hoses were connected and by nightfall the ship was ready for sea again. Not so with the 'pussers' stores', which had closed up at noon for the weekend and would not reopen until Monday morning to supply fresh meat and vegetables.

'Being in all respects ready for sea,' quoted my orders, *St Loman* was to sail for New York via St John's, Newfoundland and Halifax, Nova Scotia, without delay, and repeating the Admiralty statement: 'Nothing must delay the sailing of these ships.'

The lack of fresh meat, milk and vegetables was not enough to delay us. At dawn on Sunday morning *St Loman* sailed from Greenock and by sunset became a patch of dirty coal smoke headed west on a lonely ocean.

St Loman's voyage on passage to within about one and a half day's steaming from St John's was uneventful and clear enough for us to get both sun sights and star sights. The first vessel to be sighted was the hull of a large tanker in ballast. No response came to our Aldis lamp signal, and on closing we saw that the ship had been torpedoed in her fore end, so that the foreward tank section had broken away at its bulkhead on the starboard side, from which jagged plates rose and knifed down in the heavy Atlantic swell. It seemed that her rudder was jammed hard to starboard, most likely trying to avoid the torpedo. This factor combined with the westerly wind and swell created a slow swing to starboard as the 'headsman's axe' formed by the jagged plates swung up and down, moving right-handed.

The tanker proved to be the Shell tanker *Diala* which I recalled had been torpedoed some months previously at the start of an outward-bound convoy, but had been able to return to a UK port under escort as her Captain stated that the *Diala*'s engines were able to be operated. Now it seemed that having been repaired, and attempting again the outward-bound passage, the *Diala* had suffered a similar fate, but this time far from a home port, and had been deserted by her crew (see p. 118).

I made the signal to the Naval Officers-in-Charge at Halifax and St John's, repeated to the Admiralty, advising of the tanker's position and condition, then stating that it was proposed to put a towline aboard pending the arrival of a salvage tug from St John's.

The swell was fairly heavy but with a calm sea so I put *St Loman*'s forward whaleback against the stern of the tanker while my chief engineman Jimmy Dell, leading four other 'pirates', jumped aboard as *St Loman* went full astern with her helm hard to starboard, in order to swing her away from the menacing 'headman's axe'. With a couple of feet to spare the jagged plates of the tanker sliced down as *St Loman* swung clear with almost excruciating slowness, but answering my prayer for clearance.

St Loman continued swinging to starboard with the engines now to slow ahead to come alongside the *Diala*'s stern as before, with the towing spring ready for hauling aboard to be made fast to the stern bollards of the tanker. Jimmy Dell caught the heaving line and with the help of one of the four seaman hauled in the towline and made it fast. The other three seamen were busy throwing down a couple of dozen frozen chickens they had found in the officers' galley freezer which bounced like small bombs on *St Loman*'s foredeck. Then as the two ships came together all hands jumped back aboard with a couple of sextants and two portable typewriters, together with a very small plaque, holding a Diala shell, from the ship's office. It was the custom of Shell tankers to name their ships after shells and display the shell selected in a plaque on the bulkhead of the ship's office.

The four men aboard the tanker were being hampered by their 'loot' and by this time I was just about 'cussed out', so that as the last man made it back on board, once again that 'headsman's axe' was starting to rise up with the heavy swell then, hesitating at its zenith, begin its deadly downward chop. This time it just grazed the bulwarks amidships as my last expletive of relief was 'Dear! Oh dear! Oh fucking dear!' Later, Ossie Dodwell, my first lieutenant with me on the bridge, remarked that he did not know whether to laugh or cry!

Several lengths of *St Loman*'s anchor cable had been secured to the towing hawser and led aft down the ship's starboard side, thus acting as a spring, and slowly my little ship began pulling the massive, derelict tanker towards St John's.

The next day the salvage tug hove in sight and requested the transfer of our anchor cable and towing hawser. This being carried out *St Loman* took station ahead of the tow acting as the A/S escort.

The following morning the tug reported that the tow had parted and she carried no replacement hawser, thus she was returning to harbour at maximum

The British Tanker Diala, *January 1942. Torpedoed in fore end, losing it and exposing jagged steel plates, drifting about 400 miles East of St Johns N.F.*

speed and disappeared in the overcast.

Chief Engineman Jimmy Dell reported that *St Loman* was low on coal, but at half, or three-quarters speed had enough for about two days' steaming, or less, with which to make St John's. Late that same evening we made harbour and made fast alongside three other A/S trawlers which had arrived two or three days ahead of us. By this time the *St Loman*'s stokers were starting to sweep out the coal bunkers, and by next morning the ship was cold and lifeless without the semblance of a head of steam.

The base flashed a signal ordering *St Loman* to move alongside the store ship. I replied: 'No steam. Request tug.'

'Why?' queried the base.

'No coal,' came the answer.

Now the base engineer officer came aboard to find *St Loman*'s bunkers swept clean of any coal. Several sacks of coal were put on board and steam began hissing through the pipes and warmth returned.

I met up with the commanding officers of the three trawlers who had received orders to proceed to a collier anchored in an inlet off the Belle Isle Straits. Due to the ice pack this meant two days steaming to get around it, and another two days to return whereas there were large stocks of coal on the docks at St John's. Two days' steaming could take our ships to Halifax, and four days to New York. It was decided to request that coal should be made available in St John's.

Thus the four of us met with the NOIC's chief of staff with our request: 'All we need is three to four days' coal to get to Halifax or New York. There is plenty of coal on the docks in St John's and we save a delay of four days.'

'It is only a few hours' steaming to the collier!' he said, gesturing to his wall chart.

Our spokesman went to the chart and tracing with his finger outlined the detour caused by the ice pack. 'There is an ice pack here, and another one here. Getting around them makes three days steaming to get to the collier and another three days to come back. Having done that it is another three days to New York. Admiralty orders state that nothing is to delay these ships!'

The chief of staff ushered us into the office of the NOIC St John's and related our objections to his orders.

'That coal on the docks is for the people of St John's!' quoth the NOIC rather petulantly. Then, concluding, 'The trouble with you reserve officers is that you are truculent, argumentative, and non-cooperative!'

'Yes, sir!' we answered in unison. 'Do we get the coal in St John's?'

The NOIC snarled, 'Yes, and now get out!'

All of *St Loman*'s ship's company were glad to comply with the NOIC's instructions to 'get out' and leave what they called 'Newfy John's' for Halifax, Nova Scotia, where our burnt-out asdic gear and electrical wiring was to be replaced under the supervision of an 'electrical gentleman' from the shore base.

The 'electric gentlemen' were a recent addition to the officer ranks of the Royal Navy. It seemed that regarding these electronic engineers, being neither officers nor ratings, the personnel people had devised the term 'electrical gentlemen' to define their functions, together with the green band between their lieutenant's stripes.

As my captain's cabin was located under the wheelhouse, the panelling of the deckhead was taken down for about a week while a succession of shore carpenters, electricians and fitters came and went. At long last the electrical gentleman informed me that the A/S work was done and a carpenter would be along to put back the panelling. After waiting for a couple of days I was tired of the exposed wires and insulation hanging down and getting a screwdriver put the panelling back in place. Soon after, a union carpenter came barging into my cabin demanding to know who had done the union carpenter's job.

'Now you hear this!' I snapped at him. 'This is my ship and this is my cabin. I give the orders, not union carpenters! I am the non-union man who got the job done after waiting two days for you to show up to do a five-minute job. Now get off my ship!'

A Canadian, Lieutenant 'Pete' Willis RCNVR, who had been put on board as an A/S officer before *St Loman* sailed from Greenock, stated that Canadians regarded Halifax as the 'arsehole of Canada', despite its magnificent anchorage. The main street of the town had little in the way of architectural quality and its perpetually rain-soaked, flagstoned road sloped down to the docks.

There were no 'taverns or alehouses' as these sailors' ports of call were termed, being forbidden to cadets or apprentices in their indentures. Hard liquor appeared to be available only by the bottle from the liquor stores. Thus down the street were men sprawling on the sidewalks in various stages of intoxication and all clasping the necks of liquor bottles to their breasts without the contemporary disguise of brown paper bags. Halifax appeared wet, cold, and miserable and thus Pete Willis's definition of Halifax in relation to the rest of Canada had some apparent justification. I was reminded of my father commenting on his family move from Yorkshire to London: 'From Hell, Hull and Halifax, good Lord deliver us!'

Thus there were no more regrets on sailing from Halifax for New York, than on leaving St John's. Heading south, we glimpsed Sable Island in the mist at the tip of Nova Scotia. *St Loman* felt her way through the fishing vessels on the Newfoundland Banks to pass Boston and sight Long Island in the early morning mist. There was an American destroyer and what appeared to be a PT boat off the western end of Long Island, but neither took any notice of us.

Sub Lt Jones had come up on the bridge. 'Jonesy, watch over the side for the indication that we are coming in to the swept channel for entering New York harbour!' He looked at me quizzically and started looking over the side as suggested.

Then came his shout of surprise: 'Just look at that stuff!' There floating by was the refuse from the lavatories of the city, bloated condoms, faeces and soiled paper floating out to sea.

The first channel buoys came into sight and I conned *St Loman* up the channel to enter New York harbour without any challenge or interest being displayed by ship or shore. By now the morning sun had burnt off the mist, thus we could admire the spectacular Manhattan skyline while avoiding the many tugs and ferryboats travelling between Staten Island and the Battery.

Now the sudden flash of a signal lamp came from the end of a large wooden warehouse building on the end of Staten Island pier. After a brief interrogation we were ordered to dock inside. Entering, we found the A/S trawler *Stella Polaris* berthed alongside and made fast ahead of her at 11 a.m. as 'Up Spirits!' was being piped aboard both ships. Soon the heavy and heady scent of navy rum was wafting up the bridge and wardroom voice pipes from the mess decks.

I joined my three officers in their little wardroom for the traditional ritual of a mid-morning gin, and as we were filling our glasses the black shoes of a US Navy lieutenant started to come warily down the steep stair ladder to deliver my orders from the Staten Island naval base and the first from our new command.

'Have a gin, Lieutenant?' came the welcoming question from 'Ossie' Dodwell, my first lieutenant.

'As you are the only British ship I'm visiting this morning I may accept gladly. Last week, four of your ships docked at this same time. As I have done this morning I took the base orders aboard and was greeted with the same question when I entered each wardroom.

'This I assumed to be a British naval custom and thus it would have been discourteous or even insulting to refuse, particularly as the glass put into my hand was fast being filled from a Plymouth gin bottle. "Lime?" I quickly accepted expecting some possible dilution of the half-full glass. Not a chance, only a squeeze from half a lime dropped into my glass.

'Now raising their full glasses to me with the salutation "Bottoms up!" the captain and his officers drank deeply. I followed their example and as the burn in my throat faded excused myself to board the next British ship.

'"Pink gin?" greeted me on entering the next wardroom. "Pink gin," I replied, having never had this drink before. I hoped also the "pink" might mean more dilution of the neat spirits offered previously. But this was no soft drink either.

'The first lieutenant splashed a couple of drops of pink angostura bitters into the bottom of my glass. Turning it bottom upwards his deftly trained hand twirled the glass around so that the bitters coated the inside from bottom to top. Then, reversing the glass, he filled it with Plymouth gin.

'I am still not quite sure how I made the next two visits, but I do know that on my way back to the base, I was weaving!'

Scanning the base orders quickly as the US Navy lieutenant sipped a well-watered pink gin as he had requested, I gathered that a tug and harbour pilot would be due next morning and both *St Loman* and *Stella Polaris* were to be taken up to the Bethlehem Steel Company yard located in New Jersey at Hoboken on the Hudson River waterfront, north of Upper New York Bay.

'We don't have any major engine room defects,' I told him, 'but I do need an anchor and cable to replace what was lost in a tanker salvage attempt when on passage to St John's, Newfoundland. Your navy is not wasting any time to start checking out their assigned A/S ships. My chief engineman has already made up his defects list.

'Now, I am rather curious at the apparently casual way in which we made our entry into New York Bay. In the UK and Canada, we are challenged by the port signal stations to identify our ships when making our approach.

'Near the Ambrose Light vessel was a US destroyer. She took no notice of us and appeared to be swinging for compass adjustments. Then there were two or three patrol launches, or PT boats. They did not pay us any attention either, so we made our entrance to the ship channel and steamed into New York Bay, flying a nice clean white ensign for the occasion.

'Then at long last we received the welcoming interrogation signal lamp from your Staten Island base giving us docking instructions.'

The lieutenant looked thoughtful. 'The destroyer making adjustments was on passage to Norfolk, but the PT boats or motor launches should have made contact with you. I'll mention it to the base commander.

'Now there is something that you might explain to me, commander, regarding the three distinct designs of gold braid or stripes worn by British navy officers. Your liaison officer in New York, Commander English, wears three straight gold stripes. Your three officers have wavy gold stripes, whereas you wear lattice pattern stripes and the executive curl resembles the Jewish "Cross of David".'

'Possibly, Lieutenant, the US Navy may be more democratic and less discriminating than the British,' I commented with a smile. 'The straight, thick gold stripes worn by Commander English indicate that he is a regular navy officer. The thinner wavy gold stripes indicate that the wearer is a Royal Navy Volunteer Reservist. More than likely to be a keen yachtsman in his private life and member of the volunteer reserve in peacetime. My lattice stripes mean that, to quote, I am one of those who go down to the sea in ships to make our living on the great waters. Professional sailor. Professional sailor of the Royal Navy Reserve.

'In peacetime our Royal Navy shipmates have come up with such brief and humorous definitions for the three different stripes as follows:

'RN straight stripes denote "Officers and gentlemen".

'RNVR wavy stripes indicate "Gentlemen".

'RNR lattice means "Sailors".

'Some further elaborations as to the meaning of the various letters are that RNVR means "not very reliable", and RNR stands for "really not required".

'Your US Navy stripes do not make such distinctions, which are a holdover from the First World War, in our case, but I have heard that when a US navy officer is introduced, the words "Annapolis man" are made as an added aside. Would that apply to you, Lieutenant?'

'No, sir! If anything it would be "Ninety-Day Wonder!", my initial training period . . .' was his laughing response.

'Then you are one of us! Have another pink gin, Lieutenant!'

The following morning the harbour pilot came aboard. Soon after we cast off, the *St Loman* was threading her way through the busy tracks of the ferries and tugboat tows between Manhattan Island and the Jersey shore to reach the repair berths at the Bethlehem shipyard on the Jersey side of the Hudson river.

While we were still making fast, a US navy officer flourishing a large clipboard and writing paid leapt aboard, to be taken down to the wardroom by the duty quartermaster.

'I am Jordan, your progress chaser,' he announced as introduction. 'You will have your defects lists ready, I hope?' Jordan scanned the lists I handed to him quickly, remarking, 'Is this all? What about this wardroom for example? You need new sofas, and those two commodes should come out and be replaced with proper washbasins, cabinets and mirrors. Ventilation is inadequate and a blower system is going to be essential here and in the mess decks. It can get hot on this coast in the south.' As he spoke, he scribbled notes on his clipboard pad.

Obviously, this was a golden opportunity to obtain the many improvements required in the barren former fish hold, now serving as the seamen's and stokers' mess deck and living space fitted with two-tier, steel-frame bunks with straw mattresses.

'Let's take a walk around the ship, Lieutenant Jordan, and Mr Dodwell, my first lieutenant, or Number One, will come with us,' I suggested, leading the way up on deck.

Undoubtedly, Lieutenant Jordan was 'an Annapolis man' who knew his own navy ships and ship repairers. He made a note of the dented bulwark on the port side of the foredeck where the jagged plates of the tanker *Diala* had given us a parting nudge. Coming up from inspecting the seamen's mess deck, Jordan commented, 'That place has all the comforts of a dank, dark prison. Your officers' wardroom and sleeping area are as bare and inviting as a baboon's bottom!'

'I could not agree with you more, Mr Jordan. My quarters are the peacetime fishing skipper's cabin below the wheelhouse, panelled in polished walnut. My bunk is over a three-drawer chest with the telltale compass hung above it. A massive sideboard stretches across the forward end with two large settees on the starboard side, and the after end faces a table with two swivel armchairs. There is a small bathroom and lavatory, all superbly fitted out for the ship's master, a man of great and most valuable knowledge and experience in finding and locating long cod fish in the northern waters of the Arctic Circle.

'You will find the petty officers' mess in the stern, which again is the peacetime quarters for the trawler engineers, stokers and seamen. Cramped, but warm and comfortable just the same.

'Now you remarked that we had no refrigeration, but for some time I have been considering that the large lazarette store below the fantail could be quickly and easily insulated to be used as a big icebox.' I led the way aft and the coxswain lifted up the lazarette hatch for inspection. Jordan glanced down quickly, and writing again busily, commented, 'Good suggestion, sir! I will get it done right away.'

An hour later the shipyard manager and superintendent were being briefed by Lieutenant Jordan in my cabin, and by noon the *St Loman* was swarming with shipyard workers showing great interest in reading the engraved brass plate, which was 12x18 inches, fixed on the forward bulkhead of the captain's cabin, between the two ports, which bore the heading:

HMS *St Loman*. Actions & Awards.
1939-40. 15th A/S Striking Force & Norwegian Operations.
April-May 1940.
1940-41 Destruction of enemy submarine.

Decorations and names of officers and men were listed. This plate had been the suggestion of the Harland shipyard manager when the *St Loman* was being refitted in Belfast.

On either side of *St Loman*'s funnel two yellow or 'gold' stars had been painted by Seaman Sands, a peacetime signwriter, who enjoyed the reputation of having been a boy signalman at the Battle of Jutland in the First World War. A great deal of interest and respect was now being shown for our 'ugly old duckling'.

Lieutenant Jordan now left the two shipyard executives in my cabin to go ashore. As he went, it seemed to me the executives were 'licking their lips' somewhat, so I broke out the Scotch whisky bottle. Pouring about 'three fingers' into each of three glass tumblers, I said, pouring, 'Sorry, gentlemen,

Sands paints up the 2nd U-boat Star

125

about the lack of ice cubes as is customary in the US. For dilution, I can offer just plain water from my bathroom carafe. There are no refrigeration facilities on board, but as soon as you get that lazarette fitted as a giant icebox, then I promise that you'll get a civilized drink of Scotch with ice in our entertaining!'

'Straight or neat as you would say, Captain, your Johnnie Walker, Black Label, will do just fine. Your lazarette is now a top priority on our defects list!' replied the yard manager picking up his glass.

Silently, we all appreciated the famous brand. After catching his breath, the yard manager, adopting an apologetic tone of voice, made a statement of Bethlehem Steel policy, so it seemed.

'If this was a merchant ship job, then we would give three thousand dollars to the captain and his chief engineer so as to enjoy themselves ashore while work on their ship was being carried out, but with a navy job you will understand that things have to be done differently. Since you have no friends ashore, then every evening this week we would like to show you and your Number One that we've got about everything on this side of the Hudson river that you'll find in Manhattan!'

The Bethlehem yard manager and his superintendent were as good as their words. Late on that Monday afternoon, they were down in my cabin again discussing the work in progress with me and Ossie Dodwell. This routine was repeated until we cast off *St Loman* early on the Saturday morning to return to the Staten Island navy base.

It never took them very long to 'kill a bottle of Scotch', then our yard managers would suggest, 'Let's go ashore and get a drink!' Our hosts could drink like fish with a whale of a thirst at the steakhouses, bowling alleys, and finally at night clubs offering music hall style entertainment, snacks and liquor well into the small hours of the morning.

Nothing was barred for the entertainment of two British navy officers, for as one very curvaceous singer finished her act there came a whispered inquiry, 'How would you fancy that one, skipper? It's available!'

'Not this evening!' I replied, wondering how it might have been itemized on the expense account for Bethlehem Steel; possibly as a 'blanket entry'?

CHAPTER XI

The following Monday morning I reported to Captain L.E. Lindsay USN, Commander Patrol Forces, Third Naval District. With him as his aide was the young lieutenant who had brought our orders on board when we had arrived from Halifax. In common with the commanders of the other A/S trawlers, I had anticipated that a coastal convoy system similar to that which was a successful operation in the UK would have been planned and set up ready to put into action.

In the UK, attacks by enemy aircraft were the most frequent events, as U-boats in the North Sea, outward-bound to their assigned operational areas on the North Atlantic convoy routes, would concentrate on making fast and safe passage to pass into the Atlantic via the Fair Isle channel and south of the Shetlands. Thus U-boat commanders stayed clear of coastal areas, making full speed on the surface with their diesels during the hours of darkness, and during periods of poor visibility by day, to avoid sightings and subsequent attacks by allied aircraft of Coastal Command.

It was therefore a great disappointment to learn that the 24 British A/S trawlers were to be assigned to reinforcing the US coastguard cutters and small armed patrol craft in their patrols of the Eastern Sea Frontier of the US from New York to Key West.

The A/S trawlers *St Loman*, *Arctic Explorer*, *Wellard*, *Northern Chief* and *Lady Rosemary* were to be assigned to the Third Naval District and based on Staten Island. Other A/S trawlers would be working out of Morehead City, NC, Charleston, SC, and Jacksonville, Fla.

The US Navy had set up a number of protected anchorages on the East Coast, where merchant shipping, keeping close inshore and on the comparatively shallow continental shelf, could be anchored during the night hours when the US Navy blimps, providing daylight air cover, returned to Lakehurst, NJ. Major protected anchorages were Hampton Roads, Delaware Bay and Chesapeake Bay. Heavily-laden tankers drawing 38-40 ft were often literally 'bumping' along in depths of 7-8 fathoms.

U-boat commanders had made a visible graveyard of US shipping off Cape Hatteras, marked by the masts and upper structure of ships torpedoed close inshore. This had developed as the favourite location in which to lay in wait for ships 'turning the corner' on their way north. Furthermore the first U-tanker, the U-459, was working in an area of operations about 500 miles NE of the Bermudas. The latter had been considered an essential prerequisite for any efficient U-boat operations on the American seaboard. The medium-sized U-boat could remain at sea for an average of 41 days, but when supplied by U-tankers, attained a sea endurance of 62 days on the average, and up to 81 days if supplied twice. Eighty-one days was the limit for U-boat crews, stretched to their limits between combat and replenishment of their U-boats before fatigue symptoms would develop. Cape Hatteras was the shortest distance between combat and replenishment for the U-boats.

As Captain Lindsay completed outlining our patrol procedures, his aide asked, 'Would you tell the Captain how you brought your ship into New York harbour?'

As the Captain listened intently I made a similar brief and factual report to the one I had made to his aide on berthing at Staten Island the previous week.

'Commander, my patrol craft have orders to contact and investigate every vessel approaching New York harbour past the Ambrose lightship and the pilot cutter. Now this is an order! When you are out there on patrol, challenge our patrol vessel. If you get no response then shoot them up! It will make them learn fast that we are in a war now!'

His aide followed up with another request. 'There are a lot of buoys off Long Island and the Jersey shore, and it could be just possible that some of them might be marking the location of supplies for U-boats put there by German sympathizers. You might investigate a few of them to see if they are only marking fishermen's traps.'

'It is just possible that something of that nature might be happening, Lieutenant,' I replied. I will check several of the buoys as the opportunity offers itself.'

The *St Loman*'s fishermen crew members had been very keen to 'investigate' the buoys when we were coming in. 'Now you know, and I know, just what is down there!' I had told them. 'The last thing we need to be met with is a complaint from American lobstermen that the British are stealing their catch in broad daylight.'

Returning from my meeting I went down to *St Loman*'s wardroom with its newly upholstered sofas and toilet facilities, to meet up with my three lieutenants and relate the high points of my visit to the base.

'The US Navy don't seem to have learnt that A/S striking forces such as we initiated in 1939 seldom catch U-boats on patrol activities. So! Here we are back to 1939-40 looking for U-boats who can see our black, soft coal funnel smoke on the horizon, and outrun us with their diesels making fifteen knots on the surface. The best chance that we could make an A/S contact is that one of these US navy blimps might catch a U-boat with its crew sunning themselves on the surface in the warmth of the Gulf Stream, and mark the spot of the crash-dive made by the commander. Unfortunately, Captain Lindsay tells me that the blimps only fly by day, and then in good weather, operating over the inshore coastal route for merchant ships. Possibly the blimps can't work at night or in poor visibility for fear of getting lost, and that's just when U-boats are getting themselves set up for target locations like Cape Hatteras.

'Well gentlemen, that's the patrol situation, New York to Norfolk is our operational area, and for bunker coal and boiler cleaning we will be going to Newport News or Norfolk.

'Now for the better news! Jonesy, your gun's crew may be able to get in some practice as Captain Lindsay has given me orders to "shoot up" any patrol vessel not responding to our challenge. So to carry out those orders we will close one of those sleeping guardians late one evening and have a star-shell illumination display!

'Ossie is going to have Pym Grace the coxswain organize some grappling hooks and lines as we have instructions to investigate just what may be marked by some of these buoys. Just before the crack of dawn might be the appropriate time when everything is rather shrouded by that white morning mist on this coast. The Captain's aide thinks that some buoys might be for marking U-boat supplies put down by a fifth column group ashore. Of course, any lobster pots would be likely to spill out on the deck when hauled in, and should be reset with the bait put back before being put back overside. It may put up the price of lobsters in New York, but after all, there's a war on. They will understand!'

During the following four weeks, *St Loman* made her A/S sweeps up and down the coast between New York and Norfolk. Mindful of Captain Lindsay's request, I chose a clear, late evening off the New Jersey shore, south of Sandy Hook, to challenge one of his sleeping patrol craft. After the third challenge by *St Loman*'s Aldis lamp signal, Lieutenant Jones's trigger-happy gun crew loaded with a star shell and then lobbed it over the sleeping patrol launch. The response by the awakened crew finding themselves starkly illuminated by the descending light was to burst their engines into a full-speed run towards the safety of the Jersey shore!

When dawn was breaking I attended to the request made by Captain Lindsay's aide. Much to the delight of my former fishermen sailors, they threw the grappling hooks with unerring aim around the lines below each buoy as it came amidships, and then hauled in the four or five lobster and crab pots or traps. Expertly they shook out the live contents, then, resetting the rotting fish bait, returned the traps overside. There were no supplies for U-boats attached to any of the buoys by Fifth Column sympathizers in New York, but over a hundred fine lobsters and hard-shell crabs were liberated to provide a gourmet treat for all hands!

The record the US Coast Guard had been maintaining of all the wrecks of both known and unknown sunken vessels off the Eastern Sea Frontier proved to be of great use in checking out all our sonar or asdic contacts picked up during our A/S sweeps. When in doubt, the dropping of a practice depth charge would prove the existence of a wreck below by bringing up several large conger eels inhabiting the bones of the wrecked vessel.

Weather during the February-March period was reasonably pleasant compared to that of the North Atlantic, and at the end of March *St Loman* was due for coaling and boiler cleaning.

My custom was to require a pilot for the first time entry of a major port likely to have net defences; thus the Norfolk pilot came aboard. He proudly observed to me and Ossie, soon after coming up on the bridge and setting the initial course for entering the swept channel: 'There have always been pilots in our family. My father was a Norfolk pilot, as was his father, and my great grandfather, who was the pilot on the *Merrimac* during the war – not so long ago, you will remember!'

As he moved over to the wing of the bridge, Ossie asked, *sotto voce*, 'What war is he talking about?'

'Ossie, my boy, he's a Virginian, and Virginians fought the war he is talking about, as he will tell you! It's not the Great War of 1914-18. Nor this World War, but the war between the States; that is his war memory!'

Berthing about 5 p.m. that afternoon, I made my courtesy call to the duty officer at the naval base. 'You have just come in from sea, Commander, so you'll be needing fresh milk, vegetables, meat and bread?' he enquired.

'The stores can deliver our order tomorrow. It's late, they are probably closing,' I said.

The duty officer grabbed his telephone. 'We are here to serve you! Your ship's requirements will be delivered by the time you return aboard.' I thought back to *St Loman*'s arrival in Greenock on a Sunday afternoon before being sailed for St John's, Newfoundland on 'hard tack' because the stores were closed until Monday! When I returned to the *St Loman* ice cream was being taken aboard with the other stores!

The following morning Ossie and I visited the US navy post exchange operation to invest in white and khaki uniforms and caps to convert to British appearance with our own cap badges and buttons, and then toured the base facilities to admire the residences of the admiral and staff captains, ending up at the US Naval Officers' club with its magnificent dining room and bar. Scapa Flow was never like this, or likely to be at any time!

In the evening we made a brief visit to the city of Norfolk finding the streets filled with a sea of white sailors' caps and uniforms. The only bars appeared to be those of The Veterans of Foreign Wars and the Rifle Club. Returning to *St Loman*'s wardroom we met Commander, The Earl of Carrick, RNVR, relieved of a corvette command and appointed British Naval Liaison Officer in Norfolk.

The Earl of Carrick was a professional company chairman and director in peacetime, and had brought his very attractive, and we gathered, wealthy American-born wife with him on his assignment. Carrick may not have convinced fiesty Admiral Stevenson RN of his abilities as an escort ship commander at the new working-up base at Tobermory, Scotland, but he was an ideal selection as our liaison officer in Norfolk. A telephone call regarding services and supplies heralded by the announcement, 'This is Commander, The Earl of Carrick' received immediate attention and quick response, as was evidenced by the duty officer's reception when I had reported at the base on arrival and requested supplies. Nevertheless, as regards the pay situation, Carrick could only confirm that New York had not received the pay documents for any of the ships.

Now the three most important factors for ensuring the happiness of any British naval vessel's crew are their leave, pay and rum issue at regular intervals. While shore leave, and the rum issue may be under the control of the commanding officer, there is nothing that can be done regarding the extraction of pay for the ship's company when the base paymaster at a new base is awaiting the receipt of pay documents.

It had been my experience that pay documents moved like cold molasses from one base paymaster to the next, thus prior to our sailing from Greenock, my Canadian A/S officer, Lieutenant 'Pete' Willis, who had been assigned responsibilities for the crew's pay, canteen, and the officers' wardroom gins and whiskies, had gone smartly to the paymaster's office to draw a fortnight's pay for all hands. On arrival at St John's he had obtained another two weeks' advance, and when arriving in Halifax, Nova Scotia, made a repeat performance. Thus on arrival at New York there was over two weeks' pay being held in the ship's safe, together with the canteen funds until the next fortnightly pay became due.

When Commander English had come aboard in New York, he told us that pending the arrival of the pay documents for all the ships transferred to the US Navy, it had been arranged for an advance of $15 to each officer, and $5 for crew members. In addition a payment of $1 per day had been authorized as a 'higher cost of living allowance' while the ships were based in the US. An exchange rate of about $4.75 US to the pound sterling was in effect.

At this time commanding officers were instructed to inform their ship's companies that no mention of any kind was to be made to civilians ashore as to why their ships were assigned to be operated by the US Navy Department. It seemed that there had been a great deal of criticism in both the US Congress and the news media regarding the sinkings of US ships in coastal waters by German U-boats, and the apparent unpreparedness of the US Navy Department in anticipating and meeting this situation. The last thing that the US Navy Department required was to have the US news media announcing that British A/S ships were being used to combat U-boats in American coastal waters!

The *St Loman* was due for boiler cleaning in Norfolk and seven days' shore leave at rest and recreation camps in the Raleigh-Durham city area had been arranged for two watches. Lieutenant Willis had been given leave to Canada from Halifax, and would be standing by the ship with the watch aboard. He had already made contact for female company with a civilian in the US Navy stores office, and the question of spending money was uppermost, as he suggested getting another pay advance for the ship's company. 'As the ship has seven days' leave coming up skipper, it would be good to get another advance of a fortnight's pay set up for the ship's company!'

'Well, as you should know, Pete, the only British Navy paymaster on this coast is in New York, and they are not going to pay out anything more until our pay documents are in their hands, and then only when they're good and ready!

'Now I recall that in peacetime the British Consuls in foreign ports had funds available for taking care of DBS, or Distressed British Seamen, put ashore from British merchant ships. So it could be worth a try at getting a lump sum advance for the *St Loman* amounting to two or three weeks. Get up to the British Consul's office around lunchtime and present our story. You know the rough passage we had from Greenock to St John's. How we sailed on a Sunday morning at short notice after coming in from convoy duty at sea the previous afternoon. The ship's pay documents are still in transit, and the crew need to go on R & R at the camp in Raleigh-Durham.'

Pete Willis returned early in the afternoon smiling like the cat that swallowed the canary. 'Any problems?' I asked.

'No problem at all. The Consul seemed to have had an excellent lunch indeed. Said something about possibly calling Washington, but was rather expansive and changed his mind. I drew another month's pay, cashing the check at the bank.'

After drawing their fortnight's pay for all hands, the two watches due for boiler cleaning leave left in charge of Pym Grace, the coxswain for the R & R camp facility in Raleigh-Durham, NC, in a US Navy bus. Pete was duty officer aboard having had leave in Canada, and Ossie, Jonesy and I boarded a US Dakota transport aircraft for New York for a few days of exploration while located at the Barbizon Plaza hotel at 59th Street off Central Park.

The manager of the Barbizon Plaza had been a purser in the Cunard passenger line, and having room vacancies on the outbreak of the war, had contacted the British purchasing agency being established in New York with a proposal that he would always have single rooms reserved for Allied navy, army, and air force officers on passage through New York and at an established minimum rate of $9 per diem. This included a 'continental breakfast' consisting of a box containing a small thermos flask of coffee with rolls and butter.

Officers had the facility of being able to sign their bar and dining room bills while resident in the Barbizon Plaza. Payment was made to the hotel by the British agency, and, of course, subsequently debited to the individual officers against their navy, army, or air force lodging and provision allowances. In addition the Barbizon manager's room rate was the very lowest in Manhattan, nevertheless it proved the old adage 'what we lose upon the roundabouts, we make up on the swings!'

At the end of the downstairs dining room was a 50-ft bar fitted with comfortable armchair stools. Starting around noon and extending to early evening these bar stools supported an almost solid mingled-colour line of dark navy blue, army khaki, and sky-blue uniformed officers' backs.

Ossie had been transferred to another transport aircraft to meet with Jonesy and me at the Barbizon Plaza for lunch. Refreshed, Ossie and I visited the sights on Broadway, stopping in at Jack Dempsey's bar, where the famed Manassas Mauler was reputed to make brief social appearances. Jonesy went to explore the facilities of the Stage Door Canteen arranging to rendezvous with us at the Astor Hotel. Our meeting was possibly prompted by the words of a then popular ditty: 'She had to go and lose it at the Astor. It really was the only one she had!'

As soon as we found ourselves a table, we were greeted by two gentlemen at the adjoining table identifying themselves as 'Eighth Avenue cloak and suiters'.

They were entertaining their lady designers and were most curious about the design of the RNR braid with its executive curl, which they took to be the 'Cross of David'. I explained that it was not a Jewish affiliation in the British Navy. Although they seemed to be a little disappointed, they proved to be the most hospitable New Yorkers we met during this brief leave and insisted on picking up our bar tab and entertaining us to a steak dinner.

After four relaxed days came a call from Commander English's office in New York with reservations by Pullman train and the Chesapeake ferry so that we could return to Norfolk to meet the Commander visiting ships in Charleston and Morehead City at that time.

A couple of days later the two watches on leave returned to the *St Loman* from their reputed 'rest and recreation' at the camp near Raleigh-Durham, escorted by the coxswain, Pym Grace.

'Good God!' Coxswain! What have you been doing with this pallid bunch of wraiths moving like zombies?'

'Sir, we are really glad to be back on board again! On either side of our holiday camp were two camps of girl guides. What girl guides! Young tarts of sixteen or seventeen years old, attaching themselves, one, two or even three at a time to an available sailor to cuddle up both day and night!

'That was not all, sir! People with homes in Raleigh and Durham were making telephone calls to the camp every evening inviting three or four British sailors to come in for a party. We couldn't very well refuse, could we, sir?'

'No, Pym, you are quite correct for that was the kind of extreme Southern hospitality that would have been most discourteous and very hard for lonely sailors to refuse. Besides, it no doubt gave you an opportunity to exchange the tender clutches of those young girl guides for more adult embraces.'

The following day, with the Earl of Carrick in attendance, Commander English came aboard.

'Having any problems with the troops, Warwick? Some of the crews aboard the other ships are almost mutinous! Getting no pay to speak of for two or three months, I can hardly blame them! I have tried to expedite matters with New York and at last the paymaster tells me that he has received the various ship's pay papers.'

'No, sir, no problems,' I said. 'Except that the men on leave might be said to be suffering from an overdose of Southern hospitality! When boiler-cleaning leave was given, the crew were just about paid up to date.'

Commander English was now looking puzzled and incredulous. 'How could that be when the only payment since your arrival was the dollar advance made in New York?'

'I try to be a little ahead when it's possible, sir. I had Lieutenant Willis draw an advance of two weeks' pay for all hands when we sailed from Greenock. Then on arrival at St John's another two weeks' pay was drawn. At Halifax, we anticipated a little with a further two weeks' funds to be retained in the ship's safe with the canteen funds, so that the hands could be paid on their fortnightly due date. That arrangement has kept the ship's company pay situation current, so to speak, until recently when boiler-cleaning leave and pay became due in Norfolk.'

'How did you manage to make a pay advance for boiler-cleaning leave, Warwick?'

'Well, sir, we did have some funds in the ship's canteen account, but not enough, so I had Lieutenant Willis contact the British Consulate office in Norfolk. I recalled from my merchant navy days, that British Consuls in foreign ports of call always had funds available for DBS care and repatriation. DBS refers to "Distressed British Seamen" left ashore from their ships due to injury, sickness and hospitalization. It seemed to me that British navy men going on leave without any pay might also be considered to be in the distressed category!

'The British Consul was most cooperative and advanced HMS *St Loman* a month's pay by cheque which Lieutenant Willis cashed at their bank.'

'Good God, Warwick! I don't know what Washington is going to say!'

'What I do know, sir, is that Washington has advised the Consul not to make any more advances. Lieutenant Hartnell, commanding *Northern Dawn* was so advised by him when making a request a day or so later. Another pink gin for you, sir?'

'Yes, indeed! I need it after that! Now what other situations have you for discussion?'

'The major one, as you know, is for the US Navy Department to set up a coastal convoy system similar to that in the UK. The minor gripes by the troops concern paying Staten Island ferry fares while US navy men travel free of charge. Then when they patronize the same bars, they have been getting some static to the effect that they should be fighting their war and not be "tourists"!'

Commander English sipped his pink gin thoughtfully, before saying, 'There isn't very much that I or Carrick can do. The ferries are operated by the City of New York. As to the "tourists" jibe, perhaps I can take this up with the British press and public relations staff in New York. As regards coastal convoys, I gather that there is a political situation in the US Navy Department to be decided with the Commandant of the Eastern Sea Frontier and others. However there is no reason why you, as commanders of A/S ships assigned under the orders of the US Navy, should not make your recommendations, based on your previous experience.'

'A reverse flow of this paperwork might be effective in more ways than just one, Commander. If we are going to be effective in catching and destroying German U-boats, then it is essential that they must risk coming within range of our asdics when attempting to sink coastal shipping. The recent attack on a U-boat by *St Loman*, and incidentally the torpedo attack by another U-boat on *St Loman*, might well introduce a "Confidential Memorandum on the Development of Convoys and Escort Forces in the Western Approaches". Fortunately we have a couple of typewriters salvaged from that derelict tanker, MV *Diala*, when on passage to St John's, for making copies.'

Commander English started to smile as he searched in his breast pocket to produce a cartoon drawing of a foundering A/S trawler under a mass of papers.

'This was given to me on one of the ships I was visiting last week. I'm sending it to Washington to try to stem the flow of paperwork being poured into your ships by two navies!'

CHAPTER XII

Two days later *St Loman* received orders to make coastal patrols north from Norfolk, while working in cooperation with the daylight patrols being made by US Navy blimps based on Lakehurst, NJ. I had suggested they might make night patrols for hunting U-boats in a similar manner, but Commander English reported that it was considered that the U-boats might shoot down the blimps, and, in addition the blimps might get lost without their familiar daylight landmarks.

One afternoon a US Navy blimp, coming from the vicinity of Atlantic City, exchanged identification signals. The weather was fine, sunny and clear with a slight, short sea running, being whipped up by the stiff offshore breeze. *St Loman* was patrolling just inside the 8-9 fathom line marking the end of the continental shelf. It was considered likely that U-boats might rest on the bottom at this depth during daylight hours, then surface to periscope depth in the late afternoon to make their way towards the coastal shipping lanes.

Towards sunset a southbound, medium-sized tanker in ballast was heading for the Gulf, taking advantage of her unloaded draft to keep close inshore, where the depths shoaled to 5-6 fathoms, and loaded northbound tankers drawing 35-40 ft could be bumping their keels on the shallows.

Suddenly the blimp's signal lamp came to life, spelling out 'periscope observed', and, making a sharp dive towards the sea, it dropped a marking flare, then circled around and came back to drop another one.

St Loman was already at action stations and fast closing the blimp's flares with Leading Seaman Houghton carrying out his phlegmatic asdic sweep. With his usual, unshaven hangdog expression remaining unchanged, he reported: 'Firm contact, seventeen hundred yards, fine on the starboard bow.'

Pete Willis, A/S officer, was on the second set of headphones: 'Possible U-boat contact, skipper! Do you want to run in now for a five-charge attack or investigate it further?'

'We are closing the periscope sighting spot and with that tanker in sight and closing; let's attack first and investigate afterwards, Pete. Houghton has a good ear for U-boat contacts!'

'Set all charges to one hundred feet!' shouted Pete into the binnacle voice pipes as *St Loman* swung to starboard to steady on the asdic bearing. Pete was watching his recorder stylus markings intently as the range shortened. Then came his firing orders, followed by the quivering explosion astern and a rising column of water boiled up by some 1,500 lb of explosive detonating below.

Opening the range to about 1,700 yards from our U-boat contact, I rang down for 'slow ahead', and as Houghton regained firm contact, brought *St Loman* head on to the target and began to steam towards the attack area where the blimp was now circling.

'Port and starboard throwers reloaded! Request settings,' came up the voice pipe from the A/S rating in charge.

'Three charges on the rails ready for settings!' came the report from aft.

The 4-inch gun's crew had their armour-piercing shell ready to slam into the breech.

'Check out your contact, Pete, and we'll steam slowly over it. Then turn to come head on again when the range is about fifteen hundred yards.'

'There is no movement, skipper. He's probably sitting quiet on the bottom. Perhaps another five-charge attack might bring up something?'

The tanker had altered course to hug the shoreline more closely. The evening sun was already resting its lower rim on the distant haze of the shoreline, as the blimp's signal lamp began flashing and sending: 'Have reported attack position to base. Destroyer due to make contact in morning. Looks like some light oil on surface of attack area. Due to return to our base at sunset.'

The observers in the Navy blimp seemed to be correct as a film of diesel-type oil was smoothing down the ruffled waters.

Ossie came up from aft where he had been taking charge of the depth-charge rails. 'What do you think, skipper? Put him to bed with another five-charge attack, then have the hands stand down for supper?'

'Sounds like the right way to finish the evening, Ossie! Take her in, Pete, and use hundred and fifty feet settings so as to settle the charges well down and not shake the engine room so much, as it will give a little more time to increase the distance.

'Full ahead! Stand by for five-charge pattern set to one-fifty feet.' Pete and Houghton hunched over the A/S recorder once more. Down below, *St Loman*'s reciprocating engine, the old 'three legged, up-and-down job', began pounding hard as engineman Jimmy Dell was trying for the maximum distance from the hammer blow of the exploding depth charges in the ship's wake astern. The range indicator markings shortened on the recorder roll paper, as the echoes returned faster.

'Fire one!' A depth charge plopped off the rails astern, as the port and starboard throwers amidships fired their respective depth charges lashed to their 'T' shaped stalks in two graceful parabolas.

'Fire two!' Another charge left the rails, followed by a final third with 'Fire Three!'

The resulting five-charge pattern resembled in diagram the Five of Clubs with the U-boat in the centre of the card receiving a clubbing effect as the depth charges exploded around it.

Forty-eight hours was the probable survival period for a submerged U-boat, as it was unlikely that human lives would last any longer, a signal addressed to Commandant Eastern Sea Frontier confirmed the U-boat position with our intention to remain in contact for that period.

The Commandant Eastern Sea Frontier replied: 'Approved, USS *Roper* joining you at daylight.'

This was good news to hear, as the US destroyer *Roper*, joining us in the morning, had sunk the first U-boat, U-85, off Cape Hatteras on 14 April 1942. We would not be having a complete novice working with us.

On *St Loman* the hands stood down for supper and the watches were set for the night. Pete Willis took the first watch, 8 p.m. to midnight. Ossie always liked the middle watch of midnight to 4 a.m., when he would be relieved by Jonesy taking the 4 a.m. to 8 a.m. morning watch.

During that night *St Loman* carried out a square-mile A/S sweep. In the centre of this area lay our dormant U-boat as *St Loman* steamed slowly around. There was no moon, and it was dark to seaward, but the coast outline was reflected by the shore lights of Atlantic City.

After joining Ossie and Jonesy at their little wardroom table for a meagre supper of corned beef, boiled dried peas and potatoes washed down with strong tea, I returned to my cabin below the bridge.

Changing my day clothes for those worn at night, I went up on the bridge to 'sleep, perchance to dream' on the straw donkey's breakfast mattress. Lying near to the A/S in the still of the night I could hear the faint reverberations of the asdic oscillator feeling out with searching fingers.

Perhaps I did 'worry too much' as the skipper of another ship had once remarked to me, but I considered that I would worry less by sleeping on the bridge, and most importantly would be on the spot with my night vision intact to be able to see in the night darkness of the sea.

As the bridge lookouts changed and the asdic ratings made their reliefs, I would rouse up to stretch and take the inevitable mug of 'pusser's kye', a piping hot, sweet concoction brewed with naval issue cocoa, sugar, and, it was said, an addition of some custard powder for additional body!

Dawn broke bringing a slight misty rain and an overcast sky. A darker blob on the horizon started flashing a signal requesting the bearing and range of the U-boat contact from our position. USS *Roper* closed and confirmed our contact. Then came a seeming excited signal flashing: 'We have contact with hydrophone effects!'

St Loman remained with engines stopped while holding asdic contact at right angles to the *Roper*'s attack course so that when making the depth-charge attack she would be 'crossing the T'. The wake boiled under the destroyer's stern as *Roper* gathered speed to run in with a thundering 14-depth charge attack on the contact *St Loman* was holding. It was right on!

St Loman now steamed slowly through the attack area to find that increased quantities of light diesel oil were being brought to the surface by *Roper*'s attack. This could be an indication that one of the U-boat's external fuel tanks had been fractured, while the pressure hull remained intact. Past experience had shown that the German U-boats could accept the most extreme punishment from several depth-charge attacks, as could their crews working to repair internal damage caused.

St Loman now signalled to *Roper* that she would remain in contact with the U-boat until dawn the next day, and then return to base at Staten Island. *Roper*, on completing a brief search, proceeded to Norfolk.

The weather was clearing and with the dropping of the wind the seas were relatively calm. Somewhat ghoulishly perhaps, *St Loman* maintained little more than steerage weigh to slowly patrol the area while checking the now silent and motionless U-boat hull at regular intervals.

The sun came out to clear the overcast sky and burn off the misty rain, and visibility was good by late afternoon with little wind and an almost calm sea.

As was my usual procedure I had gone up on the bridge and was on my mattress when Ossie relieved Pete Willis at midnight to take the middle watch. There was no moon and it was darker on the seaward side than to the western shoreline dimly silhouetted by the shore lights. Ossie and I chatted a little over our pusser's kye before I went to doze on my straw mattress.

Around 2 a.m. in the morning the alarm bells for action stations brought me up to my feet on the bridge.

'Have you got another one, Ossie?'

'No, skipper, someone has fired a torpedo at us!'

'What are you doing?'

'Full ahead skipper!'

Impassively, Seaman Houghton was checking bearings with the hydrophone facility of his A/S diaphram.

'It's on the starboard side!' came his laconic comment.

Ossie and I went out on the starboard wing of the bridge. Sure enough there it was making a white bubbling wake about 45° off *St Loman*'s bow.

'Hard to starboard!' we yelled in unison down the wheelhouse voice pipe. The ship's bow began to swing slowly towards the approaching track of the torpedo, bringing it parallel to the ship's side, when the order: 'Amidships, steady as she goes!' followed, and the torpedo passed by amidships, clearing and crossing the stern.

'Watch the lookout aft!' I shouted to Ossie. 'It's going to scare the hell out of him!' Sure enough there came a loud yell from the gun platform aft with the frantic gesticulation at the torpedo track crossing the ship's wake astern.

Now as the *St Loman*'s course was steadied on the reverse track of the torpedo, Jonesy and his 4-inch gun's crew were busy firing star shells to illuminate the darkness on the seaward side.

Houghton, listening on his hydrophones, reported high-speed diesels fading into the darkness of the seaward side. A fruitless search was made on the last bearing obtained until dawn broke, when *St Loman* returned to her motionless victim. Then for good measure a farewell gesture of our five-depth charge attack was delivered.

St Loman, patrolling slowly around her U-boat contact, would have been silhouetted against the light of the shoreline to be silently stalked by a revengeful hunter, now long gone into the darkness, trimmed down with conning tower awash at 17-18 knots to *St Loman*'s 9-10 knots on clinker-making coal.

The torpedo was most likely the compressed-air-driven variety usually carried in a U-boat's stern tubes, thus enabling a quick take-off from the target when it missed!

A French-built and named A/S trawler *Jacques Duhamel* recently assigned to stand by a burning tanker making a pillar of smoke by day and of fire by night, was reported missing. *St Loman* had been more fortunate.

In due course I made my U-boat attack report to our dual headquarters, British and American, with the multiplicity of carbon copies. Our A/S recorder graph paper had to go to the A/S Warfare Department in the Admiralty for evaluation, much to the disgust of the US Navy who also required it.

On the subject of evaluations, during May 1942 approval was given for the promulgation, as it was termed, to HM ships of the assessments of attacks on U-boats and a 'Return of U-boat Casualties' was to be included in future issues of the report made monthly by the A/S Warfare Division.

The assessments made were extremely conservative under the headings of:

'A' 'Known Sunk'.
'B' 'Probably Sunk'.
'C' 'Probably Damaged (A)'.
'D' 'Probably Damaged (B)'.
'E' 'Probably Slightly Damaged'.

The report stated: "'Probably Damaged (A)" indicated a promising attack, believed to have damaged a U-boat seriously and which may have proved fatal, but on which a higher assessment is withheld pending receipt of intelligence indicating that the attack was probably successful.

"'Probably Damaged (B)" indicated that the U-boat was seriously damaged and had to return to port.'

The May Report (see p. 143) concluded that 'It must be remembered that as far as "Known Sinkings" are concerned, our intelligence may, in some cases, be many months late in its receipt. Only if prisoners are captured, or bodies or definite U-boat wreckage are blown to the surface, can a "Known Sinking" be recorded at once. Thus the list of "Known Sinkings" can be accepted as fairly accurate up to, say, the end of 1941, but must be considered incomplete thereafter."'

Pages 144 to 159, 'Return of U-boat casualties' and pages 160 to 162, 'Estimate of U-boats operating in May' (1942) from the Report of the A/S Warfare Division are reproduced on the following pages.

I was particularly interested in the return made on page 158, 'Italian U-boats probably slightly damaged. 8 May 1941. HMT *St Loman*, HMCS *Columbia*. 300 miles west of Aran Island.'

Due to the exploitation of ULTRA information the positions of U-boats become known from around early 1941 which would account for the knowledge that an Italian submarine was operating in an area 300 miles west of Aran Island on the north coast of Ireland. There is a 9-10 fathom bank in this area on which the submarine was sunk. This depth would have made an ideal resting place for the submarine during daylight, and being adjacent to the convoy routes to and from the entrance of the North Channel.

Prior to being joined by the Canadian destroyer, *St Loman* had marked the submarine's position with a well anchored dan buoy flying a red flag and providing a check for the two fourteen-depth-charge attacks made by *Columbia* on our oil-bleeding target and with which we held contact for the 50 hours estimated as the submerged life with fully charged batteries.

THE U-BOAT OFFENSIVE

(a) REVIEW FOR MAY

In the middle of this month coastal convoys between Hampton Roads and Key West were instituted and an immediate effect was apparent. During the first half of the month U-boats sank a considerable tonnage off Cape Hatteras and in Florida Strait, but in the latter half scarcely showed themselves off the coasts of Virginia and Florida. Logically enough in pursuit of easy prey, the U-boats sought out the remaining soft spots where traffic had to pass through focal areas and operated actively off the mouth of the Mississippi and in the Yucatan Channel between Cuba and Nicaragua. Shipping casualties continued at a high rate, but some reassurance may be sought from the fact that at any rate until the end of May, though not for very much longer, the U-boats held off from escorted shipping.

It appears inevitable that the convoy system should be progressively extended until all important shipping routes can be afforded some measure of protection by escorts and organised air cover, but it is plain that, in proportion to the extension of the area so patrolled, the strength of escort available in any one place is thinned out and that the process of affording adequate protection universally is still far from completed. As the U-boats discover that wholly unprotected targets are becoming rarer, they will be more ready, of necessity, to risk attacking lightly-protected convoys. Nevertheless their heyday in North American and West Indian waters is drawing to its end.

It is estimated that a considerable force of U-boats was again operating from Biscayan ports, the total number of U-boats based in them having further increased. Additional U-boats from new construction are thought to be coming out fairly constantly from Germany to the Bay north-about Scotland and it is plain that at present more boats must be entering operational service than are being sunk.

At the same time such a weight of effort was exerted against convoys between Iceland (c) and Russia as clearly implied the presence in northern Norwegian waters of some 20 U-boats. A fair amount of damage was caused by this northern group, including the loss of HMS 'Edinburgh.'

One heavy and concerted attack on a convoy in the North Atlantic was carried out during the month. ON 92 was the unlucky exception to the general statement that in recent months transatlantic convoys have enjoyed immunity from U-boat attack. Four of five U-boats were concerned and seven ships were sunk.

Convoy SL 109 was also attacked near the Cape Verde Islands but, thanks to the excellent offensive measures employed by the escorts, only one ship was sunk.

At the end of the month there were indications of increasing U-boat strength in the Caribbean Sea and in the area north-east and north of Brazil; these areas may be expected to prove dangerous for some time to come.

SECTION 1
RETURN OF U-BOAT CASUALTIES

Approval has now been given for the promulgation of HM ships of the assessments of results of attacks on U-boats and a 'Return of U-boat Casualties' will be included in future issues of the Report.

The Return will contain particulars of attacks on German, Italian and Japanese U-boats which have been assessed as causing damage in varying degree.

Assessments have been made under the following headings:-

'A'	....	'Known Sunk.'
'B'	....	'Probably Sunk.'
'C'	....	'Probably Damaged (A).'
'D'	....	'Probably Damaged (B).'
'E'	....	'Probably Slightly Damaged.'

'*Probably Damaged* (A)' indicates a promising attack, believed to have damaged a U-boat seriously and which may have proved fatal, but on which a higher assessment is withheld pending receipt of intelligence indicating that the attack was probably successful.

'*Probably Damaged* (B)' indicates that the U-boat was seriously damaged and had to return to port.

The particulars given in this issue cover attacks of which assessments have been made or received from the beginning of the war until 1st June, 1942. The return, as published, may require subsequent modification.

It must be remembered that, as far as 'Known Sinkings' are concerned, our intelligence may, in some cases, be many months late in its receipt. Only if prisoners are captured, or bodies or definite U-boat wreckage are blown to the surface, can a 'Known Sinking' be recorded at once. Thus, the list of 'Known Sinkings' can be accepted as fairly accurate up to, say, the end of 1941, but must be considered incomplete thereafter.

PART A
German U-boats known sunk

No.	U-boat	Ship or Aircraft concerned	Date	Position
			1939	
1	'U 39'	H.M. Ships 'Faulknor' 'Foxhound' and 'Firedrake'.	14th September	150 miles west of the Hebrides.
2	'U 27'	H.M. Ships 'Fortune' and 'Forester'.	20th September	60 miles west of the Hebrides.
3	'U 12'	*Probably mined.*	8th October	
4	'U 40'	Mined.	13th October	Dover Strait.
5	'U 42'	H.M. Ships 'Imogen' and 'Ilex'.	13th October	400 miles west of Land's End.
6	'U 16'	H.M. Ships 'Puffin' and 'Cayton Wyke', *after detection by Dover indicator loop system.*	22nd October	Goodwin Sands
7	'U 35'	H.M. Ships 'Icarus', 'Kingston' and 'Kashmir'.	29th November	120 miles east of the Shetlands.
8	'U 45'	*Possibly* 'Sirocco' (Fr.).	20th November	140 miles west of Bordeaux.
9	'U 36'	? H.M. Submarine 'Salmon'.	? 4th December	?85 miles south-west of Lindesnes.
			1940	
10	'U 53' ?	H.M.T. 'Northern Duke'.	After 29th January	Unknown.
11	'U 55'	H.M. Ships 'Fowey' and 'Whitshed', and aircraft of 228 Squadron.	30th January	120 miles west of Ushant.
12	'U 41'	{ Either H.M.S. 'Antelope'.	5th February	170 miles west-south-west of Land's End.
		{ Or 'Simoun' (Fr.).	23rd February	South-west of Cape St. Vincent.
13	'U 15'	*Rammed and sunk by German warship.*	February	Baltic.
14	'U 33'	H.M.S. 'Gleaner'.	12th February	Firth of Clyde.
15	'U 63'	H.M. Ships 'Narwhal', 'Escort', 'Inglefield' and 'Imogen'.	25th February	80 miles east of Dencansby Head.
16	'U 54'	*Circumstances unknown.*	Between 16th February and 23rd March.	–
17	'U 44' ?	H.M. Ships 'Greyhound' and 'Havock'.	? 10th April	? In Vest Fjord.
18	'U 1'	*Believed sunk by a submarine.*	? April	–
19	'U 22'	*Circumstances unknown.*	After 8th April	–
20	'U 64'	Aircraft of 700 Squadron (H.M.S. 'Warspite').	13th April	Hersangs Fjord.
21	'U 49'	H.M.S. 'Fearless'.	15th April	Entrance to Vaags Fjord.
22	'U 50'	{ *Possibly either* H.M.S. 'Imogen'.	27th April	120 miles north of the Shetlands.
		{ Or H.M. Ships 'Amazon' and 'Witherington'.	29th April	70 miles north-east of the Shetlands.
23	'U 13'	H.M.S. 'Weston'	30th May	9 miles south-east of Lowestoft.
24	'U 102'	? H.M.Y. 'Viva II'	? 21st June	? 60 miles south-west of Belle Isle.
25	'U 25'	*Possibly either* H.M.S. 'Vansittart' *or mined in the North Sea.*	1st July	210 miles west of Ushant.

26	'U 26'	H.M.S. 'Gladiolus' and Sunderland F.B. No. 510.	1st July	240 miles west of Ushant.
27	'U 122'	*Circumstances unknown.*	Early July	
28*	'U 51'	H.M. Submarine 'Cachalot'.	20th August	50 miles west-south-west of Belle Isle.
29	'U 32'	H.M. Ships 'Harvester' and 'Highlander'.	30th October	200 miles west by north of Bloody Foreland.
30	'U 31'	(1) Aircraft of Bomber Command.	11th March	Schillig Roads+
		(2) H.M.S. 'Antelope'.	2nd November	110 miles north-est of Bloody Foreland.
31	'U 104'	*Possibly* H.M.S. 'Rhododendron'.	21st November 1941	80 miles south of Rockall
32	'U 70'	H.M. Ships 'Arbutus' and 'Camellia'.	7th March	150 miles north of Rockall.
33	'U 47'	? H.M.S. 'Wolverine'.	? 8th March	? 180 miles north-west of Flannan Island.
34	'U 99'	H.M.S. 'Walker'.	17th March	240 miles north-west of the Butt of Lewis.
35	'U 100'	H.M.S. 'Vanoc'.	17th March	240 miles north-west of the Butt of Lewis.
36	? 'U 551'	H.M.T. 'Visenda'.	23rd March	190 miles east-south-est of Reykjanes.
37	'U 76'	H.M. Ships 'Scarborough' and 'Wolverine'.	5th April	435 miles west of the Butt of Lewis.
38†	'U 65'	*Circumstances unknown.*	About mid-April	–
		Possibly H.M.S. 'Gladiolus'.	29th April	260 miles north-west of Barra Head.
39	'U 110'	H.M. Ships 'Aubretia' 'Broadway' and 'Bulldog'.	9th May	550 miles south-west of Reykjanes.
40	'U 147'	H.M. Ships 'Wanderer' and 'Periwinkle'.	2nd June	150 miles west of Skerryvore.
41	'U 138'	H.M. Ships 'Faulknor', 'Fearless', 'Foresight', 'Foxhound' and 'Forester'.	18th June	100 miles west of Cape Trafalgar.
42	'U 556'	H.M. Ships 'Gladiolus', 'Nasturtium' and 'Celandine'.	27th June	300 miles south-west of Iceland (c).
43	'U 651'	'H.M. Ships 'Malcolm', 'Violet', 'Scimitar', 'Arabis', 'Speedwell'.	29th June	200 miles north-west of Rockall.
44	'U 401'	H.M.S. 'Wanderer' and H.No.M.S. 'St. Albans', H.M.S. 'Hydrangea'.	3rd August	620 miles west of Land's End.
45	'U 452'	Aircraft of 209 Squadron and H.M.T. 'Vascama'.	25 August	320 miles west-north-west of the Butt of Lewis.
46‡	'U 570'	Aircraft of 269 Squadron.	27th August	80 miles south of Dynholar, Iceland (c).
47	'U 501'	H.M.C. Ships 'Chambly' and 'Moosejaw'.	10th September	60 miles west of Sebesteds Fjord, Greenland.
48	'U 207'	H.M. Ships 'Leamington' and 'Veteran'.	11th September	310 miles west of Reykjanes, Iceland (c).

* See Part D. No. 8.

† See Part C. No. 15

‡ This U-boat surrendered and is now H.M. Submarine 'Graph'.

49	'U 111'	H.M.T. 'Lady Shirley'.	4th October	140 miles south-west of Palma, Canary Islands.
50	'U 204'	*Probably* H.M. Ships 'Mallow' and 'Rochester'.	19th October	Off Cape Spartel.
51	'U 580'	*Rammed by German Ship 'Hamburg'* (?).	? November	Baltic area.
52	'U 433'	H.M.S. 'Marigold'.	16th November	38 miles east-north-east of Gibraltar.
53	'U 579'	*Rammed by U-boat or German Ship.*	Some date before 29th November.	Baltic – off Memel.
54	'U 95'	H.Ne.M. Submarine '021'.	28th November	60 miles east of Gibraltar.
55	'U 206'	*Circumstances unknown.*	Probably late November or early December.	Atlantic area.
56	'U –'?	H.M.A.S. 'Nestor'.	15th December	50 miles south-south-west of Cape St. Vincent.
57	'U 131'	H.M. Ships 'Stork', 'Exmoor', 'Blankney', 'Audacity', 'Pentstemon' and 'Stanley'.	17th December	280 miles south-west of Cape St. Vincent.
58	'U 434'	H.M. Ships 'Stanley' and 'Blankney'.	18th December	270 miles west-south-west of Cape St. Vincent.
59	'U 574'	H.M.S. 'Stork'.	19th December	330 miles west of Cape Sines, Portugal.
			1941	
60	'U 567'{	Possibly either H.M.S. 'Deptford'	21st December	500 miles west by north of Cape Finisterre.
		Or H.M.S. 'Samphire'.	21st December	460 miles west by north of Cape Finisterre.
61	'U 451'	Swordfish aircraft of 812 Squadron.	21st December	Off Cape Spartel.
62	'U 79'	H.M. Ships 'Hasty' and 'Hotspur'.	23rd December	30 miles north-east of Bardia.
63	'U 75'	H.M.S. 'Kipling'.	28th December	30 miles north-east of Mersa Matruh.
64	'U 557'	*Circumstances unknown.*	Probably December.	Mediterranean.
65	'U –'?	H.M. Submarine 'Unbeaten'.	12th January	Eight miles south-west of Cape Spartivento.
66	'U 93'	H.M.S. 'Hesperus'.	15th January	300 miles west of Cape St. Vincent.
67	'U 581'	H.M.S. 'Westcott'.	2nd February	Between Fayal and Pico, Azores.
68	'U -'?	H.M.S. 'Sharpshooter'.	24th March	60 miles south-south-east of Bear Island.
69	'U 85'	U.S.S. 'Roper'.	14th April	Off Cape Hatteras.
70	'U –'?	H.M. Ships 'Vetch' and 'Stork'.	14th April	450 miles north-west of Cape Finisterre.
71	'U 352'	U.S.C.G. 'Icarus'.	9th May	60 miles east of Wilmington, Delaware.
72	'U –'?	H.M. Ships 'Eridge', 'Hurworth' and 'Hero'.	28th May	70 miles north-east of Tobruk.

PART B
German U-boats probably sunk.

No.	U-boat	Ship or Aircraft concerned.	Date	Position
			1940	
1	–	H.M. Submarine 'Tuna'.	1st September	140 miles east of May Island.
2	–	H.M. Submarine 'Tigris'.	2nd September	40 miles west of Belle Isle.
3	–	H.M. Submarine 'Tribune'.	8th September	35 miles south-west of Flannan Island.
4	–	Aircraft of 821 Squadron.	14th September	25 miles north of Cape Wrath.
5	–	H.M.C.S. 'St. Laurent' and H.M.S. 'Viscount'.	2nd December	330 miles west of Donegal Bay.
			1941	
6	–	Aircraft of 210 Squadron.	6th January	80 miles north-east of Rockall.
7	–	H.M.S. 'Walker'	17th March	240 miles north-west of the Butt of Lewis.
			1942	
8	–	Aircraft of 230 Squadron.	9th January	Eight miles north of Sidi Barrani.
9	–	U.S.N. Aircraft (Patrol Squadron 82).	1st March	30 miles south-west of Cape Race.
10	–	U.S.N. Aircraft (Patrol Squadron 82).	15th March	250 miles south-east of Cape Race.
11	–	H.M. Submarine 'Seawolf'.	18th March	85 miles west-north-west of Aalesund.
12	–	Aircraft of 58 Squadron.	16th May	30 miles north of Santander.

PART C
German U-boats probably damaged (A).

No.	U-boat	Ship or Aircraft concerned.	Date	Position
			1939	
1	–	H.M.S. 'Broke'.	9th September	Six miles east of Aldeburgh.
2	–	H.M. Ships 'Exmouth' and 'Eclipse'.	9th September	360 miles south-west of Cape Finisterre.
3	–	H.M. Ships 'Intrepid' and 'Vesper'.	14th September	75 miles west-south-west of Milford Haven.
4	–	H.M. Ships 'Fortune' and 'Firedrake'.	23rd September	55 miles north-east of Kinnairds Head.
5	–	H.M. Ships 'Esk' and 'Express'.	24th September	500 miles north of Lough Swilly.
6	–	H.M.S. 'Eclipse'.	15th October	25 miles south-west of Lizard Head.
7	–	H.M. Ships 'Inglefield', 'Intrepid', 'Ivanhoe' and 'Icarus'.	14th October	83 miles west-south-west of Berehaven.
8	–	H.M. Submarine 'Sturgeon'.	14th October	Skaggerak.
9	–	H.M. Ships 'Inglefield' and 'Ivanhoe'.	16th October	300 miles west of Berehaven.
10	–	Aircraft of 269 Squadron and H.M. Ships 'Afridi' and 'Woolston'.	18th October	Off St. Abb's head.
11	–	H.M. Ships 'Somali' and 'Fame'.	31st October	Off Kinnairds Head.
			1940	
12	'U 23'?	Aircraft of 269 Squadron and H.M. Ships 'Speedwell' and 'Niger'.	21st February	30 miles south-east of Duncansby Head.
13	–	Aircraft of 269 Squadron.	4th August	170 miles north-north-west of Rockall.

148

14	–	H.M. Ships 'Deptford' and 'Keppel'.	25th September	120 miles north-west of Bloody Foreland.
			1941	
15*	–	H.M.S. 'Gladiolus'.	29th April	260 miles north-west of Barra Head.
16	–	*Either* Aircraft of 224 Squadron.	22nd June	110 miles west of Oronsay.
		Or Aircraft of 217 Squadron.	24th June	150 miles north-north-west of Ushant.
17	–	H.M. Ships 'Gladiolus' and 'Nasturtium'.	25th June	600 miles south-west of Iceland (c).
18	–	H.M.S. 'Jervis'.	18th December	40 miles west-north-west of Alexandria.
19	–	H.M.T. 'Kingston Cyanite'.	19th December	18 miles west of Ras el Tin.
20	–	H.M. Ships 'Kipling' and 'Legion'.	27th December	10 miles north-east of Tobruk.
			1942	
21†	–	Aircraft of 203 Squadron.	2nd January	220 miles east of Malta.
22	–	H.M. Ships 'Rochester' and 'Tamarisk'.	6th February	380 miles north of San Miguel, Azores.
23†	–	H.M. Ships 'Keppel', 'Volunteer', 'Badsworth' and 'Leamington'.	18th March	125 miles west of Bloody Foreland.
24	–	H.M. Ships 'Leamington', 'Grove', 'Aldenham' and 'Volunteer'.	27th March	640 miles west by south of Land's End.
25‡	–	Aircraft of 502 Squadron.	1st April	135 miles south-west of Brest.
26	–	Aircraft of 500 Squadron.	28th April	60 miles north-west of Rockall.

*See Part A. No. 38

† Nationality uncertain. See Part H, No. 11.

‡ Nationality uncertain. See Part H. No. 12.

PART D
German U-boats probably damaged (B)

			1939	
1	–	O.R.P. 'Blyskawica'.	7th September	The Minches.
2	–	Aircraft from H.M.S. 'Courageous'.	10th September	300 miles west of Ushant.
3	–	Aircraft of 269 Squadron.	15th September	50 miles east of Aberdeen.
4	–	Aircraft of 204 Squadron.	20th September	West-south-west of Land's End.
5	–	H.M.S. 'Forester'.	22nd September	East of Fair Isle.
6	–	H.M.S. 'Echo'.	19th November	270 miles west-south-west of Ushant.
7	'U 41'?	H.M. Ships 'Versatile' and 'Witherington'.	25th November	150 miles west-south-west of Land's End.
			1940	
8*	'U 51'	Aircraft of 210 Squadron.	16th August	170 miles north-west of Tory Island.
9	–	Aircraft of 233 Squadron.	25th October	100 miles south-west of Stavanger.
10	–	H.M.S. 'Beagle'.	5th November	80 miles north-west of Blacksod Bay.

* See Part A, No. 28.

1941

11	'U 93'	Aircraft of 502 Squadron.	10th February	40 miles south of Rockall.
12	–	H.M.S. 'Douglas'.	28th April	250 miles north-west of Barra Head.
13	'U 96'	F.S. 'Leopard' and H.M.S. 'Churchill'.	24th February	290 miles north-west of Rockall.
14	–	Aircraft of 269 Squadron.	5th May	130 miles west of the Butt of Lewis.
15	–	H.M. Ships 'Burnham' and 'Verbena'.	21st May	260 miles south-south-east of Cape Farewell.
16	–	H.M.S. 'Folkestone'.	2nd July	390 miles north-north-west of Graciosa Island, Azores.
17	–	H.M. Ships 'Lavender' and 'Petunia'.	5th July	840 miles west of Cape Ortegal.
18	–	H.M.S. 'Pimpernel'.	27th July	350 miles north-west of Cape Finisterre.
19	–	H.M.S. 'Zinnia' and S.S. 'Volturno'.	5th August	180 miles west of Arran Islands.
20	–	Aircraft of 1404 Squadron.	12th August	220 miles west-south-west of Ushant.
21	–	H.M. Ships 'Faulkner' and 'Wild Swan'.	13th August	300 miles west of Figueira da Foz (Portugal).
22	–	Aircraft of 220 Squadron.	26th August	225 miles west by north of the Butt of Lewis.
23	–	Aircraft of 240 Squadron.	4th September	260 miles west of Fastnet Light.
24	–	Aircraft of 221 Squadron.	8th September	260 miles west-south-west of Ushant.
25	–	H.M.C. Ships 'Skeena' and 'Alberni'.	10th September	130 miles north-east of Cape Discord.
26	–	Aircraft of 210 Squadron.	14th September	220 miles west of Skerryvore.
27	–	Aircraft of 221 Squadron.	16th September	250 miles west of Land's End.
28	–	Aircraft of 240 Squadron.	27th September	270 miles west of Fastnet Light.
29	–	Aircraft of 240 Squadron.	16th October	590 miles west by north of Achill Head.
30	–	H.M.S. 'Veronica'.	17th October	485 miles west of Barra Head.
31	–	H.M.C.S. 'Pictou'.	17th October	700 miles west of Barra Head.
32	–	Aircraft of 53 and 209 Squadron	30th October	160 miles west-south-west of Ushant.
33	–	H.M. Ships 'Verbena' and 'Landguard'.	2nd November	700 miles west of Ushant.
34	–	Aircraft of 233 Squadron.	7th November	50 miles south of Nazaire.
35	–	U.S.S.R.S. 'Briz'.	25th November	80 miles west-south-west of Cape Kanin.
36	–	Aircraft of 812 Squadron.	30th November	Off Cape Spartel.
37	–	Aircraft of 502 Squadron.	1st December	290 miles west-south-west of Ushant.
38	–	Aircraft of 233 Squadron.	13th December	160 miles east of Gibraltar.
39	–	Aircraft of 812 Squadron.	16th December	Off Cape Spartel.
40	–	Aircraft of 812 Squadron.	19th December	Off Cape Spartel.
41	–	H.M.T. 'Arctic Ranger'.	22nd December	Off Almina Point.
42	–	H.M.A.S. 'Napier' and H.M. Ships 'Gurkha' and 'Foxhound'.	28th December	70 miles north-north-east of Tobruk.

			1942	
43	–	Aircraft of 815 Squadron.	25th January	Near Mersa Matruh.
44	–	U.S.C.G. 'Campbell'.	26th January	200 miles south-east of Halifax.
45	–	H.M.S. 'Chelsea'.	5th February	425 miles west of Islay.
46	–	Aircraft of 612 Squadron.	18th February	60 miles south-west of Reykjanes.
47	–	Aircraft of 224 Squadron.	12th March	220 miles west of the Butt of Lewis.
48	–	H.M.S. 'Tynedale'.	27th March	130 miles west by south of St. Nazaire.
49	–	U.S. Submarine 'R.I.'.	16th April	650 miles south-east of Portland, Maine.
50	–	Aircraft of 233 Squadron.	1st May	115 miles east by south of Cartagena.
51	–	U.S.C.G. Aircraft.	15th May	50 miles north-north-east of Cape Hatteras.

PART E
German U-boats probably slightly damaged

			1939	
1	–	H.M.S. 'Inglefield' and 12th Sub-Division.	9th September	250 miles west of Cape St. Vincent.
2	–	H.M.S. 'Volunteer'.	16th September	48 miles south of Lizard Head.
3	–	H.M.S. 'Kelly'.	17th September	English Channel.
4	'U 33'	Aircraft of 228 Squadron.	18th September	70 miles south-east of Fastnet Light.
5	–	Aircraft of 204 Squadron.	19th September	250 miles west-south-west of Land's End.
6	'U 35'	H.M.S. 'Ardent'.	21st September	55 miles west-south-west of Land's End.
7	–	'Admiral Mouchez' (Fr.).	2nd October	30 miles north of Le Havre.
8	–	H.M. Ships 'Whirlwind' and 'Walpole'.	16th October	Irish Sea.
9	–	Aircraft of 224 Squadron.	20th October	100 miles east of Kinnaird's Head.
10	–	Aircraft of 228 Squadron.	21st October	70 miles west-south-west of Berehaven.
11	–	Aircraft of 224 Squadron.	12th November	40 miles west of the Naze.
12	–	Aircraft of 206 Squadron.	3rd December	40 miles north-north-west of the Texel.
			1940	
13	–	Aircraft of 224 Squadron.	16th February	100 miles east-north-east of Duncansby Head.
14	–	H.M.S. 'Fortune'.	20th March	170 miles north-north-east of Muckle Flugga.
15	'U 19'	H.M.S. Zulu.	9th April	40 miles north-east of Fair Isle.
16	–	Aircraft of 224 Squadron.	17th April	South of Bergen.
17	–	H.M. Ships 'Deptford' and 'Whitehall'.	22nd May	120 miles south-west of Ushant.
18	–	H.M.S. 'Arabis'.	31st May	30 miles south-south-west of Start Point.

151

19	–	Aircraft of 217 Squadron.	4th June	41 miles south of Land's End.
20	–	H.M.S. 'Deptford'.	8th July	250 miles west of Ushant.
21	–	H.M. Ships 'Walker', and 'Periwinkle'.	31st July	70 miles north-west of Tory Island.
22	–	S.S. Clintonia'.	2nd September	40 miles south of Rockall.
23	–	S.S. 'Makefjell'.	9th September	40 miles west of Barra Head.
24	–	S.S. 'Harlingen'.	22nd September	330 miles west of Bloody Foreland.
25	'U 99'	H.M.S. 'Folkestone'.	17th October	200 miles north-west of Rockall.
26	–	M.V. 'Cardita'.	11th December	230 miles west of Cape Wrath.
27	–	S.S. 'Newton Pine'.	13th December	840 miles south of Cape Verde Islands.
28	–	H.M. Submarine 'Tuna'.	18th December	Off the Mouth of the Gironde.
29	–	S.S. 'Everleigh'.	25th December	420 miles north-west of Rockall.
			1941	
30	–	H.M.T. 'Northern Reward'.	25th February	270 miles north-west of Flannan Island.
31	–	Aircraft of 10 Squadron.	9th March	300 miles west of Dingle Bay.
32	–	S.S. 'Treverbyn'.	29th March	340 miles north-west of Rockall.
33	–	Aircraft of 107 Squadron.	11th April	Off Christiansand.
34	–	Aircraft of 107 Squadron.	16th April	80 miles south-west of Rekefjord.
35	–	H.M. Ships 'Inglefield' and 'Maori'.	28th April	200 miles north-west of Rockall.
36	–	H.M. Ships 'Leamington', 'Gladiolus' and 'Roxborough'.	28th April	160 miles north-north-west of Rockall.
37	–	Aircraft of 269 Squadron.	30th April	60 miles west of the Butt of Lewis.
38	–	Aircraft of 220 Squadron.	4th May	230 miles west of Sumburgh Head.
39	–	H.M. Ships 'Bulldog', 'Amazon' and 'Rochester'.	7th May	500 miles north-west of Rockall.
40	'U 201'	H.M. Ships 'Amazon', 'Nigella' and 'St. Apollo'.	9th May	370 miles north-west of Barra Head.
41	–	H.M.T. 'Notts County'.	30th May	400 miles north-west of Flannan Island.
42	–	H.M. Ships 'Walker' and 'Heliotrope' and H.No.M.S. 'Bath'.	25th July	60 miles west-north-west of Malin Head.
43	–	H.M. Ships 'Dianella' and 'Kingcup'.	26th July	650 miles west of La Rochelle.
44	–	H.M.T. 'Fleur de Lys'.	28th July	350 miles west of Oporto.
45	–	H.M. Ships 'Fleur de Lys' and 'Rhododendron'.	28th July	270 miles west of Oporto.
46	–	Aircraft of 221 Squadron.	29th July	110 miles west of Ushant.
47*	–	Aircraft of 221 Squadron.	29th July	330 miles west of La Pallice.
48	–	Aircraft of 206 Squadron.	31st July	160 miles west of Ushant.
49	–	Aircraft of 221 Squadron.	31st July	160 miles north by west of Cape Ortegal.
50	–	{ Aircraft of 221 Squadron. / Aircraft of 502 Squadron. }	0937 on 5th August / 1420 on 5th August.	200 miles west of Slyne Head.

* Possibly an Italian U-boat.

51	–	Aircraft of 221 Squadron.	5th August.	280 miles west of St. Nazaire.
52	–	Aircraft of 210 Squadron.	19th August	325 miles west-south-west of Valencia.
53	–	Aircraft of 221 Squadron.	24th August.	410 miles west-north-west of the Butt of Lewis.
54	–	Aircraft of 502 Squadron.	24th August	385 miles north-west of the Butt of Lewis.
55	–	Aircraft of 502 Squadron.	26th August	300 miles west of Vaago Is. (Faroes).
56	–	Aircraft of 269 Squadron.	27th August	128 miles south of Reykjanes.
57	–	H.M.S. 'Walker'.	28th August	300 miles west-south-west of Slyne Head.
58	–	Aircraft of 269 Squadron.	11th September	310 miles west of Reykjanes.
59	–	Aircraft of 209 Squadron.	12th September	500 miles west of Reykjanes.
60	–	H.M. Submarine 'Clyde'.	28th September	Tarrafal Bay, San Antonio, Cape Verde Islands.
61	–	Aircraft of 1404 Squadron.	5th October	230 miles south-west by west of Land's End.
62	–	H.M.S. 'Londonderry'.	10th October	280 miles south-west of Cape Blanco.
63	–	H.M.S. 'Beverley'.	23rd October	170 miles west of Cape Clear.
64	–	Aircraft of 53 Squadron.	11th November	250 miles west-south-west of Ushant.
65	–	H.M.S. 'Totland'.	29th November	170 miles north-north-west of Graciosa Is., Azores.
66	–	Aircraft of 502 Squadron.	30th November	130 miles south-west of Ushant.
67	–	Aircraft of 202 Squadron.	6th December	20 miles south-west of Cape St. Vincent.
68	–	Aircraft of 203 Squadron.	6th December	50 miles north of Bardia.
69	–	U.S.S. 'Brooklyn'.	14th December	80 miles south-east of Antigua.
70	–	Aircraft of 120 Squadron.	22nd December	475 miles west-north-west of Cape Finisterre.

1942

71	–	H.Ne.M.S. 'Isaac Sweers' and H.M.S. 'Legion'.	8th January	50 miles north-west of Mersa Matruh.
72	–	Aircraft of 815 Squadron.	11th January	50 miles north of Tobruk.
73	–	H.M.S. 'Arrow'.	13th January	95 miles west-north-west of Alexandria.
74	–	F.S. 'Roselys'.	26th January	90 miles west-north-west of Achill Head.
75	–	U.S.N. Aircraft (Patrol Squadron 82).	28th January	300 miles east-south-east of Cape Breton.
76	–	Aircraft of 230 Squadron.	29th January	45 miles north-north-east of Sidi Barrani.
77	–	H.M.C.S. 'Summerside'.	3rd February	680 miles west of Achill Head.
78	–	Aircraft of 230 Squadron.	8th February	40 miles east of Sidi Barrani.
79	–	H.M.S. 'Hyacinth'.	9th February	45 miles north-east of Bardia.
80	–	Aircraft of 206 Squadron.	14th February	145 miles west-north-west of Broadhaven.
81	–	H.M.S. 'Lamerton' and H.No.M.S.	11th March	90 miles west of Flannan Island.

		'Newport'.		
82	–	Aircraft of 224 Squadron.	13th March	150 miles north of Rockall.
83	–	Aircraft of 228 Squadron.	13th March	165 miles north of Rockall.
84	–	U.S.N. Aircraft (Patrol Squadron 82).	15th March	30 miles south of Narrangansett Bay.
85	–	H.M. Ships 'Gossamer' and 'Hussar'.	29th March	180 miles north-east of Kirkenes.
86	–	H.M.S. 'Orib'.	13th April	130 miles north of Berlevaag.
87	–	Aircraft of 502 Squadron.	14th April	400 miles west of Jersey.
88	–	U.S.S. 'Rowan'.	22nd April	650 miles east of Jacksonville, Florida.
89	–	U.S.S. 'Woolsey'	29th April	70 miles south-east of New York.
90	–	U.S. Aircraft Scouting Squadron 1 D.3.	1st May	Near Ambrose Lightship.
91	–	Aircraft of 120 Squadron.	3rd May	500 miles west-south-west of Ushant.
92	–	Aircraft of 58 Squadron.	5th May	100 miles north-north-west of Cape Ortegal.
93	–	U.S.N. Aircraft (Patrol Squadron 31).	19th May	300 miles east of Martinique.
94	–	Aircraft of 228 Squadron.	21st May	60 miles east of Rockall.
95	–	Aircraft of 608 Squadron.	22nd May	155 miles west of Statlandet.

PART F
Italian U-boats known sunk
1940

1	'Macalle'	Wrecked on a reef.	14th June	65 miles south-east of Port Sudan.
2	'Galileo Galilei'	H.M.T. 'Moonstone'.	19th June	Off Aden.
3	'Diamante'	H.M.S. 'Parthian'.	20th June	45 miles north-north-east of Tobruk.
4*	'Evangelista Torricelli'	H.M. Ships 'Kandahar' and 'Kingston'.	22nd June	11 miles west-south-west of Perim.
5	'Luigi Galvani'	H.M.S. 'Falmouth'.	23rd June	Entrance to Persian Gulf.
6	'Liuzzi'	H.M. Ships 'Dainty' and 'Ilex'.	27th June	100 miles south-east of Crete.
7	'Argonauta'	*Believed sunk by flying boat.*	? June	Mediterranean.
8	'Uebi Scebeli'	H.M. Ships 'Dainty' and 'Ilex'.	29th June	165 miles west of Crete.
9	'Rubino'	Flying Boat L.5804.	29th June	50 miles south-west of Corfu.
10	'Provana'	*Believed to have been sunk by French forces.*	30th June, or 2nd July	Western Mediterranean.
11	'Iride'	Aircraft (H.M.S. 'Eagle').	22nd August	Jezel Marakeb.
12	'Gondar'	H.M.A.S. 'Stuart' and Flying Boat L. 2166.	30th September	80 miles west-north-west of Alexandria.
13	'Berillo'	H.M. Ships 'Havock' and 'Hasty'.	2nd October	80 miles north-west of Mersa Matruh.
14	'Gemma'	*Italian* M.A./S.B.	6th or 7th October	In Dodecanese Islands.
15	'Durbo'	H.M. Ships 'Firedrake' and 'Wrestler'.	18th October	60 miles east of Ceuta.
16	'Lafole'	H.M. Ships 'Hotspur', 'Gallant' and 'Griffin'.	20th October	Off Alboran Island.

* See Part K. No. 4.

17	'Foca'	Circumstances unknown.	Between mid-September and 31st December	Eastern Mediterranean.
18	'Faa di Bruno'	Possibly H.M.S. 'Havelock'.	8th November	150 miles south-west of Rockall.
19	'Tarantini'	Probably sunk by mine.	Mid-November	Off Bordeaux.
20	'Naiade'	H.M. Ships 'Hyperion' and 'Hereward'.	14th December	Off Bardia.
			1941	
21	'Nani'	? H.M.S. 'Anemone'.	? 7th January	? 70 miles west of Outer Bailey Bank.
22	'Negbelli'	Circumstances unknown, possibly mined.	Late January or February	Aegean Sea.
23†	'Anfitrite'	H.M.S. 'Greyhound'.	6th March	Off Cape Sidero.
24	'Pier Capponi'	H.M. Submarine 'Rorqual'	31st March	17 miles south of Stromboli.
25	'Marcello'	Circumstances unknown.	Between 22nd February and 14th April	Atlantic Ocean.
26	Name unknown	Aircraft of 204 Group.	1st/2nd May	Derma Harbour.
27	'Salpa'	H.M. Submarine 'Triumph'.	27th June	50 miles north-west of Mersa Matruh.
28	'Glauco'	H.M.S. 'Wishart'.	27th June	210 Miles south-west of Cape St. Vincent.
29	'Jantina'	H.M. Submarine 'Torbay'.	5th July	Off Mykoni.
30	? 'Tembien'	H.M.S. 'Hermione'.	2nd August	100 miles south-south-east of Cape Bon.
31‡	'M. Bianchi'	H.M. Submarine 'Severn'.	7th August	220 miles south-west of Cape St. Vincent.
32	'Mareggior Francesco Baracca'	H.M.S. 'Croome'.	8th September	270 miles north-east of San Miguel, Azores.
33	'Adua'	H.M. Ships 'Gurkha' and 'Legion'.	30 September	100 miles east-south-east of Cartagena.
34	'Fisalia'	Possibly H.M.S. 'Hyacinth'.	28th September	30 miles north-west of Jaffa.
35	'Malaspina'	Circumstances unknown. ?	Between 8th September and 10th October.	Atlantic Ocean.
36	'Ferraris'	Aircraft of 202 Squadron and H.M.S. 'Lamerton'.	25th October	300 miles west of Cape St. Vincent.
37	'Perla' class.	H.M. Submarine 'Upholder'.	8th November	90 miles east by north of Malta.
38	'Marconi'	Circumstances unknown.	? November, probably later	Atlantic Ocean.
39	'Caracciolo'	H.M.S. 'Farndale'.	11th December	25 miles north-east of Bardia.
			1942	
40	'Saint Bon'	H.M. Submarine 'Upholder'.	5th January	15 miles west-north-west of Messina.
41	'Sirena' class.	H.M. Submarine 'Thorn'.	30th January	Off Brioni Island, Adriatic.

† See also Part J, No. 8.
‡ See also Part K, No. 6.

42	'Ammiraglio Millo'.	H.M. Submarine 'P.34'.	16th March	75 miles south-east of Strait of Messina.
43	'Argonauta' class	H.M. Submarine 'Unbeaten'.	17th March	Southern approaches to the Strait of Messina.
44	'Setembrini' class.	H.M. Submarine 'Upholder'.	18th March	Near Brindisi.

PART G
Italian U-boats probably sunk
1940

1	–	H.M. Submarine 'Cachalot'	24th September	110 miles west-south-west of Belle Isle.
2	–	H.M. Submarine 'Thunderbolt'.	15th December	Off the mouth of the Gironde.
			1941	
3	–	H.H.M.S. 'Psara'.	11th March	11 miles south of Falkonera.
4	–	H.M. Ships 'Jaguar' and 'Juno'	30th April	130 miles north-west of Alexandria.
5	'Squalo' class	H.M. Submarine 'Tigris'.	5th July	140 miles west of Bordeaux.

PART H
Italian U-boats probably damaged (A)
1940

1	–	H.M.S. 'Decoy'.	10th June	67 miles north of Sollum.
2	–	H.M.T. 'Jade'.	14th September	Off Cape Delmara (Malta).
3	–	H.M.A.S. 'Vampire'.	4th October	Off west coast of Crete.
4	–	H.M. Trawlers 'Victorian' and 'Bandolero' and Flying Boat L.2166.	14th October	Off Alexandria.
			1941	
5	–	H.H.M. Submarine 'Triton'.	9th January	Off Othoni.
6	–	Aircraft.	9th January	Off Dahlak Island (Red Sea).
7	–	H.M.A.S. 'Vendetta' and Flying Boat L.2166	18th March	Off Serpho (Aegean).
8	–	H.M.A.S. 'Vampire'.	19th April	Off Cape Colonna.
9	–	S.S. 'Berkel', H.M. Ships 'Sandwich' and 'St. Wistan' and S.S. 'Empire Storm'.	21st April	300 miles west of Slyne Head.
10	–	H.M.S. 'Duncan'.	28th October	530 miles west of R. Minho (Portugal).
			1942	
11*	–	Aircraft of 203 Squadron.	2nd January	220 miles east of Malta.
12†	–	Aircraft of 502 Squadron.	1st April	135 miles south-west of Brest.

* Nationality uncertain. See Part C, No. 21.
† Nationality uncertain. See Part C, No. 25.

PART J
Italian U-boats probably damaged (B)
1940

1	? 'Balilla'	H.M.A. Ships 'Voyager', 'Stuart' and H.M.S. 'Decoy'.	14th June	Off Alexandria.
2	? 'Perla'	H.M.S. 'Kingston'.	26th June	140 miles south-east of Massawa.
3	? 'Salpa'	H.M. Ships 'Dainty', 'Ilex', 'Decoy' and 'Voyager'.	29th June	160 miles west of Crete.
4	–	H.M.S. 'Hostile' and H.M.A.S. 'Stuart'.	1st July	100 miles north-north west of Tobruk.
5	–	H.M. Trawlers 'Coral' and 'Jade'.	1st July	Off Malta.
6	? 'Beilbul'	'H.M.S. 'Hasty'.	7th July	100 miles north-west of Alexandria.
7	–	Flying Boat L.5803.	9th July	70 miles south-east of Cape Spartivento.
8‡	'M. Bianchi'	*Struck bottom.*	3rd November	Strait of Gibraltar.
9	'Brim'	*Struck bottom.*	4th November	Strait of Gibraltar.
10	–	'H.M.C.S. 'Ottawa' and H.M.S. 'Harvester'.	6th November	140 miles south-west of Bantry Bay.

1941

11	'Bagnolini'	{ H.M.T. 'Northern Pride'.	1st January	170 miles south of Rockall.
		Aircraft of 217 Squadron.	3rd January	60 miles south-west of Ushant.
12	'Cappellini'	S.S. 'Eumaeus' and Aircraft of 710 Squadron.	14th January	Off Freetown.
13	–	H.M.S. 'Camellia'.	21st March	260 miles west of River Shannon.
14	'Glauco'	H.M. Trawlers 'Scottish' and 'Loch Oskaig'.	14th April	40 miles west of Cape Roca.
15	–	H.M.S. 'Flamingo'.	25th April	50 miles south of Hierepetra (Crete).
16	–	H.M.A.S. 'Stuart' and H.No.M.S. Kos 22.	8th May	30 miles west of Alexandria.
17	–	H.M. Ships 'Winchelsea' and 'Vanquisher'.	15th May	350 miles west of Blacksod Bay.
18	–	H.M. Ships 'Hibiscus' and 'Rhododendron'.	15th May	360 miles west of Westport.
19	'Smeraldo'	*Probably* H.M.S. 'Defender'.	29th June	40 miles north of Bardia.
20	–	Aircraft of 233 Squadron.	13th October	90 miles north of Cape Ortegal.

1942

21	–	Aircraft of 203 Squadron.	1st April	30 miles north of Cape Bougaroni.

PART K
Italian U-boats probably slightly damaged
1940

1	'Cappellini'	H.M.S. 'Watchman'.	12th June	Off Ceuta.
2	–	H.M.A.S. 'Voyager' and H.M.S. 'Decoy'.	15th June	Off Alexandria.
3	–	H.M. Ships 'Diamond' and 'Coral'.	17th June	Off Valetta.

‡ See also Part F, No. 31.

4* 'Evangelista Torricelli'	H.M.S. 'Khartoum'.	21st June	Off Perim.
5 –	S.S. 'Baron Erskine' and S.S. 'Baron Newlands'.	26th June	16 miles north of Cape Sigli.
6† 'Anfitnite'	Flying Boat L. 5804.	28th June	70 miles south-west of Zante.
7 –	H.M.S. 'Hasty'.	8th July	100 miles north-west of Alexandria.
8 –	H.M.A.S. 'Voyager'.	11th July	90 miles south-east of Malta.
9 –	Flying Boat N.9020.	12th July	30 miles east of Cape Passaro.
10 –	H.M. Trawlers 'Coral' and 'Jade'.	12th July	Off Malta.
11 –	H.M.T. 'Beryl'.	19th July	Off Valetta.
12 –	H.M.S. 'Wishart'.	28th September	50 miles south-south-east of Cape St. Vincent.
13 –	H.M.A.S. 'Vampire'.	10th October	120 miles south-south-west of Zante.
14 'Argo'	H.M.S. 'Harvester'.	5th December	170 miles west of Slyne Head.
15 –	S.S. 'Sarastone'.	22nd December	360 miles west of Oporto.
		1941	
16 –	H.M.S. 'Hyacinth'.	2nd April	170 miles south of Scarpanto.
17 'Baracca'	H.M.T. 'Fleur-de-Lis'.	14th April	70 miles south-south-west of Cape St. Vincent.
18 –	H.M.T. 'St. Loman' and H.M.C.S. 'Columbia'.	8th May	300 miles west of Arran Islands.
19 –	H.M. Ships 'Kandahar' and 'Jervis'.	9th May	60 miles south of Malta.
20 –	Aircraft of 209 Squadron.	15th May	330 miles west of Blacksod Bay.
21 –	H.M.C.S. 'St. Francis'.	20th May	370 miles west of Skelligs.
22 –	H.M.A. Ships 'Parramatta' and 'Stuart'.	27th June	Off Ras el Ranais.
23 –	H.M.A.S. 'Nestor'.	22nd July	60 miles north-west of Cape Bougaroni.
24 –	H.M.S. 'Hotspur' and H.M.A.S. 'Vendetta'.	30th July	60 miles north of Ras el Melh.
25 –	Aircraft of 202 Squadron.	6th August	160 miles west-south-west of Cape St. Vincent.
26 –	Aircraft of 204 Group.	Night of 11th/12th August	Bardia Harbour.
27 –	H.M.S. 'Peony'.	7th October	Off Sidon.
28 –	Aircraft of 203 Squadron.	15th October	50 miles west-south-west of Kavo Krio (Crete).
29 –	Aircraft of 39 Squadron.	19th October	140 miles north of Bomba.
30 –	H.M.S. 'Gorleston'	1st November	830 miles west of Ushant.
31 –	Aircraft of 203 Squadron.	25th November	130 miles west of Crete.

* See also Part F, No. 4.
†See also Part F, No. 23.

PART L
Japanese U-boats known sunk
1942

1	–	*Circumstances unknown.*	Before 7th January	–
2	I.60	H.M.S. 'Jupiter'.	17th January	Western end of Sunda Strait.
3	–	H.M.A.S. 'Deloraine' and U.S.S. 'Edsall'.	20th January	60 miles west of Darwin.
4	–	Possibly U.S.S. 'Drayton'.	25th January	Near Pearl Harbour.
5	–	*Circumstances unknown.*	Before 20th May	–
6	–	*Circumstances unknown.*	Before 20th May	–

THE U-BOAT OFFENSIVE

(a) REVIEW FOR MAY

In the middle of this month coastal convoys between Hampton Roads and Key West were instituted and an immediate effect was apparent. During the first half of the month U-boats sank a considerable tonnage off Cape Hatteras and in Florida Strait, but in the latter half scarcely showed themselves off the coasts of Virginia and Florida. Logically enough in pursuit of easy prey, the U-boats sought out the remaining soft spots where traffic had to pass through focal areas and operated actively off the mouth of the Mississippi and in the Yucatan Channel between Cuba and Nicaragua. Shipping casualties continued at a high rate, but some reassurance may be sought from the fact that at any rate until the end of May, though not for very much longer, the U-boats held off from escorted shipping.

It appears inevitable that the convoy system should be progressively extended until all important shipping routes can be afforded some measure of protection by escorts and organised air cover, but it is plain that, in proportion to the extension of the area so patrolled, the strength of escort available in any one place is thinned out and that the process of affording adequate protection universally is still far from completed. As the U-boats discover that wholly unprotected targets are becoming rarer, they will be the more ready, of necessity, to risk attacking lightly-protected convoys. Nevertheless their heyday in North American and West Indian waters is drawing to its end.

It is estimated that a considerable force of U-boats was again operating from Biscayan ports, the total number of U-boats based in them having further increased. Additional U-boats from new construction are thought to be coming out fairly constantly from Germany to the Bay north-about Scotland and it is plain that at present more boats must be entering operational service than are being sunk.

At the same time such a weight of effort was exerted against convoys between Iceland (c) and Russia as clearly implied the presence in northern Norwegian waters of some 20 U-boats. A fair amount of damage was caused by this northern group, including the loss of H.M.S. 'Edinburgh'.

One heavy and concerted attack on a convoy in the North Atlantic was carried out during the month. O.N.92 was the unlucky exception to the general statement that in recent months transatlantic convoys have enjoyed immunity from U-boat attack. Four or five U-boats were concerned and seven ships were sunk.

159

Convoy S.L.109 was also attacked near the Cape Verde Islands but, thanks to the excellent offensive measures employed by the escorts, only one ship was sunk.

At the end of the month there were indications of increasing U-boat strength in the Caribbean Sea and in the area north-east and north of Brazil; these areas may be expected to prove dangerous for some time to come.

(b) ESTIMATE OF U-BOATS OPERATING IN MAY

Week	Southward and westward of a line drawn from Belle Isle Strait to 44°N., 40°W., and thence along the fortieth meridian to Brazil (North and Central American Waters.)		Northward and eastward of a line drawn from Belle Isle Strait to 44°N., 40°W, and thence along the forty-fourth parallel to Cape Finisterre. (Cape Farewell – Iceland (c) – Western Approaches).		The North Atlantic Command. (The Southern part of the North Atlantic Ocean to 40°W.)		The South Atlantic eastward of the fortieth meridian.	
	German	Italian	German	Italian	German	Italian	German	Italian
4th-10th May	26	1	11	–	4	2	–	2
11th-17th May	24	1	12	–	7	2	–	2
18th-24th May	28	1	13	–	5	1	3	3
25th-21st May	26	–	19	–	5	1	3	4

(c) MERCHANT SHIPPING LOSSES

The figures of tonnage lost by U-boat attack during April have increased to approximately 413,000 gross tons since the last report was rendered. Compared with this tonnage the provisional figures for losses in May of approximately 588,000 gross tons show an appreciable increase over April; it is, in fact, the peak figure for sinkings by U-boat for the present war.

The following table gives the losses due to U-boats during the past twelve months classified according to areas:-

	Atlantic				Mediterranean		Indian Ocean, Far East and Pacific		Elsewhere (including North Sea and Barentz Sea)		Total	
	North		South									
	No.	G.T.	No.	G.T.	No.	G.T.	No.	G.T.	No.	G.T.	No.	G.T.
1941												
June	56	294	–	–	–	–	–	–	–	–	56	291
July	22	94	–	–	–	–	–	–	–	–	22	94
August	23	80	–	–	–	–	–	–	–	–	23	80
September	49	186	2	16	3	3	–	–	–	–	54	205
October	27	141	1	5	2	2	–	–	1	3	31	151
November	10	50	1	5	1	7	–	–	–	–	12	62
December	8	35	1	6	7	27	8	38	–	–	24	106
1942												
January	41	256	–	–	–	–	12	50	–	–	53	306
February	67	399	–	–	–	–	6	25	–	–	73	424
March	83	491	–	–	–	–	7	28	2	11	92	530

April	57	338	3	17	2	7	5	32	3	19	70	413
May	115	558	1	5	1	4	2	12	2	9	121	588
(provisional)												

Note – Tonnage is given in thousands of gross tons.)

As the table shows, the bulk of the losses again occurred in the North Atlantic area where the U-boats were particularly active throughout the month.

The following table gives the distribution of the losses by U-boat over the month divided into three periods of approximately ten days:-

	British		Foreign		Total	
Period of month						
	No.	Gross Tons	No.	Gross Tons	No.	Gross Tons
1st-10th May	11	58,357	26	119,524	37	177,881
11th-20th May	16	89,987	38	191,610	54	281,597
21st-31st May	11	39,415	19	89,486	30	128,901
	38	187,759	83	400,620	121	588,379

This table shows that the losses were consistently heavy throughout the period, but that the heaviest sinkings occurred in the middle of the month between 11th and 20th.

As regards the foreign tonnage referred to above, the U.S.A. suffered the loss of 42 ships aggregating 215,566 gross tons; Norway 11 ships of 56,244 gross tons; Panama six ships of 35,762 gross tons; the Netherlands seven ships of 25,734 gross tons; Honduras three ships of 9,740 gross tons; Mexico two ships of 10,067 tons; Brazil two ships of 11,688 gross tons; Sweden two ships of 10,220 gross tons. Russia, Belgium, Yugo-Slavia, Latvia, Nicaragua and Dominica each lost one ship. Incidentally, the sinking of the two Mexican ships brought that country into the war on the side of the United Nations.

As for tanker losses, the total of 28 vessels so far recorded was slightly higher than in April but lower than the March figure of 31. Six British tankers were sunk, twelve American, three Panamanian, five Norwegian and two Mexican.

The following table gives losses in convoy by U-boat compared with total losses by U-boat during the last six months:-

Month	Total sunk by U-boat		Sunk in Convoy by U-boat		Remainder		Proportion of Tonnage Sunk which was in Convoy
	No.	Tons	No.	Tons	No.	Tons	Per cent
December	24	106	5	21	19	85	20
January	53	306	2	12	51	294	4
February	73	424	7	42	66	382	10
March	92	530	2	11	90	519	2
April	70	413	3	19	67	394	5
May (provisional)	121	588	11	55	110	533	9

(Note – Tonnage is given in thousand gross tons.)

The proportion of tonnage sunk in convoy by U-boat showed a slight upward tendency. Two attacks were made on Sierra Leone Convoys, S.L.109 being attacked on 12th May, when one ship was lost, and O.S.28 on 21st May. Two ships of the latter convoy were sunk – (one being a Royal Fleet Auxiliary is not included in the figures for mercantile losses).

O.N. convoys suffered rather heavily; O.N.92 was attacked on the night of 11th May and lost five ships, two more being sunk on the following night when the attack was resumed. One straggler from O.N.89 was also sunk on 3rd May.

A P.Q. convoy to North Russia was heavily and continuously attacked with torpedoes and bombs from 25th to 27th May and lost seven ships, one of which was attributed to U-boats. One ship was also lost by U-boat attack from Convoy Q.P.11 on 1st May.

As against the above losses, it is satisfactory to record that 536 ships arrived in United Kingdom ports in twenty ocean convoys with the loss of only one ship – the vessel lost in the Sierra Leone convoy mentioned above.

The introduction during May of convoys by the United States Navy between Key West and Hampton Roads and vice versa, and convoys with British escorts, mainly for tankers, between Halifax and Trinidad and Aruba – Curacao to Trinidad and reverse should tend to lessen the losses, particularly of tankers, in the Western Atlantic and Caribbean areas.

As I had previously discussed with Commander English, a confidential memo on the 'Development of Convoys and Escort Forces in the Western Approaches' had been prepared by me for the Commander, Inshore Patrol. His acknowledgment appears on the following page.

The Anti-Submarine Warfare Division reporting on 'The U-boat Offensive' commenced the review for May (see p. 143) with the announcement: 'In the middle of this month coastal convoys between Hampton Roads and Key West were instituted and an immediate effect was apparent.'

Commander English, making a social call, remarked over his pink gin: 'It seems that you fellows will be getting the coastal convoys you have been demanding. You have been joined by the tanker operators refusing to sail any more tankers up from the Gulf until they get coastal convoys.

'Warwick, you will be getting orders to attend the first coastal convoy conference at Ninety Church Street, New York. As the senior officer of the escort group made up of US Coast Guard cutters you will brief the masters of the merchant ships. There are ships bound for Baltimore and Philadelphia that will break off for protected anchorages in Delaware and Chesapeake Bays. The remainder, together with a US Navy destroyer, are bound for Norfolk, Newport News and Hampton Roads.'

'That's good news, sir! Now the U-boats must run the gauntlet of our asdics to make their attacks.'

'The other good news for you, Warwick, is that you won't have to pay on

Really Not Required

Headquarters of the
Commander Inshore Patrol
Third Naval District

Federal Office Building, 90 Church Street
New York, N.Y

From: The Commander, Inshore Patrol

To: The Commanding Officer, H.M.S ST LOMAN

Subject: Receipt of your Confidential Memo on the
             Development of Convoys and Escort Forces
             in the Western Approaches.

Reference: Subject of Memo dated May 1st 1942.

1.   This is to acknowledge receipt of the
reference which is being forwarded to the Commandant,
Third Naval District, 90 Church Street, New York.
Prior to forwarding this paper it was shown to the
Convoy Officer of the Eastern Sea Frontier who made
several copies for his own use.

2.   The paper has been read with interest
by all who have seen it so far, and I am sure it will
be a valuable contribution to anti-submarine warfare
in the U.S. Atlantic Coast Area.

H.M. JENSEN

Copy to: CESF
         ComThree (with copy of report)
         Comdr. English

the Staten Island ferries any more. Seems that the mayor was informed of the discrepancy regarding Allied service personnel.'

'That's right, sir, I had a note from "the Little Flower", as New Yorkers call the Mayor of New York City, Fiorello La Guardia. He seems to be a political executive sincerely concerned with his little people. You may recall that in the recent newspaper strike he was reading the comics over the radio to his city's children so that they could keep up with their favourite characters.'

'You mean that you wrote to him, Warwick?'

'Why yes! The hands expected the skipper to do something about it. The mayor seemed to be an understanding and very approachable type. So I mentioned that on the municipal buses running between Greenock and Gourock, the "clippies" should not accept fares from Allied servicemen, except when a girlfriend was with them. Seems that he got the reference right, sir.'

'Good God, Warwick! You are as bad as these Americans who slap me on the back the first time we meet, and insist on taking me out to lunch, when I really don't want to go, and can't very well refuse!'

'You and your American methods! I've been told that before in peacetime marketing, sir, but the important thing is to get the job done.'

As predicted by Commander English, I was ordered to attend the southbound convoy conference at 90 Church Street, New York, as senior officer of the escort group consisting of four small Coast Guard cutters and a US navy destroyer on passage to Norfolk, Virginia.

Prior to the conference, I took the destroyer commander aside and said: 'Sir, you are a senior commander in the US Navy, so you should take over from me as the senior officer of this escort group.'

'No, sir!' he replied, 'you have two years' active duty in anti-submarine and convoy escort operations. We have got to learn, and learn fast! The best and fastest way I can learn is to be under your orders.'

Some time later I related this exchange to Commander English, concluding with a question: 'Sir, these Americans have the right attitude. Now, would you put yourself under the orders of a lieutenant of another navy, admitting that you lacked his operational experience? I think you would have bluffed it through.'

'Yes, Warwick, you are right.'

After I had outlined the convoy escort procedures to the assembled masters of the dozen merchant ships of various nationalities, the Captain of a British ship drew me aside:

'You are British?'

'Yes, sir!'

'In command of a British Navy escort ship and the senior officer of this escort group of US Navy ships?'

'Yes, sir!'

'Then why don't we hear about this instead of just those over-age, four-stacker destroyers being lent to us?'

'That's a good question, Captain! The silence may be due to the political situation in the US Congress. The Secretary of the US Navy has been asked just how and why US shipping has been unprotected from German U-boats operating off the Eastern Sea Frontier. The announcement that twenty-six British Navy escort ships, manned by trained and experienced officers and men have now been assigned to the US Navy to deal with the U-boat situation, is hardly desirable publicity for the US Navy Department.'

At daylight next morning, the convoy formed into two columns. I assigned the destroyer the forward screening position with *St Loman* on the port or seaward side, and the Coast Guard cutters on either beam and the convoy flanks.

On arrival at Hampton Roads the Coast Guard cutters went to their base in Norfolk, and the *St Loman* to the Newport News coal tips for topping up her bunkers.

A northbound convoy was forming, and the Norfolk convoy officer attending the convoy conference warned me that the masters of American ships were rather independent.

'I don't anticipate any problems,' I replied. 'We have had American ships in our North Atlantic convoys.'

'That's so, but the ships of the commodore and vice-commodore are fifteen-knot cargo vessels, whereas the rest are eight- and ten-knot ships making a convoy speed of about eight knots. The masters of those fast ships are not going to care about being delayed in making New York!'

The next morning the convoy formed up in two columns and was headed north with the two 15-knot ships leading each of the two columns. The four Coast Guard cutters were assigned as previously with *St Loman* on the starboard or seaward bow of the convoy columns making 8 knots, plus the additional flow of the Gulf Stream.

Then, as if the two 15-knot leaders had looked across at each other and said: 'The hell with crawling along at eight knots! Let's go full pelt to New York,' off went the commodore and vice-commodore ships. The flashing of *St Loman*'s signal lamp was disregarded. These were two independent American masters! *St Loman* could just about make 9 knots on the clinker-forming coal obtained in Newport News.

'Jonesy, get your four-inch gun's crew up and load with star shell. Ready?

Now put a star shell across the bows of both of those ships. It will make a pretty firework without the risk of putting a hole in their hulls by getting too close.'

Andy Morrison, the gunner, put two star shell bursts at a little over masthead height and about two hundred yards ahead of each ship. Both the merchant ships stopped engines and hove to. *St Loman* drew abeam of the commodore and vice commodore, and on her loud hailer made the polite request: 'Would you please take up your correct stations in the convoy?'

'Yes, sir!'

Without further incident the convoy made New York, and I docked at our Staten Island berth. The next morning, I went to the base for debriefing: 'What was the weather like, Commander?'

'It was a little bumpy.'

'Now, Commander, that's carrying the British understatement too far! Our Coast Guard cutters said it was the worst weather in the past five years.'

'Well, compared to winter in the North Atlantic, it was just a little bumpy for my ship.'

'Did you have any problems on the way north?'

'No, sir, nothing of consequence!'

'I have news for you! The word has gone out – don't fool with these British escort ships, or they'll shoot you up!'

Commander English came on board at noon with the request for Able Seaman Wright to be transferred to UK. This was 'Darkie Wright', as his shipmates referred to him. His father was a West Indian seaman and his mother a Hull woman. In England there was no particular problem with his going to the local pubs with his shipmates. New York was different, so 'Darkie' Wright was returning to the UK.

I asked Ossie to tell the coxswain, Pym Grace, that 'Darkie' Wright was to be vittled out to Saker II and to bring him up to my cabin so I could wish him well and express my regret for the loss to *St Loman* of a good able seaman.

When Wright left, Grace mentioned that Seaman McGovern had requested seeing me on a personal matter, and this seemed as good a time as any. Andrew McGovern was a young fisherman from Granton, a small fishing port on the Firth of Forth. Handing me a letter in an envelope he said, 'I wished to see you, skipper, about this letter I just received from my wife, and to get your advice as to what I might do.'

It seemed from her letter that McGovern's wife had a brief affair with another man in Granton. She had been lonely, missing her husband, and had made a mistake which she now regretted and wished had never happened, as she did truly love him. This was why she was telling about it and wanting to know if he wished to break up their marriage because of it.

'Granton is a small port, McGovern. I expect that everyone tends to know all about everybody's affairs. If your wife had not told you, then sure enough some busybody would have made it their business to let you know about the affair.'

'That's right, skipper! Most people in Granton know each other.'

'McGovern, this is something that a chaplain should advise you about. In the UK I would give you compassionate leave in all probability, but we are on foreign service. Now, tell me, do you love your wife enough to forgive her mistake and keep your marriage intact?' I hoped I was saying the right thing.

'Yes, skipper, and I do truly need and love her,' he assured me.

'Then here's the all important matter. Can you truly forgive and really forget this one mistake, or might it rankle always in the back of your mind and memory so that you might bring up this one infidelity at some future time?'

'Skipper, I can forgive, and will do that!'

'You asked me for my advice, McGovern, so I suggest that you write to your wife to tell her in your own words that you understand her indiscretion because you are missing and loving her very much and need and want her as your wife, as always. Now here is your wife's letter. You'll need it to reply!'

I was thoughtful for a while after McGovern left my cabin. Then I found the *St Loman*'s crew list with the addresses and names of the next of kin, and addressed a memorandum to Mrs McGovern:

From: The Commanding Officer, HMS *St Loman*
To: Mrs Andrew McGovern

Your husband asked me to see him on a personal matter. He gave me your letter to read and asked my advice. I told him that I was not qualified to advise on your marital affairs. Being on foreign service, he would understand that compassionate leave could not be granted, as I might have been able to do when based in the UK. I asked Andrew if his love for you would enable him to really forgive and completely forget your indiscretion, of which he may soon learn from some neighbour or friend. Andrew replied that he wished to remain happily married and could and would do as I had suggested.

While your family affairs are no business of a ship's captain, the health, happiness, and fighting heart of every man is very much his concern, and an essential duty.

One miserable and unhappy man with no heart in him, as Andrew is at this time, can infect others in a small, happy ship's company.

You have a duty to put back the heart and happiness that Andrew is now lacking. He is a good fighting man or I would not be writing this confidential memorandum.

The British A/S trawlers based on Staten Island were the coastal convoy escort commander's with four or more Coast Guard cutters under his orders and running north and south between Hampton Roads and New York. Other groups of A/S trawlers operating from Norfolk, Morehead City and Charleston provided similar anti-submarine escort for the other sections of the Eastern Sea Frontier to and from Key West.

As a result, the U-boats began to seek easier, unprotected targets in the Gulf and Caribbean creating the need for the later assignment of 10 British corvettes to this area.

An isolated experiment for minelaying by U-boats was experienced off Norfolk when magnet/acoustic mines were laid in the swept channel. The first indication was a mine being set off on the day before a convoy sailed to New York. As *St Loman* was leading the starboard column out of the swept channel, I had ordered all hands on deck wearing their lifejackets, the exceptions being the duty engineman and stokers, until *St Loman* cleared the swept channel.

Wearing lifejackets was not customary and 7 a.m. was time for breakfast. I could hear some muffled grumblings about having to be up on deck wearing a lifejacket and not getting breakfast. There was a dull explosion astern of the *St Loman* as a rusted cargo carrier leading the column stopped and slowly began to settle into the water while the crew lowered the boats to abandon ship. All hands were clear with the exception of two stokers who came up from below as their ship began to capsize and float bottom upwards. Nonchalantly, they walked up the ship's side as she slowly rolled over and then stood upright waiting for the nearest Coast Guard cutter to take them off.

I picked up the loud hailer microphone: 'Those of you grumbling about the old man making you wear your lifejackets on the upper decks and being late for breakfast can now see the reason for it!'

German mines were usually set to avoid being set off by minesweepers by not being triggered until several passes had been made by a sweeper or target.

The convoy continued without further incident taking an inshore course much to the dismay of three heavily loaded tankers and a British passenger ship converted for troopship duty in the Norfolk shipyards and now on passage to New York. Since these four ships were literally scraping their bottoms in the shallows despite the calm sea, I advised the commodore to set a course into the deeper waters from the 6-7 fathom line.

All went well until the late afternoon when, passing the Avalon Shoal off the New Jersey coast, the troopship rammed her bows into the shallow end of it. Fortunately, the three tankers passed clear, but the troopship remained stuck with her engines going astern.

A sea-going harbour tug in the convoy was signalled to join *St Loman* at the troopship, but we got no response from her. Using the loud hailer, I closed the nearest Coast Guard cutter: 'The troopship is aground. Tell the tug master that if his tug doesn't join us you can open fire on his ship.'

'Yes, sir!' came the delighted reply from the officer of the watch as his little ship boiled off to close the tug about 2,000 yards ahead. After a few minutes abeam, we saw the tug turning back to join us.

Fortunately, the sea was almost dead calm. Ossie had checked his tide tables to find that the tide was still rising. The tug was instructed to take a bow wire on the troopship's port side and, facing aft, to tow astern. *St Loman* took up the corresponding bow wire on the starboard side.

The chief officer on the forecastle head said that his soundings indicated that only the troopship's bow section was hard aground. The tug and *St Loman* pulled in unison as the troopship went full astern and with the help of the rising tide she finally slid off the Avalon Shoal into deep water. Towing wires were cast off and all ships resumed their stations in the northbound convoy. 'Nae bather at all!' observed 2nd Engineman McCullam, coming up to spit over the side.

The British public relations staff had arranged for the New York correspondent for Lord Beaverbrook's London *Daily Express* to make a convoy trip on the *St Loman*, and I was to meet him at his apartment in Manhattan that evening and bring him down to the ship to sail with the early morning convoy.

At the Thompson apartment I was met by Dixie Tighe, a well-known American newspaper correspondent in her own right, who was sporting a femme fatale negligee, 4-inch heels and actively gesticulating with a foot-long silver cigarette holder.

Following a round of drinks, and after my promising Dixie to return her husband safely from his convoy reporting assignment, Thompson and I left for an evening at the Barberry Room, a nightclub frequented by newspapermen. Here Moriaty and Manson were holding a table for us.

An informed onlooker might have seen us as an incongruous group. The New York newspaper correspondent for a major British daily newspaper, the well-respected music critic for the *New York Times*, a young British naval officer, and a former New York speak-easy operator, now the owner of these glittering four-floor-to-ceilinged mirrored walls that enclosed the night spot and reflected an endless impression of limitless hospitality.

'We will make you an honorary member of the MTM Club, Moriaty Thompson Manson,' said Moriaty. 'Every so often these young girls hit New York to make it as top models and toasts of the town, then after a year or two they fade away. When they are in vogue, just to be seen with them at a lunch or dinner will command a fee of several hundred dollars. Now we have a syndicate on one young lady, who, while no longer up in that top flight, is still very charming and decorative. We invite her to join us from time to time, at our expense. She may be in this evening.'

'Unfortunately Tommy and I have an early morning sailing date, so I'm afraid we shall miss her, as we have to make the Staten Island ferry. Another time perhaps, and a future pleasure to come,' I reluctantly replied.

It was a short walk from the Staten Island ferry terminal to the US Navy pier where the British trawlers seemed to be quietly asleep in their berths, but a duty quartermaster appeared to give his salute as Thompson and I crossed the gangway.

Down in the wardroom we found Jonesy clad in his bathing trunks and cleaning the ship's .45 navy revolvers. Ossie and Pete were resting on their bunks and turned out for introduction to our guest and passenger. As we were due to sail shortly the inevitable 'pusser's kye' was being brewed in the galley. It made a new taste experience for Thompson when Alfie, the officers' steward, brought a steaming jug down to the wardroom.

Jimmy Dell, chief engineman, knocked on the wardroom door to announce that he had a head of steam, followed by Pym Grace, coxswain, to report that all hands were aboard. I introduced them to the New York correspondent of the London *Daily Express*, requested them to make Thompson welcome, and take him around the ship to visit the seamen, stokers, and petty officers in their quarters. Thompson would be interested in their varied experiences in the Norwegian operations, the Dunkirk evacuation, British Channel patrols, and North Atlantic convoys. There were many tales to be told.

The duty watch had quietly cast off fore and aft, leaving the sole wire back-spring. With the single screw going astern *St Loman*'s bows would be swung out into the dock. Ossie, now on the bridge, was initiating this operation, as I took Thompson up to my cabin and told him to make use of my bunk and bathroom as his own.

I went up to join Ossie on the bridge and ordered the back-spring let go by Leading Seaman Cuthbert, who tossed it off the bollard and jumped aboard. At slow ahead *St Loman* cleared the dock to enter New York Bay joining the dim shapes of merchant ships now getting under weigh, making dim, slow-moving shapes in the early light of dawn. 'Can you see anything, skipper? I can't see a damn thing!'

'It's all right, Ossie. I have cat's eyes!'

At the convoy conference, the master of an American merchant ship had complained of the apparent compulsory pilotage when entering the Delaware Bay area. 'The British escort heads the column and leads the way into the protected anchorage in Delaware Bay. Here the pilot vessel is anchored and then pilots come aboard who just direct us where to drop anchor!' he grumbled. It was apparent that the pilot vessel was not taking chances from a U-boat torpedo.

This proved to be a short trip and uneventful for our guest reporter, as all the ships in this convoy were bound for Philadelphia and Baltimore, anchoring in Delaware Bay until their berths came available. Next morning five merchant ships were escorted from the Delaware Bay anchorage to New York.

The sun shone every day with blue skies and calm seas. Thompson enjoyed himself listening to the sailors' yarns, and as an honorary crew member was qualified for his 11 a.m. tot of 'Nelson's blood' at the midday 'up spirits'. The navy nickname for the sailor's rum issue goes back to the Battle of Trafalgar, where legend has it that the body of the great admiral, stricken by a French sharpshooter firing from the mast of an adversary locked alongside, was brought back to England preserved in a cask of navy rum. On arrival at Portsmouth the cask was opened to find the well-preserved naval hero inside, but the cask to be completely dry of any rum. The seamen of HMS *Victory* had been able to siphon it out using straws from their mattresses during the voyage home.

On the following early morning convoy sailing from New York, Ossie and I returned from a quiet social evening with some new American friends at their New York apartment to find Jonesy in the wardroom being entertained by four journalists, each of whom had brought a bottle of Scotch whisky.

One of them, Rader Winget, introduced his group: 'Skipper, you have here the worldwide press association coverage offered by Reuters, Associated Press, United Press, and the Press Association. We will inform the world press of the coastal convoys now being escorted by British A/S ships assigned to the US Navy.'

'Mr Winget,' I replied, 'the officers and men of HMS *St Loman* are most flattered and appreciative of your group's selection of our ship as your medium for obtaining first-hand information and experience. You and your associates will be free to ask any questions and to talk freely with all and any members of this ship's company. The hospitality that you have brought, while most welcome, is not further required. You are now our guests. It is fortunate that our assignment to the US Navy does not include their ban on the carriage and consumption of hard liquor. Thus from now onwards the drinks will be on us!

'Now as to sleeping quarters, there will be a duty officer's bunk to be kept warm, and the wardroom settee with adequate blankets. Then in my captain's cabin is another settee and a bunk which I do not use when at sea as I find sleeping on the bridge quite adequate. You might wish to flip coins to decide who gets what and where. Breakfast will be around eight a.m. when the ship should be south of the Ambrose light vessel after sunrise.

'Sleep well, gentlemen, and excuse us, as we must take the ship to sea. See you on deck at daylight?'

At daylight we were joined by our four Coast Guard cutters, and later on the navy blimp appeared from Lakehurst, New Jersey. Two bodies crawled out of the wardroom hatchway, to be joined by the other two from my cabin under the wheelhouse. They climbed up to the bridge to be revived by boiling mugs of 'pusser's kye'.

During the next two days our guests were strictly business. Ossie reported them diving down into the seamen's mess decks, and then visiting the petty officers quarters aft, followed by hectic sessions on the wardroom typewriter, a salvage souvenir from the tanker *Diala* encountered on passage to St John's, Newfoundland.

As an entertainment and instructional benefit for our journalist guests, Ossie selected the location of a small wreck from the US Coast Guard records. Our asdic operator obtained a good sounding echo, and practice action stations for a U-boat attack were carried out by Lt Pete Willis who dropped one depth charge on the target wreck set to 50 ft. This produced a most gratifying explosion accompanied by a rising mushroom-shaped boil of seawater.

Sharing his headset, Pete provided each of the four journalists with a hearing of the actual 'ping' of the asdic contact. This would have compared realistically with that from a U-boat 'playing possum' on the ocean floor.

Shortly after the depth-charge explosion subsided four or five large conger eels floated to the surface to be joined by a small shoal of herring-sized fish called 'menhaden' from an American Indian word translating as 'they fertilize'. The only suitable uses for them are for making oil and fertilizer as the fish are a mass of small bones: a worthwhile catch for local fishermen.

Rader Winget was standing next to me on the bridge. I told him: 'A few weeks ago, Rader, we would not have let you and your associates listen to the reverberations and echoes from asdic contacts, as in the UK this would have been regarded as "Top Secret", but I listened to a radio station "soap opera" in which the captain of a Coast Guard cutter, and the unpopular lover of the Commandant's only daughter, made a successful attack on a U-boat. All the asdic sounds which you have heard from our sonar gear were broadcast on the radio. It was fantastically correct!

'Shortly afterwards, Lieutenants Dodwell and Jones visited the CBS studios in Manhattan with the cast of "Young Doctor Kildare" and asked the effects staff about the Coast Guard feature.'

'Did you find it to be realistic? The Coast Guard were very cooperative indeed!' was the response. So much for security between the two navies!

The London *Daily Express* carried a feature page by their New York correspondent, C.V.R. Thompson, headlined: 'My trawler has five stars'.

Unfortunately, from my point of view, Thompson had made a human interest embellishment in writing, 'On entering the wardroom, I found the commander in his seagoing attire of bathing trunks and a .45 revolver.' With the approach of cold weather, this gave rise to *St Loman* being greeted with Aldis lamps flashing, 'It's getting a little cold for the bathing trunks and .45.'

Rader Winget met Ossie and I a couple of weeks after his trip and was most apologetic. 'I have to eat my words boasting about the power of the media coverage by the four major press associations, as the US Navy in New York are making the publication of my stories and those of my associates very difficult for any publications circulating in the United States. As Tommy Thompson has succeeded in getting into some West Coast papers, we are hoping to make a breakthrough.'

CHAPTER XIII

Spring and summer passed on the Eastern Sea Frontier with no loses due to the vigilance of the coastal convoy escorts forcing U-boat commanders to move their theatre of operations down to the Gulf and the Carribean. This resulted in ten British corvettes being added to the original assignment of British A/S ships and their trained crews, enabling the US Navy to convoy the vital tanker traffic carrying oil and aircraft gasoline from the Gulf refinery ports to the UK.

In order to move their U-boats from their previous mid-Atlantic operational areas to the convoy assemblies off Halifax, Nova Scotia, and extend to the Gulf and Carribean, U-boat tankers and supply submarines were located about 340 miles north-west of Bermuda. This resupply of diesel fuel and essential stores enabled the U-boats to double their former operational sea time. While this stretched the endurance of U-boat crews to the limit, U-boat Command was able to initiate 'wolf pack' convoy attacks by several U-boats. Fortunately all communications between U-boat Command and their U-boats were being read by the Admiralty to enable very effective rerouting of Western Ocean convoys on passage in mid-Atlantic as U-boats reported their patrol line positions in the Atlantic.

In December 1941, U-boat Command had planned a multiple U-boat, or 'wolf pack', attack on Convoy HG.76 sailing from Gibraltar to Liverpool. This became a test of effectiveness between several U-boats and a strong convoy escort group, supplemented by an additional striking force and the 'pocket carrier' HMS *Audacity*, newly developed for convoy escort duty with Swordfish aircraft.

Four U-boats were sunk during the course of this engagement over several days resulting in no repeat of similar 'wolf pack' attacks being made on the Liverpool-Gibraltar convoy routes.

The following narrative histories of three U-boats sunk in the course of the attacks on Convoy HG.76 over the period 14 to 23 December 1941, taken from the A/S Warfare Division Journal of February 1942, are illustrative of the impact made on the attacking U-boats (see p. 175).

174

NARRATIVES

(a) THE HISTORIES OF THE THREE U-BOATS SUNK IN THE COURSE OF THE ATTACKS ON CONVOY H.G.76

'U 131'

'U 131' left the building yard at Bremen about the beginning of August, 1941, and proceeded to Kiel, which was her base during her trials. Generally nothing worth recording happens during trials but with 'U 131' it was different. A Russian submarine attacked her with a torpedo while she was engaged in tactical exercises; another U-boat fired a torpedo which passed directly underneath her; finally she became entangled in some anti-torpedo nets. It took her a day and a half to extricate herself and in her struggles she did some damage to her hydrophones which, to her ultimate undoing, were never properly repaired.

After about three months in the Baltic she returned to Kiel and took in stores and ammunition in preparation for her first war cruise. While the U-boat was at Kiel there was a heavy raid, which did a great deal of damage to the docks around her.

On the night before 'U 131' sailed upon her first and last war cruise, there was a party. An officer prisoner told how they danced until half past one in the morning and then moved on to a cellar for more drinking and dancing; deck chairs were provided there for those completely overcome. The climax of the evening was a 'pas seul' by the Captain in a woman's dress.

This may have had something to do with the accident which occurred the following afternoon, when 'U 131', northward bound, collided with a Norwegian freighter. Her stern was slightly stove in and she had to return to harbour for repairs, which took a week. Starting out again, this time without a party and without mishap, she sailed up the Norwegian coast as far north as the latitude of Bergen and then turned westward to enter the Atlantic.

There 'U 131' gained the solitary success of her short career and sank a merchant ship, claimed to be of 6,000 tons, with the expenditure of six torpedoes. In the course of her patrol she sighted two other ships, which were never in much peril from her. The first of these was sighted at night, fully illuminated; the U-boat had orders not to attack such a ship but nevertheless pursued her. The merchantman suddenly switched on three searchlights, which made the U-boat suspicious of a trap, and she gave up the chase.

Later on she came up with a 12,000 ton liner and gave chase. At the critical moment the port Diesel engine failed and long before it could be repaired, the quarry had passed out of sight.

The only other incidents of 'U 131's' patrol, apart from repeated crash dives to avoid the attention of patrolling aircraft, was the meeting with a lifeboat containing fifteen Portuguese, to whom the Germans gave provisions and cigarettes.

When the U-boat sailed from Kiel, on 17th November, they expected to reach Lorient in time for Christmas leave. About 12th December, orders came that they were to set a southerly course and make for the Gibraltar area. Hopes of Christmas ashore, all the more welcome by reason of the bad weather, were dashed and there was deep depression on board.

'U 434' and 'U 574'

'U 434' was built at Danzig and was one of the first U-boats constructed there to be sunk. Prisoners did not think highly of the workmanship of the firm which, incidentally, employs a number of Dutchmen. Soon after the U-boat sailed on her first war cruise it was found that the gearing for the venting and flooding valves was partly defective. Later on, overheating of one of the Diesels developed, due to the fact that a substitute had been used for the insulation of the water circulator.

On 26th October, 1941, 'U 434' left Kiel and proceeded northwards through the Kattegat. On rounding the Skaw she found herself in the teeth of a gale and ran for shelter. Putting in at Arendal, in Norway, she stayed there for three days and then crept along the coast to Kristiansand, where she remained for a few days before proceeding into the Atlantic.

Her mission was the same as that of 'U 574', a sister ship of HMS 'Graph', who followed her westwards about a fortnight later. They were to join with other U-boats to destroy a convoy then assembling off Halifax. The U-boats proceeded to within about twenty-four hours of Newfoundland – near enough for a rating to be able to test the difference between the temperature of the Gulf Stream and the surrounding area off Labrador – only to have the orders for the attack on the convoy cancelled. Acting under fresh instructions, the U-boats put about and at the end of November 'U 434' and 'U 574' were off the Azores.

Convoy O.S. 12 was in the neighbourhood of the Azores about this time and from Vice-Admiral U-boats came orders to attack it. The efforts of both U-boats ended in failure. 'U 434' made contact with the convoy and, while waiting for 'U 574' to join her, tried unsuccessfully to shadow it and lost it. 'U 574' was meanwhile trying, equally unsuccessfully, to attack it but found the escorts too much for her and gave it up as a bad job at the end of the second day. The convoy thus escaped the pair of them, but lost one ship to another U-boat.

On 2nd December the two U-boats met. The weather was too bad for them to get alongside and they communicated with each other by means of a life jacket towed by a light line. Orders for their future movements had been received by 'U 434' who passed them in this way to her sister ship.

'U 434' had by this time been at sea for about five weeks, 'U 574' for rather more than a fortnight. The latter boat, however, seems to have had the worst of the weather, particularly during the westward passage of the Atlantic, and the battering which she had received had caused the inexperienced ratings to suffer severely. Many of them were sick and ill.

Christmas was not far off and there were hopes that their cruise through the autumn storms would end at Lorient in time for leave at home. Instead, 'U 574' was to make for Vigo, take on stores sufficient for a six weeks' cruise and then return to her patrol area off the Azores. She was, of course, to return before the end of the six weeks if she had used all her torpedoes. When these orders came she had her original complement of fourteen torpedoes intact, 'U 434' had similar orders to repair to Vigo for stores and then continue her cruise; she too had all her torpedoes to fire.

The effect of these new orders on the crew of 'U 574' was described by a prisoner as 'deplorable', but their Captain, an able officer of the sternest character, suppressed their murmuring. When the U-boat was making use of territorial waters off the Azores and again off the coast of Portugal, he did, however, allow the crew, on two occasions, to come on deck to admire the view.

'U 434' had been at sea for longer than 'U 574' but the crew do not seem to have been so downcast at the new orders. Possibly the Captain thought it kinder not to make them known; at all events, when the boat turned northwards, most of the crew thought that their course was set for Lorient or St Nazaire.

The two U-boats followed each other up the Portuguese coast, with about a day between them. 'U 574' led the way, making not more than five knots, as oil was so low, that she could only use one Diesel. Both U-boats sighted ships sailing independently but, to their disgust, they were always neutrals.

'U 434' who was apparently off Lisbon on 9th December, came into contact with the strongly guarded Convoy O.G.77, but after two wearing days she lost it without getting any reward for her pains. Her Captain wanted to lie in wait for some British and American ships which he heard were loading cargoes in Lisbon, but the crew had been without bread and potatoes for five days and in face of their discontent he gave up the project. As it was, the two U-boats entered Vigo within a few hours of each other.

'U 574' entered the anchorage at about 2200 on 13th December, and made fast on the seaward side of a German merchantman, which was herself moored parallel with the shore. The Master of the supply ship, a man reputed to be in close touch with the Gestapo, would from time to time dress himself as a corn chandler and go through the length and breadth of Spain to buy provisions. On 27th November the supply ship had received three lorry loads of stores.

By 0330 'U 574' had completed her embarkation of oil and provisions and, casting off, put out to sea. Probably the U-boats passed each other, for 'U 434' reached the port in the early morning of the 14th. There was not time for her to complete her embarkation of supplies before daybreak and she therefore submerged alongside the supply ship. When it was dark, she rose to the surface and took on oil and stores, leaving the harbour before dawn, as 'U 574' had done.

The corn-chandling Master had been thorough in his scouring of impoverished Spain; a few hundred eggs, many pounds of onions, a couple of hundred oranges, as well as lemons, grapes and tangerines, bacon, asparagus, matches, wine, beer and soap, were among the provisions taken on board the U-boats.

Even these good things did not cheer the listless spirits in 'U 574', on her way to patrol the Western Approaches to the Straits of Gibraltar, in the hopes of catching a British cruiser, before returning to her area off the Azores. 'U 434', if one prisoner is to be believed, was now under orders to proceed to Genoa.

The Three U-boats in Contact with Convoy H.G.76

The memorable voyage of Convoy H.G.76 is fully described in the earlier pages of this report. The first U-boat to come in contact with it was 'U 131', who sighted it on 16th December. She directed the other two U-boats to the position; both of them were spectators of the action in which she was destroyed.

On the same night 'U 131', thanks to her hydrophones having been indifferently repaired after her struggles in the anti-torpedo net, rose to periscope depth to find herself in the middle of the convoy. As soon as he had recovered from his surprise, the Captain endeavoured to make something of his unexpected opportunities, but his chosen target, an escort vessel, foiled two or three of his manoeuvres, and deciding that discretion was the better part of valour, he submerged and allowed the convoy to pass over him.

At 0925 next morning, being then about twenty-two miles on the port beam, he surfaced for a quick look round and was spotted by one of HMS 'Audacity's' aircraft. The U-boat also saw the aircraft and knew that in a very short time the escort would be in full cry after her. She therefore dived. HM Ships 'Stork', 'Blankney', 'Exmoor', 'Stanley' and 'Pentstemon' formed the striking force, the sloop and the two 'Hunt' class destroyers being the first to reach the scene. While they were investigating various contacts, 'Pentstemon', coming up astern with 'Stanley', obtained a contract, which, though it gave rather different echoes, was attacked with a pattern of ten depth charges.

'U 131' was the object of this attack and three of the charges were very close. A large quantity of water came in aft and the U-boat, lying at an angle of nearly 40°, began to sink. Oil poured into the Diesel room from a leaking tank and the electric motors were damaged, though not to the point of being unworkable. Fortunately for the crew the lights were not put out.

Down went the U-boat to a great depth. Under the tremendous pressure steel plates began to crack and paint peeled off in blisters. Just in time, the Captain managed to get the boat into some sort of trim. The tanks were blown and 'U 131' came to the surface with less than twenty pounds of pressure left. 'Stanley' sighted her and at once the pack were in full cry.

The U-boat had come up some ten miles from the destroyer and hoped to get away on the surface. Driving the damaged engines as hard as they could go, she steered away from the striking force. One of 'Audacity's' fighters joined in the pursuit and dived to machine gun the bridge but the Germans saw her coming and, manning their 2-cm. and 3.7-cm. guns, shot her down. The body of the pilot was afterwards recovered by 'Stork' and was buried at sea next day.

The destroyers were closing fast and, when the range was seven miles, they opened fire. The U-boat could not reply as her one effective gun was trained forward and, with shells straddling her, the order to scuttle was given. At 1330 she sank.

Ten miles away 'U 434' lay watching the action. She avoided the escorts who came within three miles of her and followed in pursuit of the convoy. At 0400 on the following morning she lost contact and the Captain, as he went below, told the Chief Quartermaster to steer what course he pleased. He kept a course of 030°, for two hours and then altered to 043°, which he held until he was relieved by the First Lieutenant. At 0800, as he was taking over, the latter picked up his telescope and sighted 'Stanley', 'Blankney', 'Exmoor' and 'Deptford' dead ahead. With the words: 'Quartermaster, your reckoning has justified itself – four destroyers,' he rang for full speed ahead.

When the range was three miles 'U 434' dived to periscope depth and fired a torpedo. As soon as she realised that it had missed, she went deeper. She had left a trail of oil and wake and this was observed by 'Stanley'. The destroyer, with her Asdics out of order, reduced speed and began to drop depth charges one by one in the form of a square round the position. She had completed three sides of the square when 'Blankney' came up, obtained contact and gave her the U-boat's range. She then dropped a fourteen charge pattern, which 'Blankney' followed with one of six charges.

'U 434' had barely begun her dive from periscope depth when the depth charges began to burst around her. The conning tower hatch was damaged almost at once and water began to pour into the control room. As depth charge after depth charge burst around her, the lights failed, the steering gear became useless, and more water began to come in forward. Such a shaking did the U-boat get that the stern torpedo went off of its own accord. The single gauge which remained intact showed that she was sinking rapidly.

Within a few seconds of utter disaster, the Captain gave the order to surface and, though the boat was by this time almost unmanageable, it struggled to the surface. At once both destroyers opened fire and 'Blankney' increased to ram. They need not have troubled; with the least possible delay, the Captain gave the orders to scuttle and abandon ship.

'U 574' had also watched the shooting down of 'Audacity's' fighter by 'U 131', but she did not stay to witness the destruction of the U-boat. She was herself sighted by 'Stanley' but dived in time to be out of the way of 'Blankney' and 'Exmoor' when they searched for her. After remaining submerged for the afternoon, she surfaced and sighted the convoy in the distance, but a rain squall obscured it almost at once. 'U 574' made for its estimated position but the appearance of a corvette caused her to dive and it was not until the following evening (18th December) that she was again in contact.

At dusk the U-boat began the pursuit of a large merchant ship. She was seen by 'Pentstemon' and an hour later, when she was manoeuvring into a position for firing her torpedoes, she sighted two corvettes steering towards her. Breaking off her attack, she escaped on the surface at high speed, diving when she had put the pursuing ships some distance behind her.

The U-boat was able to keep in touch with the convoy and in the early hours of the following morning, she closed it and, submerging, used her hydrophones to keep in contact with it. After about two hours, the Captain went to periscope depth but, being unable to see anything, he came to the surface. Some miscalculation had been made and the U-boat surfaced very close indeed to the convoy, too close for comfort in the opinion of some of the crew. The Captain was not a man to waste his opportunities, however fortuitous, and there were plenty of targets. A number of merchant ships were passing and behind them were 'Stork' and then 'Stanley', who sighted the U-boat. 'Stork' was moving fast and altered course at the critical moment; taking the destroyer as his target, the U-boat Captain fired a salvo of three torpedoes from a range of 1,200 yards. They hit and 'Stanley' blew up in a terrifying flash of flame, which 'set the sea on fire' and silhouetted 'U 574' against the night.

She turned away and endeavoured to escape at full speed on the surface but 'Stork' was hard on her heels and she had to dive. The sloop soon obtained contact and after a pattern of five charges had been dropped, a little late, she made a second attack, this time with ten charges.

This second pattern, which exploded immediately above the U-boat, was considered 'fatefully accurate'. It put both electric motors out of action and as a result of a short circuit, a small fire broke out in the Control Room. A group of compressed air bottles was shattered and a rib supporting the pressure hull fractured. A certain amount of water came in.

The Captain seemed careless of the fate of the U-boat and her crew. The Engineer Officer protested that the boat was doomed and that, if anyone was to come out alive, the order to surface must be given at once. The Captain, preferring the certainty of death to the risk of capture, was unmoved, until at last the Engineer Officer, who for several days had been suffering the agonies of an ulcerated stomach, burst out 'Either you leave the boat or I do. I cannot take any more responsibility.' The Captain then gave way and ordered the crew to put on their life-saving gear, and blew the tanks.

On coming up to the surface, 'U 574' found 'Stork' 200 yards away running in for a third attack. Star shells, 'Snowflake' and gunfire greeted her and the stubborn Captain soon had to give up his ideas of stealing away undetected. He gave orders to abandon ship. The Engineer Officer opened the valves to scuttle the U-boat and then, picking up his revolver, shot himself.

It is difficult adequately to describe the last act of this drama. The stage was brilliantly lit by 'Snowflake' and had for backcloth the intense darkness of that December night. A ship in the vicinity would have seen 'Stork' pursuing the U-boat at her full speed, the U-boat just within her turning circle, her guns' crews, unable to depress their guns enough to fire, shaking

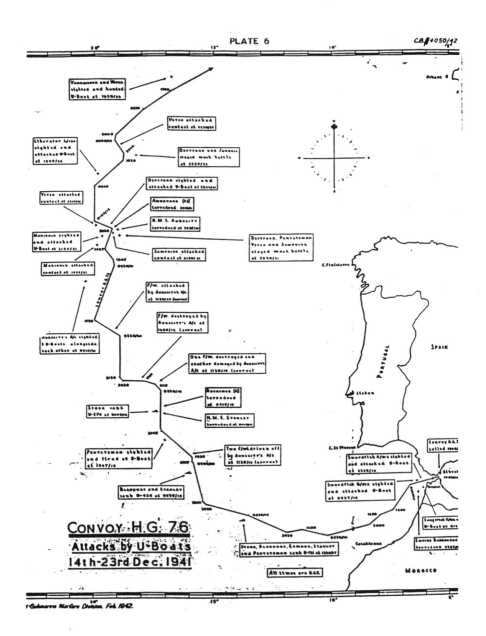

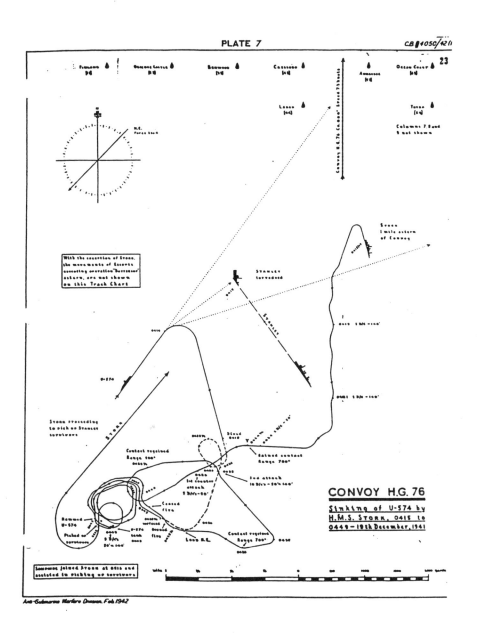

PLATE 7

CONVOY H.G. 76

Sinking of U-574 by H.M.S. STORK, 0415 to 0449 – 19th December, 1941

their fists and roaring curses at their enemies, who were sometimes only a few feet from them. After eleven minutes, in which 'Stork' made three complete circles, she caught 'U 574', rammed her, rode over her and finished her off with a pattern of depth charges.

A number of the crew abandoned ship during the chase but the Captain did not; he made no effort whatsoever to save himself and went down with his ship.

Convoy H.G.76 came into harbour on 23rd December. Thus it came about that some of the Germans had their wish and spent Christmas ashore after all.

(b) MONTHLY RETURN OF VESSELS CONVOYED AND LOSSES DUE TO ENEMY ACTION WHILST IN CONVOY

	No. of Ships Convoyed.			Total Ships Con-voyed for Month	Lost by Enemy Action			Total Lost for Neutral
	British	Allied	Neutral		British		Allied	
N. America and Canada outwards	178	93	7	78	1	–	–	1
Orfordness-Methil	725	158	12	895	3	–	–	3
Methil-Orfordness	588	109	9	706	2	–	–	2
Gibraltar outwards	26	3	–	29	–	–	–	–
Gibraltar homewards	10	2	–	12	–	–	–	–
Halifax homewards	108	61	6	175	–	–	–	–
Sydney, N.S., home-wards	68	51	3	122	–	–	–	–
Sierra Leone homewards	75	11	2	88	–	–	–	–
Sierra Leone outwards	98	24	2	124	–	–	–	–
Channel convoys	111	–	–	111	–	–	–	–
Oban to Methil	182	44	6	232	–	–	–	–
Methil to Oban	223	67	11	301	–	–	–	–
Belfast to Bristol Channel	116	42	10	168	–	–	–	
West Channel convoys	182	197	16	395	–	–	–	–
Archangel to U.K.	7	5	–	12	–	–	–	–
Milford Haven to Holyhead	26	20	4	50	–	–	–	–
Holyhead to Milford Haven	7	2	2	11	–	–	–	–
U.K. to Iceland	19	15	–	34	–	–	–	–
Iceland to U.K.	14	11	1	26	–	–	–	–
Totals	2,763	915	91	3,769	6	–	–	6

(c) ANALYSIS OF U-BOAT OPERATIONS IN THE VICINITY OF CONVOY H.G.76 14th-23rd DECEMBER, 1941

Note – The detailed reports and track charts forwarded by 'Stork' and the co-ordination of records by Captain (D), Liverpool, have proved of the greatest value in the production of this analysis.

Events Prior to the Sailing of Convoy H.G.76

The sailing of the Convoy was postponed as there were indications of a number of U-boats in the area west of Gibraltar.

During the fortnight commencing 26th November, a large number of attacks on U-boats were made by both surface vessels and aircraft. The available forces at Gibraltar had recently been strengthened by Hudson aircraft of 233 Squadron and also Swordfish aircraft of the Fleet Air Arm.

These naval aircraft led the way in a new form of offensive by attacking the U-boats at night, and several promising attacks were carried out.

In the second week of December many U-boats were still operating West of Gibraltar and Convoy O.G.77 was approaching with a normal escort of one Group. In the hopes of offensive action, the patrol in the Straits was temporarily lifted and the Escort Group thus released was sent out to reinforce the outward bound convoy. The convoy was apparently reported by 'U 434' off Lisbon but came through unmolested by the enemy and arrived at Gibraltar on 13th December.

It had been intended to sail Convoy H.G.76 on 15th December but owing to the congestion in the harbour caused by the arrival of the outward bound convoy, and also to the possibility of an air raid, F.O.C.N.A. ordered it to sail during the afternoon of 14th December.

'Empire Barracuda' and four tankers bound for the Middle East via the Cape sailed four hours later.

Particulars of Convoy H.G.76:-

Number of ships	32
Number of columns	9
Speed	7.3 knots
Commodore's ship	'Spero' (51)

Particulars of Escorts on Sailing:-

H.M.S. 'Exmoor'	H.M.S. 'Rhododendron'
H.M.S. 'Blankney'	H.M.S. 'Vetch'
H.M.S. 'Stanley'	H.M.S. 'Pentstemon'
H.M.S. 'Stork'	H.M.S. 'Marigold'
H.M.S. 'Black Swan'	H.M.S. 'Convolvulus'
H.M.S. 'Deptford'	H.M.S. 'La Malouine'
H.M.S. 'Fowey'	H.M.S. 'Carnation'
H.M.S. 'Samphire'	H.M.S. 'Jonquil'

H.M.S. 'Audacity'

Escorts left and joined the convoy during passage as follows:-

Date.	*Ship.*
1000/15	H.M.S. 'Carnation' left.
1330/15	H.M.S. 'Campion' joined.
0830/16	H.M.S. 'Hesperus' joined.
1350/16	H.M.S. 'Coltsfoot' joined.
1600/16	H.M.S. 'Campion' left.
1730/16	H.M. Ships 'Hesperus', 'Black Swan', 'La Malouine', 'Fowey' and 'Coltsfoot' left.
1100/18	H.M. Ships 'Exmoor' and 'Blankney' left.
1600/23	H.M. Ships 'Vanquisher' and 'Witch' joined.
0915/25	H.M.S. 'Volunteer' joined.

Attack on a U-boat by Swordfish Aircraft X/812

At 2325, 14th December, whilst 6½ miles on the starboard beam of the convoy, Swordfish X/812 obtained an A.S.V. contact at a range of 3½ miles. On investigation this was found to be a U-boat which was steering towards the convoy. Having circled twice to confirm its identity, the aircraft came up astern of the U-boat and dropped three depth charges, set to 25 and 50 ft., at 2330. The first two fell 80 ft. ahead, whilst the third fell 60 ft. on the starboard bow as the U-boat took evasive action to port. Unfortunately the Swordfish was not fitted with R/T and it was therefore difficult to inform the convoy's surface escort of the attack.

'Stork' (S.O.), who was stationed ahead of the convoy, had heard the depth charge explosions and saw two calcium lights about three miles ahead, but it was not until some time later that a report was received from the aircraft.

'Stork' carried out an A/S search but, finding nothing, detailed 'Deptford' and 'Rhododendron' to continue the hunt until 0400/15. Nothing further however, was seen.

It is to be noted that the U-boat was closing the convoy when sighted by the aircraft, and it was undoubtedly due to the prompt action taken that the convoy was not attacked.

Further Events During Night 14th-15th December

Shortly after midnight a signal was received from Admiralty stating 'D/F at 2130Z/14 indicates that a German U-boat has made a first sighting report of either H.G.76 or tankers escorted by "Wishart"' (Admy.'s 2350A/14.)

At 0135 Swordfish X/812 sighted another U-boat, some ten miles astern of the convoy, but no offensive action could be taken as the aircraft had dropped all its depth charges in the first attack. The U-boat dived as soon as the presence of the aircraft was realized.

The Sinking of 'Empire Barracuda'

The 'tanker convoy' had sailed from Gibraltar at about 2000/14 and the four ships had formed up in two columns.

The convoy was escorted by H.M.S. 'Wishart' and three corvettes, who were stationed ahead, astern and on either beam. When clear of the Straits, the convoy set a course of 250° and commenced zig-zag No. 11.

At 0305, 15th December, in position 35° 28' N., 06° 15' W., 'Empire Barracuda' (21) sighted two torpedoes approaching from the starboard beam. Before any avoiding action could

184

be taken, one torpedo struck forward and the other aft. Immediately after the explosions the conning tower of the U-boat was momentarily sighted about half a mile away on the starboard bow.

The ship began to sink rapidly and disappeared within ten minutes. While H.M.S. 'Coltsfoot' was picking up survivors, she obtained a doubtful contact and dropped depth charges. Having completed the rescue of the survivors she returned to Gibraltar.

The movements of the remainder of the escort are unknown, but it is believed that the convoy maintained its original course and continued its voyage without further incident.

Attack on a U-boat by Swordfish Aircraft B/812

At 0537/15 Swordfish B/812 sighted a U-boat in position 210° Cape Trafalgar 24'. Two depth charges set to 25 and 50 ft. were dropped about six seconds after the U-boat submerged. One fell on the forward edge of the swirl and the other 160 ft. ahead. No evidence of damage could be seen.

Events during 15th and 16th December

The Senior Pilot of 'Audacity' states: 'As only four aircraft were available, flying had to be kept to a minimum as, under conditions obtaining in "Audacity", there was always a bigger risk than in other carriers and our normal wastage had so far been about four aircraft per convoy trip. In consequence, aircraft were not normally flown off on A/S patrols unless there was a probability that U-boats were in the vicinity.'

Note – H.M.S. 'Audacity' was formerly a German merchant ship s.s. 'Hannover', 5,537 tons. She was intercepted and taken in prize by a Naval patrol in March, 1940. She had since been reconstructed and was the first auxiliary aircraft carrier to be commissioned.

Aircraft A/S patrols were carried out on 15th December as it was possible that the convoy had been reported, but nothing was sighted. No flying was done on 16th December as there was no indication that U-boats were in the neighbourhood.

After this date there were practically always U-boats or Focke-Wulfs in contact, so that flying was nearly continuous, although after 17th December, there were only three serviceable aircraft.

Taking advantage of the two days lull, the Commodore practised altering course by visual and sound signals and also emergency turns. These exercises proved invaluable later on, as throughout the period of attacks the convoy kept excellent order. One night when an attack took place, the convoy was in the middle of an 80° wheel, but the turn was completed in excellent order, according to the Commodore, 'just as if no attack was taking place.'

The Sinking of U 131*

As a result of U-boat warnings from both Admiralty and F.O.C.N.A. during the night of 16th/17th December, 'Stork' closed 'Audacity' before daylight on 17th and requested her to carry out an aircraft A/S search at dawn.

At 0925/17 an aircraft reported a U-boat on the port beam, 22 miles away. 'Stork' therefore set course for this position at full speed and ordered 'Blankney', 'Exmoor', 'Stanley' and 'Pentstemon' to do likewise.

* See page 178

'Blankney' arrived on the scene first and immediately commenced signalling to 'Stork' passing the following messages:- 'Several non-sub. echoes here,' 'Rattle effect,' 'Oil,' 'No contact'; at 1045 a doubtful contact was obtained which was attacked at 1057, with six charges set to 150 and 250 ft. Contact was then lost and not regained.

'Stork' was unable to confirm any of these reports except the first one. As soon as the depth charges had been dropped, 'Exmoor', 'Blankney' and 'Stork' formed up in line abreast 1-2 miles apart and commenced a sweep to the westward. 'Stork' believed that, as the U-boat had been shadowing the convoy on a westerly course, she would probably continue on this course even though forced to dive.

Meanwhile 'Stanley' and 'Pentstemon' were joining the hunt and at 1049 'Pentstemon' gained a firm contact at a range of 1,100 yards. After investigation, a deliberate attack was carried out at 1106 with ten charges set to 150 and 385 ft.

A poor contact was regained astern but this was lost at 1110. After a further search 'Stanley' and 'Pentstemon' set course to close 'Stork', who had ordered them to join if they were not in contact.

Having swept 12 miles to the westward, 'Stork' carried out two turns to port, thereby altering the direction of the sweep to 090° and transferring it in order to cover fresh ground to the south.

At 1247 'Stanley' reported an object on the horizon bearing 130° but this was immediately followed by 'U-boat on surface bearing 060°.' Course was at once altered towards and ships were ordered to proceed at utmost speed. In the ensuing chase the two 'Hunt' destroyers drew ahead, closely followed by 'Stanley'.

At 1307 a relief aircraft from 'Audacity' who had been ordered to attack with machine gun fire, was shot down by the U-boat.

The three destroyers opened fire at about seven miles range: the shooting of 'Exmoor' appearing to be particularly accurate. The U-boat fired a few rounds at 'Blankney' but sank at 1330, prisoners being picked up.

It appears that U 131 was damaged by 'Pentstemon's' attack and had later struggled to the surface.

Believing the object sighted on the horizon by 'Stanley' at 1247 to be a U-boat, 'Exmoor' and 'Blankney' were ordered to search while the other escorts rejoined the convoy.

Events during night 17th/18th December

During the afternoon Admiralty had signalled that the convoy was probably being shadowed by a U-boat (Admy's 1538A/17.)

The course of the convoy was therefore altered at 2200 to 350° and 'Stanley' was stationed on the outer screen, on the port quarter of the convoy.

No attack developed, however, during the night.

The Sinking of U 434*

At 0906/18 'Stanley' reported a U-boat six miles on the port quarter and 'Blankney', 'Deptford' and 'Exmoor' were ordered to assist in the hunt.

Meanwhile the course of the convoy, which had shortly before been altered to 310° was altered to 000°.

* See page 178

'Stanley', whose asdics had been out of action the whole trip, closed the U-boat at full speed and it dived when she was still three miles away.

When still about one mile away from the diving position, oil and wake were observed to starboard. 'Stanley' therefore reduced to 12 knots and commenced dropping single charges in the form of a square round the position. Three sides of the square had been completed and 19 depth charges dropped by the time 'Blankney' arrived on the scene at 0923. At 0929 'Blankney' gained a firm contact and when the range was 800 yards, speed was increased to 18 knots. Doppler became marked opening and strong hydrophone effect was heard. 'Blankney' states that the U-boat took violent avoiding action and that it passed down the port side about 50 yards away. A pattern of six charges was fired at 0934.

Contact was immediately regained and ranges and bearings were passed to 'Stanley', who fired a fourteen-charge pattern with deep settings.

'Blankney', going slow, was in to 600 yards by the time 'Stanley's' charges had all fired and she decided to attack at once before the U-boat Commander had time to recover from the previous attack. 'Blankney' therefore dropped a six-charge pattern with medium settings at 0942. Six minutes later, while the throwers were still being reloaded and Asdic contact held, U 434 surfaced 2,000 yards away. 'Blankney' increased speed and both destroyers opened fire. The U-boat swung stern on and in hitting it a glancing blow, 'Blankney' damaged her port side. A whaler was lowered and an attempt was made to board U 434, but it sank too quickly. Prisoners were picked up.

At 1100/18 'Blankney' and 'Exmoor' set course to return to Gibraltar, having taken part in the sinking of two U-boats.

During the forenoon two Focke-Wulfs were engaged by aircraft from 'Audacity', but unfortunately, guns in both the fighters jammed. Although both Focke-Wulfs got away, one of them is believed to have been damaged.

'Stork' remarks that the dusk A/S air search was carried out a little too early and revealed no U-boats. At 1847, 'Pentstemon', who was stationed six miles on the port beam of the convoy, sighted a U-boat bearing Red 60°, at a range of five miles. A report was made to the Senior Officer, who ordered 'Stanley' and 'Convolvulus' to join the hunt.

'Pentstemon' increased speed and altered towards, but found that the U-boat, who was steaming on the surface at high speed, was rapidly drawing further ahead. Fire was opened with the 4-in. gun; spotting, however, was difficult in the failing light. At 1920 'Pentstemon' commenced firing starshell, but the U-boat could not be seen.

'Stanley' and 'Convolvulus' had arrived by now and the former ordered an A/S sweep to be carried out. Nothing was seen or heard until 2049 when 'Convolvulus' reported torpedoes passing from port to starboard.

The three escorts illuminated the area but no contact was obtained. At 2107 and 2137 two depth charges were dropped by 'Pentstemon' on orders from 'Stanley'. Course was then set to rejoin the convoy.

Weather during night 18th/19th December

Wind	N.E. Force 3.
Weather	Fine but cloudy.
Sea	Slight swell.
Visibility	2-4 miles. No moon.

The Torpedoing of 'Stanley'

At 0345/19, 'Stanley', who was stationed astern of the convoy on the outer screen, reported by R/T 'U-boat in sight'. Having very little idea of her exact position, 'Stork' ordered her to indicate her position by illuminating, but 'Stanley' at about 0355 amended her signal to 'Torpedoes passed from astern'. In point of fact, at this time she was on the port quarter of the convoy.

'Stanley' had made her pendants twice by light, and 'Stork' was in the middle of replying, when at 0415 in position 38° 12' N., 17° 23' W., 'Stanley' was torpedoed, probably on her port side, and blew up in a sheet of flame several hundred feet high.

At the same time torpedoes were reported to have passed astern of 'Stork' and 'Largo' (44).

'Stork' remarks:- 'It appears likely that the U-boat which was being hunted earlier in the evening had followed the escorts back to the convoy on the surface. In future, when ships were rejoining the convoy at night, I always ordered them to use an indirect route.'

The Sinking of U 574*

As soon as 'Stanley' was torpedoed 'Stork' altered course to port and ordered '"Buttercup" astern'. (*See* Appendix 'B'.) She then proceeded at 15 knots, dropping single charges, and at 0424½ contact was gained, range 700 yards. 'Stork' states:- 'Movement was very slight and the U-boat's position suggested that she was waiting for a ship to stop and pick up 'Stanley's' survivors, thus providing her with another victim.'

The contact was immediately counter-attacked and five charges set to 50 ft. were fired at 0426. This pattern was fired nearly a minute late, as the depth-charge crews, with very little warning, had to change from the organisation of firing single charges to that of firing a pattern.

The explosion of this pattern affected the dynamo and contact was temporarily lost. Having opened the range 'Stork' turned to starboard and regained contact at 900 yards. The U-boat commenced moving rapidly right as the range closed, but 'Stork' made a large and rapid alteration to starboard and ten charges set to 50 and 140 ft. were fired at 0432. This attack appeared to be very accurate.

Again the dynamo gave trouble and contact was once more lost. On opening out, however, 'Stork' regained contact at a range of 700 yards. A third attack was commenced, but when the range had decreased to 500 yards strong hydrophone effect was heard and at 0438½ the U-boat surfaced 200 yards ahead.

Speed was increased in order to ram and a ten-charge pattern was set to 50 and 150 ft.

The Commanding Officer, 'Stork' states:- 'The ensuing chase lasted 11 minutes and I was surprised to find later by the plot, that "Stork" had turned three complete circles. The U-boat appeared to be turning continuously to port just inside "Stork's" turning circle at a speed only two or three knots less than the latter's best. I kept her illuminated with Snowflakes, which were quite invaluable in this unusual action. Some rounds of 4-in. were fired from the forward mountings until the guns could not be sufficiently depressed, after which the gun's crew were reduced to fist-shakings and roaring curses at an enemy who several times seemed to be a matter of a few feet away rather than yards.

'No men were seen to leave the U-boat, although they must in fact have done so, judging from the position in which prisoners were later picked up. Eventually at 0448 I managed to ram her just before the conning tower, from an angle of about 20° on her starboard quarter, and roll her over.

'She hung for a few seconds on the bow and again on the asdic dome and then scraped aft, where she was greeted by a ten-charge pattern at shallowest settings.'

'Stork' now proceeded to search for 'Stanley's' survivors and soon heard cries for help which sounded English. Five Germans were, however, picked up. She then set course for the wreck of 'Stanley'. So violent had been the explosion that there seemed little hope of there being any survivors. Cries were heard, however, and 25 men were picked up.

At 0528 'Stork' signalled by R/T:- '"Stanley" sunk by U-boat. U-boat sunk by "Stork".'

Movements of 'Samphire'
'Samphire' had been carrying out 'Operation "Buttercup" astern', when 'Stork' ordered her to close. Hoping to be in at the kill 'Samphire' increased to full speed.

At 0516 men were seen to be in the water and thinking them to be survivors from 'Stanley' both boats were lowered. At 0545, however, a signal was received from 'Stork' stating:' 'Search for "Stanley's" survivors, bearing 020° 1-2 miles, until 1000 and then rejoin'. On recalling the boats it was found that the 13 survivors picked up were all German.

The wreck of 'Stanley' was then closed and, although a number of dead bodies were seen in the water, only three survivors could be found.

Movements of the Convoy and the other Escorts
After the attack the convoy continued on its course while the remainder of the escort carried out 'Operation "Buttercup"' in accordance with 'Stork's' orders.

The Torpedoing of 'Ruckinge' (11)
At 0515, 19th December, in position 38° 20' N., 17° 15' W., 'Ruckinge' (11), leader of the port wing column, was struck by a torpedo on her starboard side amidships. Just before she was hit, a torpedo was sighted approaching from the starboard bow but too late to take any avoiding action. No rockets could be fired as the bridge was wrecked. The Master did not consider that this ship would sink immediately, but, as the escorts were busy attacking U-boats, he was afraid that the ship would probably be torpedoed again. The order was therefore given to abandon ship and both boats were lowered, being intended to return to the ship at daylight.

Movements of the Escort
All escorts remaining with the convoy appear to have carried out starshell searches but nothing was seen.

The Rescue of Survivors from 'Ruckinge'
'Finland' (13), rear ship in the column, observed the explosion and approached within half a cable of the sinking ship. Hailing brought no response, so 'Finland' cruised around in the vicinity and picked up 25 men from a lifeboat. It was discovered that another boat containing 14 persons had also left the ship. A further search was therefore carried out by 'Finland', but owing to the intense darkness nothing was found. At 0700, not considering it prudent to tarry any longer in an area which was believed to be infested with U-boats, 'Finland' proceeded at full speed and eventually rejoined the convoy at 1115.

At about 0800 'Stork' arrived at the wreck of 'Ruckinge' and discovered the missing boat. She ordered 'Samphire' to close as soon as she had completed searching for 'Stanley's'

189

survivors, while she herself set course to rejoin the convoy.

'Samphire' closed 'Ruckinge' at about 1030 and the First Lieutenant went on board. At 1132 a W/T message was received from 'Stork' with orders to sink the merchant ship and the boarding party was therefore recalled.

On his return the First Lieutenant stated that the ship had a 25° list to port which appeared to be increasing. He brought back the Confidential books which had been found on deck in a weighted bag. It appeared that they had been thrown from the bridge but, owing to the list, had fallen on deck.

As soon as the boarding party had returned 'Samphire' commenced shelling the wreck; this operation was watched at a respectful distance by a Focke-Wulf. At 1250 it was seen that 'Ruckinge' was slowly sinking and was on fire, so course was set for the convoy which was rejoined at 1413.

Events during 19th December

Soon after 1100 two Focke-Wulfs arrived in the vicinity of the convoy. The first one was soon set on fire and shot down by two fighters. In his report the Senior Pilot states: 'Hot return fire from the Focke-Wulf destroyed the Pilot's hood, passing through where his neck should have been. Fortunately he had got his neck near his boots just in time.'

'Stork' states: 'The aircraft presently returned leaving a very dead Wulf.'

The second Focke-Wulf was damaged but succeeded in escaping. 'Audacity' now only had three serviceable aircraft and the weather was such as to make solid cloud cover available. It was essential, therefore, to have two aircraft, one above and one below the clouds, for each Focke-Wulf.

At about 1600 another Focke-Wulf appeared, using different tactics – presumably in an attempt to avoid 'Audacity's R.D.F. It was sighted flying very low over the horizon, some ten miles ahead of the convoy.

Two Grumman Martlets shot down the Focke-Wulf by means of a combined quarter and head on attack. One fighter broke away a little too late and struck it a glancing blow with his port mainplane and tailwheel. On landing, several pieces of Focke-Wulf were discovered adhering to the Martlet.

Earlier in the afternoon another of 'Audacity's' aircraft sighted a U-boat some miles on the port beam of the convoy. 'Deptford', 'Marigold' and 'Convulvulus' were ordered to search, but they were unable to gain contact. On their return to the convoy just after dark, these ships were mistaken for a U-boat by one of the escort. Starshell and Snowflake were fired but this period of illumination did not prevent the remainder of the night from passing peacefully.

Events during 20th December

The routine Focke-Wulf visit was duly paid during the afternoon. The Senior Pilot states: 'We had a long chase with one Martlet above the cloud layer and one below. After 45 miles he peeped out of the cloud and was at once pounced on. He therefore returned to his cloud at once and went home.'

Both Martlets had eventful dogwatch patrols. The first one sighted a Portuguese ship which opened fire and then a Vichy French four-engined flying-boat. The second fighter sighted and reported two U-boats ahead of the convoy.

The convoy course was altered 80° to starboard to 020° at 1730. This course was maintained throughout the night. 'Stork' decided not to send a striking force, because it was too late in the day, too far and there was nothing fast enough to send. The aircraft were therefore ordered to make the U-boats dive and this was successfully accomplished. As an additional precaution the port side of the screen was reinforced.

Up to this time 'Audacity' had remained in the centre of the convoy at night, but as two U-boats were known to be in contact at dusk, the Commanding Officer decided to leave and zig-zag at 14 knots, going about 30 miles to starboard of the convoy and rejoining at dawn. An escort was therefore requested and 'Rhododendron' was ordered to escort 'Audacity'.

No attack developed during the night which passed without incident.

Events during 21st December

At 0910/21 the dawn aircraft A/S patrol disclosed two U-boats alongside each other with a plank between them some 25 miles astern of the convoy. They made no attempt to dive when approached by the Grumman Martlet but opened fire with their Oerlikon guns from the conning tower. They appeared to be repairing damage to the port bow of one of the U-boats. The pilot discovered that the Oerlikons did not seem to be capable of firing above 70°; he therefore came right over the top and, diving down, shot three men off the plank. After this episode work ceased and the two U-boats made off on the surface at slow speed, steering away from the convoy.

R/T reports were made to 'Stork' but unfortunately the aircraft R/T microphone then failed and communication was interrupted.

'Stork' states: 'I appreciated this situation as the two, having collided during the night, were transferring either the whole of one crew to the other or perhaps a working party. It was a long way off and I had nothing above 15 knots, but it seemed too good a chance to miss. I sent "Deptford", "Pentstemon", "Vetch" and "Samphire"; a strong force in case the enemy should elect to fight it out on the surface. I also requested long range aircraft from Plymouth or Gibraltar but these were not available.'

At 1126 this hunting force was reported to be only 12 miles from the position but the relief aircraft could find no trace of either U-boat, and the surface force never gained contact.

At 1215/21, however, a Martlet was seen making steep dives and turns. 'Samphire' closed the position but before she arrived there, a metal tank was sighted. This was approximately 60 ft. long by 30 ft. beam, with two fins protruding upwards about 4 ft.

It was thought that this might be part of a military landing craft which had been washed overboard from a ship in an O.S. Convoy. The Commanding Officer, 'Samphire', believed that the aircraft had sighted and attacked a U-boat lying alongside this object and not alongside another U-boat.

It should be noted, however, that both U-boats are reported to have fired at the aircraft with their Oerlikons.

Later another aircraft from 'Audacity' reported two more U-boats on the port beam of the convoy. 'Marigold' and 'Convolvulus' were therefore sent to hunt, but whilst closing the position the aircraft reported that the U-boat had dived. On reaching the area this aircraft was seen to be circling and diving on the position where the U-boat had submerged.

Attack on a Contact by 'Marigold'

At 1528 'Marigold' obtained an echo dead ahead at a range of 1,500 yards. On the run in, a considerable patch of disturbed water was seen ahead; as the recorder was not working, time to fire was taken from this, a pattern of depth charges set to 100 and 300 ft. being fired at

1532.

Three minutes later a contact was gained but on investigation, this was considered to be a non-sub.

'Convolvulus' was not in contact and an independent close search was carried out till 1600, when 'Convolvulus' ordered a search in company.

At 1630 'Convolvulus' received orders from 'Stork' to conduct a search for another U-boat which had been sighted by aircraft and course was set towards the new position.

Further events during 21st December

At this stage it became clear to 'Stork' that the convoy was likely to be continuously shadowed and attacked whatever route it took, therefore the shorter the better. C.-in-C., Western Approaches, later approved 'Stork's' proposal to proceed home by the most direct route.

At 1510 a U-boat was sighted from 'Stork's' foretop about 12 miles ahead.

'Stork' states: 'The net of U-boats around us seemed at this stage to be growing uncomfortably close in spite of "Audacity's" heroic efforts to keep them at arm's length. I realised that a drastic alteration of course was essential after dark, and decided to stage a mock battle of starshell, depth charges, etc., by "Deptford's" force (which had not yet rejoined) away to the south-eastward, commencing one hour after dusk.'

On the previous night 'Audacity', with one corvette, had zig-zagged independently well clear of the convoy. On the night of 21st December she asked 'Stork' for a corvette and proposed operating on the starboard side of the convoy. This request had to be refused as at that time there were only four escorts in the immediate vicinity of the convoy. 'Stork' also suggested that 'Audacity' should take station to port, since the U-boat attacks were anticipated to starboard.

The Commanding Officer of 'Audacity' however, decided to stick to his original idea of going to starboard as all the U-boats so far reported appeared to be on the port side of the convoy.

'Stork's' plan to evade the U-boats was unsuccessful for two reasons. First, a merchant ship fired a snowflake at dusk by accident and gave away the exact position of the convoy. Secondly, when 'Deptford' commenced her mock battle some 12 miles away at 2030, several of the ships in the convoy again let off snowflakes. 'Stork' states however: 'I do not believe that this second fact made much difference, as the first attack occurred only a few minutes later and the U-boat was merely provided with a perfect aiming mark.'

The Torpedoing of 'Annavore' and 'Audacity'

Weather–

Wind	N.E. Force 2
Weather	Overcast
Sea	Calm
Visibility	1 mile

The Torpedoing of 'Annavore' (53)

At 2032, 21st December, in position 43° 50' N., 19° 45' W., 'Annavore' (53), rear ship of the centre column, was torpedoed, probably on her port side amidships. The ship, which was loaded with 5,000 tons of iron ore, sank like a stone and disappeared within a minute, there being only four survivors.

Movements of the Convoy and Escort

The Senior Officer at first believed that the torpedoed ship was on the starboard side of the convoy, and '"Buttercup" starboard' was therefore ordered. 'Stork' states:- 'This was a mistake; had I realized the victim was the rear ship of the centre column, I should have ordered '"Buttercup' astern."' 'Deptford's' force was ordered to rejoin at full speed.

On the unsuccessful completion of '"Buttercup" starboard,' all escorts engaged in the operation set course to rejoin the convoy.

At the time of the attack the convoy was in the middle of a turn in succession from 020° to 290°, but in spite of everything the turn was completed in good order.

A few seconds before the explosion, 'Finland' (11), now leader of the port wing column, had sighted a U-boat fine on the port bow about 200 yards away. The helm was put hard aport in an endeavour to ram the U-boat and an alarm was sounded on the steam whistle.

The U-boat at once crash dived and owing to lack of speed 'Finland' missed ramming by about 30 ft. The U-boat passed down the port side of 'Finland' and then crossed ahead of the next astern. Unfortunately the 12-pdr. gun could not be used, as the ship astern was in the line of fire.

The Torpedoing of 'Audacity'

'Audacity' left the convoy at 2000 and when clear of the escort, commenced zig-zagging.

At 2030 the mock battle commenced astern and two minutes later the convoy was attacked to port. Both of these incidents caused illumination to be used and this lighted up 'Audacity' who was at the time some ten miles on the starboard beam of the convoy.

At 2035 a fitter on 'Audacity's' flight deck saw a torpedo approaching from the port side. He ran towards the bridge but before he could give the warning the torpedo struck the port side of the engine room. Two white rockets were immediately fired.

The engine room flooded and the lights went out. Confidential books were thrown overboard and the order was given to go to 'Abandon Ship' stations, the 4-in. gun and pom-pom remaining manned.

As soon as 'Stork' had observed that 'Audacity' had been torpedoed, 'Convolvulus' and 'Marigold' were despatched to her assistance. These corvettes were just seen approaching when a U-boat was sighted on the port beam at a range of about 500 yards. Fire was immediately opened with the pom-pom.

A survivor from 'Audacity' states:- 'Torpedoes were then seen approaching and those so inclined, including myself, lay down, then rose smartly into the air twice in succession as they hit us. One struck under the bridge while the other exploded in the ward room.'

The Commanding Officer immediately ordered abandon ship and the aircraft carrier sank by the bows ten minutes later. Just before the ship sank, the aircraft, with the exception of one which had been lashed down, crashed over the side and caused a number of casualties in the water.

Survivors were picked up by 'Convolvulus', 'Marigold' and 'Pentstemon'.

Attack on a U-boat by 'Marigold'

'Marigold' was proceeding to rescue the survivors of 'Audacity' when at 2124 the R.D.F. Operator reported a contact on the port bow, range 3,500 yards. Full ahead was immediately ordered and a wake was soon seen. Starshell was fired but nothing was illuminated. The R.D.F. Operator held the contact however and reported that it was moving rapidly left. Course was immediately altered towards but when it was moving rapidly ahead, range 2,500 yards, the Operator reported the contact moving rapidly right. A round of starshell fired on the starboard bow revealed a wake. Course was altered to starboard but at this moment the target again altered course and moved rapidly left again. By this time 'Marigold' had steadied, the target was reported to be 'Red 40° range 2,000 yards.' A starshell was fired on this bearing and again a wake was revealed. The ship was turned to port and when the R.D.F. Operator reported 'Target dead ahead,' another round of starshell was fired. This clearly revealed a U-boat dead ahead on an identical course.

A round of H.E. was fired from the 4-in. gun but the fall of the shot was not observed. The range was now rapidly decreasing but when it was 1,000 yards the R.D.F. Operator lost contact.

By this time, however, the H.S.D. had contact by asdic and orders were given to set a pattern of ten charges to 100 and 225 ft.

Contact was lost at 150 yards and depth charges were fired at 2132, time to fire being taken from the recorder which was tracing clearly.

Efforts were made to regain contact but these failed and at 2150 'Marigold' signalled 'Stork' that she was proceeding to the assistance of 'Audacity'.

Attack on a Contact by 'Samphire'

After taking part in the mock battle, 'Samphire' was rejoining the convoy when, at 2146, a contact was obtained on the starboard quarter, range 1,000 yards. Course was altered towards and hydrophone effect was detected. At 2150 'Samphire' fired a ten-charge pattern of depth charges set to 100 and 225 ft. Contact was temporarily lost but was regained at 2157 at a range of 1,500 yards.

Having fired another pattern of charges at 2202, speed was reduced and the area was illuminated astern with the searchlight. One of the pom-pom's crew reported that an object had been sighted astern soon after the depth charges had exploded, but the Commanding Officer could not confirm this.

At 2207 contact was again established and, although the echo was faint, a pattern of five charges set to 150 feet, was dropped seven minutes later.

No further contact was gained until 2236 when a faint echo was heard at close range, but during investigation it faded away. A further search was carried out but at 2300 lights were seen and course was set to investigate. These lights turned out to be the corvettes picking up 'Audacity's' survivors, so 'Samphire' acted as an A/S screen until the rescue work was completed.

Attack on U-boat by 'Deptford'

At 2244, 21st December, whilst 'Deptford' was zig-zagging on the port beam of the convoy, she detected hydrophone effect on her starboard side.

Altering course towards, 'Deptford' illuminated the bearing with starshell and a U-boat was sighted on the surface closing to attack the convoy. As soon as the U-boat realized that she had been detected, she turned away and crash dived. A counter-attack with a ten-charge pattern set to 100 and 225 ft. was at once carried out. It is remarked that this attack was probably inaccurate as it was carried out by eye. Contact was regained astern, range was opened to 1,700 yards and a deliberate attack was then commenced, a full pattern set to 150 and 385 ft. being fired.

In both these attacks the recorder failed to give a satisfactory plot in Scale 10 under a range of 600 yards, and during the second attack contact was lost at this range. It is therefore believed that the U-boat was deep.

The same conditions prevailed for the third attack, but on this occasion an attempt was made to counter any anti-asdic tactics by keeping the transmission interval at 1,700 yards.

A further attack was carried out with five charges set to 385 ft.

'Deptford' now considered it desirable to rejoin the convoy, the primary object of preventing an attack on the convoy having been achieved. Two more charges set to 500 ft. were dropped, however, and a search of the area was commenced. No signs of oil or wreckage could be seen, but eight minutes after the deep charges exploded, a double underwater explosion was heard on the bearing.

'Deptford' states that the U-boat was still moving after the last attack, but it is not clear whether she was in contact when she set course to rejoin the convoy at 0105/22.

Attack on a Contact by 'Vetch'

At 2314, 21st December, whilst 'Vetch' was on the port beam of the convoy keeping a listening watch, strong hydrophone effect was reported on the port bow. Course was altered towards, and the target commenced moving rapidly right. On increasing to 15 knots, however, H.E. contact was lost, so speed was again reduced to 9 knots.

At 2316 contact of a wake was obtained by echo at a range of 1,000 yards. The range rapidly increased and contact was lost. At 2320 a pattern of five charges set to 100 ft. was fired in the approximate position of the last contact. An unsuccessful search was made of the area until 2340, when course was set to rejoin the convoy.

'Vetch' states: 'The initial H.E. contact was strong and clear of a fast-running Diesel motor of a U-boat on the surface. Shortly after, the velocity distinctly increased and then began to fade on a steady bearing.'

It is not clear whether 'Vetch' fired any illuminants during this haunt.

Events during 22nd December

The Commanding Officer, 'Stork', states: 'At 0517 I was aroused by an unusually ominous crash and came up to find "Deptford's" stem about one-third of the way into the port side of my quarter-deck. The damage was serious enough, but not vital, since the main engines and the steering gear (by an inch or two) had not been touched. The after cabin flat was wide open to the elements but the wardroom flat and the tiller flat were tight.

'I was able to go ahead at 10 knots in about ten minutes time.

'At dawn on 22nd December, therefore, it was difficult not to take a somewhat gloomy view of the situation:-

(a) "Stork" was completely out of action for A/S: it had been even necessary to shift all depth charges forward to lighten her stern. Maximum speed, 9 to 10 knots.
(b) "Deptford" was reduced to 11 knots, without any A/S.
(c) Most of the R.D.F. sets in the group were broken down.
(d) "Audacity" and her gallant aircraft had gone.'

The day passed uneventfully, however, and a Liberator aircraft escorted the convoy during both the forenoon and afternoon.

195

Attack on a U-boat by Liberator L/120

At 1245, whilst covering Convoy H.G.76, Liberator L/120 sighted a U-boat on the surface about 7 miles away. At this time the aircraft was about 10 miles on the port bow of the convoy.

The U-boat dived as soon as it sighted the Liberator and had completely submerged when the aircraft was still 1¼ miles away.

When reaching the estimated position of the U-boat, five depth charges were dropped set to 50 ft. The first one exploded at the head of the swirl and all the others fell along the track, the fifth falling 240 ft. ahead. Five seconds after the last depth charge had fallen, a large upheaval of water was seen about 100 ft. to 250 ft. ahead of the diving swirl, and a large oil patch appeared.

Contact was made with the convoy and the aircraft states that when leaving its patrol, a corvette was seen to be approaching the scene of the attack.

No mention of this, however, is made in any of the surface escorts' reports.

It is to be noted that the Liberator had to fly nearly 800 miles to meet the convoy and found it after a short search. This was a most creditable feat.

Further events during 22nd December

At 1115 the Focke-Wulf paid his daily visit and circled the convoy at a respectful range – occasionally fired at by 'Stork'.

At 1600 the relief Liberator reported two U-boats on the port bow; these submerged shortly after the aircraft had sighted them.

'Stork' remarks:- 'In considering my night intentions, there was clearly one thing not to be done and that was to continue on a steady course and passively await attack. I could think of nothing better than last night's ruse (which had not really had a fair chance). Course for home was 047°. I took the precaution of arranging for no snowflakes from the convoy, and carried out the following plan:-

(a) An alteration of 80° to port by the convoy to 327° – necessarily in two bites, commencing at 1920.

(b) A mock battle by 'Deptford' and 'Jonquil', commencing at 2225, in a position in which the convoy would have been had it steered 070° from 1920.

(c) The convoy to alter course back to 047°, commencing at midnight – having transferred itself some 32 miles to the north-westward of its original track.'

All went according to plan and the night passed without any major incident.

At 2220/22, however, 'Vetch' picked up a contact on the port beam of the convoy and dropped a number of depth charges. As she has sent in no report of this attack, it is assumed that it was made on a non-submarine target.

Hearing the depth charge explosions, 'Ogmore Castle' (22) believed she had been torpedoed and a number of her crew abandoned ship.

Although 'Ogmore Castle' was still doing 7½ knots, a boat was miraculously slipped without mishap.

As soon as the Master realised what had happened the ship was stopped and a search was made for the missing boat. This was recovered at 0110/23 and course was then set to rejoin the convoy.

Events during 23rd December

At 1620/23, whilst joining the convoy with 'Vanquisher', 'Witch' sighed smoke which was at first believed to be the convoy, then thought to be some 17 miles ahead.

At 1630, however, the mast lead lookout reported an object; the Commanding Officer climbed to the crow's nest himself and sighted a dark conning tower.

Speed was increased and the situation was reported by R/T to 'Vanquisher', who had by then sighted the convoy to port and was proceeding towards it. At 1644 the U-boat dived at a range of about eight miles and an enemy report was made by W/T.

At 1712 speed was reduced and an asdic search was commenced. At 1745 'Vanquisher' joined the hunt, but as nothing but non-submarine echoes had been obtained by 1833, the hunt was abandoned and course was set for the convoy.

Subsequent Movements of Convoy H.G.76

A false alarm with starshell was caused by 'Stork' on Christmas-Eve, but apart from this, the rest of the voyage passed uneventfully and the convoy arrived in the United Kingdom on 27th December.

U-boat Movements

Owing to the number of U-boats which took part in these operations, it has been impossible to determine their various movements.

It is known, however, that 'U 131' was the first U-boat to contact the convoy and that shortly after the first sighting report five or six other U-boats gained touch.

On 21st December three or more U-boats closed the convoy from the Bay of Biscay.

The only other information available is that all U-boats had lost touch by the night of 23rd December.

Conclusions

Considering the number of U-boats involved in this operation, it is surprising that more attacks were not carried out on the convoy. This can only be attributed to the excellent work done by the surface and air escort.

Extract from remarks by Commanded-in-Chief, Western Approaches

'(i) My remarks on operation "Buttercup" are briefly, that reliance should not be placed on estimates of the side of attack, offensive action being taken on both sides; more escorts should take part in the search; and delay in the commencement of operation "Buttercup" is not acceptable – on a torpedoing, any escort should order it by R/T at once.

'(ii) The object of snowflakes must be to assist in counter-attacking the U-boat and, as the position of the convoy is accurately known to the enemy, illumination of the merchant ships is acceptable, but every effort must be made to control the duration of the illumination (the possibility of using W/T for this purpose has been investigated by the Admiralty and promulgated in A.G.M. 59A).

'(iii) It is considered that at night "shaded Aldis distance" is too far from the convoy and that any use of this light is liable to endanger the escorts and convoy. If station cannot be kept by R.D.F., escorts should close to visibility distance.

'(iv) The Commanding Officer, H.M.S. "Stork" is congratulated on his conduct of the operations as a whole and both he, the Commanding Officers of all escorts concerned, and their ships' companies, are congratulated on the parts they played in the destruction of the three U-boats.'

APPENDIX A

(The following is a translation of a German account of the sinking of H.M.S. 'Audacity'. It was broadcast at 1815 on 30th December, 1941, from Frankfurt Radio Station.)

Reported: The U-boat, commanded by Senior Lieutenant Bigalk, which last week torpedoed an English aircraft-carrier, has now returned to her base.

Senior Lieutenant Bigalk: I had only been at sea for a few days when I had to crash-dive one afternoon because of an English 'plane. In the listening instrument I heard screw noises under water and took them to be coming from a convoy. I told myself that I should get to the surface as quickly as possible to see what was actually the matter, so I came to the surface very soon and only a few minutes later I saw clouds of smoke, and a few minutes after that I saw the outlines of some destroyers. Aha, there is a convoy! We were very glad to have met a convoy only a few days after our departure. First of all I approached the convoy to see how things were. I discovered a number of destroyers zig-zagging wildly and furthest to the left, next to the destroyers, I saw a large, long shadow, surrounded by several destroyers zig-zagging crazily. Suddenly a wild firing of tracer-bullets started up in the east. At this moment my other U-boat comrades, who were also going for this convoy, had probably opened the attack. The destroyers took course for the tracer-bullets; the long shadow, which I first took to be a tanker, zig-zagged first eastward, then northward, presumably to get away from the convoy. I made for the large shadow immediately, to attack it. Suddenly the shadow turned away sharply and at the same moment there was a great firing of rockets from the convoy. The whole area was as light as day. Other U-boats must have been attacking. Ten or 15 rockets hung over the U-boat as though spellbound. The destroyers nearby also started firing tracer-bullets and suddenly I saw in the light of the tracer-bullets and rockets a large aircraft-carrier lying in front of us. Good God! what a chance! – an opportunity such as a U-boat Commander does not find every day. The whole bridge was wildly enthusiastic.

Now I was in a favourable position for attack. I had to fire. I fired several torpedoes, and then came the terrible tension while waiting to see if, or if not, one of them hit its mark. Then suddenly a fiery detonation aft. A hit aft! The ship described a semi-circle portside and then stopped, unable to manoeuvre. Apparently my torpedo had smashed her screws. I turned a short distance off to load new torpedoes. Down below in the for'ard compartment there was a terrific crowding, since we had only left a few days before, and the for'ard compartment was full of provisions and all sorts of impossible things necessary for an operational cruise. My torpedo mate and my torpedo crew worked like mad. We, in the meantime, were standing on the bridge, constantly watching the aircraft-carrier, and were terribly excited lest the destroyer should approach and mess up this unique chance. But apparently the destroyers were furiously busy, for way back on the horizon there were bangs and detonations, and tracer-bullets were being fired. Our comrades were doing their work. The torpedo tubes were reported clear for action, thank God. I made another attack, approaching the ship at a crawling pace so that she should under no account hear me. The water was phosphorescing like mad, and I could only proceed very slowly so as not to be discovered by the aircraft-carrier, which had stopped. I came nearer and nearer. I didn't care any more. I had to get so near that my torpedoes could on no account miss. A gigantic shadow growing larger and larger all the time! I had approached so closely that no torpedo could possibly miss, and then I gave permission to fire. The torpedoes left their tubes. Seconds of great tension. There, hit for'ard, 20 metres behind the stem. A great detonation, in the middle; again, a great column of fire. Hardly had the column of water subsided when a strong detonation was observed for'ard. Probably ammunition or fuel had been hit. I presumed that petrol tanks or something of the kind had been blown up. I turned off, and in so doing cast another glance at the aircraft-carrier. The fore was already flooded and the deck was turning upwards. At that moment destroyers were reported starboard. They were dashing at top speed towards the aircraft-carrier, which was wildly firing distress signals – great stars bursting in the air. I was able to get away from the pursuit. I got a rain of depth charges, but that was of no avail to the English – I escaped.

Reporter: And you arrived back here safely today. We are happy and proud to welcome you today. You know from the communique that on that night when a convoy sailing from Gibraltar to England was attacked, many, many more tons were went to the bottom of the Atlantic by your comrades, besides the aircraft-carrier which you sank.

On one of his regular visits to the ships for 'pink gin and sympathy', Commander English asked me, 'Would it amuse you to come with me to a party that Commander Onions has asked me to join at the Stork Club?'

'Yes, sir, it would indeed interest me as I have read in the "gossip columns" of the New York dailies of Mr Sherman Billingsly's Stork Club. It appears to be the rendezvous zenith of the cafe society and social set's "beautiful people"!'

'That's arranged then, Warwick! Change into your white uniform, and have your DSC ribbon pinned on your chest. Meet me at 90 Church Street at about seven-thirty p.m. this evening. We can take a cab to the Stork Club from there.'

It was a humid, mid-summer of 90° in Manhattan when Commander English, with me following close behind him, was greeted and ushered into that select, air-conditioned sanctum of society by Mrs Annette Downs, the New York hostess for 20th Century Fox, and guided to a small group around tables in a secluded area.

'Let me introduce, Sir Cedric and Lady Hardwick! Commander and Mrs Onions you know already, of course. Then one of England's best-known playwrights with Miss Angela Lansbury, who is going to meet the movie-makers in Los Angeles under the wing of Sir Cedric.'

I did not catch the name of the famous playwright, who just looked up, and then remained in conversation with Cedric Hardwick for the rest of the evening. Cedric was relating how he had been primed by a radio show host for a personality interview, to conclude with: 'Good night, God bless you and not forgetting those bums the Dodgers.'

'I don't know what those bums the Dodgers meant,' he said, 'but it produced a roar of laughter from the studio audience!'

'Sir Cedric, those "bums" are the Brooklyn Dodgers baseball team and bitter opponents of our New York Giants,' explained Mrs Downs.

I was seated next to Mrs Onions, a complaining service wife. Having been fortunate enough to accompany her husband on his New York assignment, she was now relating the differences in customs and living between America and England.

Musing over this, I listened in polite silence until she drew breath to conclude with, 'I suppose that I should be glad to be living over here during the war.'

'Yes, Mrs Onions,' I said, 'there are quite a few bombs being dropped on civilians over there, and it is really quite unpleasant at times!'

Fortunately, the band struck up and I excused myself from Mrs Onions's silly conversation to dance with 'Pixie Hardwick', well known in her own right as the very competent actress, Helena Pickard. Her brother, Squadron Leader Pickard was a decorated RAF bomber pilot, Pixie told me. He had spent a little time with her in New York while making some public relations appearances there. It seemed that the gallant squadron leader had been quite an 'item' in squiring around the most attractive and bubbling Mrs Annette Downs. Thirtyish and most nobly built, she was a divorcee from Texas, with a teenage daughter being educated in New York at the Gardiner School for Girls, apparently a society institution. Decorations, in my somewhat cynical thoughts, seemed to create some romantic appeal in wartime, and in particular when following in Squadron Leader Pickard's footsteps.

In the late evening, the party members adjourned to Grand Central Station, bearing suitable offerings of farewell bunches of flowers which the ever-thoughtful Mrs Downs had ordered in advance for presentation to Angela Lansbury's parents, both being actors, and about to join a USO tour of Canadian RAF bases.

Angela's mother was the daughter of old George Lansbury, a long-term socialist member of Parliament for the East End of London, whose name Angela had adopted for her stage career. Beside her very beautiful mother, Angela appeared as a slightly plump and plain-looking teenager. I felt that there could be some conflict between her and her dazzling mother.

St Loman had become due for three or four days in harbour for rectifying some minor engine room defects and boiler cleaning. As Pete Willis elected to remain on board as the officer of the day, Ossie, Jonesy and I moved into the

Jonesy, Ossie, 'Pixie Hardwick' and the Skipper.
In the garden after lunch. Little Old Mansion.

Barbizon Plaza Hotel.

Now 20th Century Fox, in the delightful form of Annette Downs, really 'pushed the boat out' for the *St Loman*'s officers. On our first day we were driven out to the countryside for lunch at a rather exclusive restaurant with young Angela Lansbury. Annette had the inevitable camera and everyone was photographed afterwards.

Our second day's luncheon had been arranged at the Little Old Mansion restaurant in Manhattan to experience the real Southern cooking provided by Rudolph, Miss Gladys Wilcock's New Orleans chef. Miss Wilcock claimed that he was so essential that on his retirement she would close her restaurant. Pixie Hardwick and Angela Lansbury joined us and once again more photographs were taken in the small garden adjoining the restaurant. Of course the food was out of this world!

Miss Wilcock's niece, Joy, accompanied by her bosom friend Audrey Heide, heiress to a chocolate fortune, were lunching at an adjoining table. Joy announced that they had just seen the film *The Hamilton Woman* which depicted Lady Hamilton's love-and-politics affair with Admiral Horatio Nelson in the Kingdom of Naples. Audrey stated that it was absolutely shameful that Lady Hamilton had been so badly treated by the British Navy after she had inspired the great sea victories of Admiral Nelson. The film had ended with Lady Hamilton being pictured as an inebriated, poor and rejected creature in rags tottering about the rain-lashed cobblestones outside Westminster Abbey, where her one-time lover was being buried.

Ossie and I joined in the defence of our service, in all seriousness. We agreed that our navy paymasters were a heartless lot, but they were bound by the Royal Navy's bible entitled *The King's Rules & Regulations & Admiralty Instructions*. 'K R & A I', the short title by which the massive detailed coverage was known, stated very clearly that officers and men were entitled to just one wife's allowance. The compensation for their mistresses was considered a personal responsibility, no matter how inspiring the ladies may have been in regard to their contribution to victories at sea. Thus, unfair as it might seem, Lady Nelson, resident in Norfolk at that time, received all the allowance. Despite our efforts to offset the Navy's shame as pictured by Hollywood, the young ladies appeared unconvinced.

Annette Downs had set up a date for Angela Lansbury with Jonesy, providing tickets to the Radio City Music Hall. Next morning Jonesy informed us that it was 'sort of a dull date'. Ossie and I understood his meaning. At twenty-four or so, Jonesy had the build, energy and stamina of a Welsh rugby scrum-half, a position that he played well enough to be asked to play for the Royal Navy.

Sexually, Jonesy was extremely well endowed.

When *St Loman* was based in Greenock he had become engaged to a 'Wren', as the Women's Royal Naval Service were termed. She was the daughter of a Mr East, a former Navy Chief Petty Officer and now the HM Customs Officer in the port. Miss East was being true to her Jonesy, and he was always trying to be likewise.

It was said in New York City that when servicemen ran out of money, they went to the Stage Door Canteen. Jonesy was saving his money so as to marry his 'little girl', as he called her, and went to the Stage Door Canteen, where he inevitably seemed to get 'adopted' by fifty-ish ladies who seemed to shatter his weak defences with an excellent dinner and wine at their apartments, and possibly, Ossie and I would learn, 'change into something cooler'.

Joining Ossie and me at breakfast in the wardroom, Jonesy would berate himself to us. 'I'm a swine! I'm a swine. My poor little girl trusting in me to be faithful to her!'

'Who is it this time, Jonesy, that wife of the night editor for the *New York Times*, perhaps?'

'Yes! She must have been a beautiful woman in her time. She gave me a wonderful steak dinner with a bottle of red wine. Well, you know how it is . . .'

'Not quite, Jonesy, but after that what happened?'

'It was a near thing I can tell you. Just when I was up and dressed I heard the apartment door open. Her husband had come home early from his newspaper office. I was in a sweat!'

'I don't doubt it, Jonesy. Just think, as you were stepping into your white uniform trousers and reaching for your coat, that editor was coming up the first flight of the old brownstone apartment stairs.'

'I did think of that, skipper. There I was in a cold sweat and he came in saying, "Hot, isn't it?" Then he fetched a big paper tissue soaked in eau de Cologne, with another for himself, to cool our foreheads. He was home earlier than usual . . . Oh, I'm a swine! My poor little girl.'

'Don't take it so hard, Jonesy. It is just a case of a lost battle between your better self and your worser self. This evening better self said, "Jonesy don't make that telephone call! Stay on board and write to your little girl tonight." Worser self says, "Jonesy you mailed a letter to her when we docked this morning. You have been getting corned beef, dried peas and potatoes for dinner in last trip's rough weather. That's why you deserve a nice, rare, tender New York strip steak. Some red wine too? Just step ashore and make a telephone call to say that you are back and safe in harbour. No harm in that?" Better self says, "Don't pay attention to worser self. You are in a weakened state!" No

Ossie, Angela, Lansbury and Jonesy

harm in just telephoning to say Hello, you tell yourself as you step ashore.'
Next morning at breakfast we hear once more, 'I'm a swine, I'm a swine!'

Jonesy's temptations in New York were to end late in 1942. U-boats had moved down to the Caribbean where two or three operated in the hope of attacking tankers sailing from Trinidad and Gulf ports. Others were now appearing on the West and East Coasts of Southern Africa.

Commander English called a meeting of all commanders of A/S trawlers at their respective bases on the Eastern Sea Frontier to present orders to sail for Cape Town via Trinidad and Freetown. Admiralty charts covering the South Atlantic and Indian Ocean were delivered.

In *St Loman*'s wardroom my officers and I asked Commander English if the British Navy shore staff and A/S service personnel would be taking passage in the A/S trawlers. Anticipating the hazards and hardships of the long sea voyage, the staff and the commander were being flown to Cape Town, in order, as he said, to be 'ready for us when we arrived'.

On 17th October 1942 *St Loman* received a MAILGRAM from the Inshore Patrol, Third Naval District (see p. 206).

St Loman's chief engineman, Jimmy Dell, was busy getting his coal bunkers topped up. Coxswain Pym Grace was in charge of filling the stern lazarette with butter, beef and bacon and renewing the essential ice blocks. The melody wordsmiths in the seamen's mess deck were knocking out revised lyrics to the popular tune of 'Bless 'em all!' with strong emphasis on their favourite four-letter action word.

One seaman had acquired a small guitar and several others had mouth organs to strike up with the words of their parody:

> The trawlers are leaving New York
> Bound for a far distant shore
> Heavily laden with well fucked-up men
> Far from the land they adore
> Now there's many a PO just finishing his time
> And many a gob signing on
> But they'll get no promotion
> This side of the ocean
> So cheer up my lads fuck 'em all! Fuck 'em all!
> The long and the short and the tall
> For we're saying goodbye to them all

205

NRB—29539—6-4-41—200M—(H-31-32)

MAILGRAM

U. S. NAVAL COMMUNICATION SERVICE

DELIVER THIS MAILGRAM TO COMMUNICATION SYSTEM
IMMEDIATELY UPON RECEIPT FOR DISTRIBUTION AND
HANDLING AS A REGULAR DISPATCH.

FROM:

COMTHREE
COMPATFOR INSPAT 3ND

DATE ___OCTOBER 17, 1942___

MAILED AT _____

ACTION TO:
HMS ARCTIC EXPLORER
HMS ST. LOMAN
HMS NORTHERN CHIEF
HMS LADY ROSEMARY
HMS WELLARD

INFORMATION TO:

CESF
COMDR. ENGLISH, R.N.

CLASSIFICATION: *RESTRICTED_____

*CONFIDENTIAL_____

*SECRET_____

PRECEDENCE:

ROUTINE_____

DEFERRED_____

(*) If not encrypted by originator do not retransmit by radio
without thorough paraphrasing and encrypting.

The following message has been received from the Commander, Eastern
Sea Frontier:

"On departure British Trawlers from service with this command,
it is desired to express to them appreciation for duty well
done and all good wishes for their continued success."

The Commandant, Third Naval District and the Commander Patrol Forces,
Inshore Patrol, in forwarding the above message, add their recognition
of the valuable services rendered by His Majesty's Trawlers while
in Third Naval District waters. The seamanship, energy and skill
displayed by them on patrol and escort and in meeting the enemy
have been of the very highest order.

We are sorry to see them go and we hope that we may serve together
again.

Authenticated Signature: _____
(Name and Rank)
H. M. JENSEN, Captain, USN.
Assistant Commandant.

_____
D. E. LINDSAY, Captain, USN.
Commander Patrol Forces, Inshore Patrol 3NI

206

As back to their bases they crawl.
Now fuck all the skippers and their number ones
Fuck all the base staff and their bastard sons
They'll get no promotion
This side of the ocean
So cheer up, my lads, fuck 'em all!

Thus went the words of the *St Loman*'s sea-shanty men as they cast off and hauled in bow and stern lines, as the ship, going astern on her back spring, swung out her bow.

St Loman's destination was the best-kept secret on Staten Island's waterfront. Shouts of 'Have a good trip to South Africa!' came from the dockyard maties, as the ship moved past them on the dock into New York bay, down to the Ambrose Lightship heading south towards the sunshine away from the coming chill of the north-eastern states.

An early start in working our passage to Cape Town came when *St Loman* was requested to escort two new diesel-electric, ocean-going salvage tugs towing a hulk to Trinidad from Norfolk, Virginia. On delivering their tow, one tug was to be based in Port of Spain, Trinidad, while the other was to provide salvage services from Cape Town.

These two tugs carried a massive steel drum aft on which to wind and unwind a specially braided towing hawser. The tug master could unreel and reel in this towing cable at will from his controls on the bridge of the tug. The tug captain, standing on his open bridge, had the equivalent of fingertip control of his tug's two twin-screw diesels in the engine room, as the tug captain enjoyed instant, automatic control of ahead and astern speeds, and also starting and stopping both or either diesel, as required.

These two powerful twin-screw tugs had their towing hawsers fast on either side of the hulk's bow and were making a very fair speed of 8-9 knots. Possibly this speed was proving more than the timbers of the aged coal hulk could bear for it became lower in the water as the island of Trinidad came in sight. No one was on board the hulk to advise of the situation which was just as well. The hawsers were securely fast and as the hulk began to sink rapidly, we saw one tug cut its cable to avoid being pulled under. The other remained fast but was going full astern and reeling in its towing hawser until the hulk hit the sea bottom with the tug over it on the surface, still reeling in the slack of the towing hawser before cutting it free.

John Earle, the tug master, came aboard *St Loman* when our ships were alongside the US Naval Base dockside. Over a Scotch he related the loss of the hulk and tow cables. 'That hawser is a specially braided cable providing both the extra strength and flexibility. It is a long wait for a replacement and could put the other tug more or less out of action as the winding drum is specifically designed for the braided cable.

'When I saw the hulk go under, I ran the echo sounder on the bridge and found a depth of eight fathoms, thus, by coming astern as the hulk was sinking, and reeling in my cable until the hulk reached bottom, I would only lose about fifty feet of cable when floating over it on the sea floor.

'My tug's twin ship has lost about three quarters of its cable by chopping it free as soon as the hulk started to sink. She's not going to be useful as a salvage tug until a braided cable is available. It could be a two or three months' wait,' he concluded.

'Another Scotch, John, and we'll drink to your fast, advanced thinking, good seamanship and ship handling.'

St Loman's A/S officer, Lt Pete Willis, had been ashore to 'make his number' with the port A/S officer who proved to be an old acquaintance, an Australian officer. I greeted him with: 'Cobber Gott, welcome aboard once more! Here we are halfway around the world from Aberdeen where you came aboard for passage to Belfast, and an air raid experience at sea. Scotch or pink gin?'

'Scotch, thank you, skipper. It's a welcome change from Trinidad rum and Coca Cola. I always remember asking you about having air raid stations practice when we cleared Aberdeen, and you replied that it was not really necessary! I did not have to wonder why for more than ten minutes when the real thing started.'

Lieutenant Gott had an aunt living in Cape Town and asked me to contact the lady. 'I have an aunt living there, my mother's sister. Would you look her up for me and tell here where I am at present? Here is her address in Sea Point.'

'Glad to do it, Cobber, and I know that she'll give me a strong cup of tea while I tell her about your air raid experiences off Aberdeen. Then how things have quietened down since you moved to Trinidad as the port A/S officer.'

My next wardroom visitor was the base Surgeon Lieutenant.

'VD is rife in Trinidad, sir!' he told me. 'I would emphasize the need for the watch ashore to be warned of the need for condoms in case they become intimate with any of the ladies of joy ashore.'

'Lieutenant Jones is your man, doctor. He always sees to it that a packet of condoms goes with each pay packet. I shall warn the ship's company about the situation in Trinidad, and for that matter in Freetown, West Africa, our next port of call. Rather different ports and populations to what most of them have known. Could you arrange to come aboard tomorrow morning and spend some time with Lieutenant Jones?'

'Of course, skipper. Does he have any men on sick call?'

'No, doc, I want you to bring syringes and antibiotics so as to work with Jonesy to clean out the complete ship's company. Then he will instruct the men in this prevention activity every morning that the ship is alongside in Port of Spain, or Port of Pain, as it might well be called!'

'Just the watch shore would be enough, skipper.'

'No, doc, let it be understood that everyone has to have the same treatment. You can include me and the wardroom officers, so that there's no apparent discrimination between officers and men. We are all men! As to only those going ashore taking the treatment – officers and men often switch duty and shore leave activities. Then there's always a "fast Eddie" who will slip ashore for a promised knee trembler against the dockside wall, and then nip back aboard!'

'If that's the way you want it, skipper, I'll set it up with Lieutenant Jones right away.'

'Thank you, doc,' I concluded. 'We're going to be fifteen to twenty days at sea before that little convoy assigned to *St Loman* and the *Northern Dawn* makes Freetown. A sailor or stoker catching a bad dose of VD before we sail could develop a very dangerous and painful condition. Our ship would lose a good crew member through having to put him ashore for treatment at the naval hospital in Freetown. I plan to make Cape Town with all hands now on board, healthy and happy!'

The wardroom conversation now turned to the recent U-boat activities in the Caribbean and a daring attack carried out in the Port of Spain anchorage by a bold and most innovative U-boat commander about ten days prior to our arrival.

The entrance through the Boca Grande checked the comings and goings of all vessels as ships had to pass over magnetic loops on the bottom of the channel. Nevertheless the U-boat had been able to enter without observation or detection by the loops. After remaining on the bottom of the anchorage during the day, the U-boat commander calmly surfaced in the evening. He torpedoed two tankers and during the resultant confusion made his way out to sea, again without being detected by visual sighting or the magnetic loops at the Boca Grande channel entrance. Fortunately the tankers were in ballast and could be salvaged.

It was assumed that the U-boat commander, being aware of the probable existence of the magnetic loops, had waited for a merchant ship to approach the

Boca Grande entrance. Remaining submerged and keeping station on the ship's propellers with his hydrophones, he must have passed over the magnetic loops under the vessel's stern, thus ensuring that the two vessels were reported as one.

After the torpedo attacks during the late evening, no ships were reported passing out over the magnetic loops with the exception of a small tug showing her steaming lights, port and starboard, and masthead lights. A check on the movements of the harbour tugs reported that none of them had been moving at that time. The U-boat trimmed down and exhibiting steaming lights, had been the reported 'tug'!'

The US Naval Base was located in a new, tall, seven-storey, fully air-conditioned, modern office building.

The British Naval base offices occupied a couple of one-storey, wooden-frame huts on the dockside, formerly used by a stevedoring company. There was no air-conditioning, but there was the one redeeming feature of a large room set aside as an officers' club and beer bar. It was the meeting place for the officers of both navies, as one might expect.

Trinidad's steel bands in the shanty town were beating out their local songs including the recent addition:

> The Yankees come to Trinidad
> They drive all the young girls mad
> Drinking rum and Coca Cola
> Both the mother and the daughter
> Working for the Yankee dollar!

The *St Loman*'s songsmiths added some more scurrilous material of a similar nature, much less complimentary to our allies.

There was little in the way of entertainment of a higher standard, except the country club, which entailed an expensive taxi trip. Thus the officers entertained each other with visits to the wardrooms of *St Loman* and *Northern Dawn*.

Within two days in Trinidad both our ships had topped up with coal and water and such fresh vegetables as were available. When the masters of the five merchant ships and the tug captain met at the convoy office in the naval base, the shipmaster to act as commodore was appointed.

After leaving Port of Spain the convoy would form up to steam in line abreast with the salvage-rescue tug astern and in the centre of the line. *Northern Dawn* and *St Loman* would be carrying out their respective A/S sweeps on the starboard and port bows of the convoy.

Thus on the morning of the third day all ships and their escort put to sea. As our little convoy cleared the Boca Grande to form up in line abreast, the weather was simply perfect. There was hardly a cloud in the blue sky. The sea was as a blue-green millpond. Asdic conditions were exceptional, providing an excellent range of 5,000 yards when testing on a merchant ship's hull. Our five merchant ships maintained their steady line abreast steaming at 8-9 knots with the little salvage tug stationed astern of them like a Border collie driving a flock of sheep.

In the late afternoon, Trinidad was a fading dark blue shape on the hard line of the western horizon, when *Northern Dawn* hoisted her black A/S contact flag, then became almost motionless as a game dog pointing. *St Loman* crossed the course of the convoy to close *Northern Dawn*. Pete Willis and the asdic operator confirmed *Northern* Dawn's possible U-boat contact. As *Northern Dawn* began her attacking run, I signalled by Aldis lamp, 'We will hold contact and monitor your attack. When you run out and regain contact *St Loman* will make the second depth-charge attack. Suggest that we continue to make alternate attacks on the contact. Each ship to monitor the other vessel's attack position.'

St Loman and *Northern Dawn* now delivered six attacks in alternate succession, each ship crossing the 'T' three times. A thin film of diesel oil was spreading an ever widening patch as our two ships stopped engines to keep contact with their target. The echoes, formerly sharp and clear, now started to fade until they were finally lost in the bottomless depths below the calm of the stained blue sea above.

Our convoy steaming on its course was now 7 or 8 miles away and there was no alternative but to rejoin before dusk and resume our respective A/S screening stations. Perhaps it had been the bold and resourceful U-boat commander of the Port of Spain anchorage torpedo attacks that we had been hammering like two old-time road repair navvies breaking into a road surface with their rhythmical sledgehammer blows on the steel wedge without respite. The chart showed 1,400 fathoms translating into 8,400 ft of water pressure on a sunken U-boat hull. As the sun was setting astern *St Loman* and *Northern Dawn* were back in station on the convoy.

Sun-drenched days now passed uneventfully as our convoy commodore continued on his course some 12 degrees north of the equator. Pym Grace, the coxswain had found a large tarpaulin for rigging up a seawater bathing pool on the foredeck for the rest and recreation of the watch below. This bath proved to be an extremely popular innovation.

At noon each day the commodore signalled his convoy position, course and speed. Ossie and I did our own navigation for making a comparison with our morning star sights and the traditional noon sun sight.

When in New York I had been taken to a book publishers' promotion for a historical novel entitled *Forever Amber* by Katherine Windsor. The author had given the impression that she could have lived the seductions described in every chapter illustrating the life and times of Charles II of England. My three officers were now reading the book in turn, finding inspiring scenes of just one chapter a day proved enough fuel for imagination during a long sea voyage! Rationing was considered essential . . .

Another book given to me by Dorothy Wilcock was *Behind God's Back* by the author Negley Farson. This became wardroom reading in due course. The author's African visit began at Walvis Bay, the port for the former German colony of South West Africa, and described the 'stately, bare-breasted Herero women sauntering around Walvis Bay'. Walvis being a port of call after making Freetown and Pointe Noir, our wardroom readers had built up expectations of seeing the visions observed by the writer.

I recalled that when doing my sea time as a cadet aboard SS *Glamorganshire*, an aged flush-decked cargo ship chartered to the Union Castle by my owners the Royal Mail Steam Packet Company in 1929, the ship had cargo for Walvis Bay from London. All I could remember was a low line of cargo sheds with the tracery of the crane jibs above them. Over and beyond them stretched an endless vista of yellow desert sand. As an Australian would have put it, 'the great bugger-all!'

As we drew nearer to the coast of West Africa, the weather turned colder with frequent rain squalls whipping up the seas. On one such morning a day's steaming from Freetown, as was my usual custom, I was on the bridge shortly after dawn. Houghton, the most experienced of *St Loman*'s asdic ratings reported a possible U-boat contact on the port side ahead. As *St Loman* went to action stations and initiated an attacking course, the merchant ship on the port side of the convoy line abreast opened fire with her stern-mounted gun. *St Loman* completed the five-charge attack with 150 ft settings, but contact was lost after this attack. Now, the convoy having passed clear, the A/S screening station was resumed.

On arrival in Freetown the chief officer of the merchant ship opening fire gave me a copy of his report: 'At 0700 the after gun crew sighted a periscope on the port side ahead and opened fire and it disappeared. At the same time *St Loman* was closing the position to make a depth-charge attack.'

Freetown was a busy convoy terminal and assembly port. Several A/S trawlers commanded by Skipper Lieutenants had been based on Freetown to patrol the

212

approaches. These former deep-sea trawler captains were heavy drinkers and hard-case characters, and Freetown may have been an appropriate assignment for they seemed well satisfied with their port facilities.

Two visiting officers highly recommended that our wardroom should hire some young black virgins to do our laundry, cabin cleaning, and supply any other desired services while *St Loman* was alongside. It appeared to be a customary arrangement with them. From time to time several West African women would walk up and down the dockside barefoot and bare chested, much to the admiring delight of Stuart, an Aberdonian stoker, who leaned over the ships' bulwarks fascinated with what he called, 'Those firrrm titties!' Ossie rudely observed that those he had at home must be very downcast indeed.

Ossie and I took a short walk ashore and away from the port, passing by a shallow river bed with a fast running stream flowing over the smooth, rocky bottom. Here we saw the African women doing their laundry soapless, or with a minimum of soap, while pounding the garments with a small boulder against a larger boulder in the running water of the stream.

Pete Willis had sent a number of his shirts for washing by one of the Africans coming aboard and remarked how snow white they had been returned, neatly folded. I told him, 'Pete, you should take an educational walk to the local laundry where your shirts were being laundered when Ossie and I walked by. Let's have a look at your threads now, because that is what they are going to be!'

There was little in the way of shore attractions. I visited Lt Hartnell aboard the *Northern Dawn* and vice versa. Our respective wardroom officers did much the same to exchange navy gossip and experiences. Within two or three days our ships' bunkers and water tanks had been topped up. The merchant ships we had escorted from Trinidad had discharged their cargoes. Two of them were bound for Cape Town, and a mixed bag of vessels now made up the southbound convoy. The additions were a South African coastal trade steamer, whose captain and chief engineer had their wives on board, and an Indian navy sloop on passage to India via Cape Town, commanded by a Lieutenant Commander of the Indian Navy.

The convoy officer at the Freetown naval base appointed *St Loman* as the senior officer of the escort group despite my suggestion that the Indian navy sloop should have this honour. The NOIC Freetown overruled me on the grounds that *St Loman* had greater experience with A/S convoy escort operations.

After bumping over the equator and losing the star Polaris to our navigation, we passed about 30 miles to the west of the mouth of the Congo river where far out at sea the silt being brought down by that great river made a visible muddy darkness in the surface of the ocean. At night the flames of a massive jungle fire could be observed far inland.

As the merchant ships had cargo for Pointe Noir in French Equatorial Africa, one day and night was spent alongside. A signal was received from the British NOIC stating that the commanders and wardroom officers could visit the base provided that they were dressed in their white uniforms. The officers of the escort ships decided that under the circumstances they would provide their own hospitality aboard their ships.

CHAPTER XIV

On the morning of 24 December 1942, our little convoy sailed into Walvis Bay. *St Loman*, *Northern Dawn*, the salvage tug and the Indian Navy sloop docked alongside each other. Those 'stately, bare-breasted Herero women' as described by the writer, Negley Farson in his book *Behind God's Back* were nowhere in sight. As I had viewed entering Walvis Bay a dozen years previously, the same tracery of the cargo cranes' jibs rose about the low line of the cargo sheds. Over and beyond stretched the flat, yellow desert of the 'great bugger-all'.

On inquiring about Farson's visit of the pilot, we learned that he had spent a couple of hours in Walvis Bay before taking the first train up to Swakopmund and thence to Windhoek, said to be a quaint, calm, exotic city of Dutch gardens, German tidiness and African rhythms.

Shortly after arrival a hand-transmitted signal was made.

> From: *St Loman, Northern Dawn.*
> To: Officers of Walvis Bay Naval Base and all ships alongside.
> Our Christmas eve party will commence at 2000 hours.

A gigantic stag party developed, flowing to and from the wardrooms of the two ships and across the decks of all four vessels. Gin and whisky flowed easily throughout the night and until the early morning. Many songs and recitations were given.

'Christmas Day in the workhouse'.
'The Ball of Kirriemuir'.
'It was the good ship Venus'.
'In a back street in London a whore did dwell'.
'As I was going down the Strand I met two ladies hand in hand'.
'Said the major to the captain indeed it would be grand'.
'I was a servant girl at a house in Drury Lane'.
'Who's that knocking at my door? Said the fair young maiden'.

'She was poor, but she was honest and bore an honoured name'.

'The trawlers are leaving New York'.

'If you're filling pubs or sinking subs'.

'Roaming on *St Loman* with a depth charge by my side'.

'She had a wild and roving eye and her hair hung down to her whatnot'.

Pym Grace and Jimmy Dell organized an informal PO's party fuelled with the remains of the *St Loman*'s emergency stores of British army rum acquired in the evacuation of Namsos. As dawn was breaking the last of the party-goers were rolling off to their base beds or ships' bunks.

It was eight o'clock on Christmas morning when Alfie the wardroom steward brought me a mug of tea together with a signal from the base addressed to 'Commanders of Escort and Masters of Merchant Ships': 'You will prepare to sail for Cape Town at 1200 hours. Attend conference at 1000 hours'.

I greeted the base operations officer with 'Sailing us on Christmas Day is an inhuman request!'

'You are to sail at noon today regardless. The NOIC said we could not stand another night like last night! We thought you would make it to the convoy conference, but we were not so sure about the others . . .'

St Loman cast off at noon together with *Northern Dawn*, the Indian navy sloop, and our faithful salvage tug. Three merchant ships followed us to sea, bound for Saldanha Bay where the trawlers were to top up bunkers prior to arriving at Cape Town. The great level expanse of Table Mountain was a welcome and impressive sight as *St Loman* and *Northern Dawn* headed in towards the breakwater to complete their odysseys or working their passages for every sea mile between New York and Cape Town as convoy escorts, to become the last of the British A/S trawler fleet to arrive from their assignment with the US Navy.

Commander English was waiting on the dock as *St Loman* came alongside with orders for *St Loman* and *Northern Dawn* to proceed to East London for boiler cleaning and minor refits. The work would be carried out by the port facilities of the South African Railways whose security measures seemed to be a little lax, as there were some reports of minor sabotage by 'OBs' or Old Boers', as translated from Afrikaans.

On arriving at East London I was contacted by Mrs Isabelle Cresswell, President of the Women's Transport and Entertainment Club for Servicemen. Mrs Cresswell was the wife of the managing director of a South African insurance company who had organized and most effectively managed a group of local ladies as hard working volunteers who now arranged weekly dances, outings to the countryside, and picnics for small groups of ships' officers and men. In addition to East London entertainments, families of farmers in the countryside would take groups of officers and men into their homes during a 10-days' leave period.

As usual the pay documents for *St Loman* and *Northern Dawn* had not yet arrived in Cape Town and the customary pay advance as a temporary measure had been arranged by Commander English. South African Railways took their time in making their estimates for the repairs and refit, and it was several days before the estimate of time required came through.

Mrs Cresswell had arranged that two-thirds of the *St Loman*'s ship's company could have the opportunity of spending 10 days with families on the various farms around the country town of Tarkastad. As was the British Navy custom, one-third of one watch remained on board the ship during boiler cleaning and short-term refits. *St Loman*'s coxswain, Pym Grace, had no problems in setting up the farm families leave group, and the watch to stand by the ship during the refit. There were enough 'hard cases' to make up the watch aboard from those wishing to say 'near the boozers' and the lady friends with whom they had made local connections.

The British admiral stationed in Durban as Commander-in-Chief, South Africa, had made a signal to all ships giving leave in South Africa.

It seemed that personnel of 'other services', principally RAF personnel, had not behaved very well and abused the hospitality of South African families entertaining them. The Admiral concluded his signal by stating that he knew that the men of the Royal Navy could be expected to maintain their high standard of personal contact and behaviour.

When briefing the country families group, I commenced with reading the C-in-C's signal to the ship's company in the mess deck, followed by this recommendation:

'It appears from the Admiral's signal that RAF personnel visiting the farm families, as you are about to do, have been making passes at the wives, daughters and the female hired help. It is possible that mistakenly they were trading on the hero reputation earned by the RAF by Battle of Britain pilots.

'Now as the song claims, "All the nice girls love a sailor". All the other girls do, too! You do not need to make passes at the farm daughters or the hired help, because if you conduct yourselves as the gentlemen sailors of this ship are capable, and behave in a completely opposite fashion to those men of "other services", you won't need to!

'With their contrariness the ladies are quite likely to make passes at nice, shy, gentlemanly sailors from *St Loman* resting after their long, lonely and arduous convoy escort trip to South Africa. You need no further advice from me on handling any situation which is likely to occur!

'Tomorrow at noon all hands will draw a pay advance. Those leaving to stay with the farm families will be dressed in their Number One uniforms. This group will march to East London railway station under the command of the coxswain and Lieutenant Jones.

'The train for Tarkastad is due to leave East London at two p.m. You will arrive at about one-thirty p.m. and the train will only just be starting from East London. After boarding the train and stowing your baggage, five or six men from the first carriage will be free to visit the station bar for a couple or so beers, then return to their carriages, so that another carriage group can take their turn. Thus when the train pulls out all hands should be cheerful, but not excessively so!'

Everything went as planned. A train full of cheery sailors leaning out of the carriage windows waved to Mrs Isabelle Cresswell, Ossie and me, as we watched the train pull out for Tarkastad.

On watch at sea several weeks later, signalman Sid Wain standing next to me at lookout on the bridge remarked, 'You know what you said to us about not making passes at the daughters and the help?'

'Yes, why?'

'Well, it works!'

Mrs Cresswell now prevailed on me and Lt Hartnell to spend a week on a farm near Tarkastad, where a Mr & Mrs Ryan had operated a holiday guest facility. Hartnell was not too keen as he had been rather smitten by an attractive girl in East London, But Mrs Cresswell would have it that we needed to get away from our ships for a few days. So we made the two-hour railway journey to Tarkastad to be met by Molly Gray, one of the married Ryan daughters, and her South African army doctor husband on leave from North Africa.

At the farm we met with our hosts, Mr & Mrs Ryan, and their other married daughter, Peggy Norton, and another army doctor's wife whose husband was on duty in Egypt. A third young woman was a recent widow of another South African army officer. All three had young daughters and occupied the guest rondavels, or round, thatched, native-style huts constructed of sunbaked mud and whitewashed inside and out. Simple, yet attractively furnished, they were cool and comfortable.

Hartnell and I shared a bedroom in the main farmhouse and everyone sat down in the farm dining room for meals. Sitting down for the family dinner that evening, Peggy Norton remarked, 'I don't know why Mrs Cresswell sent you both up here with a trio of married women with young babies.'

'It's said that a change is a complete rest, and this is a complete change for us,' I replied.

A small concrete swimming pool had been constructed near to the main house for which fresh water was obtained by diverting a small stream in a ditch during a heavy rainstorm. This rainwater drained off a small kopje, or dimunitive kop rising up behind the farmhouse. It was peopled by several bands of baboons which would come down to steal maize corn cobs from time to time.

The week passed quietly around the pool and gathering in the evening at Major and Mrs Grey's rondavel for 'sundowners' before supper. I climbed the kopje at the invitation of Molly Grey to look at the baboons and the view of the surrounding country.

'You are in pretty good shape,' she remarked as I kept pace with her to reach the top without resting. 'I used to bring my boyfriends up here, and they were too tired to make passes at me when reaching the top.'

On returning to East London it came to my mind that the wise Mrs Cresswell had initiated us in platonic friendships with two lonely women and their children on holiday.

St Loman's boiler cleaning had been completed and steam raised, but in order to remove and replace a main bearing the whole of the engine room skylight area had been cut open, leaving a gaping hole to potential bad weather had we been forced to go to sea before being made seaworthy.

Another naval vessel which appeared to be undergoing an almost perpetual refit in East London was *Columbia*, a Dutch Navy submarine depot ship. Almost all of the officers and crew had been billeted in homes ashore, and had become comfortable residents of East London to all intents and purposes.

Eventually the day came when, despite minor sabotage by suspected 'OBs', the *Columbia* was to sail for Cape Town. The Women's Transport and Entertainment Club held a farewell party and dance for the Dutch navy officers and POs, which was attended by the British officers who observed some extremely tearful farewells at the end of the evening prior to the *Columbia*'s early morning sailing.

On the early afternoon of *Columbia*'s departure, Ossie, Jonesy, and I were being entertained to tea by a Mrs Bonsor with her two daughters, Molly and Akka (the last name being Indian for 'sister', I had been told). A telephone call came for me from the naval base asking if I would be prepared to take *St Loman* to sea despite the warning by the shipyard about the unseaworthy situation of the exposed engine room, in order to search for a U-boat which had just torpedoed the *Columbia* a few miles down the coast.

The staff car arrived post haste to take us back to the *St Loman*. The two attractive girls and their mother tearfully 'kissed the boys goodbye', quite an emotional event for our hostess and her daughters, but just a routine matter for us. Nevertheless, their very evident and sincere concern swelled our hero chests just a little. It was a good feeling!

Within an hour of the base telephone request, *St Loman* was at sea and steaming south for the *Columbia*'s last position. After steaming south for a couple of hours, the big RAF air-sea rescue launch was sighted dead ahead and heading for East London with all the officers and crew of *Columbia* on board. I estimated that by the time *St Loman* made the position of the torpedo attack, those lucky Dutch navy officers would be returning to the arms of their adopted East London families for a happy reunion and drying out!

St Loman made a 48-hour A/S sweep and search of the area, and one thing was certain, *Columbia*'s sailing time had been transmitted to the U-boat commander who had his vessel in just the right position to put one torpedo into *Columbia* and head out to sea, possibly to wait for another sailing date to be transmitted.

On the evening of the *Columbia* sinking, the German propaganda station broadcast, 'Thank you, East London, for *Columbia*!'

It was towards the end of February 1943 that *St Loman* left the hospitable East London harbour for Cape Town to work the coastal sea routes between Walvis Bay and Cape Town, and north to Durban and Beira, Portugese East Africa.

The Admiral in Durban would have credited his signal regarding conduct by navy men on leave as having been very effective, had he received a letter from Mrs Isabelle Cresswell (see p. 221).

The little fleet of some 26 A/S trawlers, reassigned from duty with the US Navy on coastal escort duty on the Eastern Sea Frontier of the USA, were now repeating similar activities on the west and east coasts of Southern Africa on the coastal sea routes from Walvis Bay, West Africa, to Cape Town, and from the latter north to Durban, and off Beira in Portugese East Africa.

Commander English was now an old hand at this type of operation and had arranged with the NOIC Cape Town, Captain Ridgeway RN, that the A/S trawlers would make two coastal convoy trips to the barren shores of Walvis Bay, alternated with one northbound convoy to Durban. Coaling would be carried out at Saldanha Bay. Thus all the ships' companies would have equal opportunity to frequent the 'fleshpots' of Durban and the Cape.

On the completion of her refit in East London, *St Loman* took her place in the

Really Not Required

Women's Transport and Entertainment Club
for Servicemen

SECRETARY :
F. I. ALGIE.
4 KING STREET.
PHONE 3866

IHC/RE

East London,

February 23rd 1943

Lt. Warwick,
Commander, Ship 2C8,
EAST LONDON DOCKS.

Dear Lt. Warwick,

        Before you leave East London harbour I would like you to know how much our Club has enjoyed looking after your Officers and men. The exemplary behaviour of your men is something of which I feel you can be very proud.

        It was my good fortune to visit all the towns where your men and Lt. Hartnell's men were enjoying country leave, and I listened to praise from all the hostesses I met. I feel very proud and pleased to know that our Club was instrumental in sending such nice men into our country districts.

        I have a request from our country hostesses to the effect that when at any future date your ship returns to East London harbour, each and every man be granted leave to return to his "family". This I feel is the highest praise any ship could hope to receive, and I trust that if at any time your ship should require repairs, you will make a special effort to return to us, to enable your officers and men again to enjoy leave with their adopted families.

        I would like to thank you and every one of your officers for your co-operation in the entertainment of your men. It has been a great pleasure to entertain such a well-behaved and happy ship.

        With every good wish from the Women's Transport and Entertainment Club for Servicemen, and may you return to us in the near future,

                Yours sincerely,

                Isabelle Cresswell

                PRESIDENT.

221

coastal convoy routine. On completing a northbound convoy to Durban with the A/S trawler *Wellard*, the two ships were assigned to meet a small convoy of four or five British merchant ships sailing from Beira in Portugese East Africa for Durban. Beira, being a neutral port, could be expected to have the German consul providing a 'listening post' with the British consul listening in.

On sailing north from Durban, *St Loman* and *Wellard* carried out an A/S sweep up the coastal route to Beira. Off Beira, the two A/S ships swept the eastward approaches in the Mozambique Channel from dusk to dawn on the convoy sailing day from Beira to ensure that a predator might not be able to sight the ships leaving Beira. As senior officer of the little escort group, it was logical for me to assume that despite our preventative measures the German consul would radio the sailing time and date to a U-boat offshore.

It was logical also to assume that any U-boat would keep well out at sea in the Mozambique Channel from our swept area and would surface at night to proceed on the surface to a position off the bulge in the coastline at Inhambane where the convoy commodore would be altering course from south to south-west to approach Durban by following the coastline. This would be approximately 50 hours after sailing from Beira.

At daybreak *St Loman* and *Wellard* had completed their A/S sweep from the centre of the Mozambique Channel to the three-mile limit off Beira where the first of the four merchant ships could be seen clearing the harbour breakwater. This was a bulk carrier and the appointed commodore contacted *St Loman* by Aldis lamp to state that the four-ship convoy would be in two columns with the bulk carrier leading the starboard side.

I had assigned *Wellard* to maintain an A/S sweep on the starboard approach side of the columns with *St Loman* in the corresponding position on the port column and the seaward side. The commander of *Wellard* was comparatively inexperienced, and I considered that a torpedo attack was most likely to come from the seaward side. I was wrong.

The first two days were uneventful. The weather was indifferent with an overcast sky and a strong breeze whipping up a choppy sea. In the early afternoon of the third day, our little convoy was off the bulge of Inhambane, altering course to a south-western course to follow the coast. *Wellard* appeared to be stopped and had hoisted a black flag to indicate that she was investigating a possible U-boat contact. 'Attack . . . Attack!' I had my signalman flashing on his Aldis lamp, as *St Loman* steamed at full speed to pick up *Wellard*'s contact, towards which her bows were pointing.

Ldg. Seaman Houghton, picked up the A/S contact just as there was a loud explosion from the commodore ship, which disappeared within minutes. Cracks in the steel used in the construction of bulk carriers can open at a speed of several metres a second leading to the loss of a vessel and its crew without a trace before a 'Mayday' message can be sent. Thus, loaded with bauxite ore, the ship sunk without trace except for the two life-rafts, supported by their 40-gallon empty oil drums, on which the surviving crew members were huddled.

Wellard was still stopped and holding her investigative A/S contact as *St Loman* delivered her first five-charge pattern of depth charges set to 150 feet as I estimated that the U-boat commander would plan to go down deep, and followed it with another pattern set to 350 feet.

Wellard's commander, now convinced that his contact had been an attacking U-boat, carried out two more depth-charge attacks. Some wreckage and diesel oil was appearing as *St Loman* made the fifth depth-charge attack to further shake the survivors viewing the destruction of their attacker from a grandstand view.

Coming aboard *St Loman* in Durban, when we landed the surviving crew members, the commanding officer of Wellard seemed over-pleased with himself.

'Why didn't you attack without delay? You were screening a convoy approach,' I asked.

'Well, we got the U-boat!'

'That's right,' I replied, 'but we might have saved those four men lost in the engine room, if you had attacked right away.'

Reporting to the operations staff officer in the Durban 'War Room', I had outlined how we had swept up the coast to Beira and then the east and west approaches in the Mozambique Channel. Nevertheless, the U-boat commander was located just in the right spot off the convoy turning point. The chief of staff drew back the black curtain covering the operations chart. 'There was a W/T signal from Beira received by a U-boat lying east of Beira in the Mozambique channel,' he commented.

'Interesting. It would have been nice to have known about it!' I answered. 'Did the W/T signal come from the German consulate, while the British consulate obtained the D/F report?' A faint smile was his only reply.

St Loman was about due for boiler cleaning and my chief engine man Jimmy Dell was complaining about leaking boiler tubes, a common complaint due to multiple depth-charge attacks. Thus *St Loman* was berthed at Maydon Wharf, a long walk from the centre of the city of Durban along the promenade. Maydon Wharf was an industrial complex starting at the end of the Durban seafront promenade. Lever Brothers' soap and detergent factory occupied the first block of buildings on the wharf, and there was the terminal for the trams from the city to make their turnaround.

Intending to visit the city centre around noon, I had walked up the wharf side from the *St Loman* to where Lever's warehouse offices had their Hollerith machine computers operating in the open air under a projecting roof for processing the production, sales and shipment data to the Lever marketing areas in South Africa. At first the IBM operation appeared to be working of its own volition until I observed a slender, lithe, tanned, brown-haired female figure flitting expertly around the machines to feed in the punched data cards from which the printouts of marketing information were being developed.

I became far more interested in the operator than the operation being supervised by Mrs Marjorie Plasket, who told me that she was on assignment from the IBM offices in Johannesburg to produce Lever's quarterly figures. Everything had stopped for lunch, giving me the opportunity to suggest that Marjorie should join me at Durban's famous Edward Hotel on the seafront. I hailed a taxi.

Over lunch I learnt that Marjorie was single, divorced and lived in Johannesburg where she worked at IBM. While on the IBM project in Durban she had taken a bed-sitter and bathroom at a residential complex in the city.

It was Friday, and as I took Marjorie back to complete her afternoon's work at the Lever warehouse, she asked me if I could be her escort to a friend's wedding and reception on Saturday afternoon. Possibly the white navy uniform I was wearing would be typical of a wartime wedding guest.

It was an attractive little church ceremony at a suburban area on the outskirts of Durban followed by a friendly little hotel reception attended by a few friends and acquaintances of the young bride and groom. After the reception, in the early evening, Marjorie and I took a table in the roof garden of the hotel where we danced to a band playing soft sentimental songs and music under a star-studded tropic sky, as the soft breeze carried the scent of bougainvillaea from the garden below.

Marjorie told me that an American air force officer she had been dating in Johannesburg had made a rather strange suggestion that in event of his death his body would be sent to her for burial, as he had no close relatives in America. I remarked thoughtfully, 'You seem to be following in the footsteps of the air forces in New York and Johannesburg!'

It had been a long and somewhat pent-up odyssey since leaving New York and all at once the unwinding had begun. It was early in the morning when I left Marjorie's little apartment room to find my way in the bright moonlight down to Durban seafront, then along the Indian Ocean past the Boer War hero statue of the horseman, Dick King. I mused that my father's sister Annette had asked me to contact his kin folk when first visiting South Africa, and I had found no trace left of the Victorian era of Paul Revere. I continued walking with my thoughts to where *St Loman* lay quietly at Maydon Wharf, startling the dozing quartermaster at her gangplank.

'You're a different man this morning, skipper!' remarked the discerning Ossie. 'Relaxed, not so tense as you have been in past weeks. Whoever she is, I'm grateful to her for you being easier for us to live with in the wardroom!'

The following Monday *St Loman* was due to sail for Cape Town and the Walvis Bay assignment. Marjorie knew of a small establishment at Umlanga Rocks, reached by train from Durban. She made reservations for that weekend where we dined on the largest and fattest oysters I had ever experienced.

As *St Loman* turned seaward on the Monday I waved a hand towards the corner of the Lever building where a slim little figure might have been standing.

On arrival at Cape Town *St Loman* was assigned a berth alongside the *Northern Duke* commanded by Lt Wright RNR, who invited me aboard shortly after we made fast. *Northern Duke* was one of the German-built trawlers and had been working out of Morehead City when we had been assigned to the US Navy. Thus when the British trawler fleet sailed for Cape Town, *Northern Duke* was several hundred miles on her way, and being without convoy escort duties, arrived in South Africa at the end of November.

Prior to joining the Navy, Lt Wright had been a 3rd officer on a British tanker when war was declared. Although he was only 30 years old, his hair was snow white, although in tight curls. Nevertheless his eyebrows were jet black, making it apparent that his hair had gone prematurely white. Wright caught my quizzical glance to answer the unspoken question:

'Yes, it went white overnight! I was third mate on a British tanker about two days out of Milford Haven when war was declared. We were in ballast on passage to the port of Abadan in the Persian Gulf. A U-boat surfaced, told us to abandon ship then put two torpedoes into her. It was early evening and the sea was relatively calm; we lowered two lifeboats and pulled away from the ship as she sank. Being in ballast, there was no oil fire created. Yet when we were picked up a day later my hair had gone dead white, although I had been under no great stress.'

'Your story reminds me of one of Joseph Conrad's tales,' I told him, '*The Black Mate*, where the chief mate of the clipper ship *Sapphire* had lost his ship in the Indian Ocean and had his master's certificate suspended for a year. During that year Mr Bunter's hair went white, like yours, and like you he was in the prime of life. Since only a young man could be signed on as the chief mate of a clipper ship, Mr Bunter had dyed his hair as black as a raven's wing

225

and was recognized by the policemen on the East India dock gate as "The Black Mate".'

'Yes, Warwick, I remember the story, and I have thought about dyeing my hair like Mr Bunter to get back my old job with Shell Oil after we win this war!'

'By that time you won't have to fake up Mr Bunter's excuse. He had to convince Captain Johns of the *Sapphire* that he had seen a ghost, causing him to fall down the poop ladder, so that after several days in his cabin with his head bound up he could reveal that his hair had turned white from the shock of seeing the apparition.'

'Another pink gin, Warwick?' Wright enquired. 'It's what we call "Skeleton Coast" salvage in our wardroom! It came off *Dunedin Star*, the thirteen thousand-ton Blue Star passenger-cargo ship bound from Liverpool to Cape Town. She had sailed independently from Liverpool with a full cargo of munitions and other war material, with about a hundred aboard, including twenty-one passengers.

'After crossing five thousand miles of the U-boat-patrolled Atlantic safely, and only three days steaming from Cape Town on the twenty-ninth of November 1942, the *Dunedin Star* hit what was believed to have been the Clan Alpine shoal. It's three to five miles off the Kaokoveld coast, four hundred miles north of Walvis Bay.

'Bumping over the shoal tore away the duct keel beneath the engine room and water rushed in. With every pump in the ship working, the chief engineer reported to the captain on the bridge that the ship could float for three or four hours at the most.'

'I have some idea how he felt,' I interrupted him. 'The *St Loman* was rammed by a ten thousand-ton ship straggler off a coastal convoy north of the Firth of Forth. We had to steer for a sandy beach to go ashore if the pumps didn't keep the water below the main fires in the engine room. Fortunately, by reversing the condenser pump, the *St Loman* made it to the dockside in Aberdeen for Christmas 1941.'

'Well,' he went on, 'the Captain of the *Dunedin Star* was lucky enough to find a sandy beach to run up his leaking liner. That's how we saw her, lying in the boiling surf, hard and fast on the shore when *Northern Duke* came up from Walvis Bay to stand by the wreck to protect it, and the salvage party on board from possible U-boat attack.'

When the *Dunedin Star* was beached, the two nearest ships were the British freighter *Manchester Division* and a Norwegian motor ship *Temeraire*. Both ships would take about 48 hours to reach her position.

Meanwhile the *Dunedin Star* was rolling and bumping with every swell. A sandbank had begun to form on both sides and amidships, while at the same time the current was scouring away the sand from under the bow and stern leaving them unsupported. As the hull was already weakened by the bottom damage when hitting the Clan Alpine shoal, eventually the strain would cause the ship to break her back into two half sections (see p. 228).

The Captain weighed up the choices of remaining on the wreck until help arrived in two days' time, or make a landing to wait ashore, and made the decision to abandon ship. The ship's stout motor lifeboat was the only boat capable of negotiating the surf by keeping the lifeboat end on to the incoming waves with the help of a strong rope made fast to the wreck and paid out foot by foot from the motor boat as she edged nearer to the beach.

The first trip was made with 21 passengers, including 8 women, 3 babies in arms, a number of elderly men, reinforced by several Royal Navy men on their way to Alexandria. The launch made two more trips with crew members before being disabled by heavy seas and cast up on the beach, leaving 63 people on the beach and 43 more still on board the wreck about 500 yards away in the surf.

At dawn on the third day the *Manchester Division* and the *Temeraire* had come up during the night. It was arranged between the two rescue ships that the *Temeraire*'s motor lifeboat should try to get the remainder of the crew off the wreck. The motor boat went alongside the wreck several times transferring the men to the *Manchester Division*. By about eleven o'clock that morning the Captain of the *Dunedin Star* was the last to leave his ship. A police convoy was coming overland to help those on the beach and aircraft would be dropping food to them.

'How did you get into the bonded store of the *Dunedin Star*? It must have been close to Christmas when *Northern Duke* arrived on the scene?' I asked.

'You're right. In fact, we were the only ship standing by on Christmas Eve. The two minesweepers *Crassula* and *Nerine* of the South African Navy, based on Walvis Bay, had left to ferry cargo salved by about twenty men of the Witwatersrand Rifles, back to Walvis Bay. Thus, at the same time as *St Loman*'s group was celebrating in Walvis Bay, we had about fifty soldiers, sailors, and airmen having a party in the listing lounge of the *Dunedin Star*!

'While my orders were to stand by the wreck and provide protection from possible U-boat attack, it was suggested that *Northern Duke* might try to salvage the mails for the Eighth Army in North Africa.

'Prior to Christmas Eve, *Northern Duke* had dropped anchor as close as it was prudent and clear of the surf, and then we paid out the cable until close to the stern of the wreck, going slow ahead on the engines to maintain steerage

THE DUNEDIN STAR, the 13,000-ton Blue Star ship, bound from Liverpool to Cape Town, was wrecked on the Kaokoveld coast, 400 miles north of Walvis Bay, on November 29, 1942, it has now been officially disclosed. The Union Government organised the rescue of the 106 survivors by land, sea and air, the rescue taking nearly three weeks. The ship broke her back and thousands of tons of potatoes soon strewed the uninhabited coast.

way.

'The Coxswain and a couple of the seamen rigged up a Carley float with a cable paid out from the stern of *Northern Duke,* and getting aboard *Dunedin Star,* pulled another line to be reeved through a block on the mast and back to *Northern Duke,* then as fast as the salvage party brought along the mail bags, we hauled them aboard. After the party on Christmas Eve, we salvaged most of the gin and whisky from the bonded store, leaving the beer, as water was in short supply.

'We sailed for Cape Town on Christmas Day and docked late one night about five days later to alert all the trawler wardrooms that there was salvage work to be done right away to hide the cases in the bunkers.

'Next morning I was awakened by South African Customs men requesting a search of *Northern Duke,* stating that as we had been able to transfer the mail, we would have also gone into the bonded stores! Naturally I protested, saying that it was enough risk to men's lives to salvage the essential mail for the Eighth Army, let alone liquor! On the conclusion of their fruitless search, I demanded and received an apology . . . Have another pink gin, Warwick!'

Lt Jones, the *St Loman*'s gunnery officer, now came to me with a problem over the missing sighting telescope for the 4-inch gun.

'Just what did happen to it, Jonesy?' I enquired.

'Andy Morrison, the gunner, says that a staff gunnery PO in New York took it ashore for adjustment and never returned it, but as Andy never uses it and prefers the open sights, he didn't worry about it.'

'Now it is my turn to worry about it!' I said. 'I am responsible for everything. Of course neither you nor Andy obtained a receipt from the staff PO, and it's an odd's on chance that he could have flogged it ashore in New York. If the shore staff require any accounting for the telescope from me, then you and Andy have a poor excuse.'

'That's the situation, skipper. The Cape Town gunnery officer is due aboard tomorrow for an inspection of the four-inch gun.'

'Jonesy, you had better see Ossie right away and get out his deck logbook for that time when the US Coast Guard cutters reported the worst weather on the Eastern Sea Frontier in the past ten years. As I recall, the port life-raft, lashed to the foremast rigging, was damaged, and you might find Ossie's entry as to the four-inch gun telescope being knocked adrift and lost overboard at that time. I will need to see that a proper entry was made regarding the damage to the life-raft and the loss of the telescope overboard in that heavy weather. I can explain the loss of the telescope, if I should be asked about it. Ossie must produce his deck logbook to show the entry. Entries are always made in pencil by prudent deck officers; only the fair logs are in ink and those are not made up in wartime on these ships. Do I make myself quite clear, Jonesy?'

'Yes, skipper, I will see Number One right away!'

The staff gunnery officer was rather perplexed as to how the telescope could have been knocked adrift, and undoubtedly had his suspicions, despite the production of the deck log records.

At a staff cocktail party later, the NOIC Cape Town, Captain Ridgeway, observed to me, 'Warwick, you cover up for your officers!'

'We have been together for a long time, sir,' I replied.

It is customary for all ships in the Royal Navy to have a specific crew complement of officers, petty officers and ratings for the most economic and efficient operation and fighting effectiveness of each individual type of ship and class. By promoting experienced and well-qualified men to higher ranks could result in a ship's company being 'over complement'. A base manning officer observing this situation, and also short of qualified leading ratings, would be expected to replace the newly promoted men with inexperienced recruits.

Disregarding deserved recommendations for promotion and advancement would avoid the possible loss of some of the best men in the ship's company, but those ratings and petty officers would lose the opportunity to earn extra pay and promotion.

Ships' captains in wardroom conversations would warn me, 'Warwick, if you make promotion recommendations for your best seamen, you are going to lose them to the base manning officer!'

'Maybe so,' I would reply, 'but I feel that I will get the best out of my ship's company if the word gets around that good men getting their job done earn promotion, which means extra pay!'

That extra pay did follow for the *St Loman*'s three asdic ratings, Sutton, Sullivan, Houghton and also for Able Seamen Cuthbert and Brown, who all made leading seamen.

It might be said, like the mills of God, those of navy paymasters also 'grind slowly but exceeding small!' Visiting the paymaster's office on learning that the *St Loman*'s pay papers had been received at the Cape Town base, I found that the five able seamen recommended for promotion had received it nine months previously and were due for a lump sum in extra pay earned through their promotion.

'You and you officers don't do as well, Commander. You are not due to draw a month's pay for another month or more,' remarked the paymaster lieutenant.

I was incredulous. 'We were at least two months on passage without a monthly pay settlement, with only a small advance drawn in Freetown. So! How come, paymaster?' Then the awesome thought struck me. 'Do you mean to say that we have been paying fifty cents of that magnificent one US dollar "higher cost of living allowance per diem" as a deduction for UK income tax?'

The lieutenant grinned and nodded. 'Yes, that's the situation. The only exception is your Canadian officer, Lieutenant Willis, as neither Canadians, Australians, nor South African personnel on active service pay income tax!'

'Well, it just shows that because the UK declared it, then it is our war to pay for!'

That evening Ossie and I went to Savini's in Cape Town, a favourite watering hole for all ranks and services. No sooner had we sat down at a table when came the shout of: 'Champagne for our skipper and Number One. We only drink champagne in our ship!'

Nearby were the *St Loman*'s five new leading seamen clutching fistfuls of pound notes. There was no denying the large bottle of sparkling South African wine that the waiter plonked down on our table. Toasts were duly exchanged after which I suggested to Ossie that we might quietly make an exit to the Officer's Club.

At the Officer's Club a visit to a local night club was suggested. It appeared that one paid an entrance fee and bought a bottle of Cape brandy. The club then supplied and charged for 'set-ups' with ginger ale. The latter was essential to kill the fire and taste of Cape brandy. Ossie had invited the receptionist at the Officers' Club to join us. She turned out to be one of the very few ladies present as the club was full of South African army officers on leave from North Africa where General Rommel's Afrika Korps was now beating a retreat westwards.

A tall, dark-haired party girl in a form-fitting, long, white evening gown was entertaining a group of young army lieutenants at the neighbouring table. They were too busy drinking to be using the dance floor. Ossie got up to dance with his date and I looked over at the vibrant nineteen-year-old and was invited to the dance floor.

Her name was Joan Taytasac, of French Huguenot descent, and the French showed through.

'Do you know Lieutenant Ronald Smith?' she asked. 'He was the gunnery officer on an armed merchant cruiser being refitted in Cape Town. He and Diana, my sister, decided that they could not live without each other and were married in Cape Town.'

'Where is your sister now?' I replied.

'Bubbles is in Liverpool, where Ronnie is the destroyer base gunnery

231

officer. We were inseparable and I do miss her so much. We did just everything together.'

It was early morning when Ossie and I left the night club to drop off our dates by taxi and then back to the ship. Joan worked at a florist shop and I had her telephone number with a date for lunch next day.

Over our lunch Joan was more talkative than ever, fuelled by a bottle of her favourite white wine. The Bernkastel was excellent, although, of course, rather more expensive than the average South African vintages. When we parted on busy Adderley Street, Joan planted a torrid, lingering kiss on me, much to the delight of the passing crowd, doubtless thinking that a serviceman was getting his just welcome.

That afternoon I had planned to carry out my promise to my one-time Australian shipmate, Lt Gott, now resident A/S officer in Trinidad. Walking to his aunt's house along the seafront, I knocked on her door, to be greeted by a charming, elderly Australian lady who welcomed me in for a strong brew of tea, remarking that I shouldn't be wasting my shore leave having tea with an old lady.

'Not at all!' I said. 'In fact this is a period of calm relief after my rather

On St Loman*'s foredeck*
S/Lt. Atkinson, Lt. Warwick, Lt. Dodwell, S/Lt. Jones

exciting lunch!'

'You have still got a little smudge of her lipstick on the corner of your mouth.' My hostess wetted the corner of her handkerchief and removed the tell-tale evidence.

As we chatted, I learned that her nephew's father had been awarded a posthumous Victoria Cross in 1918, and that was the reason for his volunteering for overseas service. There were old scores from the First World War to be settled in the Second.

CHAPTER XV

During March/April 1943 there had been little reported U-boat activity in the Indian Ocean. A couple of sporadic attacks were considered to have been made by two U-boats, Italian and German. U-Boat Command was preparing for their spring battle in the North Atlantic while at the same time General Bernard Montgomery's Eighth Army was driving General Erwin Rommel's Afrika Korps across North Africa. In 1940 during the German invasion of Norway, U-boats had been withdrawn from the North Atlantic to act as supply ships to the German Army advancing northwards in Norway. Now several U-boats were being diverted from the North Atlantic to supply a retreating German Army.

U-boat captains were personally assured by their Führer that their supply assignment was essential to the survival of the Afrika Korps. Subject to continuous air surveillance and attack in the shallow, clear waters of the Mediterranean after the deep, dark and more secure waters of the Atlantic, both commanders and their crews were most unhappy.

Springtime in England was the start of the South African winter, and there was a marked chill in the air as *St Loman* and *Northern Dawn* escorted a northbound convoy to Durban. One moonless night, under a cloudless, star-studded sky, the luminous discharge of St Elmo's fire, often regarded as a portent of bad weather, heralded the approach of a violent electrical storm.

The extremities of the mast and yardarms flickered and glowed with the fingers of blue-red fire reaching for the heavens. Then the storm broke. Lightning flashes came as giant, photographic, magnesium light flashes. Just for a second, the sea and all the ships were revealed in stark, naked brilliance, then plunged back into the black of night. Then came the rain in torrential, blinding sheets, seeming to alternate with the lightning flashes.

Almost as quickly as it came, the storm left us. I moved out from the shelter of the bridge deck house and was joined by Able Seaman Sands, the duty lookout.

'Quite a show of the heavenly fireworks, skipper!'

'Yes, Sandy. It must be ten years since my last experience in this ocean.'

'Will you be seeing that young lady in Durban, skipper?'

'Yes, I hope so. Do you have a girlfriend in Durban, Sandy?' Sands had been a boy signalman in the First World War. His dark, short, curling hair was now flecked with white.

'Aye, skipper, I have one in Durban, and one in Cape Town. I like the one in Cape Town best, as when we go out she gives me the money to pay, but the one in Durban pays the tabs herself. That looks bad, don't you think, skipper?'

'Yes, Sandy, indeed it does, and furthermore there's no chance of any change staying in your pocket either!'

'Aye, that's true, but then I always send an extra pound or two to the old lady. There's no one like the old lady, is there, sir?'

'You're right, Sandy, we're always faithful to them in our fashion!'

Ossie Dodwell had just come up to take the middle watch, and, joining him on the other wing of the bridge, I remarked that Sands and I had been comparing his dates in Cape Town and Durban. Ossie had his own date in Cape Town on his mind.

'Skipper, I've dated the receptionist at the Officers' Club several times. As you know the club is lit dimly. Then there is the blackout on the streets, and her apartment has rather secluded lights. So I had never seen her in broad daylight. Last week, after we had joined you and Joan at the night club, I met her for lunch and saw her in daylight for the first time. It gave me quite a shock to see how much she was made up to hide the ravages of time, as you might say. Why, I even felt embarrassed about being seen with her in broad daylight!'

'Now, come, come, Ossie! You're no youthful Adonis either. I found her quite an interesting conversationalist, in contrast to my nineteen-year-old date. As my wise old father would quote to you "At night all cats are grey, while many a good tune is gotten out of an old fiddle". Makes good small talk in addition.'

'You're right, skipper. I'd best stick to taking her out at night.'

'That could depend, Ossie, on what she thought when seeing you in daylight for the first time! Incidentally how do you get on with Noreen in Durban – the young widow living with her mother?'

'That's no problem. We go out in her car and park on the far end of the sea front. Noreen then opens the car door to let out her little dog to run around and guard the car.'

'Seems like a well-trained dog, Ossie, not lacking in experience!'

The following extract is from the Monthly Anti-Submarine Report for June 1943:

THE U-BOAT OFFENSIVE

(a) REVIEW FOR JUNE

Late in May the enemy accepted the fact of decisive defeat in the Spring Battle, which he had no doubt hoped might decide the War of the Atlantic in his favour, and retired from the battlefield of the North Atlantic convoy routes. During June he maintained only outriders in this field and apparently sent his main forces to scour new territory in search of targets outside ranges of shore-based aircraft.

Fortunately, the story of the month's endeavours can be summed up in the single word 'Failure'. Shipping casualties were extraordinarily low. In the area 500-700 miles to the south-west of the Azores U-boats were sighted on several occasions and it is probable that they were present in force, apparently still seeking to employ the pack tactics, familiar in the North-Western Approaches, in an area where immunity from air attack may have been counted upon. In the whole month one ship was sunk in this area: the cost of this futile operation to the enemy is not known but U.S.S. Bogue's aircraft made several attacks, apart from the one after which survivors were recovered.

Whilst maintaining this intended offensive against troop and supply convoys between the United States and Morocco, the enemy was also busy planning and preparing for U-boat raids on shipping in distant areas such as Rio de Janeiro, the Cape of Good Hope and the Caribbean, the fruits of which he could not gather before July. In consequence the month was an interim and in the result a quiet phase.

Owing to the dispersal and redisposition of the U-boat forces, the opportunities to attack U-boats were comparatively rare but, judged by the reduced scale of targets, the rate of killing remained satisfactory, though inevitably lower than the unacceptable casualty rate which forced the enemy to withdraw from the main battlefield.

Pending a renewal at the enemy's choice – if and when morale can be sufficiently restored – of the main and only vital and decisive struggle in the North-Western Approaches, battle was joined on our initiative in the approaches to the Bay of Biscay. On the 24th June the Second Escort Group made history with two kills in the newly but now permanently embattled area to the north-west of Cape Ortegal. At the fringe of enemy air dominion, surface escorts joined the Coastal Command pioneers in marauding sallies against U-boats on passage into and out of the Bay of Biscay through which all U-boats, wherever they may be bound or wherever they have been operating, must pass from and to their bases. For the time being this is the vital contest: 'They shall not pass' is the aim and, if it be made good in whole or in substantial part, there may never be any renewal of the Battle of the North-Western Approaches.

(b) ESTIMATE OF U-BOATS OPERATING IN THE ATLANTIC AND INDIAN OCEANS IN JUNE

Areas as shown in Plate 3	North-Western Approaches		Arctic		South-Western Approaches		Western Atlantic		Azores		Freetown		South Atlantic		Indian Ocean	
	German	Italian	German	Italian	German	Italian	German	Italian	German	Italian	German	Italian	German	Italian	German	Italian
31st May – 6th June	25	–	6	–	20	–	20	–	10	1	6	–	7	1	3	–

7th-13th June	25	–	7	–	15	–	10	–	25	–	6 1	7	1	3	–
14th-20th June	10	–	7	–	10	2	30	–	25	2	3 2	8	2	2	–
21st-27th June	10	–	6	–	10	–	35	–	20	2	2 1	3	–	6	1

(c) MERCHANT SHIPPING LOSSES

The mercantile tonnage lost by U-boat attack during June, as recorded to date, amounts to 101,000 gross tons and is the best monthly total since November, 1941. The quiet period in U-boat activity which began about 10th May continued throughout June and the number of U-boats operating during the month was substantially less than in previous months.

A rather more detailed analysis of the numbers and tonnage sunk by U-boats gives the following results:-

	Independents		In Convoys		Stragglers		Dispersed Ex Convoy		Total	
	No.	G.T.	No.	G.T.	No.	G.T.	No.	G.T.	No.	G.T.
January, 1943	10	48	15	107	8	45	1	3	34	203
February	11	63	34	212	12	72	1	5	58	352
March	20	114	70	416	13	72	2	11	105	613
April	22	135	25	150	7	40	–	–	54	325
May	18	97	25	124	5	31	1	5	49	257
June	15*	79*	4	22	–	–	–	–	19	101

(Tonnage is given in thousand gross tons.)
* This includes one ship sunk in Muscat harbour.

Of the four ships lost in convoy, one sinking occurred in the Cape of Good Hope area, two in the Mediterranean, and one in the Pacific. No convoy losses occurred in the North Atlantic.

During the month 14 ocean convoys of 591 ships arrived in the United Kingdom without loss and 15 outward ocean convoys of 572 ships reached their destinations without loss. In the same period 172 Western Atlantic and Caribbean convoys of 1,742 ships reached their destinations without loss and one convoy, originally of 35 ships, lost one ship (by mine) before arrival.

The following table shows tonnage losses by U-boats compared with tonnage losses by Aircraft and other enemy causes during the last six months:-

Month	Total Losses All Causes	By U-boat		By Aircraft		By Other Causes	
		Losses	Percentage	Losses	Percentage	Losses	Percentage
January	244	203	83	26	11	15	6
February	377	352	93	7	2	18	5
March	680	613	90	66	10	1	–
April	344	325	94	3	1	16	5
May	278	257	93	20	7	1	–
June (Provisional)	110	101	92	6	5	3	3

U-boats once again claimed the highest proportion of the total tonnage sunk at 92 per cent.

The analysis of attacks shows a considerable reduction in the number of attacks by U-boats during June. There were 14 attacks on single ships resulting in 11 being sunk, two escaping with damage, and one escaping undamaged, giving percentages of 79, 14 and 7 respectively. The percentage of ships lost was rather below the average for the previous nine months. Five convoys, in which 184 ships were subjected to risk of attack, were attacked by U-boats, resulting in two ships, or one per cent, being sunk and 99 per cent being undamaged.

No surface craft attacks were recorded.

As regards attacks by enemy aircraft, there were five on single ships resulting in no losses, while two ships escaped damaged and three undamaged or 40 and 60 per cent respectively. There were only two attacks on convoys or groups, in which 11 ships were subjected to risk of attack, and of these two were sunk, one escaped with damage and eight were undamaged, giving percentages of 18, 9 and 73 respectively. The percentage of ships sunk was relatively high in comparison with the percentage rate for the previous nine months and may indicate greater precision in bombing but, as the figures are rather small, no precise conclusions can be drawn from the June results alone.

General remarks

The Mercantile losses from all enemy causes fell to 110,000 gross tons in June which represents the third lowest monthly total since the war began. A satisfactory feature was the very small loss of tonnage in the North Atlantic which only amounted to just over 15,000 tons. The Indian Ocean with 43,000 tons took priority of place, for the first time, as the worst area for losses during the month.

The total of Allied and Neutral tonnage (ships of all tonnages) sunk by enemy action since the war began now amounts to rather more than 18 million gross tons of which nearly 12¾ million gross tons, or 70 per cent, has been sunk by U-boats.

The usual exaggerated claims of tonnage sunk were broadcast by the enemy. One in particular from Calais on 1st July claimed that 'the British and Americans were deprived, in June, of a total tonnage of 513,000 tons. This figure does not include Japanese successes in the Pacific and Indian Oceans. The British and Americans are, therefore, not justified in claiming June as an especially lucky month.'

It was late August 1943 when Captain Ridgeway, the Naval Officer in Charge, Cape Town, requested my presence in his office.

'Warwick, I have just received a signal from A/S Warfare Division at the Admiralty to the effect that you are being promoted to Lieutenant Commander, and are to return to the UK to take command of a bigger and better ship.'

'I cannot have a better ship, sir!' I replied.

Ridgeway shook his head a little testily. 'I understand your meaning, Warwick, but a new frigate now building is a much better ship command.'

I was to take passage on a troopship now on her way from North Africa to Durban and Cape Town carrying 'walking wounded' officers and men from the Eighth Army. The battleship *Resolution*, accompanied by a fleet oiler and two destroyers, would form the little group bound for the UK.

'Captain Ridgeway, I have been in command of *St Loman* for a little over three years. After handing over to my relief, it would enable me to make a clean break by leaving to meet the troopship in Durban, rather than wait in Cape Town.'

'I know how you must feel, Warwick, and it's a reasonable request that I will approve.'

Returning on board *St Loman* I met my three officers to advise them of my pending transfer to the UK, and to bring the wardroom wine accounts together with the ship's canteen accounts up to date ready to be handed over to my relief.

Two days later *St Loman* was due to sail for Walvis Bay under her new commander. At that time my standard navy uniform trunk was packed and locked, accompanied by a large seaman's canvas kit bag. A taxi had been ordered to take me to the Cape Town railway station. Then I went down to the mess deck to face my ship's company for the last time.

'Captain Ridgeway, the NOIC, told me that I was being relieved to take command of a better ship. I replied that I could not have a better ship than *St Loman*. That reply did not go down too well with him. He said that he knew what I meant, but a new frigate building in the UK was a better ship!

'I recall that evening in Belfast, when the watch ashore started to cross the gangway of the ship alongside just as her quartermaster sang out: "Here comes *St Loman*'s watch ashore, rolling along with their medals going clank! clank!" I felt very proud indeed.

'Over the past three years or more, I have cussed out most of you from time to time, and I know that under your breath you've called the "old man" a right bastard in reply. Nevertheless, through both the rough times and the smooth, we have had a very happy ship, so much so that the seaman from Newfoundland you call "Newfie John", who was on leave at home when we sailed from New York, travelled over three thousand miles to join us in Cape Town, despite being torpedoed in one ship on the way!

'In the words of the old ditty, the best, the very best of friends must part. There is something sticking in my throat and I cannot say anything more except "Thank you, one and all" and shake your hands.'

As I shook hands with *St Loman*'s best asdic operator, Ldg. Seaman Houghton, he told me, 'Skipper, you've called me a silly bastard at times, but I'd rather sail with you than any other bastard!' That was a compliment straight from the heart.

My taxi, loaded with my gear, was waiting on the dockside. I crossed the gangway, *St Loman* was already coming gently astern on the back spring, swinging her bow out to starboard. Now, all lines cast off, she headed out into Table Bay.

The taxi driver remarked to my back, 'They say that it's harder for a captain to leave his ship than his wife. Is that so?'

'See for yourself!' I replied turning to meet him with tears running unashamedly down my face.

There had been another reason for asking Captain Ridgeway for permission to travel to Durban for boarding the troopship coming from North Africa. Joan Taytasac was as hell-bent as ever to join her married sister Diana, who had succeeded in joining her husband, Lt Ronald Smith RNVR, in Liverpool, where Ronnie had obtained the post of gunnery officer for the Western Approaches escort group base. It was probably helpful that Ronnie's father was a very well-connected family lawyer, and had established the young couple in the charming guest house of his home. It was not all hardships in wartime England!

When in New York, Miss Gladys Wilcock of the Little Old Mansion Restaurant had observed to me, 'What you know about women wouldn't fill a nutshell, and I don't mean a coconut shell!' Bearing her sage evaluation in mind, I realized that being at a loose end in Cape Town, exposed to a vibrant nineteen-year-old with an overwhelming desire to qualify for passage to England, I would be a very vulnerable prospect, particularly as during the last evening spent with Joan on the family couch of a silent home, her parting comment had been, 'You had made up your mind that you would not, but I had made up mine that you would!' I really did not have a chance with my very best intentions!

As luck would have it, Marjorie Plaskett was again on an IBM assignment at Levers and was able to get me a small one-room apartment in her facility. Money was short, as always, but the sale of my personal sextant provided ample funds for my R & R week in Durban. The sextant was really excess baggage and my possession was the mandatory requirement when I was a cadet in the Royal Mail Steam Packet Company. The Hughes sextant that my father had bought with an export discount through his brokerage firm produced double its original cost of fifteen pounds. I thought my 'goer father' would have approved!

Four days passed pleasantly, as did the nights, but all too quickly. Marjorie left early for her supervision of the Hollerith, or IBM operations at Levers on Maydon Wharf. I checked in at the naval base and met Marjorie for lunch.

On the morning of the fifth day I was given the change in operations. As there were less than a hundred 'walking wounded' to be embarked in Durban, the decision had been made for the troopship to save time by continuing direct to Cape Town. The troop train was to leave the next day, and that morning I left quietly before Marjorie was awake, leaving a message that I was on my way.

One of the naval officers in the group was a Lt Crowley RN, from my brother Ian's term at Pangbourne College, who was returning to the UK after completing an assignment on an Australian destroyer as first lieutenant. Crowley did not have much to say except that there had been a rather mutinous situation existing since the Japanese takeover of Singapore. We arranged to share a two-berth compartment on the miserable slow train to Cape Town, when it seemed that every morning, as the blind was raised at dawn, there was the very same whirring metal windmill, greening a patch of flat brown veldt as it kept the water flowing into the cistern and trough surrounded by a small flock of sheep.

In the late afternoon, after travelling for almost three days, our train pulled alongside the troop transport in Cape Town, which I recognized as the converted passenger ship that *St Loman*, with the unwilling tug from the coastal convoy, had pulled off the Avalon shoal off the New Jersey coast. The same chief officer, who had been on her fo'csle then, was now on the gangway as I came aboard welcoming me as an old acquaintance. 'Come up to my quarters after we get to sea tonight!'

Over a quiet bottle of beer after supper he asked me: 'Did you get any salvage money?'

'The Admiralty don't pay any salvage money these days,' I replied.

'The owners made a payment to the tug of three thousand dollars and the Captain wrote a very appreciative letter to the Admiralty,' commented the chief officer.

In the morning Table Mountain was a faint blue blur as our troopship sailed, in company with the weary old battleship *Resolution*, a fleet oiler and two destroyers. We were scheduled to make 7-8 knots, but most likely would average less on our way to the UK.

Our 'walking wounded' were all up and about on the boat deck, hobbling along or steadying themselves with their crutches. It was estimated that there were a thousand on board.

'Not much hope for many survivors if this lot gets a torpedo!' remarked Crowley. 'Not enough boats and they would never be able to get into them.'

'True enough, Crowley, but a U-boat commander with his eye on earning an Iron Cross with diamonds might make the *Resolution* his first choice and tangle with her destroyer as this ship cleared the danger area!'

There was a small bar open in the evening, but after two days the beer supplies ran out followed by all the spirits, with the exception of Creme de Menthe – 'Starboard Light'. The ship's officers had their personal supplies and thanks to my salvage connections with the chief officer I was able to join him every evening for a rationed bottle of beer.

One evening in the bar I met with another college acquaintance, Mitchell Innes, a captain in the Rifle Brigade nursing a battered leg and thigh, which despite doctors' predictions he was hoping to retain after arriving in England. His brigade had been with the initial landing of the Eighth Army in North Africa. He told me, 'As reinforcements began building up we hoped that it might be a little easier for us old timers, but now that General Montgomery was planning his strategy, he was demanding that probes of the enemy lines should be made by "seasoned troops". Of course we were the "seasoned troops", and there was no relief from that duty! Monty was not going to make a move until he was sure of having the maximum force to win when the advance came. That was when I got hit in my leg and thigh. It hurt like hell and at every first aid station I was demanding more morphine injections. I was full of it, and it still hurt!'

All the walking wounded were willing to volunteer the action story causes of their various afflictions incurred in driving Rommel across North Africa. One exception was the silent army major who had escaped from a Japanese prison camp. Those who had seen him in the bathroom showers stated that his whole back was a honeycomb mass of bayonet wounds or stabs as they tried to make him supply information.

Lt Crowley and I read all the available books in the small ship's library, and ended up amusing each other by reciting various nonsense rhymes such as 'The Owl and the Pussy Cat', 'The Yarn of the Nancy Bell', 'You are old Father William'. Somehow the 30-odd days and nights passed by until the *Resolution* and her destroyer escort broke away for Scapa Flow as our ship gathered full speed to make Liverpool, England.

It was mid-September when I made it home to my lonely, but brave little mother living alone in the big flat in the massive five-storey Victorian mansion which my father had divided up into four flats some years back.

After arriving on a Thursday afternoon I spent the weekend quietly at home and on the Monday morning took the train to London and reported to Commander Frank Mason, my old acquaintance in the personnel division of the Admiralty.

Mason advised me that my new frigate was now completing at Swan Hunter & Wigham Richardson shipyard at Wallsend-on-Tyne, and was probably due for commissioning in November/December 1943. The *Rushen Castle* had all the latest anti-submarine technology, and the range and depth recording asdic coordinated with the 'squid' missile system. She would be manned by a regular

RN crew.

I was to attend two courses, a Damage Control session being held at a location near my home in Surbiton, and the Western Approaches Tactical School conducted in Liverpool by Captain G.H. Roberts RN. Each course was scheduled for one week.

It was getting near to lunchtime when Commander Mason called for a messenger.

'Warwick, the messenger will take you to Admiral James who heads the Press Division. He wants to get some decorated naval officers to give talks to factory workers employed on Admiralty supply contracts, and I have spoken to him about you.'

The messenger led me through the labyrinth of passages in the old Admiralty building to the office of 'Bubbles' James, to give the Admiral his navy sobriquet.

The English painter, Sir John Everett Millais (1829-1896) had painted a picture of a small boy blowing bubbles, which was acquired by Pear's Soap for a poster and advertising campaign. The picture was entitled 'Bubbles'.

'Good of Commander Mason to send you up to me. It's just after twelve noon and I want you to join me at the clerks' bar. It's a little facility where the Admiralty clerks could get beer in peacetime. We have continued to use it.'

The curly blond hair of the little boy in the Millais portrait had become a mass of grey, but the chubby boy's face remained, while the skin was weathered reddish.

'I am having a pint of bitter. Will you join me, Warwick?'

'Glad to, sir! It's my favourite drink. Having just left a troopship that was without beer for a month, I have some catching up to do!'

We both drank deeply. Then, drawing breath, the Admiral continued by outlining the needs for his Press Division.

'We are very short of officers to make presentations to factory workers. The RAF have plenty of these fighter and bomber pilots available who they can pull out of the air for a day or two, so as to speak, but we can't get our commanders off the sea. Now Mason tells me that you are standing by a new frigate and have a few weeks' leave.'

I put down my now empty glass on the little bar and looked thoughtful, perhaps thirsty.

'You can't buy anything here. It's for the staff exclusively. But you will have another pint.'

With our glasses refilled, I was thinking to myself that while I had made presentations to small groups of executives or spoken to a ship's company, I had never faced several hundred upturned faces. Perhaps this would be an opportunity to try it out and if I fell flat on my face in wartime I would be forgiven, whereas in an important peacetime gathering failure could be disastrous.

'What should I talk about, Admiral?'

'Experiences, that sort of thing!'

'What about security, sir?'

'They are doing more secret work than you can talk about!' I finished my pint. Admiral James refilled it. It was really the best bitter I had drunk in a long time.

'Very well, sir. I'll have a go at it!'

'Good man! I'll take you up to Mrs Rubin, our press officer, and she can work out your assignments to work in with your courses and time off.'

Mrs Rubin was very efficient and between 27 September and 16 December had me scheduled to tour and talk at 22 factories and shipyards. I not only faced several hundred faces, but several thousand in all. Mrs Rubin's Press Division list provided the meeting date, the number of employees involved, and the navy war material being produced. It was very varied and in most instances hard for the workers to visualize its importance to the war effort.

As a start, Mrs Rubin had given me companies in London and the Home Counties, as follows:

27 September   Mollart Engineering Company Ltd. 700 employees.
                    Surbiton, Surrey.
                    Precision tools and gauges. Universal ball joints.

28 September   A.H. Hunt Ltd. 150 employees.
                    Virginia Water, Surrey.
                    Electrical condensers.

28 September   G. Hopkins & Son Ltd. 450 employees.
                    London, N.7.
                    Oerlikon components. Asdic domes.

30 September   Young Accumulators Ltd. 220 employees.
                    New Malden, Surrey.
                    Batteries and accumulators for A/S gear.

1 October   Dubilier Condenser Co. Ltd. 1,200 employees.
                    London, W.3.
                    A/S apparatus. Condensers. Switches. Resistances.

4 October	Airscrew Co. Ltd. 1,100 employees.
	Weybridge, Surrey.
	Deckhouses for torpedo boats. Airscrews.

5 October   Multitone Electric Co. Ltd. 400 employees.
             Clerkenwell, London E.C.1.
             RDF equipment.

6 October   Wates Ltd. 100 employees.
             Mitcham, S.W.16.
             Power-driven surf boats. Boats for special forces.

7 October   R.B. Pullen & Co Ltd. 550 employees.
             Brentford, Middlesex.
             A/S Instruments and gear. Naval fire control.

16 November Johnson & Mathey Co. Ltd. 650 employees.
             Shepherds Bush.
             Compass pivots. Automatic parts.

17 November Powers Accounting Machines Ltd. 3,500 employees.
             Thornton Heath, Croydon, Surrey.
             Gun parts. Fuses. Ignition fuses.

18 November W. Lusty & Sons. 500 employees.
             Hackney Wick, London, E.9.
             Chart boxes.

23 November Standard Telephones & Cables Ltd. 6,000 employees.
             North Woolwich, London.
             A/S radio, telephone equipment.

24 November Erie Resister Ltd. 1,000 employees.
             Hendon, London, N.W.9.
             A/S radio. Resistance rod. Mining stores.

30 November Swan Hunter & Wigham Richardson Ltd. 1,000 employees.
             Wallsend Shipyard, Newcastle-on-Tyne.

Ship repairs. Castings and forgings.

1 December   Swan Hunter Neptune Shipyard. 1,000 employees.
Walker, Newcastle-on-Tyne.
Ship builders.

2 December   Mercantile Dry Docks Ltd. 800 employees.
Jarrow-on-Tyne.
Merchant ship repairs. Electric works.

3 December   Wallsend Slipway & Engineering Co. Ltd. 3,500 employees.
Wallsend-on-Tyne.
Ship repairs. Engines. Propelling machinery.

15 December   Johnson & Mathey Co. Ltd. 519 employees.
Exhibition Grounds, Wembley, London.
Searchlight components. Resistance wires.

15 December   Art Metal Construction Co. 171 employees.
Exhibition Grounds, Wembley, London.
Steel racks, boxes and cupboards for naval stores.

16 December   Brasse Ltd. 124 employees.
High Street, Hornsey.
Electrical insulation. Sleevings.

16 December   A. Imhof Ltd. 100 employees.
112 New Oxford Street, London, W.C.1.
Radar.

'Experiences, that sort of thing,' as Admiral James had suggested, to encourage and possibly enthuse factory workers, did not seem to me as being very effective in improving the quality and quantity of their production efforts. Shipyard and aircraft workers excepted, how could those engaged in soldering electrical terminals and connections, assembling switches, and resistances visualize the importance of their often monotonous production lines?

Thus I planned to try and personalize the essential use and importance of their manufactures in the continuing Battle of the Atlantic to ensure the safe arrival of the many convoys of merchant ships with their cargoes of crucial food supplies and raw materials, aircraft and high-octane fuel. During a normal tour of a factory I would hope to either devise or recognize the uses of their products in convoy escort ships.

At the Multitone Electric Company I found about 400 women and girls engaged in the assembly and soldering of electrical contacts on various condensors, switches and resistances. As I walked with the works manager along the production lines the girls began to sing, softly first of all, but then gathering volume as others joined in the song, 'All the nice girls love a sailor . . .' My sun and weather-burnt cheeks took on a bright red blush!

As I was to talk in the canteen after the girls had eaten their lunch, the works manager returned me to the directors' board room where the managing director, Mr Poliakoff, was waiting with the welcome Scotch whisky bottle on the table. Adequately fortified I then had to face the 'songbirds' gathered in the works canteen, and as I recall, my presentation to them was along these lines:

'Today I recognized many of the essential electronic items that make up the vital underwater and surface detection devices for seeking out and destroying German U-boats attacking our Western Ocean convoys. Our work on convoy escort ships, like your work here, requires fighting the monotony of repetition with great care and attention to detail. Of course, we must be vigilant at all times.

'The average convoy, when formed up, may consist of four or five columns with five or six ships in each column, making up a little fleet of about thirty ships.

'The senior officer of the escort group stations the ships so that with their underwater and surface surveillance gear they literally "sweep" the area through which the convoy will be passing.

'German U-boats are assigned patrol lines covering the convoy routes in the North Atlantic, hoping to sight and report the position, course and speed of convoys to U-Boat Command in Berlin. This sighting signal will be picked up by the Admiralty in London which will inform the escort commander that his convoy has been sighted by a U-boat patrol.

'The convoy commodore, on being informed, may decide to alter the course of the convoy to throw off the sighting U-boat, now likely to be taking a position astern of the convoy while passing the convoy position and course to other U-boats in the vicinity.

'The radio chatter between U-boats may be heard for two or three days as three or more may now be just out of sight astern of the convoy. Then there is silence, and the escort commander knows that "tonight is the night"!

'Most convoys will be averaging six or seven knots, or sea miles, per hour, the speed of the slowest ships. Thus the U-boats tailing the convoy, travelling at fifteen or sixteen knots on the surface, will move up either side of the slow-moving convoy out of visual sight from the screening escort vessels.

'By late evening the attacking U-boats will have passed the convoy and taken up positions ahead, and now, trimmed down, just keeping steerage speed, will be on a collision course with the approaching merchant ships.

'As individual U-boats position themselves, escorts will make surface contact with their surveillance gear and move in to force the U-boats to dive when the underwater contact gear takes over and a depth-charge attack is made. Contact will be lost temporarily, but when regained, another depth-charge attack will be made with two objectives – to destroy or bring the U-boat to the surface, but in any case to make her commander take evasive action for the survival of his U-boat while the convoy passes by unharmed.

'The first depth-charge attack will have exploded some two thousand pounds of high explosive about fifty to a hundred feet below the water and perhaps three hundred feet astern of my ship. Now, you girls can imagine how a two-thousand-pound bomb going off about a hundred yards off your stern would shake you! Those contacts you are soldering so very carefully must hold. So if little Rosie has been out with those free-spending Americans at her local pub the night before, and next morning at work says to herself "It'll do!" as she makes up our anti-submarine gear, well, it won't bloody well do! Because when that depth-charge explosion shakes shoddy work apart, my A/S set operator on the bridge may tell me, "The set's all mucked up, sir!" and "mucked" up isn't quite the word he uses!

'Because of a broken contact or assembly, we may have lost contact with a U-boat that can still torpedo ships in our convoy. U-boat commanders and their crews must be hammered hard and fast in their attacks on convoys. Our escort ships are dependent on your work for us to enable us to do that right!'

At question time there were only two questions:

'Are the girls in America still wearing silk stockings?'

'Yes, most of them, but . . .'

Here I paused to give an appraising look at the legs of the girls in front which caused skirts to be pulled down over knees.

'What goes into them, such as the legs I see here, is most important!'

The second question was 'What's his telephone number?'

'It'll be on the noticeboard in the morning!'

Mrs Rubin, the Press Officer, wrote to me on 11 October 1943: 'I enclose a very enthusiastic letter of thanks from Multitone Electric Co., whom you visited for us last week.'

Mr Polikoff, the managing director had written:

On behalf of the management of the Works Committee of this company, we should like to thank you very much for sending Lieut. Warwick to us. He gave the most successful talk we have ever had, and has produced a surprising amount of real enthusiasm among the workers. He spoke to both our factories, in which we now employ a total of 500 people.

I gained one of my best friends through my first factory tour, Arthur J Mollart, founder of Mollart Engineering Company. The ME Company had its main factory building in a commercial estate on the Kingston by-pass, near to my home town of Surbiton, with an extension in an old building that had formerly housed part of A C Motor Cars Ltd, now long defunct, and where 'AJ' had been the works manager until A C Motors went bankrupt. Next door to this small building was the old, locally popular and famous Swan Inn with its boatyard on the bank of the river at Thames Ditton.

A loud and knowing laugh was always earned when comedians working the Kingston Empire Music Hall posed the question, 'Are you married or do you live at Thames Ditton?'

'AJ', as he was called by his friends and known to the British engineering fraternity, had enlisted as a young navy engineer petty officer during the 'Great War' or First World War. Joining A C Motors after that war, he had conceived the design of a very simple yet most flexible ball joint. It consisted of a small grooved steel ball, held between three steel 'fingers', as a cricket bowler or baseball pitcher might hold a ball before making his delivery to the batsman or batter. The RAF used it for bomb hoists in their aircraft.

The ME ball joint was now in mass production on machine tools designed by 'AJ' in addition to the precision jigs, tools and gauges being made for Ford Motor Company, Rolls Royce, Hawker Aircraft and other engineering firms.

Arthur Mollart remained the lovable rough diamond from the Potteries area of central England, centred around the Staffordshire county towns of Stoke-on-Trent and Newcastle-under-Lyme, where china and earthenware manufacturing dates back to the 16th century.

The catholic Edict of Nantes in 1685 had created a great exodus of Huguenot Calvinist Protestants from France, bringing with them their very considerable and exclusive expertise in the design and manufacturing of china, earthenware and lace to England, Germany and the Netherlands. Arthur Mollart's family and relatives had been employed in the Staffordshire Potteries since the time their Huguenot forebears had arrived bringing with them the china and earthenware designs still possessed today. Work in the potbanks was a family tradition.

One evening, after sipping his favourite drink, 'A dog's nose', a somewhat powerful mixture of Guinness, black stout and gin, Arthur related his breaking of the family tradition.

'I wanted to become an engineer, and on breaking the news to my father the old man just blew up at me! "The potbank was good enough for thy father to manage, as did my father and his father before him back to the time our family settled in Staffordshire. The potbank was good enough for us, but if thee wishes to become an engineer, then I want no part of it, and thee does it on your own!" So I had to leave home and do it on my own. It was a long time before my father started speaking to me again.'

Arthur Mollart had broken his family tradition, and had become a skilled and respected machine tool designer. His son Kenneth had followed in his father's footsteps, so it seemed that a fresh industry dynasty was being born.

CHAPTER XVI

Lt Trevor Blore RANVR, formerly a correspondent with Reuters, had spent a month on board *St Loman* and after moving on to several other trawlers gained his primary objective of getting into the Admiralty's press division. When on *St Loman* Blore had suggested that we might 'write a book' and I undertook to develop some background material for him. On joining the press division Blore had no problems with censorship and at the end of 1942 his book entitled *Terriers of the Fleet. The Fighting Trawlers* by First Lieutenant, was published by Hutchinson & Co. (Publishers) Ltd. A large bookshop in Cape Town received a small shipment which quickly sold out.

I contacted Blore at the Admiralty and asked him about the financial situation regarding his 'fifty-fifty' suggested offer at the time I undertook to supply some of his background information. In common with the majority of his fraternity, Blore was always 'broke'. I recalled that shortly after he reported on board the *St Loman* in Aberdeen I had reimbursed the base paymaster lieutenant for a cheque of Blore's, cashed by him personally, which had 'bounced'. Fortunately for Blore, he had a Hungarian wife who understood his failings and kept him solvent by making him write.

It seemed that the initial printing was under 5,000 copies, with a minimum royalty, which Blore did not state. I settled with him for 25 pounds, and estimated that he had been paid at least 250 pounds by the publishers.

'Do you want to make some money?' he asked.

'After hearing your returns on the book venture, I would be interested!' I replied eagerly.

'Then I will contact Miss Howlett who handles the overseas radio broadcasts for the BBC. When you meet her she will ask if you come officially. You must reply that you come unofficially and in that case the BBC will pay you!'

Miss Howlett, a tall, raw-boned New Zealander, was smiling as she asked the question, 'Do you come officially?'

The British Broadcasting Corporation were no spendthrifts! Their fee was one guinea per minute of the recording, inclusive of all expenses, and of course

251

you produced the script for their approval and acceptance.

My first recording was made on Thursday, 7 October 1943:

> Title: RADIO NEWSREEL: Six U-boat Kills.
> Fee: About 4½ minutes. 4½ guineas (inclusive of all expenses).

The second recording was made on Friday, 12 November 1943:

> Title: RADIO NEWSREEL: The Battle of Atlantic City.
> Fee: About 3 minutes. 3 guineas (inclusive of all expenses).

The guinea was worth 21 shillings, thus for 7½ guineas I had earned in supplementary income the magnificent sum of £7 10s 6d. Nevertheless it was very acceptable pocket money and another learning experience.

The only comment on these two broadcasts came from my former signalman on *St Loman*, Sidney Wain, to the effect that 'It was just like the old skipper!'

In November I reported to the NOIC Newcastle-on-Tyne. My new frigate, HMS *Rushen Castle*, was arriving at completion for sea trials and I joined my future No.1, Lt Eric W. Clubb RNR, at his boarding house lodgings. He told me that he had spent most of his supervisory time in kicking the welded clamps and eyelets fixed by the 'lady welders' as few of these fixtures held up!

Clubb was a career merchant navy officer and asked me if I could relieve him for a week so that he could sit for the Board of Trade examination for his Mate's Certificate. He told me that the examiners had warned him that just because there was a war on, he should not anticipate any relaxation of their standards!

I arrived at Swan Hunter's shipyard at 8 a.m. every morning and at the end of the day travelled back on the double-decker tram, packed with the dockyard maties, all nattering in their 'Geordie dialect', a foreign language to a stranger in town.

On arriving in Newcastle I contacted an old business friend and former marketing services client – William P. Webster, known throughout the grocery trade as 'Wee Willie Webster', chairman and founder of Wrights Biscuits Ltd, South Shields. He had been a painful thorn in the side of the British Biscuit Makers Association, a strong cartel, setting the prices, policies, terms and conditions for their industry.

In the 1930s coal miners and shipyard workers were the traditional breadwinners in north-eastern England, but on the dole in the depression years of that time. Little extra money was coming into their homes, and a common sight was to see a miner balancing on his bike a sack of coal scavenged off the slag heaps, to be sold for a shilling.

Willie Webster, an entrepreneur and manufacturers' agent, conceived the idea of creating a biscuit manufacturing operation which could create light industry jobs for the wives and daughters of unemployed miners and shipyard workers, and contacted Angus Watson, an extremely wealthy local businessman, who had made a large fortune in the canned goods trade through selling his business to Lever Brothers.

'Mr Warwick, I went to Angus Watson and borrowed fifty thousand pounds from him personally. At the end of Wright's Biscuits' first year I paid him back his fifty thousand out of profits. Then I had the pleasure of firing every relative of his for whom I had to find a job.'

Willie Webster was the chairman and the sales force who, capitalizing on the dictatorial conduct of the cartel members with the chain stores, had made fast friends in the retail grocery trade and, in addition, invested in their companies.

Looking like a little bantam fighting cock, Webster chirped to me, 'I heard that you made a talk to the Swan Hunter yard. Would you do the same for Wrights' factory staff?'

'I would be only too glad to do that, Mr Webster, and particularly as Miss Orr has been arranging for the petty officers and leading ratings to be entertained at a party and a music hall show when my new ship *Rushen Castle* is commissioned this week.'

Miss Mary Elizabeth Orr operated as Willie Webster's managing director at Wrights, to which she had graduated from the factory production line through a night school business course and secretarial training. There were two fast-thinking minds in the chairman's office at Wrights.

The time had come for HMS *Rushen Castle*'s sea trials, and depending on their successful results, the acceptance of the ship by her commanding officer. Weather in the North Sea had been becoming rather rough, so at the informal conference with the shipyard management and the Admiralty liaison officer, it was suggested that the trials might be delayed until the weather moderated a little.

'As *Rushen Castle* will be experiencing rather worse weather in her North Atlantic convoy operations, as her future commanding officer I would prefer not to delay the sea trials for calmer weather in order to have the opportunity of seeing how my future command behaves in rough weather conditions.'

'Commander Warwick is right, and I agree with his suggestion that the sea trials should be held as scheduled,' added the RN liaison captain.

The shipyard management looked rather unhappy with this outcome, as the following day had been set for the sea trials when the ship would be operated by yard personnel, with a Newcastle pilot taking out the ship and returning her to harbour on completion of the sea trials.

My friend Arthur Mollart had obtained Admiralty clearance to be on board *Rushen Castle* during the trials and for the traditional shipyard 'party' catered for by the management, with arrangements for Saccone & Speed, the wines and spirits wholesalers, to supply the liquor through the medium of the officers' duty-free wardroom account.

Arthur Mollart was down in the engine room during the trials and reported that most of the shipyard management had been sea-sicked sober by the time I accepted *Rushen Castle*'s trials.

Rushen Castle's officers and men were now on board, with a long service regular navy chief petty officer as coxswain over the petty officers, leading ratings and ratings. She had eight officers in the wardroom, consisting of six watchkeeping deck officers, a surgeon lieutenant, and an engineer lieutenant – a major contrast to the *St Loman*'s three deck officers and a chief petty officer engineman down below!

My deck officers were all seasoned men out of escort ships, with one exception, a South African navy officer, Lieutenant Cecil Vernon Rhodes, related through his grandparents to the Cecil Rhodes of South Africa and founder of Rhodesia.

The first lieutenant, or Number One, was Lieutenant Eric W. Clubb RNR, who had been a submarine navigator in the Mediterranean. Due to a bad attack of dysentery he had been transferred to escort ships after leaving hospital. He was as thin as a rake and hoping to regain weight.

My navigator, Sub Lt Weeks, held a second officer's certificate. He was bright, young and eager to learn ship-handling.

The gunnery officer, Lt Gwinnell RNVR, was formerly a peacetime insurance company executive, soon to be addressed as 'Dad' by the younger officers.

The signals officer, Lt McMullen RNVR, was from Belfast, Northern Ireland. He was young and newly married.

The asdic officer, a former merchant navy seaman, was Lt Billany RNVR, who was hoping to qualify for his second officer's certificate so as to work on coastal shipping in peacetime.

Then came 'Doc', the surgeon lieutenant, RNVR, and the 'Plumber' or engineer officer, a lieutenant, RNVR.

The coxswain, approaching the end of his service, worked hand in glove with Lt Clubb, and his watch and quarter bill assignments were posted when sea trials were being made. Lt Clubb and I made a consensus of opinion as to the officers' deck watch assignments.

Fully stored and equipped for A/S operations, HMS *Rushen Castle* was sailed from Newcastle-on-Tyne for ten days at the Oban, Tobermory working-up base, commanded and personally operated by the legendary Vice Admiral Sir Gilbert Stephenson RN, who had the right background for an A/S Warfare work-up. He had served in the Mediterranean during the First World War, largely being concerned with anti-submarine warfare work and much involved with reserve manned small craft. His later service included Director of the Anti-Submarine Warfare Division in the Admiralty.

Just as Admiral James gained the sobriquet of 'Bubbles' from advertising for Pears' soap by Lever Brothers in the late Edwardian era, so did Admiral Stephenson become 'Monkey' Stephenson due to his most remarkable resemblance to the illustration headlined: 'Monkey Brand soap. Won't wash clothes!', a lava-based hand-soap of Lever Brothers.

Stephenson's A/S Warfare training role was a whole-ship approach concentrating on the basics, being described by one commanding officer as 'violently shaking the lethargy out of the ships sent to him'. He was equally as ruthless with his staff officers and instructional personnel in HMS *Western Isles* as with the commanding officers of ships under training.

When being entertained by Admiral Stephenson at a 'farewell dinner' on the *Western Isles*, Stephenson illustrated that his most frequently employed 'final solution' was removal of personnel whose performance had proved inadequate.

Dominating the dinner table in his rather terse and testy manner of speaking he barked:

'There was a commanding officer in a corvette. Commander The Earl of Carrick. Absolutely useless! Just useless . . . I had him out. Just like that!' He jerked his closed fist with an extended thumb over his shoulder.

'Do you know where The Earl of Carrick is now, sir?' I asked.

'No! He was absolutely useless. Absolutely useless!'

'Commander The Earl of Carrick is now the British Naval liaison officer in Norfolk, Virginia, sir . . .'

'God Bless my soul. He was absolutely useless!'

'He must have been in your opinion, as the commanding officer of an escort ship, sir. But, as the naval liaison and public relations officer at a major US naval base, Commander Carrick and his American wife are extremely popular. "Commander The Earl" was most helpful in meeting the needs of the twenty-six A/S trawlers assigned to the US Navy to escort coastal convoys on the

Eastern Sea Frontier of the US.'

'H'm. He was absolutely useless here!'

The staff officer designated for ASW training and who remained as 'tutor' for the duration of the ship's work-up, appeared to have made an excellent and comprehensive report on my ship's performance and progress. I received orders to proceed to Liverpool, the base of the Commander-in-Chief, Western Approaches Command, Admiral Sir Maxwell Horton RN.

Rushen Castle was to join B-2 Escort Group consisting of eight ships made up with four Castle class frigates, *Rushen Castle, Flint Castle, Leeds Castle* and the Norwegian Navy manned *Tunsberg Castle*, two diesel-powered and US built Captain class frigates and two H-class modern destroyers *Harbinger* and *Hesperus*. The senior officer of B-2 Group was in *Hesperus*, a senior commander RN.

B-2 Group was assigned to the Liverpool-Gibraltar regular convoy service started early in 1940. With the German occupation of France these convoys came within easy reach of U-boat bases on the Bay of Biscay coast and also the long-range aircraft operating from the Luftwaffe airfields near Bordeaux. Although potentially more vulnerable than the North Atlantic, these convoys were rather more heavily escorted.

The new construction Castle class frigates possessed the latest high technology developments for A/S Warfare. HMS *Rushen Castle*'s sonar or asdic equipment combined both a surface-range oscillator and a depth-recording asdic which was accurate plus-minus 5 feet.

The depth-charge armament consisted of a three-barrelled 'mortar' carrying three 250-pound 'aircraft bombs'. This weapon was located just abaft the fo'c's'le, below the ship's bridge, and could be trained automatically ten degrees on either side of the ship's centre line. The depth charge 'bombs' were fired automatically when the attacking ship was 500 feet from the U-boat target. The depth of the contact at the time of firing was set on the charges.

When asdic contact with a submerged U-boat was obtained the ship was conned head-on to the target followed by the order, whereupon the attacking escort ship was kept head-on to the asdic bearing shown on the recorder in the wheelhouse. At the same time the 'squid' cannon or mortar was being trained on the asdic bearing. The 'ping' of the asdic contact was relayed to a speaker on the bridge from the little radar and asdic operations room at the rear of the open bridge.

The 'squid', as it had been named, was a most accurate and lethal anti-submarine weapon. It could be activated within a few minutes for a quick and most accurate depth-charge attack at up to 15 knots. Whereas in the past the depth of the U-boat was merely estimated, now the actual depth was being recorded on the fast sinking charges. No longer could a U-boat commander dive to extreme depths to distance his vessel from the attacking escort ship's formerly estimated depth settings.

After some three and a half years being the decision maker's eyes and ears on *St Loman*'s bridge, it was a luxury indeed to have all the required information supplied by accurate and instant high-technology equipment, manned by the most capable and efficient officers and ratings, enabling me to make the right decisions.

During the last part of 1943 the route for the Gibraltar convoys was through the North Channel to the west of Northern Ireland and along a course to and from Gibraltar some way out from the Bay of Biscay. This convoy route was revised early in 1944 to south through the Irish Sea from Liverpool and closer to the Bay of Biscay and the Spanish coast when approaching Gibraltar – rather akin to sweeping our convoys' skirts across the U-boat bases in the Bay of Biscay.

Deep British minefields had been laid for the benefit of U-boats east of the southern Irish Republic coast, their presence being noted by the little black dots recorded by their asdic contacts.

Another interesting 'non-sub' was that of a 'right whale' picked up by the asdic one bright, sunny afternoon. After passing submerged across the ship's bows, the whale surfaced to a few feet below the clear blue waters of the North Atlantic, revealing the massive 125-foot ridged back of the sperm whale.

In January 1943 Admiral Dönitz had 212 operational U-boats, of which 164 were assigned to the North Atlantic. His list of 'Star Turn' U-boat captains brought up to date from the July 1942 ASW Report now contained 69 names against the previous 52 (see pp. 258-9).Without doubt the latter spearheaded the 'wolf pack' assaults on North Atlantic convoys, attaining their maximum success in March, but at the considerable loss of attacking U-boats, which during May 1943 had soared to 41 being sunk (see p. 260). At this stage U-boat warfare in the North Atlantic was broken off.

This was due to three developments. First, reconnaissance aircraft and escort vessels had been fitted with precision radar equipment, resulting in frequently surprising U-boats at night and during bad visibility. In these attacks the boats were often damaged or sunk. Passage by U-boats to and from their Bay of Biscay bases had become a most dangerous phase of their operations.

Section 2

(c) 'STAR TURN' U-BOAT CAPTAINS

The list of the more successful U-Boat commanders published in the July 1942 Report is here brought up to date and now contains 68 names against the previous 52.

Name	Rank	Date of Award of 'Ritter-Kreuz'	Date of Award of 'Oak Leaves'	Remarks
Prien, Günter	Korvettenkapitän	17.10.39	21.10.40	Dead.
Schultze, Herbert	Korvettenkapitän	2.3.40	13.6.41	
Schubart, Otto	Korvettenkapitän	18.5.40	–	Sank HMS 'Courageous'
Rollmann, Wilhelm	Korvettenkapitän	2.8.40	–	
Kretschmer, Otto	Korvettenkapitän	8.8.40	12.11.40	Prisoner of war. Awarded Swords to 'Oak Leaves' on 7.1.42.
Lemp, Fritz-Julius	Kapitänleutnant	21.8.40	–	Dead
Liebe, Heinrich	Korvettenkapitän	22.8.40	15.6.41	
Hartmann, Werner	Korvettenkapitän	2.9.40	–	
Rosing, Hans	Korvettenkapitän	3.9.40	–	
Frauenheim, Fritz	Korvettenkapitän	5.9.40	–	
Endrass, Engelbert	Kapitänleutnant	10.9.40	15.6.41	Dead.
Kuhnke, Heinrich	Korvettenkapitän	20.9.40	–	
Schepke, Joachim	Korvettenkapitän	26.9.40	20.12.40	Dead.
Jenisch, Hans	Kapitänleutnant	10.10.40	–	Prisoner of war.
Bleichrodt, Heinrich	Korvettenkapitän	29.10.40	–	
Oehrn, Viktor	Korvettenkapitän	29.10.40	–	Prisoner of war.
Lüth, Wolfgang	Kapitänleutnant	29.10.40	–	
Suhren, Reinhard	Oberleutnant-zur-see	10.11.40	3.1.42	
Schutze, Viktor	Korvettenkapitän	16.12.40	15.7.41	
von Stockhausen, Hans-Gerrit	Korvettenkapitän	20.1.41	–	
Moehle, Oskar	Kapitänleutnant	28.2.41	–	
Lehmann-Willenbrock, Heinrich	Korvettenkapitän	28.2.41	8.1.42	
Oesten, Jürgen	Kapitänleutnant	2.4.41	–	
Schulz, Wilhelm	Kapitänleutnant	8.4.41	–	
Kuppisch, Herbert	Kapitänleutnant	25.5.41	–	
Wohlfarth, Herbert	Kapitänleutnant	25.5.41	–	Prisoner of war.
Schewe, Georg	Kapitänleutnant	25.5.41	–	
Korth, Claus	Kapitänleutnant	3.6.41	–	
Hessler, Günther	Korvettenkapitän	30.6.41	–	
Topp, Erich	Kapitänleutnant	4.7.41	11.4.42	Awarded Swords to 'Oak Leaves', 17.8.42.
Metzler, Jost	Korvettenkapitän	1.8.41	–	
Schnee, Adalbert,	Kapitänleutnant	10.9.41	15.7.42	
Mützelburg, Rolf	Kapitänleutnant	23.11.41	15.7.42	Dead
Mengensen, Ernst	Kapitänleutnant	23.11.41	–	
Guggenberger, Friedrich(?)	Kapitänleutnant	20.12.41	–	Sank HMS 'Ark Royal'.
Scholtz, Klaus	Kapitänleutnant	7.1.42	–	
Kentrat, –	Kapitänleutnant	7.1.42	–	

258

Bigalk, Gerhardt	Kapitänleutnant	7.1.42	–	Dead. Sank HMS 'Audacity'.
Gysae, Robert	Kapitänleutnant	7.1.42	–	
von Tiesenhausen, Freiherr	Kapitänleutnant	27.1.42	–	Sank HMS 'Barham'. Prisoner of war.
Hardegen, Reinhard	Kapitänleutnant	18.2.42	–	
Witte, Helmut	Kapitänleutnant	7.1.42	—	
Clausen, Nikolai	Kapitänleutnant	14.3.42	–	
Mohr, Johann	Kapitänleutnant	28.3.42	–	
Ites, Otto	Oberleutnant-zur-see	8.4.42	–	Prisoner of war.
Zapp, Robert Richard	Korvettenkapitän	5.5.42	19.5.42	
Bauer, Ernst	Kapitänleutnant	18.3.42	–	
Winter, Werner	Kapitänleutnant	8.6.42	–	
Cremer, Erich	Kapitänleutnant	8.6.42	–	
Kraus, Hans Werner	Kapitänleutnant	20.6.42	–	
Merton, Karl-Friedrich	Kapitänleutnant	23.6.42	–	A well-known yachtsman.
Schultze, Heinz Otto	Kapitänleutnant	15.7.42	–	
Rosenbaum, Helmut	Kapitänleutnant	12.8.42	–	Sank HMS 'Eagle'.
Lassen, Georg	Kapitänleutnant	12.8.42	–	
Piening, Adolf	Kapitänleutnant	15.8.42	–	
Thurmann, Karl	Kapitänleutnant	24.8.42	–	
Schonder, Heinrich	Kapitänleutnant	26.8.42	–	
Hartenstein, Werner	Korvettenkapitän	19.9.42	–	
Krech, Günther	Kapitänleutnant	19.9.42	–	
Kals, Ernst	Korvettenkapitän	8.9.42	–	
von Bülow, Otto	Kapitänleutnant	21.10.42	–	
Poske, Fritz	Korvettenkapitän	7.11.42	–	
Strelow, Siegfried	Kapitänleutnant	1.11.42	–	
Müller, Günther	Kapitänleutnant	30.11.42	–	
Emmermann, Carl	Kapitänleutnant	30.11.42	–	
Dommes, Wilhelm	Kapitänleutnant	5.12.42	–	
Witt, Hans	Kapitänleutnant	19.12.42	–	
Henke, –	Kapitänleutnant	19.12.42	–	
Rasche, -	Kapitänleutnant	30.12.42	–	

SECTION 8

RETURN OF U-BOAT CASUALTIES

AMENDMENTS AND ADDITIONS

PART A
German U-Boats known sunk

No.	U-Boat	Ship or Aircraft Concerned	Date 1943	Position
126	'U-'?	H.M. Ships 'Black Swan' and 'Stonecrop'	2nd April	320 miles west of Oporto.
127	'U-'?	Aircraft (2) of 233 Squadron	5th April	10 miles south-east of Grand Canary.

* * *

No.	U-Boat	Ship or Aircraft Concerned	Date	Position
133	'U-'?	Aircraft of 224 Squadron	29th April	110 miles north-west of Cape Ortegal.
134	'U-'?	Aircraft of 10 and 461 Squadrons, R.A.A.F.	29 April	180 miles north-west of Cape Ortegal.
135	'U-'?	Aircraft of 455 Squadron	30th April	130 miles north of the Faeroe Islands.
136	'U-'?	Aircraft of 461 Squadron, R.A.A.F.	2nd May	81 miles north-west of Cape Ortegal.
137	'U-'?	H.M.T. 'Coverley'	4th May	About 150 miles west-north-west of Cape Finisterre.
138	'U-'?	H.M.S. 'Oribi'	5th May	About 400 miles north-east of Cape Race.
139	'U-'?	H.M.S. 'Snowflake'	5th May	About 400 miles north-east of Cape Race.
140	'U-'?	H.M.S. Loosestrife'	5th May	About 400 miles north-east of Cape Race.
141	'U-'?	Aircraft of 60 Squadron, R.A.A.F.	7th May	240 miles north-north-west of Cape Ortegal.
142	'U528'	Aircraft of 58 Squadron and H.M. Ships 'Fleetwood' and 'Mignonette'	11th May	500 miles west of St. Nazaire.
143	'U-'?	Aircraft of 53 Squadron	15th May	150 miles north-west of Cape Ortegal.
144	'U128'	Aircraft of the United States of Brazil and U.S. Ships 'Moffet' and 'Jouett'.	17th May	200 miles east-north-east of Bahia.
145	'U569'	Aircraft from U.S.S. 'Bogue'	22nd May	About 600 miles south-south-east of Cape Farewell.
146	'U752'	Aircraft from H.M.S. Archer'	23rd May	750 miles west of the mouth of the River Shannon.
147	'U-'?	Aircraft of 608 Squadron	28th May	70 miles north-east of Valencia.

| 148 | 'U-'? | H.M. Submarine 'Tuna' | 30th May | 200 miles north-east by north of Muckle Flugga. |
| 149 | 'U-'? | Aircraft (2) of 58 Squadron, aircraft of 10 Squadron, R.A.A.F., and aircraft of 288 Squadron. | 31st May | 270 miles south-west of Scilly Islands. |

PART B
German U-Boats probably sunk

			1943	
58	'U-'?	H.M.S. 'Tay'	6th April	400 miles south-west of Reykjavik.
59	'U-'?	Aircraft of 172 Squadron	29th April	100 miles north-west of Cape Ortegal.
60	'U-'?	Aircraft of 86 Squadron	4th May	600 miles west-south-west of Cape Clear.
61	'U-'?	Aircraft of 502 Squadron	5th May	60 miles north-north-west of Cape Ortegal.
62	'U-'?	Aircraft of 233 Squadron	7th May	180 miles south-west of Cape St. Vincent.
63	'U-'?	Aircraft of 86 Squadron	12th May	500 miles north by east of Tekceira.
64	'U-'?	U.S.N. Aircraft Pat Ron 84	14th May	360 miles south-west of Reykjanes.
65	'U-'?	Aircraft of 86 Squadron	14th May	500 miles north of Fayal.
66	'U-'?	Aircraft of 311 (Czech) Squadron	16th May	160 miles north-west of Cape Ortegal.
67	'U-'?	Aircraft of 58 Squadron	16th May	360 miles south-west of Lands End.
68	'U-'?	Aircraft of 120 Squadron	19th May	400 miles south-east of Cape Farewell.
69	'U-'?	U.S.N. Aircraft of Pat Ron 84	25th May	100 miles south-south-east of Iceland (c).

PART C
German U-Boats probably damaged (A)*

| 45 | – | Aircraft of 206 Squadron | 27th March | 210 miles north by west of Rockall. |
| 46 | – | Aircraft of 58 Squadron | 28th April | 160 miles north by west of Cape Ortegal. |

*This assessment indicates a promising attack, believed to have damaged a U-Boat seriously and which may have proved fatal, but on which a higher assessment is withheld pending receipt of intelligence indicating that the attack was probably successful.

Really Not Required

PART D
German U-Boats probably damaged (B)

1943

116	–	U.S.S. 'Charles F. Hughes'	24th February	600 miles south of Flores, Azores.
117	–	Escorts of Convoy U.C.1	About 25th February	About 600 miles south of Flores, Azores.
118	–	Aircraft of 224 Squadron	26th February	300 miles west-north-west of Cape Finisterre.

* * *

122	–	H.M.S. 'Lavender'	18th March	540 miles west of Blacksod Bay.
123	–	Aircraft of 220 Squadron	19th March	480 miles west of Blacksod Bay.
124	–	U.S.S. 'Babbitt'	19th March	540 miles west of Blacksod Bay.

* * *

128	–	H.M.S. 'Vidette'	4th April	330 miles south-west of Cape Farewell.
129	–	Aircraft of 172 Squadron	10th April	190 miles west-south-west of Ushant.
130	–	Aircraft of 190 Squadron	21st April	110 miles north-west by north of the Faeroe Islands.
131	–	Aircraft of 612 Squadron	1st May	100 miles west-north-west of Cape Ortegal.
132	–	U.S.N. Aircraft of 15 Squadron	15 May	220 miles west by south of Madeira.

Note – This assessment indicates that a U-Boat was seriously damaged and had to return to port.

PART E
German U-Boats probably slightly damaged
1943

221	–	Escorts of Convoy U.C.1	About 25th February	About 600 miles south of Flores, Azores.
222	–	Aircraft of 233 Squadron	4th March	70 miles west-north-west of Cape St. Vincent.
223	–	H.M.C. Ships 'Shediac' and 'St. Croix'	4th March	200 miles west of Vigo.

* * *

233	–	Aircraft of 141 Squadron	22nd March	70 miles west-north-west of La Rochelle.
234	–	H.M.S. 'Vanessa'	26th March	180 miles south-east of Cape Farewell.
235	–	Aircraft of 423 Squadron	5th April	440 miles west of Cape Clear.
236	–	Aircraft of 120 Squadron	6th April	390 miles south-west of Reykjavik.
237	–	Aircraft of 58 Squadron	22nd April	90 miles north of Cape Ortegal.
238	–	Aircraft (4) of 235 Squadron	24th April	Off Lister.

262

239	–	Aircraft of 172 Squadron	1st May	180 miles north-west by west of Cape Ortegal.
240	–	Aircraft of 269 Squadron	2nd May	165 miles west of Ostero, Faero Islands.
241	–	Aircraft of 612 Squadron	2nd May	210 miles north-west of Cape Ortegal.
242	–	Aircraft of 58 Squadron	7th May	225 miles west-north-west of Cape Ortegal.

PART J
Italian U-Boats probably damaged (B)
1943

| 38 | – | H.M. Ships 'Dulverton' and 'Exmoor' | 19th April | 40 miles north-west of Tobruk. |

The second and equally important Allied development was the increasingly intensive air reconnaissance out in the Atlantic.

Finally there was the Allies ever-increasing experience coupled with better ASW weaponry, giving us enormous improvement in our ability to detect and destroy U-boats. *Rushen Castle* was fully equipped to do this.

The revised convoy route from Liverpool to Gibraltar made the round trip approximately 4-5 weeks with a stay in Gibraltar of 2-3 days, and 3-4 days in Liverpool where the onshore training facilities for the asdic and gunnery officers and ratings were carried out in the Gladstone Dock facilities.

The staff gunnery officer was Lt Ronald Smith RNVR, of whom a young Sub Lieutenant on his staff commented: 'You should meet Mrs Smith; she's a humdinger!'

'Judging by her elder sister, Joan Taytasac of Cape Town, who has given me an introduction, I have little doubt of that!' I was able to reply.

Diana Smith, formerly 'Bubbles' Taytasac, lived up to her family nickname. She was an outrageous flirt as instanced on an occasion when she and her husband were out to lunch on board *Rushen Castle*. Ronnie was to come straight from the end of his gunnery class and Diana was coming from their family flat in Liverpool. Looking along from the gangway, I saw her coming and went up the dock to meet her, being greeted with two vigorous kisses on either cheek which left as much lipstick as her sister Joan had done on a similar occasion in Cape Town.

I had no doubt that the quartermaster on the gangway had observed the greeting as together we continued to walk down the dock.

'Are you going to let me take off that lipstick?'

'No, madame, indeed! I am proud to wear my decorations . . .'

Without batting an eyelid the quartermaster saluted, and I returned it as we went aboard to go to my cabin on the main deck where to Diana's relief I removed the traces of her warpaint before going down to the wardroom to wait for Ronnie to join us and meet the ship's officers before lunch.

On Saturday evenings there was a dance for the Allied officers and their partners, which Diana Smith greatly enjoyed, so that on occasions when Ronnie was duty officer, I would get a request from him to partner his wife as she liked to dance.

'It's so nice having you as a dance partner,' she remarked.

'That I can understand, Diana, for if you flirt with those French and Polish officers as you are doing with me, then they are going to take you seriously, and you'll have to make a run for Ronnie!'

'Yes, I found that out. It's dangerous!'

Ronnie and his wife lived in a little guest flat adjoining his parents' rather large residence. I gathered that he was a lawyer in his father's firm of rather influential and important Liverpool lawyers. The war was being good to the former 'Bubbles' Taytasac and her adoring husband.

On arrival in Liverpool my signals officer, Lt McMullen, told me that the Lt Cdr WRNS in charge of the CBs, or Confidential Books, at the base would be coming on board to check the *Rushen Castle*'s book personally. It was a very pleasant surprise to greet an old acquaintance from the office of Lt Paymaster George Kemp RNVR, under whom she had worked as a Petty Officer, controlling the CBs in January 1940. At that time Norah Marshall, tall, slim and red-haired, had a more than 'meaningful relationship' with the commanding officer of a locally-based minesweeper, sweeping for mines during daylight hours and back in port at nightfall for more than several pink gins with Norah Marshall.

When Norah became a chief petty officer, George Kemp recommended her for transfer to the Western Approaches Base in Liverpool, breaking off her liaison which was detrimental to her promotion. Thirty-ish, extremely capable and efficient, Norah had made it to Lieutenant Commander in charge of a major base department in two or three years.

The quartermasters used a little shelf-type desk fixed on the bulkhead outside my cabin door. After checking out the CBs with Lt McMullen I had invited Norah up to my cabin to have a pink gin and talk over 'old times' in Aberdeen.

The sliding door to the companionway was closed and we heard a visiting officer ask the quartermaster.

'Is the commanding officer aboard?'

'No, sir! He's just stepped ashore . . .'

'You really have got them trained!' Norah remarked.

'No! That is sheer initiative on his part, but I must complement the coxswain on the orders he must give to duty quartermasters!'

George Kemp and his wife had been mutual friends when we were both based in Aberdeen. When Norah and I visited them on one weekend from Liverpool, Mrs Kemp took me aside and observed, 'You could do a lot worse than marry Norah!'

In all small ships gossip and interesting stories come up via the 'galley wireless'. One I recall, in particular, on the theme of 'Ivy and her blue room' and a stoker petty officer.

Around midday when the ship was due to sail, the base chaplain came to see me.

'I understand that you have Stoker Petty Officer Harman aboard, and that he is unmarried, Commander?'

'Yes, padre, you are correct. He has come to you with some matter that might entail compassionate leave perhaps?'

'No, Commander, but a young lady has been to see me, and it seems that she is pregnant by Petty Officer Harman. Now while I would not want to wish marriage on a man, I do think that he should do the right thing!'

'Padre, we are just about to sail with a Gibraltar convoy. We should be back in Liverpool in 4-5 weeks. I will take the opportunity to discuss the situation with PO Harman and get in touch with you when the ship returns to Liverpool.'

As our convoy was formed up and heading down the Irish Sea, it was a pleasant sunny afternoon when, coming down from the bridge, I observed Stoker Petty Officer Harman come up on the boat deck for a breather from the engine room.

'Petty Officer Harman, I've heard some jokes connected with you being made in the PO's mess about "Ivy and her blue room". Now, just before we sailed, the padre was asking about your girlfriend, Ivy, who claims to be pregnant. Are you responsible?'

'Well, skipper, it was like this. I was in the Caradoc having a quiet pint, when a young tart asked me to have a drink with her. You know how it is, sir . . .'

'Yes, of course, I know how it is . . .'

'Well, of course, I bought her a beer, and we had a few more as time went by . . . You know how it is, sir . . .'

'Yes, of course . . .'

'She lives in Aintree, so I took her home on the tram. "You have missed the last tram back to Liverpool," she told me, "but if it is all right for you to rejoin your ship in the morning, then you can sleep on the sofa downstairs. But no funny business, mind you!"

'I told her that our skipper lets petty officers have overnight leave when we are not under sailing orders, so the sofa would be quite all right. That house was cold! I laid down on the sofa and was shivering. She came down from upstairs saying, "You are cold down there, I'll get you a blanket."

'There were a lot of bumps in that sofa. I was tossing and turning around trying to get comfortable, when she came downstairs again, saying, "You're not very comfortable down there, are you? You'd best come upstairs to bed. But no funny business, mark you!"

'Well skipper, I goes upstairs and gets into bed with her . . . You know how it is, sir!'

'Yes, indeed I do, Harman!'

'Since then, skipper, when we are in Liverpool I usually meet up with Ivy at the Caradoc pub, have a few drinks, then after taking her home stay overnight in the blue bedroom you have heard about. You know how it is, sir!'

'How it is now, Harman, is that Ivy, finding herself in a certain condition, has visited the base padre, telling him that you are responsible. Ivy may have been considering that the padre might help her to get you to make an allotment, but the padre is talking to me about the possibility of "wishing marriage on you" as he termed it.'

'Ivy hasn't told the padre that she is already married to a soldier serving in North Africa, skipper!'

Smiling broadly, I told him, 'If her husband was only drafted to North Africa recently, Ivy might be thinking that two child allotments would be better than just one. I promised to see the padre when we returned to Liverpool, and I will explain to him why marriage is out of the question.'

About five weeks later when we returned to Liverpool from Gibraltar, I visited the padre.

'Padre, I had a long discussion with Petty Officer Harman about his girlfriend Ivy, and it appears that marriage is out of the question as she is already married to a soldier serving in North Africa. It is just possible that her husband was drafted fairly recently. About three years ago when I was with one of the three escort groups working out of Greenock, the paymaster was interested to find that a sailor from each group was paying an allotment to the same young woman. Supposedly she could make the excuse, 'How do you know which tooth of the buzz-saw hit you?' It is just possible that Ivy was thinking of

266

getting your help to encourage Petty Officer Harman to make her a child allowance allotment.'

'Thank you, Commander, for your help in this matter. Really, I was quite taken in, as she seemed to be such a nice girl.'

'Seems that Petty Officer Harman thought the same, padre.'

Later, over a pink gin in the wardroom with the engineer officer, he matched my story with another.

'You know that old petty officer we call "Tanky" because his daily duty assignment is to check on all the fresh water and fuel tanks. Tank met up with a rather more mature lady at the Caradoc bar, also saw her home and missed the last tram back to Liverpool from Aintree. Halfway through the night she exclaimed, "I can feel that my poor dead husband is watching us!" "He can't be doing that from his grave," replied Tanky. "Oh, yes he can, as he's still in his coffin underneath the bed!"'

Lt Gwinnell, the gunnery officer, then made mention of the Gunner's Mate, a Cornishman, who was being told that his relatives in Cornwall would refuse to speak to him now that he had 'married a foreigner'– a girl from Liverpool!

CHAPTER XVII

Throughout 1943 and 1944 Gibraltar convoys experienced no losses from U-boat attacks, although intelligence reports regarding the disposition of U-boats would regularly report eight U-boats in the Irish Sea and fourteen or fifteen in the Bay of Biscay. The standing orders for convoy escorts regarding depth-charge attacks on suspected U-boat contacts were to rejoin station with the convoy as soon as the convoy had passed clear, whereas the support groups becoming available in the spring of 1943 had hunter-killer group concentration exclusively. Now, the former hunters were becoming the hunted by air and sea attacks.

There was little to do in Gibraltar, but on the Mediterranean side of the Rock there was a small strip of stone-covered beach that could be reached for bathing after going through a tunnel constructed at ground level through the base of the Rock, passing through small warehouses for stores carved out of the solid rock towards the dim light at the end of the tunnel. One of the Rock's slab sides had been developed as a rainwater catchment. Italian prisoners appeared to be engaged full time in tunnelling a motor road around the outside and inside of the Rock. The Rock of Gibraltar seemed to have as many holes in it as a Swiss cheese!

In June 1944 the southbound Gibraltar convoy, escorted by B-2 Escort Group, was halfway across the Bay of Biscay when the two H-class destroyers with the two Captain class frigates received orders to detach themselves and head north, in advance of the Allied landings in Normandy, with the knowledge that German U-boat flotillas on the French coast would be thrown into the battle. *Rushen Castle* was ordered to take over as senior officer, and on return to Liverpool I became the Escort Group commander.

This assignment carried with it an 'entertaining allowance', exclusive to escort commanders in the Western Approaches Command. How this allowance of two shillings and sixpence per diem had been obtained was shrouded in mystery. It was intended to cover the cost of entertaining convoy commodores and ship's captains attending convoy conferences that might be held on board.

This was a welcome addition to my daily allowances for command money and hard-lying payments, making a total of seven shillings and sixpence per diem. As my monthly base pay had little left over after various allotments to my family, with plenty of sea time for saving, I had adequate spending money to draw upon.

As had been anticipated the Germans threw all available units from the Biscay bases into the battle, but without success. Despite the 'schnorkel' device enabling U-boats to use their diesels when submerged, they were unable to penetrate our defences.

On 24 June, it was known that there were still two U-boats at each of Brest, Lorient and Saint Nazaire, six at La Pallice, and three at Bordeaux. Around 17 August all flotillas were withdrawn to Norway for operations. The last to leave Lorient was U-55 on 5 September 1944. Nevertheless our U-boat situation reports indicated an average of 15 operating in the Bay of Biscay area, and 8 in the Irish Sea.

Returning with base orders, Lt McMullen told me, 'I have found out that you are the only reserve officer commanding an escort group in the Western Approaches Command. All other groups are under the orders of Royal Navy commanders. Here is a copy of the assignments.' He handed me the list with the signals from the base.

'That's interesting and maybe it could be one reason for this signal scheduling *Rushen Castle* for ASW exercises in Londonderry next week – running the ruler over the newly appointed group commander and his ship!' I replied.

On arrival at Londonderry, Lt Billany and his A/S ratings went ashore for a training session, and Lt Gwinnell attended the shore gunnery school with his crew.

Now came the exercises at sea with HMS *Philante*, a large sea-going yacht based in Londonderry for testing out old and new ASW tactics and procedures in which Admiral Sir Maxwell Horton, C-in-C Western Approaches, and a submariner in the First World War, took a great interest, often going to sea himself.

The scenario was that the *Philante* would be the commodore merchant ship leading a convoy. A training submarine had already put to sea, and now submerged, would be in a position to make a simulated attack. *Rushen Castle* would be in screening station on *Philante*'s starboard side. *Philante* would fire a white rocket to announce a torpedo attack by the lurking submarine. *Rushen Castle* would then initiate an A/S search of the area from which the attack had been made. If successful in making a contact identified as a possible submarine,

269

and in carrying out a simulated attack, then at the instant when the depth charges would have been fired, a hand grenade would be thrown overside. Should the target attacked prove to be the submarine then a yellow smoke candle would be shot to the surface.

The staff ASW training officer was on the bridge and his assistant asdic officer was with Lt Billany in the A/S and radar cabin at the aft end of the open bridge. The contact echoes and reverberations from the asdic were transmitted by two speakers on the bridge.

It was a fine, clear afternoon with our imaginary convoy preceding along at about eight knots led by the commodore ship HMS *Philante*. Then up went the white rocket signalling the torpedo attack.

'Commodore torpedoed on the starboard side!' said the A/S staff officer on the bridge.

Lt Billany and his asdic crew working in their little cabin behind the open bridge had obtained a firm contact and reported 'possible submarine'.

'Action stations! Steer by asdic,' I ordered.

Rushen Castle was brought head on to the asdic compass bearing, moving in to make the simulated attack with the 'squid' forward-throwing depth-charge weapon. The echo which had been sharp and clear now recorded a rather woolly sound.

'It is a non-sub echo,' remarked the staff ASW officer rather pontifically.

'The convoy has been attacked. The commodore ship torpedoed on her starboard side. This was a possible submarine contact. We are going to attack it without delay,' I pointed out.

Lt Billany came out from the A/S cabin. 'I think it is a non-sub, sir,' suggesting that I should break off the attack.

'Continue with the attack on this contact, Lt Billany. You picked up a firm, possible submarine contact in the area from which the torpedo attack was made. U-boats can create non-sub effects when they hear that their submarine has been contacted by asdic.'

'It is obviously a non-sub,' sniffed the ASW staff expert.

Lt Billany looked at me apologetically, and went back to complete the attack. When the 'squid' was reported as having fired, I ordered the hand grenade to be thrown overside. Up came a yellow smoke candle from the submarine in response to the explosion. I said nothing and lit a cigarette.

'Who dropped that hand grenade down my conning tower, giving me a headache all afternoon?' asked the submarine commander at the post-mortem meeting on the exercise.

'I did, and now can you tell me what you were doing down there making non-sub effects?'

'I was going ahead and astern alternately on my engines to create a wake of disturbed water around the submarine. It often works quite well.'

On departure from a naval base a brief report known as a 'flimsy', from the thin paper used, goes on the commanding officer's record to the Admiralty, with a copy to the officer concerned. Mine read: 'This officer gives the appearance of being casual, but has plenty of guts and self-confidence.'

On completion of our ASW training exercises in Londonderry *Rushen Castle* sailed to join the southbound Gibraltar convoy. As we left Londonderry I was using the standard seaman's method of swinging out the ship's bows by coming astern on the back-spring. The current from the River Foyle sweeping down into Lough Foyle past the dockside aided this for a single-screw ship. Lt Clubb had his hands on the fo'c's'le paying out the bowline wire around the bollards to prevent a fast swing when the river current caught the bows. Ordinary Seaman Salmon, a raw conscript, was standing with his foot in one of the coils of the wire.

'Get your foot out of that coil, Salmon!' But it was now too late for Salmon was already flat on his back being pulled up to the iron bollard by the wire coil around his foot.

'Half ahead! Signal to the tower for an ambulance!' I tightened my teeth and lips as I watched that ship come slowly ahead to ease the tension on the wire as Salmon's leg moved against the bollard.

'Stop engines. Hard a starboard!'

A couple of seconds more and Salmon's foot would have been severed at the ankle. Fortunately his foot was only severely bruised and bleeding. On a corner of the Admiralty building is a statue of Captain Cook with his foot on a coil of rope – not very seamanlike!

Our Gibraltar convoy was delivered without incident and I was asked to report to the base admiral's chief of staff.

'Warwick, the Admiral wishes to come aboard your ship tomorrow morning at ten o'clock to experience one of the 'squid'-fitted ships working in an exercise with one of our submarines. The submarine will be towing red ball floats to indicate her submerged positions while you are making the simulated attacks. Then on conclusion, when the submarine has surfaced, you will carry out a test firing with three projectiles at a speed of about fifteen knots.

'I would mention that the Admiral takes a very keen interest in the handling of escort ships and destroyers, so in addition to the ASW exercises, he will be taking a most critical interest in how *Rushen Castle* leaves and returns to her berth in Gibraltar harbour.'

I thought to myself, 'This is yet another inspection of both a new-type ASW-fitted ship and new RNR escort commander.'

'We shall be very honoured to have you and the Admiral aboard, sir. Of course, he will be aware that *Rushen Castle* is a single-screw ship, and thus lacks the advantage in ship-handling of a twin-screw destroyer, but we will do our best in that respect.'

Returning on board I had a little conference with Lt Clubb and the coxswain to advise them of the next day's exercises and sea trials with the Admiral and his staff on board.

By that evening they had the ship ready for an admiral's inspection. Promptly at 10 a.m. his car drew up at the gangway and the Admiral and his staff were piped aboard. After a brief inspection he came up on the bridge. The gangway was put ashore and I gave the orders:

'Stand by on engines. Let go fore and aft. Hold on the wire back-spring. Half astern on engines. Stop engines. Let go back-spring. Full ahead. Hard a starboard. Amidships. Steady as she goes!'

Rushen Castle was smoothly away from the dockside and heading on her way out of the harbour entrance.

Currents in the Strait of Gibraltar and resulting layers of water caused by different temperatures are not conducive to good asdic operations, nonetheless Lt Billany and his asdic ratings made contact with our 'tame' submarine, and carried out several exercise runs until she surfaced. The red ball floats being towed by the submarine indicated the accuracy of our exercise attack runs and the Admiral was duly impressed, and even more by the 'live ammunition' effect of the three 'squid bombs' thrown 500 feet ahead of *Rushen Castle* making 15 knots.

Rushen Castle was now returning to Gibraltar. Entering the harbour for the Admiral's benefit at full ahead, I then made these four orders to put *Rushen Castle* gently back in her assigned berth alongside the dock with the gangway aboard. When in the centre of the harbour, abeam of the berthing position, the orders followed each other.

'Hard to starboard. Full astern. Stop engines. Amidships. Finished with engines.'

I saluted the Admiral saying, 'My ship's company and I have been honoured to have you aboard, sir!'

The quartermasters on the gangway were ready to pipe the Admiral and his staff officers ashore. The engineer officer came along to meet me as I left the bridge.

'I had to come up from the engine room to see how you could have put that ship alongside with just two engine room orders!'

'I could only have done it by having implicit reliance on my engineer officer and his engine room crew. Thanks for making my day, and the Admiral's!'

When escorting the Gibraltar to Liverpool convoy *Rushen Castle* was to carry two precious and unusual cargoes. The first consisted of gold ingots, each of them being encased in a wood housing. There appeared to be at least a ton of the valuable stuff which had been in the vaults of the Bank of Poland and shipped to Gibraltar for safe keeping in 1939. Now it was to be delivered to the Bank of England for the account of the Polish bank. It was stacked in the *Rushen Castle*'s magazine under lock and key in the bowels of the ship. On docking in Liverpool a representative of the Bank of England was waiting with an armoured truck and duly tallied the gold ingots into it with the aid of four seamen who received an unexpected donation of five pounds sterling.

The second cargo came in a RAF truck. It consisted of about a ton of large packages with lead weights sewed into the canvas bag containers. The RAF made a very specific request that this ton of packages should be stowed around the open bridge so that in the event of *Rushen Castle* being in danger of capture by the enemy, all the canvas bags could be thrown overside.

'Not on the top bridge of my ship!' I said. 'There is an excess of top weight making her "tender" already. As your stuff seems to be as good as gold perhaps, then it goes down in the magazine with the Bank of Poland's gold ingots. What's in those bags anyway?'

'Commander, it is two years' work by the RAF in photographing all the fortifications on the Spanish coast. It would create an international incident with a neutral country if this should become known through the capture of your ship.'

'Don't worry! In the event that your fantasy should come true, then the scuttling depth charges protecting the secrets of our asdic gear and oscillator would eliminate your secret work as well!'

There had been a change in the Gibraltar to Liverpool schedule for the northbound convoy, which required my escort group to exchange our southbound merchant ships with the northbound convoy escort, already about two days north. It had been rather foggy and overcast, and on taking over from the escort group returning with the Gibraltar-bound convoy we received this welcoming signal from the commodore of the Liverpool-bound ships by Aldis lamp:

From: The Commodore. Admiral, The Honourable, Sir Ernie Erle Plunkett

Drax RN
To: The Commanding Officer, *Rushen Castle*
We have had no sights for two days. Do not have correct position. Short-wave radio out of action. Report name and rank of SO Escort.

'What do you think we have here, skipper?' asked my No.1, Lt Clubb.

'I seem to recall that Admiral Drax was deputy chief of naval staff in 1939 and had something to do with going to Russia for a discussion on the Norwegian neutrality situation, without any results. Apparently he was moved out of the Admiralty into the pool of officers assigned as convoy commodores. Now he is going to be breathing down our necks all the way to Liverpool. I am thankful that his short-wave radio is out of action or he would be in conversation with us day and night! Ask the navigator to work up his exact position, as of the present time, and signal it to the commodore. Send this signal in response.'

To: The Commodore
From: SO Escort, *Rushen Castle*
We had star sights this morning. Will signal your exact position shortly.
SO Escort. Lt Cdr R.C. Warwick RNR.

All went quietly for the next few days, when to our regret the commodore was able to reactivate his short-range radio for a flow of signals.

While the convoy was making a landfall on the Cornish coast, a thick fog started to develop. As the convoy steamed north up the coast we arranged to radio the commodore his position by radar bearings of the shore every half-hour. Finally the convoy was heading up the Irish Sea and the time was approaching for altering course east to make the River Mersey and the swept channel.

At this same time, the outward-bound convoy would be leaving the Mersey. We advised Admiral Drax of his position and suggested that the convoy should alter course as scheduled on the charts for the in-bound convoys. There was no response to our signal, and the convoy held on its northerly course until the turn to the east was made to starboard and the east course to the river Mersey and the swept channel. Now Admiral Drax had put his convoy on a collision course with the outward-bound ships.

As his SO Escort, we signalled this situation and requested that the commodore make an alteration of 20 degrees to starboard to avoid the outward-bound ships. There was no response from Admiral Drax. *Rushen Castle* had been able to contact the SO Escort of the outward-bound convoy who was trying to contact his commodore to make a similar alteration. Unfortunately, when ships are leaving harbour, radio communications may have not been tuned in immediately on the short-wave channels with the commodore ship, but eventually the signal was received and the alteration made.

I placed *Rushen Castle* ahead of the in-bound convoy column. Steaming lights were turned on. The signalman turned on the bridge searchlight, flashing ahead as each merchant ship approached to swing past our port side. All went well and thankfully *Rushen Castle* made Gladstone Dock at full tide with the lock gates open to pass through to her berth. I had a stiff drink in the wardroom with No.1, and turned in.

As I was finishing breakfast the next morning down came an officer from the Chief of Staff, Western Approaches:

'C-in-C wants to see you.'

'What about?'

'Admiral Drax said that you had put him on a collision course with the outward-bound convoy.'

'Like hell I did!'

'You can't talk that way about an admiral!'

'I can and I will! I have chapter and verse in my signal book files!'

On arriving at Derby House I was given a preliminary interview by Admiral Horton's chief of staff before being taken in to the 'Lion's den'.

The chief of staff related a brief run-through of the incident as I had reported to him previously. Then I detailed my actions for leading in the convoy, so as to avoid possible collisions between ships of the two convoys. I produced my signal book records requesting the alterations of course to be made by the commodore, Admiral Drax.

'Why did not Admiral Drax alter course when you advised him?'

'The only reason I can give, sir, is that I am a Temporary Acting Lieutenant Commander RNR, whereas he is Admiral Sir Ernie Erle Plunkett Drax RN!'

'Commander Warwick, I consider that you have done all that I could expect from an escort commander in Western Approaches Command. When I say that it means something!'

'Thank you, sir! May I add that had I been a regular navy officer, Admiral Drax might well have put a black mark on my confidential record.'

'I will speak to Admiral Drax about it!'

Admiral Sir Maxwell Horton was described by some RN contemporaries as 'a common little man who had made good', and by others as ruthless with his staff.

Admiral Horton's chief of staff was delighted with the outcome. 'You've earned a big pink gin, Warwick! Admiral Drax is an old bachelor with no relatives. He stays with C-in-C when in Liverpool and moans to him all the time.'

Lt Philip Mountbatten RN, was the first lieutenant of a sloop working out of Gladstone Dock and occasionally made a visit to *Rushen Castle*'s wardroom. On the boiler-cleaning leave periods he would be off to London where he was reputed to be courting the young Princess Elizabeth, urged on by his famous uncle, Captain, acting Admiral, Lord Louis Mountbatten. During shore-leave evenings, he and other well-heeled young officers, including *Rushen Castle*'s South African Navy's Lt Cecil Vernon Rhodes, were dating young actresses and chorus girls at the Liverpool Theatre, as it might be said, 'on the fast track'.

Rushen Castle received orders to sail a day earlier than previously scheduled to meet with the convoy section coming from the Clyde and join the Liverpool convoy bound for Gibraltar. Other escorts of B-2 group would sail a day later with the Liverpool ships.

At 11 a.m. when due to sail at noon, Sub Lt Weeks reported to me: 'Cecil is not on board as yet. He went up to the base for the latest signals.'

'He knew we were due to sail promptly at noon today, as I was signalled this morning?'

'Yes, skipper, but he should soon be back.'

'Very well, but have him report to me on the bridge as soon as he comes aboard.'

Time passed and at 12 noon *Rushen Castle* was inside the Gladstone Dock lock gates.

'Mr Weeks, send this signal to *Flint Castle*: "Please take officer delayed at the base for transfer to us at sea tomorrow."'

Sub Lt Weeks, the navigator on the bridge, had been looking more and more confused and concerned. Eventually he came out with it. 'Skipper, Cecil joined a chorus girl taking a sleeper on the London train last night. He was returning on the afternoon train from London today.'

'He might have had the decency and forethought to get off the night train when it stopped at Crewe, instead of making a beast of himself!' I fumed.

Next afternoon at sea, as the Clyde and Liverpool convoy section formed up, *Flint Castle* signalled: 'Have your officer on board to transfer. Will lower my accident boat for exercise.'

'Number One, have the coxswain rig a Jacob's ladder on the lee side,' I ordered. 'I will put the ship alongside the *Flint Castle*'s boat and Lt Rhodes

276

can jump for it. Tell him to wait for us in my cabin while the convoy is being formed up.'

The escorts were in their assigned stations for their A/S sweeps when Lt Rhodes faced Lt Clubb and myself, looking rather sheepish and crestfallen.

'Lieutenant Rhodes, I have not studied the Kings Rules & Admiralty Instructions as to how "Absence without leave" or "Desertion in the face of the enemy" might be the crime for your potential court martial. Possibly both charges would apply. What do you have to say in defence of your actions?'

'Skipper, I did not think that the ship might be sailing yesterday afternoon.'

'Rhodes, you know that every officer and man in this ship's company should have been on board at eight a.m. on the day your ship sailed at 12 noon. All ready for duty.

'You planned to be engaged in sexual activities with the young actress in her railway sleeper cabin on the fast night express train to London, knowing that you could not be able to travel back to Liverpool so as to be on board at eight a.m.

'You knew that the night train stopped at Crewe, about halfway to London. Then you could have left your girl to go back to sleep, and take the next train back to Liverpool from Crewe, so as to be back on board in the coming morning. Since Sub Lt Weeks would cover for you, you took an extra day's leave on your own say-so!'

'Lieutenant Weeks was out with me that evening, skipper. So he knew that I was getting on the London train to return next morning.'

'Rhodes, there is no excuse for your actions. My duty and course of action should be to have you court-martialled. The girl was a casual acquaintance, hardly in the category of a dear wife or fiancée with whom you craved some precious extra hours before your ship sailed on a hazardous mission.'

There was a long silence. My thoughts went back to the meeting with Captain Ridgeway, the NOIC Cape Town. I could hear his sole criticism of my command. 'Warwick, you cover up for your officers. You should not do it!' I broke the silence.

'Lieutenant Rhodes, you bear the name of an empire builder, Cecil Rhodes, whose name is written in the history of South Africa, and to whom you are directly related in your family. Neither I nor Lieutenant Clubb trust having you on the bridge as a senior watchkeeping officer. Some excuse might be made that could be the lack of adequate training facilities in the South African Navy, but hardly this dereliction of duty, nor as an officer and a gentleman, involving a shipmate and fellow officer in covering up for you.

'Lieutenant Clubb and I have discussed the situation. A court martial, or even a court of inquiry, could create unpleasant publicity for *Rushen Castle*, the South African Navy, and the Rhodes family. This we wish to avoid.

'Sub Lieutenant Weeks has been at pains to cover your tracks, so to speak. The signal which I asked him to send to *Flint Castle* stating that you had been delayed ashore at the base provides additional cover-up.

'As your commanding officer I now require your presence on board as duty officer while *Rushen Castle* is alongside in Liverpool until such time as I decide otherwise. Have I made myself quite clear?'

'Yes, sir! Thank you.'

'Don't thank me, Mr Rhodes! Thank the fair name of your famous ancestor. Try to live up to it in the near future.'

CHAPTER XVIII

When the war with Germany ended, I asked for a command in the Pacific area. My relief in *Rushen Castle* was a RNVR officer who was a very dour Scotsman. Strict adherence to the King's Rules & Admiralty Instructions was to him as 'Those of the Medes and Persians which altereth not.'

The audit of the wardroom wine accounts revealed that Lt Rhodes had been steadily embezzling the payments made by fellow officers over several months past. Lt Clubb wrote to me saying that all the officers would contribute to the amount required to settle the account. He returned my cheque later, saying that the new commanding officer would not accept the officers' financial cover-up.

I understood that Lt Rhodes was duly court-martialled and dismissed from service with the Royal Navy.

Perhaps I should not have saved his skin in the first place, and should have recalled Admiral 'Monkey' Stevenson's 'Completely useless. Had him out just like that!'

The extracts on the following pages (see p. 280-5) taken from the monthly Anti-Submarine Report reflect the state of U-boat warfare in the latter part of 1943.

'Star Turn' U-boat captains suffered further attrition during their unsuccessful spring offensive, followed by Admiral Dönitz withdrawing his U-boats from the heavily escorted North Atlantic convoy routes, and assigning them to search for independently-sailed ships.

The history of U-536, commanded by Kapitänleutnant Rolf Schauenburg, indicates the sacrifice by Admiral Dönitz of a number of his U-boats in attempting to rescue those of his 'Star Turn' U-boat captains being held prisoner of war in Canada. The narrative details the fourth unsuccessful attempt made by an experienced U-boat captain in the Gulf of St Lawrence during September 1943, only to find that his mission had been compromised, as indicated by the number of A/S ships maintaining constant patrols in his intended rendezvous area.

(b) THE HISTORY OF 'U536' SUNK ON 20th NOVEMBER 1943, BY H.M.S. 'NENE' AND H.M.C. SHIPS 'SNOWBERRY' AND 'CALGARY'

Kapitänleutnant Rolf Schauenburg was different from most U-Boat Captains in that he brought to his U-Boat the standards of the battleship; thus, though the custom is for U-Boat crews to return from patrol hirsute and grimy, the only time that 'U536' came into Lorient her men were freshly washed and shaved. Schauenburg had been present at the coronation Review in 'Schlesien' and had later joined 'Graf Spee'. After she was scuttled, he was interned in the Argentine but soon escaped. Speaking both English and Spanish fluently, he represented himself as a cloth dealer, and travelled round South America. Twice he was arrested but he had influential friends and was released; eventually, however, even South America grew too hot for him and he returned to Germany at the beginning of 1941. After serving in minesweepers and also acting as an interrogator of prisoners of war, he took over 'U536' in the autumn of 1942.

'U536' left Kiel on her first patrol on 1st June, 1943. She had scarcely passed the Rose Garden before she was ordered to proceed to Lorient and have the new anti-aircraft equipment fitted. 'U170' and 'U535' had received the same instructions and the three boats proceeded to an area south of the Azores where they discharged their fuel to five other boats. 'U535' had been attacked and badly damaged while passing through the Rose Garden and they waited some days in the area for her to carry out repairs.

Towards the end of June, the three U-Boats set course for Lorient. They approached the Bay of Biscay from due west, intending to pass close north of Cape Finisterre, hug the Spanish coast for a short time and then alter to the north-eastward. Before they had even reached the Bay, they were three times attacked by aircraft. The first two attacks were ineffective, but not the third. On the 5th July, the U-Boats were proceeding in formation, 'U536' leading with 'U535' on her port quarter and 'U170' astern. At about 1700 Liberator aircraft 'G' of 53 Squadron sighted them. Her first attack was defeated by the U-Boats' successful avoiding action; in her second the depth-charges failed to release but her intense and accurate fire drove 'U536''s gun crews from their posts and Schauenburg, who was Senior Officer, decided that it was time to give the order to dive. As the boat submerged the sound of depth-charges exploding was heard. The Liberator in her third attack had dropped eight charges on 'U535', the lame duck of the party, who was a little slow in diving.

Once submerged 'U536' established contact with 'U170', but could not get any reply from 'U535'. The boats waited five hours and then surfaced and began a search for her. They found no trace and, knowing how badly she had been damaged by the earlier attack in the Rose Garden, presumed that she had sunk.

Soon after reaching Lorient, Schauenburg was summoned to Grand-Admiral Dönitz's headquarters near Berlin. The Captain of 'U536' must have been a man after the Commander-in-Chief's own heart – a keen seaman, a man of strong and determined character, and a Nazi who was not only fanatical but idealistic. Dönitz was planning an operation which required such a man – the rescue of prisoners of war from Canada. Their identity is not known for certain – some thought that the great Kretschmer was to be one of them while others spoke of von Knebel-Döberitz who was doubly distinguished as Dönitz's former adjutant and Kretschmer's First Lieutenant in 'U99'. At all events Dönitz was prepared to sacrifice a fair number of U-Boats in the attempt and Schauenburg's seems to have been the fourth chosen for this mission.

Whatever passed between Dönitz and Schauenburg, the latter did not take his crew into his confidence, and, when they sailed on the 29 August, they had no idea that they were to undertake a special operation. This was no doubt to be accounted for by the fact that at the time of sailing Schauenburg did not know for certain that he would be going to Canada. Before he was clear of the Bay, however, he received word that the third U-Boat detailed had been sunk and that he was to open his sealed orders and special codes. Schauenburg called his men together and gave them an outline of the operation, which though brief did not omit the fate of their predecessors. He told his officers that communication was to be established with the escaping prisoners by wireless and showed them the detailed charts of the area in which the rendezvous had been fixed. This was Chaleur Bay.

'U536' entered the Gulf of St Lawrence about the 16th September, and had a week or ten days in which to perfect her arrangements. The Second Lieutenant and a stoker were to go ashore in a dinghy specially fitted with an outboard motor. The former, a young man of 20, was looking forward to the adventure and employed himself in preparing a special 'gangster's cap'. It looked like an ordinary cap but was loaded with lead and, if he was accosted by anyone ashore, he was going to take it off politely – and then hit the man in the face with it.

Schauenburg had been ordered to be in Chaleur Bay by the 26th September but actually arrived there two or three days earlier. It was as well that he had, for he found that his charts were not up to date; the position of the rendezvous was partly to be fixed by reference to a solitary house and, in the area where the solitary house was supposed to be, he could see only a cluster of buildings. He spent several days spying out the land through his periscope and with some difficulty found the rendezvous. Once he picked up a signal which was thought to have come from the escaping men but it was not repeated and he feared that it might be a trap.

The night before they were due to arrive Schauenburg decided to leave the Bay and stand out into the Gulf where he could give his batteries a good charge. Just before he dived, he sighted a destroyer and a corvette; to seaward there were half a dozen more vessels. Schauenburg remained stopped at periscope depth and watched them. He saw the corvette take up her position near the rendezvous; after some hours she was relieved by another. It was clear that the German plan had been discovered.

The former Captain of 'U434' – one of the U-Boats sunk during the passage of Convoy H.G.76 in December, 1941 – had escaped on the 24th September only to be recaptured three days later.

Throughout the next day the U-Boat lay on the bottom of Chaleur Bay. Schauenburg decided that to attempt to carry out his orders was hopeless; all that he could do now was to get his U-Boat safely out of the Bay. When it was dark, he crept out into the St Lawrence, keeping at about 65 feet. He could hear the ships moving about the Bay; at one time he found that he was being followed but after a little the ship altered course and, though depth-charges were dropped, they were some distance away.

On reaching the open sea, Schauenburg made for the Cabot Strait. There he sighted a destroyer, apparently alone, and fired a salvo of three torpedoes. All of them missed. From the Cabot Strait the boat proceeded to the Halifax area, where she patrolled for nearly a month. A good deal of shipping was sighted but somehow or other Schauenburg never managed to get into an attacking position. It was not until early in October that a sinking was claimed – and it has not been possible to identify the claim – the ship being said to be one of over 10,000 tons.

Four electric torpedoes were fired in two salvoes without result and it was thought that they had hit without exploding. A fifth torpedo was fired and apparently found its mark. Two more ships were attacked, one of them being said to be a liner of over 20,000 tons and the other a small merchantman. Against the liner two air torpedoes were used and against the merchantman two electric, but the result was the same in both cases: a miss. It is strange that Schauenburg, who was obviously a competent officer, was so ineffective, but as one man said, 'He was always talking of giving his life for the Fatherland, but never, by any chance, of sinking a merchantman.'

About the middle of November, Schauenburg requested permission to return from his patrol as his fuel was running low, and received orders to return to Lorient. On his way he fell in with a number of U-Boats which were assembling for an attack on a convoy. By then he had only about 30 tons of fuel, but he asked to be allowed to join one of the four groups, each of 10 boats, into which the pack was divided. On the night of 17th 18th November, as 'U536' was proceeding on the surface to close Convoy S.I.139 M.K.S.30 she was detected by an escort vessel – possibly H.M.S. 'Foley', – but escaped without damage from the attack which followed.

'U536' closed the convoy about 36 hours later. She had another U-Boat – possibly 'U648' – on her port beam and heard the noise of gunfire followed by the sound of the U-Boat diving. Then came the detonations of depth-charges. These various noises did not trouble the crew of 'U536' overmuch. Their boat was over 500 ft. deep and it seemed pretty certain that 'U648' was getting the benefit of it all, but suddenly the 'ping' of Asdics broke in on these comfortable thoughts and before the men in 'U536' knew where they were a pattern of depth-charges, dropped by H.M.S. 'Nene', had descended upon them.

The attack was so sudden and unexpected that it threw them into confusion. It was also so accurate that the crew thought that the charges contained a new explosive. The boat went badly down by the stern, though there was apparently no entry of water. The Engineer Officer spent an hour endeavouring to regain trim; when at last he gave up his efforts and reported his failure to the captain, the order to surface was given.

The patrol, which had begun with such exciting things as sealed orders and a rendezvous in a remote bay, should by rights have ended dramatically with a hard-fought gun action; it was at least appropriate that two Canadian corvettes, H.M.S. Ships 'Snowberry' and 'Calgary' were in company with 'Nene', when the U-Boat surfaced.

Instead the end came quickly. While the U-Boat was surfacing, the men assembled in the control room in readiness to abandon ship. Under heavy fire from the three ships most of them made good their escape in dinghies, though a direct hit on the conning tower caused some casualties. Seventeen of the crew were eventually picked up; the U-Boat, all her vents open ran on for a little under port helm and then sank quietly by the stern at about 0245.

(e) 'STAR TURN' U-BOAT CAPTAINS

The list of the more successful U-Boat Captains published in the July 1943 Report is here brought up to date, and now contains 110 names against the previous 94. This very small increase reflects the state of U-Boat warfare at the present time. In the previous six months the names in the list rose from 69 to 94.

Name	Rank	Date of Award of 'Ritter-Kreuz.'	Date of Award of 'Oak Leaves.'	Remarks
Prien, Günter	Korvettenkapitän	17.10.39	21.10.40	Dead.
Schultze, Herbert	Korvettenkapitän	2.3.40	13.6.41	
Schubart, Otto	Korvettenkapitän	18.5.40	–	Sank HMS 'Courageous'
Rollmann, Wilhelm	Korvettenkapitän	2.8.40	–	Dead.
Kretschmer, Otto	Korvettenkapitän	8.8.40	12.11.40	Prisoner of war. Awarded Swords to 'Oak Leaves' on 7.1.42.
Lemp, Fritz-Julius	Kapitänleutnant	21.8.40	–	Dead.
Liebe, Heinrich	Korvettenkapitän	22.8.40	15.6.41	
Hartmann, Werner	Kapitäm-sur-See	2.9.40	–	
Rösing, Hans	Kapitäan-sur See	3.9.40	7.1.42	Swords to 'Oak Leaves,' S.O., U-Boats (West).
Frauenheim, Fritz	Korvettenkapitän	5.9.40	–	
Endrass, Engelbert	Kapitänleutnant	10.9.40	15.6.41	Dead.
Kuhnke, Günter	Korvettenkapitän	20.9.40	–	
Schepke, Joachim	Korvettenkapitän	26.9.40	20.12.40	Dead.
Jenisch, Hans	Kapitänleutnant	10.10.40	–	Prisoner of war.
Bleichrodt, Heinrich	Korvettenkapitän	29.10.40	23.9.42	
Oehrn, Viktor	Korvettenkapitän	29.10.40	–	Prisoner of war.
Lüth, Wolfgang	Korvettenkapitän	29.10.40	17.11.42	Awarded Swords to 'Oak Leaves' 15.4.43 and Diamonds 9.8.43
Suhren, Reinhard	Korvettenkapitän	10.11.40	3.1.42	Awarded Swords to 'Oak Leaves' 2.9.42. On shore.
Schütze, Herbert Viktor	Kapitänleutnant	16.12.40	15.7.41	Dead.
von Stockhausen, Hans-Gerrit	Korvettenkapitän	20.1.41	–	Dead.
Moehle, Oskar	Kapitänleutnant	28.2.41	–	
Lehmann-Willenbrock, Heinrich	Korvettenkapitän	28.2.41	8.1.42	
Oesten, Jürgen	Kapitänleutnant	2.4.41	–	
Schulz, Wilhelm	Korvettenkapitän	8.4.41	–	
Kuppisch, Herbert	Korvettenkapitän	25.5.41	–	
Wohlfarth, Herbert	Kapitänleutnant	25.5.41	–	Prisoner of war.
Schewe, Georg	Kapitänleutnant	25.5.41	–	
Korth, Klaus	Kapitänleutnant	3.6.41	–	
Hessler, Günther	Korvettenkapitän	30.6.41	–	
Topp, Erich	Korvettenkapitän	4.7.41	11.4.42	Awarded Swords to 'Oak Leaves', 17.8.42. On shore.
Metzler, Jost	Korvettenkapitän	1.8.41	–	
Schnee, Adalbert,	Kapitänleutnant	10.9.41	15.7.42	On shore.
Mützelburg, Rolf	Kapitänleutnant	23.11.41	15.7.42	Dead.
Mengensen, Ernst	Kapitänleutnant	23.11.41	–	
Guggenberger, Friedrich	Kapitänleutnant	20.12.41	9.1.43	Sank HMS 'Ark Royal' Prisoner of war..
Scholtz, Klaus	Kapitänleutnant	7.1.42	10.9.42	
Kentrat, Eital-Friedrich	Korvettenkapitän	7.1.42	–	

Bigalk, Gerhardt	Kapitänleutnant	7.1.42	–	Sank HMS 'Audacity'. Dead.
Gysae, Robert	Kapitänleutnant	7.1.42	31.5.43	
von Tiesenhausen, Freiherr	Kapitänleutnant	27.1.42	–	Sank HMS 'Barham'. Prisoner of war.
Hardegen, Reinhard	Kapitänleutnant	18.2.42	23.4.42	On shire.
Witte, Helmut	Kapitänleutnant	7.1.42	—	
Clausen, Nikolaus	Korvettenkapitän	14.3.42	–	Dead.
Mohr, Johann	Kapitänleutnant	28.3.42	15.1.43	Dead.
Ites, Otto	Oberleutnant	8.4.42	–	Prisoner of war.
Zapp, Robert Richard	Korvettenkapitän	5.5.42	19.5.42	
Bauer, Ernst	Kapitänleutnant	18.3.42	–	
Winter, Werner	Korvettenkapitän	8.6.42	–	
Cremer, Erich	Kapitänleutnant	8.6.42	–	
Kraus, Hans Werner	Kapitänleutnant	20.6.42	–	Prisoner of war.
Merton, Karl-Friedrich	Korvettenkapitän	23.6.42	18.11.42	
Schultze, Heinz Otto	Kapitänleutnant	15.7.42	–	
Rosenbaum, Helmut	Kapitänleutnant	12.8.42	–	Sank HMS 'Eagle'.
Lassen, Georg	Kapitänleutnant	12.8.42	8.3.43	
Piening, Adolf	Kapitänleutnant	15.8.42	–	
Thurmann, Karl	Kapitänleutnant	24.8.42	–	Dead.
Schonder, Heinrich	Kapitänleutnant	26.8.42	–	Dead.
Hartenstein, Werner	Korvettenkapitän	19.9.42	–	
Krech, Günther	Kapitänleutnant	19.9.42	–	Prisoner of war.
Kals, Ernst	Korvettenkapitän	8.9.42	–	
von Bülow, Otto	Korvettenkapitän	21.10.42	25.4.43	
Poske, Fritz	Korvettenkapitän	7.11.42	–	
Strelow, Siegfried	Kapitänleutnant	1.11.42	–	
Müller, Günther	Kapitänleutnant	30.11.42	–	Dead.
Emmermann, Carl	Kapitänleutnant	30.11.42	4.7.43	
Dommes, Wilhelm	Kapitänleutnant	5.12.42	–	
Witt, Hans	Kapitänleutnant	19.12.42	–	
Henke, Werner	Kapitänleutnant	19.12.42	4.7.43	
Rasche, Herman	Kapitänleutnant	30.12.42	–	
Brandi, Albrecht	Kapitänleutnant	23.1.43	12.4.43	
von Forstner, Freiherr Siegfried	Kapitänleutnant	11.2.43	–	
Heyse, Ulrich	Kapitänleutnant	30.1.43	–	
Paruscha, –	Korvettenkapitän	11.1.43	–	
Achilles, Albrecht	Korvettenkapitän	12.1.43	–	Dead.
Schneider, Herbert	Kapitänleutnant	22.1.43	–	
Schact, –	Korvettenkapitän	11.1.43	–	Dead.
Wuerdemann, Erich	Oberleutnant-zur-See	16.3.43	–	Dead.
Reche, Reinhardt	Kapitänleutnant	18.3.43	–	
Rostin, Erwin	Korvettenkapitän	28.6.42	–	Dead.
Trojer, H.H.	Leutnant-zur-See	26.3.43	–	
Engel, Horst	Kapitänleutnant	23.3.43	–	
Neitzell, –	Korvettenkapitän	30.3.43	–	
Seibicke, G.	Kapitänleutnant	30.3.43	–	Dead.
Folkers, Ulrich	Kapitänleutnant	30.3.43	–	

Gelhaus, Harald	Kapitänleutnant	30.3.43	–	
Heidtmann, Hans	Kapitänleutnant	15.4.43	–	Prisoner of war.
Moehlmann, Hellmut	Kapitänleutnant	17.4.43	–	
Jahn, Gunter	Kapitänleutnant	4.5.43	–	On shore.
Franken, Wilhelm	Kapitänleutnant	4.5.43	–	On shore.
Bargsten, Klaus	Kapitänleutnant	4.5.43	–	Prisoner of war.
Heydemann, Gunther	Kapitänleutnant	7.7.43	–	
Markworth, Friedrich	Kapitänleutnant	13.7.43	–	
Staats, Georg	Kapitänleutnant	15.7.43	–	
Kelbling, Gerd	Kapitänleutnant	21.8.43	–	Prisoner of war.
Maus, August	Kapitänleutnant	21.8.43	–	Prisoner of war.
Stark, Günther	Oberleutnant-zur-See	7.10.43	–	
Schöneboom, Dietrich	Oberleutnant-zur-See	20.10.43	–	Dead.
von Schöppenbach, Freiherr Egon	Kapitänleutnant	22.12.43	–	
Fenski, Horst-Arno	Oberleutnant-zur-See	22.12.43	–	
Franke, Heinz	Kapitänleutnant	22.12.43	–	

My mother was now very frail and her sister, my aunt Mabel, had come to stay with her in Surbiton. When I returned from Gibraltar my mail contained a letter from my aunt saying that my mother had quietly passed away, but the first news came with the base signals together with one from the Admiralty authorizing two days' leave to attend to family affairs while *Rushen Castle* was in harbour. My wardroom officers were very quiet and subdued when I was handed the Admiralty signal. 'Excuse me, gentlemen,' I said, getting up quietly for the solitude of my cabin to read my aunt's letter.

There was a note from my friend Arthur Mollart who was quite upset that I had not received the news from the Admiralty while *Rushen Castle* was in Gibraltar for a few days. It could have been possible for me to have flown to London and back before being due to sail with the Liverpool convoy. Arthur wrote to say that he had contacted the Mollart Engineering Company's liaison officer at the Admiralty, Commander Holbrook RN. Commander Holbrook's response was what I would have expected. It ran thus:

Commander Warwick is senior officer of the Liverpool/Gibraltar convoy escort group. He has delivered the southbound convoy safely. Now he has to escort the northbound convoy to Liverpool. The Admiralty and C-in-C Western Approaches consider that he has enough on his mind with the U-boat situation as it appears to be in the Bay of Biscay and the Irish Sea. His mother has died. There is nothing that he can do in that regard. His job and his duty is to bring the northbound convoy safely to Liverpool. Then he will receive the sad news and can take a couple of days leave while his ship is in harbour.

I went up to the base. My two days' leave was authorized. I went to Surbiton to meet my aunt who had taken care of all the funeral arrangements, and was looking after the maisonette flat there. Afterwards, I returned to my only home, my ship.

The war in Europe was drawing to its end. *Rushen Castle* was entering Gladstone Dock after escorting what was to be the last Gibraltar convoy, when the radio announcement came that the war with Germany had ended that sunny afternoon at 3 p.m.

All the escort ships in harbour had received a signal to the effect that no firing of signal rockets, flares etc. would take place. The disappointed base staff were cheered by the fact that *Rushen Castle* would not have received this signal, as she was still in the lock gates. Their hopes were justified, and we did the celebration honours with everything available.

All German U-boats had been instructed to surface and signal their positions in plain language. Being rather curious about the U-boat dispositions provided by naval intelligence, I instructed my W/T operators to keep watch and record these positions for my navigator, Lt Weeks, to plot on the charts. Intelligence was absolutely correct. About 15 or so U-boats were in the Bay of Biscay, as were the 8 or more in the Irish Sea!

American aircraft were now to be flown back to the US for service in the Pacific. Anticipating crash landings in the North-Atlantic, Castle class corvettes were to be assigned to 10-square-mile patrol stations across the Atlantic on the routes of these aircraft, acting as deep-sea rescue ships in picking up USAF pilots who might be obliged to ditch their aircraft. Radio operators would have to keep twenty-four hour watch on 3-4 radio frequencies.

This monotony was hardly my 'cup of tea'. On leave I went to see Commander Frank Mason, in personnel at the Admiralty.

'There are no destroyers available, Warwick. All I can give you is a tank-landing-and-assault ship building in Canada. You can have one of those for Pacific operations.'

'I'll take it, Commander. It is better action than going around in a ten-mile square in the Atlantic, waiting for USAF pilots to get into trouble!'

I was soon off to New York on the *Queen Mary*, and reporting to Montreal,

286

found my ship still under construction. On leave in New York at the Barbizon Plaza Hotel during August, I was able to experience Times Square on VJ Day.

After handing over to my relief in Liverpool I had gone down to the petty officers' mess on *Rushen Castle* to chat with my former coxswain. Upon asking him whether he was going to sign on for another term of service he had replied:

'Skipper, my present term of service has already expired. I'd be no good working on the outside and I am signing on once more. This is a lazy life in peacetime. Most often we only go to sea during the week and are always back in harbour for weekends!'

My next visit had been to Lt Cdr William Sitwell RNVR on board his ship *Flint Castle*. Bill Sitwell was the eldest son of General Bill Sitwell by his second wife, Constance Talbot, a novelist and close friend of Edith Sitwell of the remarkable literary trio Edith, Osbert, and 'Sachie' (Sacheverell). Bill was a 'doer', nowhere near the literary circle of his mother. He was a good ship handler and seaman who had 'knocked about a bit' prior to the war on Norwegian whale catchers and factory ships. His young brother Simon was a RAF fighter pilot decorated with the DFC.

'How was your leave, Bill?'

'I have no place to go to other than that perishing cold Barmoor Castle. Less said about it the better! Gin or whisky?'

'I'll join you with a traditional pink gin, Bill.'

'Colin, what do you think of the Admiralty offering a number of regular navy commissions to reserve officers? Of course you'd have no problems in that respect.'

'I'm not so sure about that, Bill,' I replied. 'Just recently one escort commander, who observed that he had been taken for me and seemed to have followed in my tracks, commented that "I had become a legend in my own time!" I was not sure whether this was wholly to my credit. Thinking back, for example, to my recent tangle with retired Admiral Sir Ernie Erle Plunkett Drax in regard to my version on his conduct as commodore of a recent convoy entering Liverpool. Then going back a little further to Captain Ridgway, the NOIC Cape Town, and his accusation that I covered up for my officers.

'I have also not forgotten the RN Captain, and NOIC St Johns, Newfoundland who called me together with the reserve commanders requesting coal to be made available in St Johns instead of making a six-day detour around an ice pack to a collier in Labrador, in terms I shall always remember: "The trouble with you reserve officers is that you are truculent, argumentative, and non-cooperative."

287

'Then I had some publicity in Admiralty Fleet Orders, regarding a leading seaman awarded the DSM in Norway being recommended for a reserve commission, which he was awarded. There are some other what you might call "lobbying incidents", such as getting the mayor of New York City to waive the Staten Island ferry charges for British sailors and encouraging the Commandant Eastern Sea Frontier to give us coastal convoys. Perhaps I should not have taken the initiative in getting my ship's payroll from the British consul in Norfolk, Virginia, while other ships' companies were most unhappy about not getting paid for a couple of months or more!

'The trouble with legends is that they become embellished as time goes by and the stories are retold with – yes, another pink gin, thank you, Bill!

'This may seem like a minor matter, when seemingly in jest, but in reality disclosing their true feelings, regular navy officers insist that the letters "RNR" stand for "Really Not Required", whereas "RNVR" means "Really Not Very Reliable"! If you and I took commissions as regular navy lieutenants, we would drop to the lowest seniority and pay scale, below that of any present regular officer, with the tab of "Special entry", similar to the army "ranker". In retirement we would be extremely lucky to be "passed over lieutenant commanders".

'Have another pink gin, Colin. I agree with you, it is not for the likes of us!'

Some 50 years on I had occasion to contact Sir Reresby Sitwell, Baronet, of Renishaw Hall, Derbyshire who was Bill's distant cousin. He wrote to me that rumours persisted that 'Bill ran away to sea' at least once after the 1939-45 war. Bill, his brother Simon, and their sister Anne all married at least three times. The very worst had happened to Barmoor which, when he visited previously in 1948, was very romantic with a lovely oval drawing room, fine furniture and silver, amusing statuary, and the usual rather indifferent family portraits. But Bill had sold everything, even the lead off the roof. All that remained were the walls of the castle and a few rambling roses outside.

When I returned to London from New York, I met up with my young brother who was back from Italy and Germany as an army major with the MBE, which he termed the 'lowest of all gongs'. We stood together in the Kensington flat of our cousin Isabel Kuklicke.

'Well, what do we do now?' asked my brother.

'You, Ian, are a gifted architect. There is an immediate need for your skills and expertise in rebuilding the country. Isabel has her government contacts in the Ministry of Town & Country Planning. She tells me that she has a meeting set up with the ministry people who want to put you to work now.

'My expertise is in the field of marketing consumer goods and services. The need in England is for production. I am not in great demand like you. I have thought of going to Australia, but I have no money, and a "pommy bastard" without money would hardly be welcome. South Africa is a country with a long-term future, but I doubt that I could become bi-lingual and learn Afrikaans! That leaves Canada and America. America will be in full production of all consumer goods quicker than any other country.

'I squirrelled away just a few US dollars in a New York bank. British pounds sterling can only be used and kept in England. I know some business people and have a tentative job offer that could let me look around. That is where I will try my luck. Of course, as I was told in 1939, it could be that I am again "really not required"!'